Representations of Motherhood

Representations of Motherhood

Edited by Donna Bassin,

Margaret Honey, and

Meryle Mahrer Kaplan

Yale University Press   New Haven and London

Published with assistance from the foundation
established in the memory of William McKean Brown.

The lines from "Eastern War Time" are reprinted from
An Atlas of the Difficult World, Poems 1988–1991, by
Adrienne Rich, by permission of the author and W. W.
Norton & Company, Inc. Copyright © 1991 by
Adrienne Rich. Chapter 12, "The Power of 'Positive'
Diagnosis: Medical and Maternal Discourses on
Amniocentesis," by Rayna Rapp is reprinted by
permission of Greenwood Publishing Group, Inc.,
Westport, Conn., from *Childbirth in America:
Anthropological Perspectives,* edited by Karen L.
Michaelson. Copyright © 1988 by Bergin & Garvey.

Designed by Sonia L. Scanlon
Set in Clearface type by The Composing Room of
Michigan, Inc., Grand Rapids, Michigan.
Printed in the United States of America by Vail-Ballou
Press, Binghamton, New York.

Library of Congress Cataloging-in-Publication Data

Representations of motherhood / edited by Donna
Bassin, Margaret Honey, and Meryle Mahrer Kaplan.
         p.   cm.
    Includes bibliographical references and index.
    ISBN 0–300–05762–8 (alk. paper)
    1. Motherhood in popular culture. I. Bassin,
Donna.   II. Honey, Margaret.   III. Kaplan,
Meryle Mahrer, 1947– .
HQ759.R48   1994
306.874'3—dc20   93–5933

A catalogue record for this book is available from the
British Library.

10 9 8 7 6 5 4 3 2 1

To our mothers—Estelle Bassin, Mary Honey, and Sarah Mahrer—and our children—Ari Bassin-Hill, Ezra Bassin-Hill, John Honey Fitzgerald, and Ian Mahrer Kaplan

Contents

Representations of Motherhood

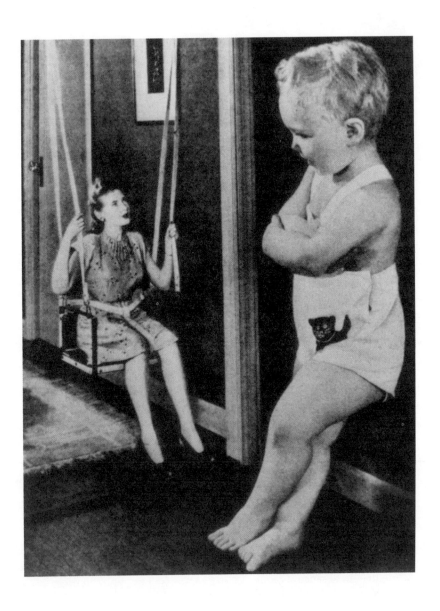

DONNA BASSIN

MARGARET HONEY

MERYLE MAHRER KAPLAN

Introduction

All three of us had strong reactions to the picture reproduced on the facing page. In a certain respect, this 1940s depiction of mom captures the overdetermined motivations for this project. A tiny mother, shrunk, strapped, and held captive in an infant swing, looks up at her massive toddler. The imposing toddler— clearly a boy—towers over her, arms folded, leaning on the wall as if he were in control of the space and master of her life. It is as if he belonged there, as if making demands, dominating, keeping her in her place, doing what pleases him were his right. Her reaction to this monster baby who holds her hostage is a mixture of apprehension, intimidation, curiosity, and helplessness. As she sits there in her pumps and dress, hanging in space (all dressed up with nowhere to go), this ladylike, nonresistant mother represents one feeling that mothers, especially mothers in isolated nuclear families, often have: the baby is in charge, controlling time and space—baby's needs and pleasures define the day.

Although it depicts one aspect of the mother's feelings, the picture perhaps goes too far. The mother is so infantilized and subjected that looking at the picture is painful. Instead of celebrating the nostalgic vision of the all-giving, ever-present, self-sacrificing mother, this picture suggests the horror of the mother dominated by her child. While the picture presents an infantile wish to be in charge, it re-presents that wish and shows that the absence of mother as a person big enough, with enough agency to be a real participant in a relationship, is a nightmare.

We can compare the picture with Toni Morrison's views about children's demands:

There was something so valuable about what happened when one became a mother. For me it was the most liberating thing that ever happened. . . . Liberating because the demands that children make are not the demands of a normal "other." The children's demands on me were things that nobody else ever asked me to do. To be a good manager. To have a sense of humor. To deliver something that somebody else could use. And they were not interested in all the things that other people were interested in, like what I was wearing or if I were sensual. Somehow all of the baggage that I had accumulated as a person about what was valuable just fell away. I could not only be me—whatever that was—but somebody actually needed me to be that. (Moyers & Tucher, 1990, p. 60; emphasis added)

In contrast to Morrison's view of motherhood as a freeing, generative experience, the picture is deliberately ironic. It does not represent the mother as a person; it does not depict liberation, reflection, or resistance through motherhood. The mother here is obscured and infantilized. At the same time, for us, the picture shows the importance of treating the mother as a person, as a subject, rather than as subjected.

Our associations to the picture are many. We identify with the dominated mother and the empowered baby. We laugh out of horror and understanding. We long for a representation of a mother who is not infantilized, as well as of one who is not larger than life. We do not want the mother and baby to change places—the horror of an engulfing, demanding mother does not fix the picture. We want a mother who is a real person. From our 1990s perspective as feminists and as mothers, the picture demands a response. We believe this volume is a good start.

The book is dedicated to the exploration of mother-as-subject, from a variety of lenses and through the experiences of a number of women. It draws on a history of feminist thought that has argued that seeing the mother as a subject, a person with her own needs, feelings, and interests, is critical to fighting against the dread and the devaluation of women. The book is also based on the notion that, as in our reaction to the picture, *representations* of motherhood reverberate with the complexities of our own maternal bonds. Motherhood is tied to infantile experience and relates to complex, ongoing, deeply personal feelings. Representations of the mother in popular culture, in the courts, in medicine, and in psychology tap and shape our complex feelings about motherhood.

Although the picture of the towering baby and dominated mother highlights power issues between mother and child, the predominant image of the mother in white Western society is of the ever-bountiful, ever-giving, self-sacrificing mother.[1] As in the picture, this mother is not a subject with her own needs and interests. This image resonates with a mother who lovingly anticipates and

1. See Loevinger et al. (1970) for documentation of middle-class women's adherence to the vision of the good mother; and Chodorow and Contratto (1982) and Pope et al. (1990) for more current indications of the attraction of this image.

meets the child's every need. She is substantial and plentiful; she is not destroyed or overwhelmed by the demands of her child. Instead she finds fulfillment and satisfaction in caring for her offspring. This is the mother who "loves to let herself be the baby's whole world" (Winnicott, 1973, p. 83).

Feminists have long argued against this vision of the mother, suggesting it is a socially supported *myth* designed to keep women in their place (Comer, 1974; Dally, 1982; Ehrenreich & English, 1978; Gordon, 1982; Heilbrun, 1979; Kristeva, 1981a, 1981b; Mitchell, 1971; Plaza, 1982; Rich, 1976; Riley, 1983, Ruddick, 1980, 1989). In the 1970s, feminist theory directed considerable attention to dismantling the ideology of motherhood by understanding its patriarchal roots and by underscoring that it did not represent the experiences of mothers themselves. As a result, the mother's subjectivity, her ability to reflect on and speak of her experience, has become an important ingredient in altering myths and changing social reality.

Jessie Bernard (1974) was one of the first feminist critics to explore the tension between the image of the all-giving mother and the actual lives of women. In her sociological analysis, the image of the selfless, ever-patient mother was described as a nineteenth-century Victorian invention that women had found unsuitable for decades. Bernard, pointing to women's entry into the workplace, called for a balance between work and family within women's lives and for shared parenting as ways of moving beyond stereotypical views of motherhood. She celebrated rebellion against maternal myths and found that women of all classes had dared to say that "although they love their children, they hate motherhood" (p. 14).

In her landmark book *Of Woman Born,* Adrienne Rich (1976) spoke of a disjunction between what she called the "institution of motherhood" and her experience of mothering. Rich's blending of the personal with the sociopolitical realities that constitute motherhood was a powerful form of analysis that demonstrated the ways in which social myths permeate and complicate the lived experience of mothering. Despite the self-consciously feminist nature of Rich's critique, she continued to be "haunted by the stereotype of the mother whose love is unconditional," a phenomenon that suggests the difficulty of challenging institutional constructions of motherhood. And, indeed, Rich wrote poignantly about the ways in which her own maternal anger and rage were experienced as monstrous parts of herself in the face of prevailing stereotypes.

The introduction to a recent volume of *Signs* (Pope, Quinn, & Wyer, 1990), devoted to analyzing the ideology of the entirely nurturant mother, speaks to the intractability of the myths surrounding motherhood: "In the collision of reality with mythology, it is the mythology that tends to prevail, as the language and the conventions of the story shape not only what is thought but also what can be said, not only what is heard but what can be understood" (p. 445). In fact, the authors indicate that the "ideology of mothering can be so powerful that the failure of lived experience to validate often produces either intensified efforts to achieve it or a destructive cycle of self- and/or mother-blame" (p. 442).

In an analysis informed by both sociology and psychoanalysis, Chodorow and Contratto (1982) focus attention directly on the intransigence of images of motherhood. They argue that individuals' visions of the mother have an "unprocessed quality," and the infantile roots of the image actually merge with culture. Because the mother is so tied to our earliest, most primitive experiences, maternal images have a uniquely archaic pull. We have an infantile wish for a mother who is less a person than an all-powerful figure who is fully responsible for our well-being. Growing up involves confronting the mother's separateness and accepting the fact that she has a life of her own. Culture, however, complicates this process by supporting and perpetuating our infantile longing for the mother who is a selfless caretaker. Chodorow and Contratto note that both feminist and conservative writers share the same view—that "perfection would result if only a mother would devote her life completely to her child" (1982, p. 65). Their formulation suggests the difficulty of moving beyond our infantile associations to the maternal, and they argue for the necessity of collective action to reshape social arrangements and cultural myths.

Adorno and his colleagues (1950) emphasized in their work on the authoritarian personality that the power of ideologies resides in the fact that people resonate differently with them. Cultural myths are of varying appeal: the same ideology can satisfy very different needs, and different ideologies can resonate with the same need. As an example, we can recall the political debate that erupted around television's depiction of the character Murphy Brown's decision to become a single mother. Conservatives were appalled, whereas progressives and feminists alike celebrated this vision of independent womanhood. The debate following the 1992 presidential election made it apparent that within certain sectors of our society, Hillary Rodham Clinton's status as a suitable first lady, mother, wife, and lawyer had become a hotly contested issue.[2]

In contemporary American society women face enormous pressures both to have successful and demanding careers and to still be the fully available, need-satisfying maternal figure. In a recent study, Kaplan (1992) found that white women who grew up in the fifties created images of motherhood that were both reparative and critical of their own mothers. Although each image was unique, these women all struggled with a vision of a new mother, one who clearly has needs of her own, but must reconcile these needs with those of her child. However, rather than seeing solutions to these conflicts in social or political terms (that is, adequate day care, shared parenting, parental leave), these women continued to create representations of the mother as she who shoulders the burden of care. No doubt the ideological pull of the all-giving mother re-

2. In the midst of the 1992 presidential campaign, the *New York Times* ran a series of front-page stories on conflicts surrounding both the realities and the mythologies surrounding mothers in contemporary American society. When one focuses on images of motherhood—working/non-working, single/married, gay/straight—it is clear that representations of motherhood evoke strong personal feelings and demand a political response.

mains a powerful force in the lives of all women, and to the extent that this myth is to be unhinged, a political as well as a personal response is required.

A review of the history of modern capitalism suggests that the contours of motherhood began to shift when work moved outside of the home (Erhenreich & English, 1978). With the growth of industrialization, men, women, and children were no longer involved in home-based, partially shared work endeavors. Instead, married women in families with any means (typically white families, working class and above) were left inside of the home in a now "private" realm that was distinctly different from the public sphere.[3] The limits and isolation of the domestic arena threw into question the place and function of women. And, increasingly, child rearing became women's primary responsibility. In the process, nurturance was privatized and devalued, and the position of women was further diminished—either through devaluation or through an equally difficult mixture of idealization and debasement (Benjamin, 1978, 1980; Dally, 1982).

In response to this major social shift, the early feminists chose to revalue motherhood, and they used maternal values of collectivity and nurturance to argue against the individualistic values of capitalist culture. Gordon (1982) describes feminists' involvement in the mid-nineteenth-century voluntary motherhood movement, noting that feminist demands for women's rights were located in a greater respect for motherhood, "the only challenging, dignified, and rewarding work that women could get" (p. 45).

At the turn of the century, increasing attention was focused on childhood as a distinct and important phase of life, and the child's growth and future became key social goals.[4] The movement began in 1888 with a child study society formed by mothers; ten years later there were child study and mothers' clubs scattered across the country. They arose as a means of professionalizing motherhood and addressing the increasing complexity of the mother's tasks (Ehrenreich & English, 1978). The movement, championed by feminists and nonfeminists alike, provided a means for mothers to join together and develop a body of knowledge about child development. Mothers in the movement saw themselves as partners with other "experts," and they chose to share their findings with psychologists as a way of developing their expertise. The movement's expertise, however, was eclipsed by that of male experts, and the growing trend toward the professionalization of mothering meant that mothers were increasingly scrutinized. By the 1930s this takeover was complete (Ehrenreich & English, 1978). Instead of joining together to make meaning of motherhood and child development, experts interceded and began to focus on the mother's role in child development. Ironically, the mother actually *lost* rights in the home at the same time as she gained responsibility for the child's emotional well-being (Weiss, 1978).

3. Much feminist writing in the seventies and eighties focused on the distinction between public and private domains (see Rosaldo and Lamphere, 1974; Elshtain, 1981). See also the early work of Chodorow (1974) and Benjamin (1978).

4. Histories of childhood have become key building blocks of feminist analysis. See, e.g., Aries (1962), deMause (1974), Harris (1987), Hunt (1970), and Wolfenstein (1955).

Although the World War II period was marked by women's large-scale entry into the labor force and the development of both public and private day-care centers, there was a concerted postwar shift to return women to the home (Bader & Philipson, 1980; Riley, 1983). Within American society, moves back to the home were associated with the contemporary growth of the suburbs and the development of single-family housing. The combination of maternal isolation and devaluation contributed to experiences of stress, feelings of inadequacy, and overdependence on children, a situation far different from that in cultures in which mothering is valued and shared (Bader & Philipson, 1980; Kitzinger, 1978; Minturn & Lambert, 1964; Rubin, 1976; Stack, 1974; Weiss, 1978).

The second wave of feminism can be understood as a response to the postwar period. Building on the highly influential work of Simone de Beauvoir (1952), theorists argued that mothering was the source of women's devaluation and lack of transcendence (Ortner, 1974). To be a person, for the most part, meant to be a person like a man.[5] Personness and subjectivity necessitated moving beyond, or avoiding altogether, home and motherhood. Betty Friedan's *The Feminine Mystique* (1963) deemed home "a prison." Juliet Mitchell (1971) saw child rearing as an "instrument of oppression," and Shulamith Firestone (1971) went so far as to entitle a chapter "Down with Childhood" and called for a total severance of the tie between women and motherhood.

The need for a turning away or avoidance of motherhood was also addressed by Adrienne Rich (1976). She articulated the ways in which maternal hatred, "matrophobia," can be understood as "a womanly splitting of the self, in the desire to become purged once and for all of our mothers' bondage, to become individuated and free" (p. 236). For Rich, the mother represents "the victim," the "unfree woman," "the martyr" in ourselves. In the face of this association, white feminist women are likely to perform what Rich calls "radical surgery" to attempt to break the blurred connection between our mothers and ourselves.

It is important to recognize that women of color have often presented a different vision of their mothers, one that includes ongoing connection and recognition of the mother's social position, her strengths and her struggles on behalf of her family and community. In the last decade white feminists have turned to African-American representations of the mother in order to develop visions of maternal strength and to find models for mother-daughter relationships that allow for both generational change and mutual respect. Toni Morrison, Alice Walker, Audre Lorde, and others have become key voices in the attempt to explore maternal subjectivity.

In recent years changes in family and work life, advances in medical technol-

5. The equal rights agenda still suffers from the assumption that equality must equal sameness. Maternity laws have become one contested area: Should childbirth be treated like a disability (something that applies to men and women) or as a uniquely female case? Should maternity leaves be extended to men? Snitow's (1990) discussion of a divide within feminism is helpful to understanding this issue: whether to strengthen and give political recognition to the unique aspects of being a woman or to tear down that category in favor of equality equals sameness.

ogy, and the multiplicity of interpretations and practices put forth by the women's movement have continued to contribute to the shifting ground of what motherhood means. Feminist responses have been multiple and varied. Some theorists view motherhood as a wellspring of psychological development and social change (Benedek, 1970a, 1970b; Klein, 1937/1964; Kristeva, 1980a, 1980b, 1981a, 1981b; Oakley, 1979; Ruddick, 1980, 1989).[6] Others emphasize motherhood's repressive aspects and see it as central to women's devaluation and assignment to silence and Otherness (Firestone, 1971; Mitchell, 1971; Ortner, 1974). Still others try to avoid the dichotomy by shifting attention away from motherhood and toward views of womanliness, sisterhood, or the shared position of the daughter (Arcana, 1979; Chernin, 1983; Chevigny, 1983; Friday, 1977; Gilligan, 1982; Morgan, 1970).

Reflecting on her 1970s consciousness-raising group, Ann Snitow writes about a divide that keeps forming in feminist thought. She sees this divide arising between the need to strengthen the identity of "woman" and the need to tear down that category in favor of equality and similarity to men. It is notable that Snitow makes a clear connection between motherhood and this division: "We used to agree in those meetings that motherhood was the divide: Before it you could pretend you were just like everyone else; afterward you were a species apart—invisible and despised" (1990, p. 32). Snitow's words make it apparent that even among feminists motherhood is likely to be a source of difference and controversy.

During the last two decades we have also witnessed the blossoming of American psychoanalytic feminism. This work has examined the importance of the mother-daughter connection, the persistence of infantile ties and their impact on our associations to the maternal, and the effects of women's mothering on gender-based social relations (Chodorow, 1971, 1974, 1978, 1979, 1981, 1989; Benjamin, 1978, 1980, 1987, 1988; Dinnerstein, 1976; Flax, 1978). With theoretical ties to the British object-relations school, these writers alter the traditional script of psychoanalysis by looking at the preoedipal period in which the mother is the prominent figure in the child's life.[7] Although these theorists share common questions and concerns, their theories turn on very different representations of the mother.

6. See Kaplan and Broughton (in press) for a review of theories of motherhood in women's development.

7. The struggle to expose the paradoxes inherent in our unconscious associations to the maternal image has been a crucial component in feminist attempts to address the question of maternal subjectivity. It is worth noting, however, that classic psychoanalytic writings, such as the work of Melanie Klein (1932) and Judith Kestenberg (1956), offer rich accounts of the development of maternal subjectivity. The work of these theorists is only just beginning to be mined for its contribution in this regard (see, e.g., Bassin, 1982). A recent volume entitled *Female Psychology* illustrates the growing body of psychoanalytic literature surrounding questions of maternal subjectivity. This book presents an annotated psychoanalytic bibliography on experiences of motherhood for the mother herself (Schuker & Levinson, 1991).

To Chodorow (1978), for example, the mother is a woman worthy of identi-fication; her daughter grows in close connection to her. Flax (1978), in contrast, sees the mother as devalued and unable to support her daughter's strivings and achievements. Dinnerstein (1976) adds yet another vision, in which the abso-lute, terrifying, and magical power of the mother is emphasized. And Benjamin (1988) speaks of a mother who is very much a person in her own right, a woman who tries to facilitate *both* connection and separateness in relation to her child.

Despite differences in their attempts to make meaning of motherhood, these theorists have continued to recognize the relation between the objectification of the mother and the objectification of all women; and they acknowledge that if the mother is treated as *less or more* than a person, then all women will be subjected to dread, devaluation, and ambivalence.

Developmentally, much feminist theorizing and practice has progressed from a relatively infantile view of the mother as a need-satisfying other who exists only to serve the relational and physical demands of the child to a view that sees the mother as distinct from her role and practice as nurturant provider. Our reluctance to see mothers other than from the perspective of their daughters speaks to the pull that infantile memories have on our ability to effect change.[8] Even feminist theory has insidiously sought a new idealized mother, one who can put aside her own needs and see her daughter not as a continuous other but as an autonomous and separate self (Chodorow & Contratto, 1982). And indeed, the pull of early memories coupled with our wish to have—and be—the perfect mother is a dilemma we struggled with as we put together this book. Even in our attempts to focus directly on maternal subjectivity we frequently found our-selves and our contributors shifting to the vantage point of the child seeking the need-satisfying mother and then struggling to construct a full vision of the mother herself.

Our purpose in this book is to focus attention on the complex issue of how motherhood is represented. In particular, we are interested in how women appropriate, resist, and create a multiplicity of meanings about motherhood. Our concern with representation acknowledges the constructed, complex, and often contradictory nature of maternal images and maternal practice. By bring-ing together a multiplicity of theoretical perspectives, we are attempting to broaden the ground on which motherhood is constructed.

We do not wish to replace an outdated and politically repressive theory of maternal practice with a new, more politically correct one. And we do not seek to

8. Many feminists have chosen to write from the seemingly shared vantage point of daughters (Arcana, 1979; Chernin, 1983; Friday, 1977). In fact, sisterhood became a model for women's relationships. *Sisterhood Is Powerful,* the name of the highly influen-tial anthology, forged a motto for the women's movement. The attractions of sisterhood have included close, ongoing, mutually caring relationships among women who could join together and help each other without the issues of authority, dependence, power, and oppression that seemed inherent in mother-daughter and male-female relationships. Sisterhood also allowed for the possibility of sexualized relationships while emphasizing connections that were both nurturant and empowering.

develop yet another way to tell the mother how to think, feel, or behave. Rather, we are interested in presenting a range of inquiries into the complex and multi-dimensional process of motherhood. Motherhood is overdetermined on many levels; it is complicated on a social and cultural level, and it is difficult on a personal plane (we all have mothers). The difficulty is compounded to the extent that we are mothers ourselves. There is, however, great value in this complexity. As Klein (1937/1964) and Benedek (1959, 1970a, 1970b) suggest, as parents we can relive our own childhood and our images of our parents. In the process we can move beyond infantile views and question cultural notions of the mother (Kaplan, 1992).

Much of the ambivalence that was characteristic of feminist writing on motherhood in the 1970s to the mid-1980s has been replaced with pleasure in bearing witness and representing maternal experience. For many, there is satisfaction in speaking the unspoken and placing motherhood on the feminist landscape. Otherness—which in the early 1970s was tied to oppression and devaluation—has for some become a key facet of uniquely female experience and a source of liberation from patriarchal values. French feminist writers like Kristeva (1980a, 1980b, 1981a, 1981b), Cixous (1981), and Irigaray (1981) have emphasized the salient role that motherhood plays in providing access to unappreciated and previously unspoken female experiences.

This book has been many years in the making. Theoretically and politically it began with the work of female novelists, poets, and academicians such as Maya Angelou, Harriet Arnow, Jessica Benjamin, Nancy Chodorow, Dorothy Dinnerstein, Jane Lazarre, Audre Lorde, Toni Morrison, Gloria Naylor, Tillie Olsen, Grace Paley, Sara Ruddick, Adrienne Rich, Alice Walker, and Virginia Woolf. These feminist writers have all attempted, each in her own distinctive prose, to rescue the mother from her status as object. Without the carefully crafted thoughts of these generative theorists and of our own contributors we would not have been so able to rescue our hostage mother from her swing.

The chapters of this volume present the perspectives of numerous disciplines, including art, film, literature, psychoanalysis, political science, philosophy, and sociology, and focus on various topics that elaborate the question of mother-as-subject. What has been seen in the past as sentimental or natural behavior is now being reexamined. Refocusing our vision on maternal experience reveals the sophistication of the process of mothering as a complex experience grounded in social, psychological, and political realities. Whereas history has recognized maternal work almost exclusively in terms of its impact on the child, contemporary culture is beginning to articulate the mother as a subject in her own right. An increased curiosity and interest in the self-experience of the mothering subject is evident in our literature and popular culture (for example, Bergum, 1989; Burke, 1986; Cahill, 1982; Greenberg, 1979; McBride, 1973; Shreve, 1987; Spencer, 1984). As many feminists have come to engage in their own mothering or other generative experiences, our daughterly longing toward mother has shifted toward an appreciation of her selfhood. The time is right for us to redirect our gaze and explore mother-as-subject.

As editors we are attempting to push forward a vision of the maternal place as generative for women's psychological development as well as for cultural and political change. Our contributors' work serves as so many possible interpretive nets. Within this volume they consider ways in which various established discourses have excluded the maternal voice, as well as other more marginally based discourses that can be seen as making room for an exploration of mother-as-subject. Several chapters focus critical attention on dominant patriarchal discourses; others explore the importance of literary and psychoanalytic texts in the development of maternal narratives. The process of naming and reflecting upon aspects of maternal experience that traditionally have been left unspoken, including the maternal body, maternal pleasure, and maternal hatred, is explored in other chapters. The potentially subversive character of mother-as-subject is a theme that runs implicitly through this volume with attention both to how mothers are perceived in the political arena and to how listening to the maternal voice disrupts deeply held views of women and motherhood.

Each chapter, like the unique voice and experience behind it, is in a category of its own. But in our many readings, we discerned a series of motifs that speak to the complexities of maternal experience. We have chosen to use these themes as an organizing framework for the volume. No doubt other readings and anchorings will suggest themselves as readers bring their own interpretive frameworks to this book.

The Acknowledgment and Appropriation of Maternal Work

The five chapters in this section address maternal work as an experience grounded in social and political realities that cultivate particular ways of being and knowing for the mother herself. They set about to dignify the craft of motherhood, and they explore the ways in which maternal activity shapes and helps direct women's relation to the social order. Instead of viewing the mother as subjected to tradition, these feminist authors treat her as activist and social critic, confronting societal issues as she struggles to both protect and develop her child. Her engagement with maternal work, in turn, contributes to the development of her sense of self, to her politicization, and potentially to the restructuring of the social order.

In a footnote to her chapter, Sara Ruddick compares the attitudes toward their mothers of white feminists, African-Americans, and other daughters of color. She suggests that white feminists' attitudes often reflect a sense of betrayal engendered by their mothers' compliance with the oppressor's system. In contrast, women of color respect their mothers' struggles. This insight is echoed by the other authors in this section, as they work to broaden the subject of feminist analysis in order to understand the position and experience of their own mothers, and to move beyond the perspective of themselves as middle-class daughters, beyond the experience of white middle-class women. They bring into view the essential elements of motherwork and explore mothers' politicization within oppressively patriarchal communities. These authors talk about the maternal faculties of memory, survival, loss, and regeneration as aspects of maternal subjectivity; they focus on motherhood as an engaged struggle with the political and economic realities of so many women's lives.

This section, and indeed the entire book, owes much of its conceptual frame to the philosopher Sara Ruddick, whose description of mothering as a practice grounded in action and thought has laid a critical foundation for thinking about maternal subjectivity (1980, 1989). Over the past decade, Ruddick has argued that motherhood, like other complex activities, engenders a sophisticated way of thinking. She analyzes the reflective thought that is a direct outgrowth of the central demands of motherhood—preservation, growth, and social acceptability—and calls our attention to the ways in which such thinking is potentially at odds with an individualistically oriented and militaristic society. Maternal thinking includes nurturance and a binding connection to others that is central to a politics of peace.

In her earlier writing Ruddick (1980, 1989) has suggested that although there is a maternal vantage point, anyone engaged in maternal practice, male or female, can develop maternal thinking. In her chapter here she seeks to reimagine pregnancy and birth, to reconnect and redistinguish natal experience and mothering, and to define it as an activity requiring a unique form of commitment and responsibility. While recognizing that many who mother are not birthgivers, Ruddick argues that fully breaking the connection between birthgiving and motherhood can minimize recognition of this uniquely female activity, reproduce envy-based social devaluation of woman as breeder, and ignore key aspects of many women's experiences of motherhood.

In thinking about the pregnant woman, Ruddick introduces a new point of emphasis in her work. The maternal self not only is a thinking and socially constituted self but is a bodily and sexualized self as well. What she calls natal thinking is rooted in the bodily self's active, responsive waiting throughout pregnancy. The pregnant woman deals with predictable pain, reckons with the complexities of control (appetites, activities, fears), and engages with distinctive issues of self and other. Her self is physically and emotionally entangled with that of an emergent being. Although natal thinking is distinct from maternal thinking, birthgiving is the beginning upon which all mothering depends. Many women draw upon the birthgiving experience in mothering.

Jane Lazarre, a novelist, has been writing from a maternal and feminist vantage point for many years. Her book *The Mother Knot* holds a significant place in writing about maternal subjectivity: she was "out there" and speaking as a mother at a time when subjectivity and motherhood were rarely connected, let alone explored. She shared her anger, ambivalence, and love of motherhood. Her work is a personal exploration of what it means to be a mother who writes.

In more than twenty years of writing and mothering, Lazarre has come to see that beneath the domestic contradictions in the two projects of her life lies a deeper coherence. They require similar struggles for a clear, often painful, vision of her limits, for a capacity to endure inevitable loss, and for an increasing ability to notice accurately the disparities between the world and her own perspective on it.

Lazarre's chapter, "Fictions of Home," from her new book *Worlds beyond My Control,* adds important elements to visions of maternal subjectivity. The mother in this story wrestles with feelings of separation and connection rooted in maternal experience. Lazarre's own experience is heightened by the fact that her child and her husband are black. The story presents a similar configuration of white mother and black child who is now a teenager. The story turns on a visit to a homeless shelter, where privileged mother and son spend an evening caring for the homeless. Fictions of home—fictions of regularity, belonging, place, and affiliation—are used by the mother as well as by the homeless. Lazarre's fictions infuse and confront the realities of having or not having a home, of being black or white, and of being a mother to a son who is no longer a child. He must develop his own fictions as he confronts his connections to mother, to black people, and to the homeless.

Patricia Hill Collins, a sociologist, enriches the texture of motherwork through her analysis in chapter 3 of the specific tasks of mothering in nonwhite, non-middle-class life that form and illuminate the subjectivity of women of color. The voices she hears—those of African-American, Native American, Asian-American, and Hispanic women—express important aspects of generativity and community. These women speak to sources of power and collaboration between mothers and daughters that have gone unrecognized in most white feminist writing. For racial ethnic women, the dichotomy between work and family is a less commanding factor than for middle-class white women. The mother is a person struggling within a particular social, economic, political context. The "subjective experience of mothering and motherhood is inextricably linked to the sociocultural concerns of racial ethnic communities—one does not exist without the other." Conflicts that have been central to a middle-class white understanding of maternal experience—conflicts surrounding gender roles and the search for individual autonomy—are less relevant for racial ethnic women, who must struggle with maintaining recognition and identity as a subordinated group within the larger society. It is in her discussion of issues of survival, power, and identity for mothers who are part of an oppressed racial ethnic community that Collins makes a most important contribution to our understanding of maternal subjectivity as necessarily socially and politically informed.

Jean Bethke Elshtain, a political scientist, builds on the connection between motherhood and political action. Her chapter provides an important counterexample to representations of motherhood as buttressing the status quo. She focuses on a particular instance in which the state has been challenged in the name of motherhood. Drawing on extensive interviews with Las Madres, the Argentine mothers of the Plaza de Mayo, Elshtain illustrates how these women occupy public spaces as mothers to protest the torture and disappearance of their children. She argues that these women transgress the boundary between private and public and turn the state's proclaimed piety on the sanctity of the family against it.

In Elshtain's view these mothers speak a double language: the anguish of a mother's loss and the protest language of human rights. These mothers use their grief, their symbolic role as guardians of life and death, not hysterically but deliberately for political activity in a repressive state. Elshtain examines the extent to which a politics of motherhood as a rebellious and critical force has been effective within a Catholic society. The mothers of the disappeared have transformed the image of the Mater Dolorosa, the grieving and weeping face of the Virgin Mary as the ideal-typical female identity, into that of the caretaker of memory and defiant witness to acts of terrorism and oppression.

Marianne Hirsch, a literary theorist, explores in the next chapter the relation between motherhood and feminism as it was elaborated in the United States in the 1970s and 1980s. She argues that during this period the dominant voices were those of daughters treating mothers as women identified and constructed within patriarchy. In Hirsch's view, feminist writing and scholarship, which continues in large part to adopt daughterly perspectives, can be said to collude with patriarchy in placing mothers in the position of object, of Other—thereby keeping mothering outside of representation and making maternal discourse a theoretical impossibility.

In this chapter, she joins Collins, Elshtain, and Lazarre in seeking to flesh out visions of the mothering subject under reigns of oppression and terror. Hirsch's literary examples are chosen from within one particular and closely circum-scribed feminist tradition—that of African-American writers of the 1970s and 1980s, a generation of feminist writing in the process of defining itself in relation to a maternal past conveyed orally for the most part. These writers focus on issues of continuity and separation, connection and disconnection from a past full of stories that have been handed down without necessarily being written down. Hirsch uses Toni Morrison's *Beloved* to explicate an alternative narrative space where an African-American mother named Sethe speaks as both daughter and mother.

In light of the violent reality of an oppressive slave culture, the master oedipal narrative, with its "invisible and repressed mother," is challenged by this novel. In the many surfaces of Morrison's book, the actuality and the metaphor of slavery for the mother—the lack of ownership of self—plays back and forth. Hirsch examines Sethe's killing ("putting her babies where they'd be safe") of her baby Beloved, whom she is not free to nurture and who, as the child of a slave, will never be free. Despite the unspeakable violence of Sethe's murder of her daughter, the story addresses the unspeakable "violence of the symbolic murders of a people." To the degree that Beloved represents memory itself, she portrays a resistant voice and a proactive stance toward the denial of maternal selfhood. As Hirsch understands it, Morrison, like Collins, Lazarre, Elshtain, and Ruddick, suggests that the narrative of maternal subjectivity must include the active use of memory for oneself, for succeeding generations, and for the linkages between the two.

The Paradoxical Nature of the Maternal Position

Traditional portraits of the mother have tended to freeze the process of theorizing maternal subjectivity by erasing the tensions between subject and object, mother and child, fantasy and reality, past and present. The mandate of psychoanalysis has been to interpret and uncover deeply buried associations that the seemingly everyday act represents, in the hope that self-conscious choice can come to prevail over previously unconscious fantasies. The task of feminism, on the other hand, has been to transform and change the structures that have created and continue to support infantile and regressive systems. Much of feminist theorizing about the maternal has been concerned with effecting reform on a more immediate and conscious level. The discourse on motherhood, however, has been hampered by our failure to understand and contend with a myriad of unconscious associations to the mother and to maternal practice in general.

The chapters in this section address the more intractable and difficult domain of the unconscious maternal universe. They move beyond contrasts between myths of motherhood and maternal experience and proceed from the assumption that mothering is a process riddled with paradoxes. Their authors grapple with the multifaceted and conflicted dimensions of the mothering experience. Through the lens of psychoanalysis, they address our primitive and deeply embedded associations to the maternal image, contend with issues of maternal hatred and ambivalence, speak to the necessity for and the difficulty of recognizing the mother as a subject in her own right, and highlight the generative and creative aspects of the mothering process.

Janine Chasseguet-Smirgel, a French psychoanalyst, addresses in chapter 6 our most primitive and deeply embedded associations to mothers and maternity in general. Her work is an exploration of the psychodynamic origins of the all-powerful and invading maternal presence. In Chasseguet-Smirgel's view, these early images are an inevitable outgrowth of "infantile helplessness"—the state of dependence into which we all are born. That we are sent into the world in less than finished form colors both our need to cling to the person upon whom we are most dependent and our desire to escape from her. This fact of human nature, according to Chasseguet-Smirgel, infuses our cultural associations to the maternal and women in general, frequently creating a tidal wave of ambivalence and hostility. Apocalyptic fantasies, goddess worship, and images of the witch/whore are all manifestations of the primitive maternal imago.

Chasseguet-Smirgel's work helps us understand on a deeper level why tendencies to both overidealize and thoroughly devalue women prevail in our representations of motherhood. Her insistence on recognizing the difference between the mother as an internal and primitive psychological object and the actual mother of everyday life is most useful to our understanding of the tena-ciousness of negative maternal images. In Chasseguet-Smirgel's analysis, change can come about only when we understand the importance of working at the level of psychic fantasy as well as the level of reality.

In chapter 7, Jessica Benjamin, a psychoanalyst and sociologist, shifts the focus from representations of the internal fantasy mother to our capacity to recognize a more differentiated, reality-bound mother. Over the years Ben-jamin's work has been characterized by her emphasis on the paradoxical nature of psychological life. At the heart of her work lies a concern with the devaluation and domination of women. Why, she asks, do the tensions that are an inevitable part of our psychic life collapse, leaving in their wake a flood of complicated power struggles that more often than not result in the subjugation of women?

In Benjamin's view, mothering is a process riddled with paradoxes. Striking the right balance—or maintaining the tension—between the child's developing sense of her or his own agency and the mother's sense of her self and subjectivity is a complex and conflicted process. This is experienced in a thousand different ways as children grow. The mother who takes pride one day in her child's ability to dress himself rushes him the next day, against his will, to dress so she can make an early morning meeting. Such conflicts are basic to life. They inevitably color the young child's sense of his or her mother's omnipotence. For the mother they color her sense of self. Learning to navigate and work through feelings of power and powerlessness is essential to the well-being of both the child and the mother.

Benjamin works at the level of theory to help us reconceptualize a number of traditional psychoanalytic assumptions about the mother. She takes issue with the classic account of the oedipal crisis and its emphasis on the father as savior of the child from the murky and fluid maternal universe. In her revised narrative, the operative metaphor is built on the dynamics of mutual recognition, a pro-cess that implies that the child has the capacity and need to recognize the mother as a subject in her own right and in turn to be recognized by her. This recasting of psychoanalytic theory away from the nursing dyad as the governing metaphor and toward a model of development premised on intersubjective re-latedness has numerous implications for our understanding of the importance of maternal subjectivity.

Elsa First, a psychoanalyst, contributes in her chapter to our understanding of the mother's subjectivity by expanding representations of motherhood to include the profoundly ambivalent feelings mothers have for their children. She undermines the sentimental idealization of the mother by addressing the most unspeakable but potentially most empowering aspect of maternal practice—maternal hatred. She calls attention to the previously unrecognized feminist implications of the work of the British psychoanalyst D. W. Winnicott. First argues that Winnicott's writings are marked by "a characteristic rhetorical de-vice: the setting up of casual, resident, and subtly subversive analogies between a psychoanalyst's way of being with the patient and a mother's way of being with her child." Winnicott also recognizes that mothering and psychoanalyzing are both skilled and complex practices that arouse profound hate as well as profound love within the mother and the analyst. Just as the analyst must learn to contain and acknowledge the negative responses aroused in her by the patient, so the mother, by accepting her own hate of the child's impositions, communicates acceptance to her child. As every psychoanalyst must struggle with hatred if she or he is to remain honest, so, in Winnicott's view, must every mother struggle as consciously as possible with legitimate hatred for her child. First argues that Winnicott was perhaps the only psychoanalyst to see this struggle, to acknowledge and integrate hatred as central to child rearing, not just as a problem for supposedly unloving, inadequate, or abusive mothers.

Donna Bassin, a psychoanalyst, explores in chapter 9 potentially generative aspects of the maternal image through the processes of memory and mourning. Drawing on a study of the culture of nostalgia as manifested in the artifacts of the 1950s and in an analysis of two women, Bassin explores the ways in which our dynamic memories of the maternal image can be used to grow beyond infantile wishes of the mother. For Bassin, this process is contrasted to the pathology of mourning as manifested in nostalgic sentimentalization of the past—a longing for the all-giving, ever-present maternal figure where memories are static and sentimental as opposed to dynamic and generative.

It is our resistance to the difficult task of mourning our childhood that binds us to a pattern of nostalgic craving. In contrast, Bassin suggests, through mourning we can recover and revitalize an active, generative maternal image within the self. Bassin's contribution to our understanding of mother-as-subject rests on a psychic transformation whereby the mother as Other—not-me, artifact, and keepsake from the past—becomes a dynamic aspect of the self. It is this process of transformation that enables us to experience our own sense of self as mother. To the extent that we are able to convert our wistful longings for a maternal presence into an understanding of our own sense of agency and accomplishment, that investment in our own maternal sense of self can occur. Rather than feel a stagnant longing, we can locate possibilities for change in our engagement with the artifacts of culture.

Myra Goldberg, a writer of fiction, has created a story that explores contemporary representations of motherhood (as breadwinner, fixer, moral organizer) as well as more traditional images of comforter and body. By exploring the multiple positions mothers occupy within the family, Goldberg in chapter 10 gives the reader the opportunity to consider how the narrative mirrors the position of mother in our society.

This story takes its fictional heroine to the hospital for a serious and mutilating operation and then brings her home. In the face of this life-threatening illness, an illness of the heart, Rosalind struggles to find herself amid a backdrop of conflicting and contradictory demands. How competent, professional Rosalind looks at herself and at her children when she is weakened and how her children, age eleven and seven, look at and mirror different dimensions of their scarred mother are important themes of this short story.

The constant play of consciousness on the world around us is important to our understanding of maternal subjectivity. The story moves from the mother's point of view to each child's and to the narrator's. Goldberg invites us to explore the ways in which the maternal subject both constructs and is constructed by the multiplicity of relationships that compose her life. In this way, her story encapsulates the themes emphasized by the other authors in this section. In a confrontation with the mother of her childhood, Rosalind struggles with her most primitive and persistent associations to the maternal image. The paradox of recognition is felt poignantly as we see Rosalind from the perspective of those whom she nurtures. And Rosalind's own maternal ambivalence and distaste are echoed most clearly in her relationship with her eldest daughter, Nana—whose name evokes the overdetermined nature of our maternal associations. And yet there is optimism in this drama—the generative and potentially transformative aspects of the maternal image are in evidence as Rosalind heals both physically and emotionally in proximity to her own mother.

The Cultural Construction and Reconstruction of the Maternal Image

Images of the maternal shape and are in turn reshaped by cultural practices. The chapters in this section address the maternal image as it currently appears in a range of discursive arenas: law, medicine, film, visual art, and technological culture. These authors emphasize the interconnection between the power of cultural practices and the development of the maternal subject who can both appropriate and contest these images. They explore the relation between the technological world, with its metaphors of phallic power, intrusion, and control, and the maternal universe. They speak to the multiple and shifting meanings that maternal representations occupy in different arenas of mass culture and social institutions. And they focus attention on the paradox of attempting to articulate the meaning of motherhood in cultural arenas that find it difficult to comprehend the lived nature of women's experiences.

Barbara Kruger and Therese Lichtenstein's collaboration of text on text-over-image is an instance of the multiple and shifting meanings any representation can have. Kruger, who deals in critiques of representation, is one of a group of women artists who gained recognition in the 1970s. Her work, based on a multiplicity of representations, suggests an alternative to essentialist notions of woman and the binary opposition of gender difference manifest in popular culture.

In her interview with Kruger, Lichtenstein, an art historian and critic, explores Kruger's understanding of the construction of subjectivity through social control and ideology. Drawing on images and text from history and current culture, Kruger deliberately forces a disjunction between seeing and understanding. The disjunction both mirrors and complicates the distinction between image and experience. Kruger's placement of the text on top of the photographs is a deliberate disruption of any simple viewing, designed to compel the viewer to realize her own subjectivity in relation to cultural artifacts. Kruger wants a self-conscious audience, aware of their own symbolizing and interpreting processes. She opens the door for the viewer to make meaning. As she says, "I am trying to deal with a serious topic in an anecdotal and comedic way, to engage the viewer and make them laugh but also to rearrange their conceptions of what is possible."

Rayna Rapp's chapter moves us out of the domain of the maternal image in popular culture to explore the ways in which the maternal is currently being constructed through the discourse and practices of medical technology. Through her study of women's experiences of prenatal diagnosis (specifically, amniocentesis), Rapp, an anthropologist, investigates the ways in which reproductive medicine increasingly shapes cultural practices and colors the subjective experience of sex, gender, family, and motherhood. Rapp focuses on what she sees as a shift from the image of the long-suffering, ever-present, self-sacrificing madonna to the individual woman making choices. She argues that medically based discourses promote themes of privatization and distancing, in which individual women are encouraged to keep their feelings and concerns to themselves. Such discursive practices do not promote the development of a shared language or shared understandings across communities of women or between women and their medical caregivers.

Although the possibility of making informed judgments appears to support the feminist battle for reproductive choice, Rapp uses a broad cultural focus to raise questions about the impact of this medical discourse on our understanding of maternal practice in general. She calls attention to the fact that in the current, polarized abortion debate and in our understanding of ourselves as objects of medical care and study, we are being handed yet another image of the mother—mother as an agent of quality control, the one who decides the fate of the acceptable child. Like that of the madonna, this vision is embedded within a patriarchal discourse that privileges the abstract and rational over the experiential. Rapp's work gives voice to the complexities of the decisions with which mothers-to-be are confronted as they contend with the experience of birth in a technological world and provides an example of how the technical is infusing the maternal.

In a different but related domain, Margaret Honey, a developmental psychologist, explores in chapter 13 the presence of a maternal voice within the gender-polarized world of high technology. In Honey's view, the discursive and symbolic nature of technological cultures is largely phallic. Like the worlds of sports or high finance or the military, the technological universe excludes maternal values such as nurturance and care and confines them to the privatized domestic world of the home. The question for Honey is how women who work within such phallic universes can give voice to their needs and desires.

In an inquiry designed to counter traditional deficit models of women's relationship to technology, she explores how women interpret and make meaning within the boundaries of such a "phallic universe." Honey's research is based on interviews with women and men who are deeply engaged in computer-related activities in their professional work lives. Her analysis is grounded simultaneously in a critique of the discourse of technological culture and an affirmation of the work of psychoanalytically oriented feminist theory.

Although focused on the technological terrain of the computer, Honey's research raises numerous questions about how women give voice to their desires in worlds governed by a kind of disembodied, hyperrational, and highly militaristic form of reasoning. Her analysis points to the paradoxical nature of the maternal voice, which she reads as both expressive and defensive. Although the women she interviewed do wish to humanize and demystify the often dangerous and elusive elements of the high-tech universe, the maternal voice also functions like a safety valve, ensuring women a ready point of exit and thus precluding their deep engagement with the technology itself. In the final analysis, Honey's work urges us to pay attention to the paradoxical nature of expression within a phallic world.

Adria Schwartz, a psychoanalyst, uses the controversial issue of surrogacy to explore in her chapter how contemporary legal discourse, coupled with advances in reproductive technologies, has called into question our understanding of who occupies the space of mother. Traditional associations to the mother as the one who gives birth and nurtures the child cannot survive these technical and legal developments. The quest for the symbolic control of the term *mother* powerfully illustrates how language defines and constructs reality. Is she the egg that holds the genetic code, the womb that sustains and nurtures, or the person who practices maternal work?

Through an analysis of the dramatic case of Baby M, Schwartz focuses our attention on the meaning of motherhood within contemporary legal culture. Despite the fact that Marybeth Whitehead was Baby M's biological mother, throughout all legal proceedings she was consistently referred to as "the surrogate." William Stern, in contrast, was referred to as the natural and biological *father*. And as the "expert" trial testimony of psychologist Lee Salk made clear, "Mr. and Mrs. Stern's role as parents was achieved by a surrogate uterus and not a surrogate mother." In this instance the legal community privileged the patriarch while constructing mother as a disembodied part-object.

Schwartz's analysis highlights the fact that legal discourse is incapable of acknowledging, let alone recognizing, the lived psychological and emotional experience of women who mother. Our legal system assumes that heterosexual coupling and reproduction is the norm and insists that there can be only one legal mother. Borrowing from the postmodern interpretation of gender as a shifting and at best ambiguous construct, Schwartz begins to think through a "new parenting subject, which would be less unitary and more conditional, free of constrictions of gender altogether." She brings us to a new way of thinking about the category mother, one allowing for the adult's desire to be the mother and based on a notion of *relationship* that can account for multiple subjectivities and is free from the polarities of gender.

Through an examination of representations of motherhood in Hollywood films, E. Ann Kaplan, a film theorist, investigates in the next chapter the ways in which our culture's largely unconscious and deep-seated hostility toward women plays itself out in the domain of popular culture. In particular, Kaplan explores what she sees as a newly emergent and ambivalent representation of motherhood, most clearly illustrated in such films as *The Good Mother* and *Baby Boom,* as well as in a new generation of films that privilege the fetus/baby over the mother (*Look Who's Talking*).

Kaplan contends that popular depictions of mothers in film do not adequately address the complexities of mothers' lived experiences. Some recent films do portray new and important images of working mothers, but more often than not they tend to collapse the complex issues that women face around sex, work, and motherhood. And, as Kaplan notes, our understanding of maternal subjectivity is deeply connected to our experience as mothers who are *also* professional and sexual beings.

Susan Rubin Suleiman, a literary critic, analyzes in the final chapter seemingly unconventional representations of motherhood, taking the antipatriarchal, energetic, and humor-based avant-garde as her starting point. In Suleiman's view, it is notable that even this counterculture group comes to subscribe to the "law of the father" in its presentation of the mother. The mother of the avant-garde is an instrument of domination who stays in her place and socializes children to become conventional. This mother betrays her daughter by her submission to patriarchy and becomes the target of her children's anger. Suleiman identifies two reactions to this presentation of the mother among feminists: the rejection of motherhood, on the one hand, and the celebration of the mother as the source of opposition to patriarchy, on the other. She argues that women who have celebrated the maternal have still presented an image of a mother who lacks humor and playfulness.

Suleiman introduces an important new element in visions of maternal subjectivity: that of the playful, laughing mother. She argues that play is the activity through which people most freely and inventively constitute themselves. In Suleiman's view, to imagine the mother playing is to imagine her most strongly as a subject.

The development of this book has enabled each of us to confront personal and political issues related to maternal subjectivity. Work on the book has spanned a considerable amount of time. It started as a special issue of a journal and gradually grew into this volume. During its creation, one of us became a mother and another lost a mother. We have had a unique opportunity to share our personal interests, desires, and ambivalences with the contributors, each of whom has joined in the struggle to face issues of maternal subjectivity.

This book has enabled us to speak and be heard as mothers, to question a society that has devalued and sentimentalized motherhood, and to develop images of generative and creative women who are also mothers. We have sought to re-present motherhood by confronting existing images; as presented in this book, that re-presentation includes a number of key elements. We have focused on motherhood as an inherently political experience, a vantage point from which to understand and question society. We have explored the complex psychological experience of both having and being mothers. And we have chosen to reckon with our own images of motherhood and to confront representations of the mother in dominant Western culture.

We write this book at a time when subjectivity itself is a topic for scrutiny.[9] Specifically, what do the concepts of identity, selfhood, and self-actualization mean in a world in which people feel fragmented and subjected to multiple life changes and social positions? Is there a difference between male and female selves? If so, what is it based on? When we speak of the mother as subject, are we speaking of her as a *female* subject? Is she *the* quintessential female subject? Is motherhood—or parenthood—privileged as a particular source of subjectivity because of the opportunity for the reliving of early experience and generativity?

The contributions to this volume provide no easy or uniform answers to these questions. Nor does the book fully map the terrain of maternal subjectivity. We hope that this volume creates a space in which the complexity and multidimensionality of mother-as-subject can be explored and that these portraits of maternal subjectivity will both resonate with and enrich the lives of our readers.

References

Adorno, T. W.; Frenkel-Brunswick, E.; Levinson, E.; and Sanford, R. N. (1950). *The authoritarian personality* (abridged ed.). New York: Norton.

Arcana, J. (1979). *Our mothers' daughters*. Berkeley: Shameless Hussy Press.

Aries, P. (1962). *Centuries of childhood: A social history of family life* (R. Baldick, Trans.). New York: Random House. (Original work published 1960).

Bader, M., & Philipson, I. (1980). Narcissism and family structure: A socio-historical perspective. *Psychoanalysis and Contemporary Thought, 3*(3), 299–328.

Bassin, D. (1982). Woman's images of inner space: Data toward expanded interpretive categories. *International Review of Psychoanalysis, 9,* 191–203.

Benedek, T. (1959). Parenthood as a developmental phase. *Journal of the American Psychoanalytic Association, 7,* 389–417.

Benedek, T. (1970a). Parenthood during the lifecycle. In E. Anthony & T. Benedek (Eds.), *Parenthood: Its psychology and psychopathology* (185–206). Boston: Little, Brown.

Benedek, T. (1970b). The family as a psychologic field. In E. Anthony and T. Benedek (Eds.), *Parenthood: Its psychology and psychopathology* (109–36). Boston: Little, Brown.

Benjamin, J. (1978). Authority and the family revisited; Or, a world without fathers. *New German Critique, 4*(3), 35–57.

9. For recent analyses that deal with the issue of subjectivity, see Henriques et al. (1984), de Lauretis (1986), Flax (1990), and Butler (1990).

Benjamin, J. (1980). The bonds of love: Rational violence and erotic domination. *Feminist Studies,* 1, 144–74.

Benjamin, J. (1987). The oedipal riddle. In J. M. Broughton (Ed.), *Toward a critical developmental psychology* (211–44). New York: Plenum.

Benjamin, J. (1988). *The bonds of love: Psychoanalysis, feminism, and the problem of domination.* New York: Pantheon.

Bergum, V. (1989). *Woman to mother: A transformation.* Granby, Mass.: Bergin & Garvey.

Bernard, J. (1974). *The future of motherhood.* New York: Dial.

Burke, F. W. (1986). *Mothers talking: Sharing the secret.* New York: St. Martin's.

Butler, J. (1990). *Gender trouble: Feminism and the subversion of identity.* London: Routledge.

Cahill, S. (1982). *Motherhood: A reader for men and women.* New York: Avon.

Chernin, K. (1983). *In my mother's house: A daughter's story.* New York: Harper Colophon.

Chevigny, B. G. (1983). Daughters writing: Toward a theory of women's biography. *Feminist Studies,* 9(1), 79–102.

Chodorow, N. (1971). Being and doing: A cross-cultural examination of the socialization of males and females. In V. Gornick (Ed.), *Women in sexist society: Studies in power and powerlessness* (183–197). New York: Basic Books.

Chodorow, N. (1974). Family structure and feminine personality. In M. Z. Rosaldo & L. Lamphere (Eds.), *Women, culture, and society* (43–66). Stanford: Stanford University Press.

Chodorow, N. (1978). *The reproduction of mothering: Psychoanalysis and the sociology of gender.* Berkeley: University of California Press.

Chodorow, N. (1979). Feminism and difference: Gender, relation, and difference in psychoanalytic perspective. *Socialist Review,* 46, 51–69.

Chodorow, N. (1981). On the reproduction of mothering: A methodological debate. Reply by N. Chodorow. *Signs,* 6(3), 500–14.

Chodorow, N. (1989). *Feminism and psychoanalytic theory.* New Haven: Yale University Press.

Chodorow, N., & Contratto, S. (1982). The fantasy of the perfect mother. In B. Thorne & M. Yalom (Eds.), *Rethinking the family: Some feminist questions* (54–75). New York: Longman.

Cixous, H. (1981). Castration or decapitation? (Trans. A. Kuhn). *Signs,* 7(1), 41–55.

Comer, L. (1974). *Wedlocked women.* Leeds: Feminist Books.

Dally, A. (1982). *Inventing motherhood.* London: Burnett.

de Beauvoir, S. (1952). *The second sex* (Trans. H. M. Parshley). New York: Knopf. (Original work published 1949).

de Lauretis, T. (1986). Feminist studies/critical studies: Issues, terms and contexts. In T. de Lauretis (Ed.), *Feminist studies/critical studies.* Bloomington: Indiana University Press.

deMause, L. (1974). *The history of childhood.* New York: Psychohistory Press.

Dinnerstein, D. (1976). *The mermaid and the minotaur: Sexual arrangements and human malaise.* New York: Harper and Row.

Ehrenreich, B., & English, D. (1978). *For her own good: 150 years of the experts' advice to women.* New York: Anchor Press/Doubleday.

Elshtain, J. B. (1981). *Public man, private woman: Women in social and political thought.* Princeton: Princeton University Press.

Firestone, S. (1971). *The dialectics of sex: The care for feminist revolution.* New York: Bantam.

Flax, J. (1978). The conflict between nurturance and autonomy in mother-daughter relationships and within feminism. *Feminist Studies,* 4(2), 171–91.

Flax, J. (1990). *Thinking fragments: Psychoanalysis, feminism, and postmodernism in the contemporary west.* Berkeley: University of California Press.

Friday, N. (1977). *My mother/my self.* New York: Delacorte.

Friedan, B. (1963). *The feminine mystique.* New York: Norton.

Gilligan, C. (1982). *In a different voice: Psychological theory and women's development.* Cambridge, Mass: Harvard University Press.

Gordon, L. (1982). Why nineteenth-century feminists did not support "birth control" and twentieth-century feminists do: Feminism, reproduction, and the family. In B. Thorne & M. Yalom (Eds.), *Rethinking the family* (40–53). New York: Longman.

Greenberg, E. M. (1979). *Journey to motherhood.* New York: St. Martin's.

Harris, A. (1987). The rationalization of infancy. In J. M. Broughton (Ed.), *Toward a critical developmental psychology* (31–59). New York: Plenum.

Heilbrun, C. G. (1979). *Reinventing womanhood.* New York: Norton.

Henriques, J.; Holloway, W.; Urwin, C.; Venn, C.; & Walkerdine, V. (Eds.). (1984). *Changing the subject: Psychology, social regulation, and subjectivity.* London: Methuen.

Hunt, D. (1970). *Parents and children in history: The psychology of family life.* New York: Basic Books.

Irigaray, L. (1981). And the one doesn't stir without the other (Trans. H. V. Wenzel). *Signs,* 7(1), 60–67.

Kaplan, M. (1992). *Mothers' images of motherhood.* London: Routledge.

Kaplan, M., & Broughton, J. (in press). The mother herself: Reproduction and change in theories of women's development. *Psychoanalytic Review.*

Kestenberg, J. (1956). Vicissitudes of female sexuality. *Journal of the American Psychoanalytic Association,* 4, 453–76.

Kitzinger, S. (1978). *Women as mothers.* New York: Random House.

Klein, M. (1932). *The psychoanalysis of children.* London: Hogarth Press.

Klein, M. (1964). Love, guilt and reparation. In M. Klein & J. Riviere, *Love, hate and reparation.* New York: Norton. (Original work published 1937).

Kristeva, J. (1980a). Motherhood according to Bellini. In *Desire in language: A semiotic approach to literature and art* (237–70) (Trans. T. Gora, A. Jardine, & L. Roudiez). New York: Columbia University Press. (Original work published 1975).

Kristeva, J. (1980b). Place names. In *Desire in language: A semiotic approach to literature and art* (271–94) (Trans. T. Gora, A. Jardine, & L. Roudiez). New York: Columbia University Press. (Original work published 1976).

Kristeva, J. (1981a). The maternal body (Trans. C. Pajaczkowski). *m/f,* 5,6, 158–63. (Original work published 1977).

Kristeva, J. (1981b). Women's time. (Trans. A. Jardine & H. Blake). *Signs,* 7(1), 13–36. (Original work published 1979).

Loevinger, J.; Wessler, R.; & Redmore, C. (1970). *Measuring ego development, Volume II: Construction of a sentence completion test.* San Francisco: Jossey-Bass.

McBride, A. (1973). *The growth and development of mothers.* New York: Harper and Row.

Minturn, L., & Lambert, W. (1964). *Mothers of six cultures: Antecedents of child rearing.* New York: Wiley.

Mitchell, J. (1971). *Women's estate.* New York: Random House.

Morgan, R. (1970). *Sisterhood is powerful: An anthology of writings from the women's liberation movement.* New York: Vintage.

Moyers, B., & Tucher, A. (1990). *A world of ideas: Public opinions from private citizens.* New York: Public Affairs Television.

Oakley, A. (1979). *Becoming a mother.* New York: Schocken.

Ortner, S. (1974). Is female to male as nature is to culture? In M. Zimbalist Rosaldo & L. Lamphere (Eds.), *Woman, culture and society* (67–88). Stanford: Stanford University Press.

Plaza, M. (1982). The mother/the same: Hatred of the mother in psychoanalysis. *Feminist Issues,* 2(1), 75–99.

Pope, D., Quinn, N., & Wyer, M. (1990). The ideology of mothering: Disruption and reproduction of patriarchy. *Signs,* 15(3), 441–46.

Rich, A. (1976). *Of woman born.* New York: Norton.

Riley, D. (1983). *War in the nursery.* London: Virago Press.

Rosaldo, M. Z., & Lamphere, L. (1974). *Women, culture, and society* (43–66). Stanford: Stanford University Press.

Rubin, L. (1976). *Worlds of pain: Life in working class families.* New York: Basic Books.

Ruddick, S. (1980). Maternal thinking. *Feminist Studies,* 6(3), 343–67.

Ruddick, S. (1989). *Maternal thinking.* Boston: Beacon Press.

Schuker, E., and Levinson, N. A. (Eds.). (1991). *Female psychology: An annotated psychoanalytic bibliography.* Hillsdale, N.J.: Analytic Press.

Shreve, A. (1987). *Remaking motherhood: How working mothers are shaping our children's future.* New York: Fawcett Colurbine.

Snitow, A. (1990). Gender diary. In M. Hirsch & E. Fox Keller (Eds.), *Conflicts in feminism.* New York and London: Routledge.

Spencer, A. (1984). *Mothers are people too: A contemporary analysis of motherhood.* New York: Paulist Press.

Stack, C. (1974). *All our kin.* New York: Harper and Row.

Weiss, N. P. (1978). The mother-child dyad revisited: Perceptions of mothers and children in twentieth century child-rearing manuals. *Journal of Social Issues,* 34(2), 29–45.

Winnicott, D. (1973). *The child, the family, and the outside world.* Harmondsworth, England: Penguin.

Wolfenstein, M. (1955). Fun morality: An analysis of recent American child-training literature. In M. Mead & M. Wolfenstein (Eds.), *Contemporary cultures.* Chicago: University of Chicago Press.

Part I The Acknowledgment and Appropriation of Maternal Work

SARA RUDDICK

1 Thinking Mothers/
Conceiving Birth

Several years ago I began to ponder this question: How might a
mother, a person who thinks regularly and intently about children, think about "the world"? What styles of cognition and
perception might mothers develop? How, for example, might a
mother, a person for whom maternal thinking was a significant
part of her or his intellectual life, think about "nature," change,
the self, and other such philosophical topics?

As I began asking these questions, a fundamental difficulty
became apparent. Neither I, nor the philosophers, feminists,
and feminist psychoanalysts to whom I turned, represented
mothers as thinking people. Representations of mothers have a
way of becoming, for mothers, representations of themselves.
During most of the years that I was actively taking care of my
children, mothering was said to be love and feminine duty rather
than a thoughtful project. It was difficult for a woman of my class
and time to believe that "as a mother" she thought at all, let
alone that her "maternal thinking" was of value. Moreover, I had
a graduate degree in philosophy; during these years of domestic
responsibility and career confusion, I clung to the fragile identify of "philosopher." But Western philosophers had explicitly
and metaphorically contrasted "rational" thinking with the
kinds of particularity, passionate attachment, and bodily engagement expressed in mothering.[1] Accordingly, "as a philosopher" I

1. Many feminist philosophers have identified the misogynist character of Western ideals of rationality. Genevieve Lloyd's *Man of Reason* is
a fine introduction to this growing literature, as are, from another
tradition, Luce Irigaray's *Speculum of the Other Woman* and *This Sex
Which Is Not One*. Also of central importance is Evelyn Keller, *Reflections on Gender and Science*. The literature on feminist critiques of
rationality is vast and growing.

could imagine myself "thinking" only when I was not being "a mother" but was at "work"—teaching—or better still when I was trying to write about the transcendent objects and transcendental questions of philosophy.

I was moved to speak about mothering partly because of a feminist desire to challenge the dominant cultural ideology of mothers as naturally loving and necessarily female. But feminist thinking was of limited use in forging a representation of mothers as thinkers. Whether they were representing their mothers as victims complicit in their own oppression or as "sturdy Black bridges that [daughters] crossed over on" (Rodgers, 1979), whether as self-sacrificing angels who paralyzed their daughters' creative wills or as teachers who taught their daughters all they needed to know, feminists tended to speak as daughters trying to forge a daughter/self-respecting connection to their mothers' lives.[2] I, by contrast, was struggling to acquire and maintain a maternal perspective. Moreover, partly because they wrote as daughters, feminists writing about mothers wrote very little about the children mothers think and speak about. I was—and still am—interested in maternal thinking because of what maternal concepts might introduce into political and philosophical discussions. But maternal concepts can be reflective of mothers, and a help to them, only if they are anchored in thinking about children.

There was—and is—at least one strand of feminist inquiry, psychoanalytic feminism, that speaks both of children and of philosophy.[3] Unlike traditional

2. Marianne Hirsch (1989) speaks about the "exclusively daughterly stance" of feminists and argues for a mother-inclusive feminism. There were, of course, many women who wrote at least partly from a maternal perspective, and in recent years their ranks have grown. In thinking about mothers, I could have drawn upon Maya Angelou, Harriett Arnow, Jane Lazarre, Audre Lorde, Toni Morrison, Gloria Naylor, Tillie Olsen, Grace Paley, Ann Petry, and Alice Walker, to cite only a few notable instances of American writers. Adrienne Rich quite consciously wrote both as a daughter and as a mother; I also (though perhaps eccentrically) drew upon Virginia Woolf's expression and legitimation of maternal vision. But feminists at that time, or at least I as a feminist, tended to read as well as to write as a daughter. It is sometimes said that white feminists of various ethnic groups saw their mothers as complicit in their oppression, whereas African-American feminists— and perhaps other daughters of color—respected their mothers' struggles. This seems to me—remembering and reading as a white woman born in 1935—to simplify the complex and ambivalent feelings of women writers from white, African-American, and various other groups.

3. I am speaking in the paragraphs that follow only of feminist psychoanalysis. In certain contexts, especially in seminars of philosophy of mind or philosophy of the emotions, I have discussed Freud, Lacan, Winnicott, and other analysts and have in this setting appreciated their inestimable contribution to philosophy. Neither in my other teaching and writing nor here do I judge psychoanalysis as therapy or as theory of therapy. When I speak of feminist analysts, I am often drawing upon literary critics' appropriation of Lacan, especially, and following Lacan, Kristeva and Irigaray. More directly, as I started thinking about maternal thinking I was influenced by Dorothy Dinnerstein, Evelyn Keller, Nancy Chodorow and Jessica Benjamin, all of whom are explicitly and consciously mother-respecting. Except for Dinnerstein they have also identified themselves with an

psychoanalysis, psychoanalytic feminism aims to speak of children in mother-respecting ways. To cite one instance, psychoanalytic feminists trace women's desire to care for children to a predominantly "positive" (albeit often personally costly) feminine identity that is forged in a daughter's struggle to maintain a differentiated connection to her mother.[4] In addressing philosophy, psycho-analytic feminists draw illuminating connections among dominant ideals of rationality, norms of masculinity, and the creation of gender identities in patri-archal households and societies.[5] These psychoanalytic feminists show, for ex-ample, how and why rationality has been opposed to female bodies and feminine attachment and why, therefore, mothers should not be expected to think.[6]

Nonetheless, despite their feminist and philosophic virtues, I found these psychoanalytic tales of little help in representing mothers as thinkers. Noto-riously, many psychoanalysts try to outmother mothers, at their worst con-

---

object relations perspective. Each of these writers has been invaluable in constructing a feminist critique of dominant ideals of rationality. Yet when I read and discussed them as a mother trying to discover a mother's voice I found that voice distorted or obscured *despite* the explicit commitment of each of these writers to the moral and psychological necessity of recognizing a mother's subjectivity. I now believe that my oppositional stance toward psychoanalytic feminism, while enabling me to speak of maternal thinking, also impov-erished the concept of maternal thinking that developed. But that is the subject of another essay.

4. This thesis was first articulated by Nancy Chodorow and since then has been adapted, refined, and criticized by many feminists, including Chodorow herself.

5. Feminist critiques of prevailing ideals of reason take many forms. Feminists have shown that some philosophers explicitly or metaphorically contrast women or "the femi-nine" with what is prior to reason, with what reason must leave behind or set itself against. Hegel is an example. Other philosophers conceptualize ideals of reason that unwittingly reveal a masculine subjectivity; Descartes is the primary example and Mill, according to DiStephano's (1989) reading, a less obvious example. Other philosophers create concep-tions of individual knowers and agents that reflect masculine fears and aggression; Hobbes is a primary example. Still others, though feminists, fail to "thematize a gender subtext" (Fraser, 1989) and therefore obscure the power relations between men and women in the allegedly private and also the public sphere. Rawls and Habermas are examples. This literature is vast and controversial. See, e.g., Lloyd (1984), Keller (1985), DiStephano (1989), and Fraser (1989).

6. For example, according to object relations theory, children create their identities by separating themselves from their mothers. For most children in male-dominant societies, but especially for boys, the mother serves as the "*negative* ground of a constructed and apparently 'positive' masculine identity" (DiStephano, 1989). DiStephano, Keller, and Bordo, among others, have shown how "masculine" direction from the (m)other and a subsequent compulsive attachment to detachment are reflected in conceptions of ratio-nality. In its post-Lacanian version, feminists see psychoanalysis as diagnosing—while also expressing—a myth that has surfaced from Aeschylus through Hegel: culture, per-haps even language itself, and therefore reason depends upon "the mother's absence and on the quest for substitutes for her, substitutes that transfer her power to something that men's minds can more readily control" (Homans, 1986, p. 4).

structing a "vast apparatus of hatred of the Mother . . . An Awful Mother, worthy of a horror film" (Plaza, 1982). But this was not my trouble: feminist psychoanalysts avoid mother-blaming, or at least they blame patriarchal systems for making mothers deficient (admittedly of small comfort if you are a mother). The maternal absence I detected had a less tractable purchase within the theory. Put simply, psychoanalysis is committed to children's experience. As Marianne Hirsch aptly puts it: "In all psychoanalytic writing the child is the subject of both study and discourse. . . . The adult woman who is a mother . . . continues to exist only in relation to her child, never as a subject in her own right. . . . She remains an object . . . always represented through the small child's point of view" (1989, p. 167).[7]

Not only is a mother's voice virtually absent in psychoanalytic tales; worse, the child that psychoanalysts reveal is often a stranger to her mother. In one dominant psychoanalytic story, an infant is at first part of a mutually desiring mother-child couple. Then, still primarily attached to "the mother," "the child" moves through a stage of development that sounds like a prelude to the "real" thing—*pre*oedipal, *pre*symbolic. Sometimes, in a rhetorical elision, the mother herself is identified with "the maternal body" or is herself called "the preoedipal mother" as if she, like her child, has yet to become a social, thoughtful being. As he inches toward language, the child also often inches toward "the father" and His Law; too much "mother-love," some psychoanalysts suggest, is madness. Yet even in her father's world, the child hero of psychoanalytic stories is apt to remain as obsessed with gender difference and sexuality and as preoccupied with Mother, Father, and the passions of family life as psychoanalysts themselves.[8]

The contrast with mothers' stories about children is striking. The "dream of plenitude"—a mutually embracing, mutually desiring mother-child couple— often disappears in mothers' tales of babies who can't be made happy, jealous older siblings, altered sexual and love relationships, financial worries, and the general emotional confusion and sleeplessness that tend to mark the early weeks of mothering. To be sure, many mothers also remember moments of passionate infatuation with an astonishingly marvelous infant. But these mothers, if they are at all effective in their work, are unlikely to remember themselves as absorbed lovers in a baby couple. As Madeleine Sprengnether has remarked, "the concept of *mother*-infant symbiosis is an obvious absurdity, for a mother can only act as a mother if she perceives herself as such, as separate and different

7. Like psychoanalysts, mothers often need to see the world, including themselves, through their children's eyes. But to act effectively as mothers, they must also maintain an adult perspective that allows them to respect the realities of their own and their children's experiences amid the strong currents of their own and their children's fantasy life.

8. I want to reiterate that I am not questioning the therapeutic usefulness of this story for adult or children patients. Psychoanalysts may well have articulated the fantasies that constitute both pathological and normal defensive ways of being in the world. My question is only whether a rehearsal of these fantasies, often in the rhetorical guise of developmental truth, enables mothers to hear and speak reflectively.

from her infant. A mother who felt in every way like an infant would be worse than useless as a caretaker" (1990, p. 233).[9]

In maternal stories, infants not only begin to grow up; they keep on growing. As their children become playmates, students, friends, lovers, employees—to mention only some crude "stages"—mothers speak about a range of their children's relationships and projects and of a welter of jealousies, loves, and fears. Only some of these are concentrated upon gender identity and sexuality or upon the mothers themselves and their mates or lovers. When mothers talk about themselves, when they appear as characters in their own maternal stories, they often depict themselves as grappling with problems their children present or that the world presents to their children. But this thinking mother is not reflected in psychoanalytic tales any more than she is in philosophy or more ordinary varieties of feminism.

Thus, however much I was otherwise indebted to philosophy, feminism, and feminist psychoanalysis, I still felt that I needed to create a conceptual framework for representing, alongside the mothers we love and hate but never are, a mother who does the loving and thinking about love, someone who sees the children who see her. Now, some years later, I can briefly summarize the conceptual strategies I devised for justifying the idea of maternal thinking (Ruddick, 1989).

I began by construing mothering as a kind of work or practice. Although mothers are, culturally and individually, radically different from each other, there is sufficient commonality among children to define a "maternal" work in terms of responses to children's demands. Children are physically vulnerable for many years; they demand protection. They develop, emotionally and intellectually, in intricate, unpredictable ways: they demand nurturance. The social group that children enter requires them to learn to behave in acceptable ways; children's moral development is integral to their psychological integrity.[10] Children therefore demand training.

To be a "mother" means to "see" children as demanding protection, nurturance, and training and then to commit oneself to the work of trying to meet these demands. There is nothing inevitable about maternal response: many people, including some birthgivers, do not recognize children as "demanding"; some, including some birthgivers, respond to children's demands with indifference, assault, or active neglect; many, including many birthgivers, are unable to respond because they themselves are victims of violence and neglect. Nor does maternal commitment guarantee success: it is the continuing effort to

9. Psychoanalysts know—they after all were the ones who told us!—that the ever-attentive, plentifully bountiful (and therefore inevitably disappointing) mother is a creature of childhood fantasy. But sometimes the psychoanalytic tales appear to express the very fantasies they diagnose.

10. It is widely accepted that children, generally, require moral guidance, both for their own and the community's well-being, but I realize that I have only assumed the point here and did not make it in my book.

respond to children, often in appalling and outrageous conditions, that marks maternal work.

In construing mothering as a kind of work I do not mean to suggest that mothers are without feeling as conventional divisions between work and feeling, labor and love, might imply. Mothering—like, for example, teaching, psychotherapy, ministering, and any kind of caring labor—is a relational work in which others' responses serve as an intrinsic and primary measure of achievement. Among relational works, mothering is especially entrenched in actual and expected passion. But there is no single emotion—love—that children inspire in mothers. A mother's emotions can vary within the course of a day, and certainly over time, depending upon the behavior of her children, the space, time, and services available to her, and myriad other desires and frustrations. The maternal "love" that threads its way through maternal stories is no pure, positive affection but a mix of many feelings—of, for example, infatuation, anger, delight, frustration, fascination, guilt, and pride. Mothers are identified not by what they feel but by what they try to do.

After construing mothering as a work or practice, I invoked and adapted what I call a "practicalist" conception of reason.[11] According to this conception, most recognizable kinds of thinking—mathematical thinking, religious, psychoanalytic, and various kinds of scientific thinking, for example—arise out of and are tested by practices in which people engage. Since mothers are engaged in a practice, they tend to acquire whatever distinctive styles and tendencies of thought arise within that practice. More particularly, they will tend to acquire whatever cognitive capacities and metaphysical attitudes are required or inspired by the threefold aim to protect, nurture, and train children. Some mothers will think more than others because they have the time, or their children are especially troubled, or they are temperamentally inclined to reflecting. But maternal thinking is no rarity. Mothering is a complex project, involving many people, sustained over time, laden with conflict, requiring cooperation, and enmeshed in fundamental questions about, for example, sexuality, death, and responsibility. Why wouldn't mothers think? In retrospect it seems that only philosophical ideologies could obscure the very existence of maternal intellectual activity.

The strategy of construing mothering as a practice, reason as arising out of practices, and therefore, mothers as thinking, allowed me—and I hope encourages others who are interested—to begin exploring certain concepts and challenges of maternal thinking. Meanwhile the strategy itself, and in particular the construction of mothering as a kind of work or practice, has political and

11. In adapting a practicalist conception of reason, I drew particularly upon Wittgenstein's later work; Winch (1982), especially "Understanding a Primitive Society"; and Habermas (1971). I used these men to support the claim that reason arises within practices, that ideals of reason reflect the aims of practices, that there are distinctive kinds of practices/reasonings, and that there was no Ur-practice or reason to which lesser practices could be assimilated, no Ur-standard by which they could be judged.

philosophical consequences. One of these is to make it easy to trivialize and difficult to conceive birth. But before taking up this conundrum, let me mention some more fruitful consequences. When mothering is construed as *work* rather than an "identity" or fixed biological or legal relationship, people can be seen to engage in mothering with differing expense of time at various periods in their lives and in various and often changing sexual and social circumstances. The *work* of mothering does not require a heterosexual or any other particular sexual commitment. Mothers lead varieties of heterosexual, gay, lesbian, and celibate lives. Nor does mothering require a particular household arrangement. Mothers can care for one, few, or many children. Some may work so closely with others that it is impossible to identify one "mother"; others share their work with many mothering persons, and some work primarily in couples. Since mothers require many kinds of material support and emotional respect for their work, it would be an unusual person who would choose to mother alone. But in communities that care for their children, individual mothers can draw upon public services while creating for themselves kin and friendship arrangements that match their sexual desires, financial requirements, and personal interests.

Mothering *work* is no longer distinctly feminine. A child is mothered by whoever protects, nurtures, and trains her. Although it is a material, social, and cultural fact that most mothers are now women, there is no difficulty in imagining men taking up mothering as easily as women—or conversely, women as easily declining to mother. Although biological differences between female and male styles of mothering *might* survive in an egalitarian society, I see no reason to believe—and good reason to doubt—that these differences would make women (or men) more "naturally" suited to protect, nurture, and train children. Nor is there any reason to believe that in an egalitarian world the differences between men's and women's ways of mothering that might arise from sexual difference would be more evident than other social or individual differences among them.

To be sure, this cheering array of domestic and sexual choices is entirely foreign to most mothers' lives. Moreover, many mothers themselves endorse the sexual ideologies that restrict mothering to women. The construction of mothering as work does not in itself produce a particular sexual or gender politics. But it opens a space for imagining new sexual and domestic combinations that suit mothers and their children. And it provides a way of describing mothering that can be inserted into the languages of sexual liberation and gender justice.

Finally, and here I begin to inch in on the troubles, by construing mothering as gender-full, gender-free work it is possible to break the connection between giving birth and becoming a mother. Mothering and birthgiving, as experienced and practiced, are quite unlike each other. Mothering is a set of ongoing organized activities requiring discipline and attention. By contrast, pregnancy can appear as a condition, a state of physical being. Whereas mothering requires deliberative thought, pregnancy may appear to require only the rational capacities that Aristotle attributed to slaves: the ability to understand and obey [doctor's] orders. Mothering is moral—a relational work that involves at least two separately and willfully embodied persons. A birthgiver seems to take care of her fetus by taking care of herself. Seen from the temporal perspective of the life of a mothered child, pregnancy and birth are but moments; birthgiving is a dramatic physical event soon out of sight or in the footnotes.

There are good reformist reasons for separating mothering from birthgiving. When birthgiving is a distinct activity, birthgivers need not become mothers; the work of a birthgiver is not compromised if she carefully transfers to others the maternal responsibility of caring for the infant she has created. Adoptive or "step" mothers can be seen to be no less qualified for the ensuing years of maternal work because they have not given birth to the children they tend. Most to the point, throughout history and across the globe, women assume a vastly disproportionate burden of mothering work. When mothering and birthgiving are seen as separable activities men can no longer excuse themselves—any more than they can be excluded from—mothering work on the grounds that because birthgivers are females mothering is a "natural" female destiny.

There are also powerful psychological motives leading women and men to minimize the one aspect of child care that men cannot undertake. The (hitherto) ineradicable inequality in women's and men's ability to give birth—the bodily potentiality, vulnerability, and power that is women's alone—evokes guilt, envy, and resentment. Women who never could, no longer can, or choose not to give birth are also often moved to suppress distinctly female procreative powers, and mothers who adopt children may find it difficult to acknowledge a potentially disturbing difference in their own and birthgivers' relationship to infants they fervently desire. Finally, the fact that only females can give birth has typically been used against women. Women have suffered economically and have been controlled politically merely because they are potential birthgivers. Even women who do give birth, or perhaps especially women who give birth, must resist reductive characterizations of their bodies in terms of one activity, birthgiving. It seems best then to underline the fact that men's and women's bodies are, on the whole, far more alike than the body of either sex is like the body of the same sex of any other species. It is important, too, to underline the many kinds and occasions of bodily involvement with infants and children after birth. These physical relations can inspire distinctly maternal conceptions of bodily life that are in no way limited to women (Ruddick, 1989).

It is understandable then that someone trying to arrange a marriage between Reason and Mother would minimize birthgiving as I have done. But as the current commonplace reminds us, every understanding creates its blindnesses and contradictions. And as feminists are still trying to learn, the differences we deny come back to haunt us. Respecting differences includes respecting bodies as they are, metaphysically as well as socially, given us. To respect *female* bodies means respecting, even treasuring, the birthgiving vulnerabilities and procreative powers of females.

Let me then state the obvious. The most obsessive attention to cultural and individual variability of birthgiving cannot disguise the fact that all mothering, whether done by men or by women, depends upon some particular woman's labor. Nor can any political arrangement accord a male birth helper, whatever the degree of emotional, domestic, and financial support he provides, a procreative role "equal" to female birthgivers. Notwithstanding scientific and philosophic fantasies to the contrary, to be "pregnant" with new life is still and only to be a woman whose *body* and embodied willfulness is the ground and condition of each new and original being who lives.

This is a fact so obvious that it seems impossible to assert it seriously. Yet time after time, mothers who have read *Maternal Thinking* tell me that in disconnecting birthgiving from mothering I failed to read the facts of birth and therefore got their experience quite wrong. Most who have spoken have been birthgivers, but I have heard the same plaint from male mothers and from women who have adopted children. Then too, there is the question of being able to speak to people outside one's own small circles where reproductive possibilities flourish, at least in fantasy, and some feminists worry whether "women" exist. I have found that it is simply impossible to comprehend mothering in the world, to compare and contrast very different mothering practices, to listen to, let alone speak with, mothers, without acknowledging the ubiquitous and tenacious connections among being female, giving birth, and mothering.

Then too, while women do suffer when we are identified as and reduced to birthgivers, birthgiving women also suffer when, in a defensive reaction, they or other people minimize the complexity and activity of birthgiving or fail to acknowledge the dependence of children and mothers upon the birthgiver's successful execution of her work. Most notably, birthgivers can be deprived of infants by a contract that has turned them—by means of turning their uterus with which they are identified—into an object of property.[12] But this is only one of the ways that economic policies, political control, and medical management can conspire to control and exploit birthgivers, especially those who are poor, assaulted by racist practices, and powerless.

I want now to step back from these critically important dangers to birthgivers to take a more distant look at some of the attitudes that underlie my neglect of birth. Plato's dying Socrates denounced the body as a source of epistemological confusion and moral temptation. As Susan Bordo has been especially adept at showing (Bordo, 1993), many other philosophers, including Plato at other moments, have urged that bodies be bent, shaped, disciplined to reason's purposes. Still more generally, although often more subtly, philosophy as it has developed in the West has honored mind over body, idea over matter, intellectual creation over physical "reproduction." Often, philosophers have implicitly highlighted a particular contempt for, if not revulsion from, female birthgiving bodies (Held, 1989; O'Brien, 1983; Ruddick, 1989).

I now believe that in thinking about mothering, I acted, conceptually, within

12. There is now a vast literature on surrogacy. I take the phrase "object of property" as well as my understanding and rejection of birth contracts from Williams (1988).

this tradition of distrust and therefore unwittingly replicated misogynist divisions between, to put the point crudely, "breeders" and moral mothers. As Hazel Carby among others has reminded us, this distinction has divided mothering women since slavery and is currently enacted in the practices and rhetoric of racism and of "reproduction" (Carby, 1987). Whatever the political and psychological advantages, there is a downside, a misogynist twist in the disconnection of mothering from birth.

How then am I, are we, to reconceive birthgiving in birth-respecting ways? It isn't possible simply to reconnect birthgiving and mothering. It is true that many mothers are women who give birth and that most birthgivers become mothers. Nonetheless the activities of birthgiving and mothering are really not much like each other, and neither activity is a necessary condition for or consequence of performing the other activity well.

I am especially concerned that we do not naturalize or sentimentalize a birthgiver's bonding with her infant. A birthgiver may have good and sufficient reasons to entrust the mothering of an infant she has carefully created to other mothers. If the reasons are *hers,* then to disregard them is once again to trivialize the birthgiver.[13] Moreover, birthgivers who later become good-enough self-respecting mothers do not, simply by giving birth, find themselves unambivalently and romantically attached to their infants. Mother love is complex from the beginning, and to deny that complexity leaves many birthgivers ashamed of emotions they do feel while guiltily fretting about emotions of "natural" love they cannot muster.

The task as I see it is to represent birthgiving as distinguished from *and* connected to mothering in ways that allow us to honor both of these activities as they play themselves out in women's and men's lives. Although I have barely begun to reimagine birth, I would like to outline three moments of this project as I discern them in others' writing and through reflections on my friends' and my own birthgiving experiences.

The first moment, and a prerequisite for the other two, is to represent birth as a chosen activity requiring commitment and responsibility. In current political conditions, both in this country and around the world, it is an anticipatory utopian act even to begin to represent birth as a chosen activity. Many women do not have the knowledge or skills to control conception or to terminate a pregnancy. Many women who have the knowledge and could make use of available technologies are nonetheless deliberately denied the material conditions of choice. Some are forced into pregnancies they would choose to terminate; some cannot secure even the food, let alone the medical attention, that birthgiving requires. Nonetheless, given the technological resources and knowledge available at this time, birthgiving could become, and could be understood as, a

---

13. The widespread exploitation of birthgivers, usually poorer women within a country, and birthgivers of poorer countries, is one poignant expression of the radical injustices that mark these women's lives. This abuse, however, does not, in my eyes, make birth-respecting adoption impossible.

project that any woman can refuse and that many, at some points in their lives, can choose to undertake.

For a birthgiver to choose means, inter alia, that she takes birthgiving as her activity, a project in which she has engaged herself. Such engagement is often emotionally complex. A choosing birthgiver may, for example, experience pregnancy as an invasion of her body; she may resent the circumstances in which she became pregnant, dread releasing her child for adoption, or fear the constraints and demands of mothering. She may nonetheless claim pregnancy and birthgiving as an expression of herself, including her resentments, ambivalences, and fears, rather than as an alien condition or social expectation to which she submits. In this ideal representation the decision to initiate or to continue a pregnancy, however complex and ambivalent, becomes reflective of and preeminent among the choices that structure a person's life. That finally the choice to give birth is, or should be, only a woman's does not make it any less human.[14]

The second phase of the project is to describe unsentimentally some of the distinctive demands of the pregnancy and birthgiving project and the particular moral requirements for meeting these demands.[15] Pregnancy is an active, receptive waiting that cannot be hurried. To call that waiting a "physical condition," as I just did, obscures the *activity* of waiting. Similarly, pregnancy is not the inherently solitary project I earlier suggested. Active waiting has an intrinsic relational character. A birthgiver can take care of her fetus simply by taking good care of herself. But the point of her caretaking, and some of its details, depend upon specific needs of the potential infant to whom she aims to give birth. The active, relational waiting of birth is often emotionally and intellectually complex. For example, birth's waiting requires judgment. To cite one familiar instance: in economically privileged classes in this country and in all classes of countries that are both socially responsible and technologically advanced, birthgivers have to make judgments about what tests to submit to, what drugs to take, what actions to initiate in response to the results of tests. This requires of them an often confusing reflection on their relation to authority. More specifi-

14. Held (1989) thoroughly and provocatively discusses the chosen character of birth. I am grateful to Astrid Henry for helpful, clarifying remarks about the "choices" birthgivers might make.

15. Even after the "demise of experience" (Jardine, 1986) it is still those who thoughtfully reflect upon present and recent birthgiving, including upon the ways it is metaphorized and socially constructed, who will be best able to articulate emotional, social, and intellectual aspects of this particular labor. Since I last gave birth twenty-five years ago, and since I went through birthgiving in a state of denial, I count myself as much a listener as mothers who have not given birth. Although I am coming very belatedly to thinking about birthgiving, there are others I am just beginning to discover who have been thinking usefully about the subject for some time. See, e.g., the work of the midwife and philosopher Mary O'Brien (1983), Iris Marion Young (1984), and Virginia Held (1989). There is now also an extensive literature on the consequences of legal and medical interventions in birthgiving. For an excellent discussion of these and other issues I have raised in this chapter, see Rothman (1989).

cally it requires of them what Socrates required of any honest thinkers: that they know what they don't know and that they take responsibility for constituting someone as an expert to whom they will listen.

Third, and finally, as birthgivers reflect upon the complexities of their experience, it may be possible to imagine their acquiring cognitive and emotional capacities that they themselves trace to birthgiving experiences. This is not to say (as I once wrote and hoped) that there is a "natal thinking" comparable to "maternal thinking."[16] There is no commonality among birthgivers to give such an idea purchase. Rituals and practices of giving birth in different cultures vary at least as much—and I believe more—than those of mothering. Moreover, there are often sharp differences between one woman's several pregnancies even when there is no change in her class, cash, access to services, sexual orientation, domestic arrangements, or the father of her children.

To be sure, mothers also differ from each other individually and socially in all the ways that people differ. I have nonetheless urged that "we" constitute a work of mothering defined in response to a "human" child who, by dint of her or his vulnerability and complexity, "demands" protection, nurturance, and training. This "human" child that I describe amid the wide variety of actual children is a political creation, not an empirical finding. Might someone imagine a similar conceptual-political creation to ground natal reflections?

Perhaps. But it is clear that fetuses cannot play the same conceptual role in natal reflection as children do in maternal thinking. Mothers are provoked to think by participating along with others over many years in the daily work of responding to children's complex ongoing demands. Birthgivers undertake a temporally limited project that, though it is surely socially embedded, is also intrinsically solitary. Birthgivers understand their project according to their knowledge and fantasies of fetal life, sometimes supplemented by medical reports. But even where birthgivers come to believe that fetal life is at stake, a fetus itself is not demanding in the way that even a "cranky" teething baby is.[17] Fetuses are much simpler, far quieter, and obviously more contained than infants; their commonality—though greater than that of children—cannot serve as a rich source for identifying a responsive work. Moreover, conceptual-political creations are justified by their consequences. Philosophers and politicians who imagine the fetus as a very little demanding child misrepresent and often trivialize the work and limit the choices of birthgiving women (Ruddick, 1988).

Although birthgivers are not provoked to thoughtfulness by fetuses as mothers are by children, they may nonetheless be pushed to reflection by their

16. In an earlier version of this essay circulated as a Tulane University working paper, I was less skeptical of the idea of "natal thinking." I am grateful to Susan Wolf in particular, as well as to many other readers, for increasing my skepticism.

17. Fetal illness may provoke birthgivers to reflection, and these illnesses might be described in terms of fetal demands. But this seems artificial and is also exceptional in a way that, say, a child's demand for protection is not.

own mysterious experience. In speaking to birthgivers, I find that most allow, and many find it boringly obvious, that the experiences of pregnancy and birth are intellectually transformative. Yet, just as a decade ago I needed to create a conceptual space for what now seems the banality of "maternal thinking," today I find myself justifying the possibility of distinctive natal reflection.

Borrowing from psychoanalysis and from feminists such as Luce Irigaray (1985b, 1991) and Rosi Braidotti (1989), I begin by representing the knowing self—the "ego"—as in the first instance, and to a degree always, a bodily ego.[18] In Braidotti's words, this means recognizing the "primacy of the bodily roots of subjectivity" and therefore identifying "the body" as a site of knowledge (1989, p. 99). If the ego is bodily then throughout their lives and into their dying, embodied knowers may consciously undergo, and may also be intellectually transformed by, experiences that have been labeled merely physical.

In this weave of mind and body, the bodily ego is thoroughly social: from the beginning it is constituted in and constructed by relationships in which "the body" is held, touched, spoken to, heard, frightened, soothed, hurt, and comforted. Accordingly, potentially transformative physical experiences are imbued with meanings of past and future relationships and may therefore also be socially transformative. An adolescent, dying person, or nursing woman brings a particular history of pleasure, pain, trust, terror, attachment, or abuse to a new physical engagement. Similarly, the stark, dramatically physical experience of birthgiving is redolent of many past and future relationships. It is also marked for many birthgivers by an apprehensive anticipatory relationship with an only gradually differentiated being for whose coming-to-life they are in some measure responsible.

Among its various social/bodily characteristics, the knowing self is sexed when and insofar as it becomes a self. What Irigaray imagines as an "ethics of sexual difference" (1991) interrupts what she calls a logic of "the same, same, always the same" (1985, p. 205). This means that the "sexed," exclusively female character of birthgiving and natal knowledge will not arise as a "problem," since ways of knowing will be intertwined with "sexual difference" from the start. The sexed bodily ego, like the ego itself, is social, however. "Sexual difference" does not require that we represent only two sexes, still less that sex is fixed for life. Rather, every body is sexed in ways that, in most societies, can be related but never reduced to dominant conceptions of female/male sexual differences.

To be sexed approximately "female" is to encounter and therefore to know the world in approximately "female" ways. One, but only one, of these encounters with the world occurs for many but certainly not all females in birthgiving. When a birthgiving female engages in this bodily/social, sex-expressive project she *may* acquire, and then through reflection articulate, distinctive metaphysical attitudes, cognitive capacities, and values. Her close companions and midwifing women and men who attend her would then also be able to participate in natal reflection through imaginative, attentive listening.

18. I am very freely adapting Braidotti and, even more so, Irigaray.

Although I am just beginning to work with the concepts of a social/bodily ego and sexed subjectivities, and while I have yet to connect them in any detail with specific concepts of natal reflection, I nonetheless admit to hunches or hints of capacities and conceptualizations appropriate to natal reflection. I am currently working with four organizing ideas.

Two of these seem distinctive to pregnancy and birthgiving. I have already alluded to the idea of an "active waiting" that in its continuation (ideally) expresses a self-expressive, often self-transformative choice. This capacity to wait actively redraws familiar distinctions between passivity and action and designates a temporally extended responsibility that can require and reveal relational, moral, and intellectual complexities.

Then, second, it seems that women reflecting upon birthgiving experiences would grapple with the phenomenon of chosen (as birth is chosen) and predictable pain. There are already many representations of the pain of birthgivers. Most notably, a birthgiver's suffering is equated with a warrior's sacrifice (Huston, 1985; Martin, 1987). Conceptions of pain are not given with its experience but are created out of past and future social meaning. I would strive to develop a conception of chosen pain that refused associations of birth's suffering with sacrifice and disclaimed heroism.[19]

The other two organizing ideas have analogues in maternal thinking. "Control" is a central issue in maternal practice and a recurrent topic of maternal reflections. Typically mothers try to protect their children and teach children to protect themselves, knowing all the while that the worlds they inhabit are "beyond their control" (Lazarre, 1991). They often describe themselves as tempted by fantasies of total control that, as their best efforts crumble in the face of children's wills and the world's assault or indifference, become fantasies of despairing passivity. Birthgivers also speak about complexities of control. Even when they have consciously chosen to initiate and to continue a pregnancy, many birthgivers describe their bodies as "invaded," their feelings as "wild." They know that they cannot ensure the particular physical character or general well-being of the infant they are attempting to create. Nor, in a first pregnancy, can they imagine or, in any pregnancy, predict the particular sufferings of a particular labor. Yet they may feel in pregnancy more than at any other time responsible for "controlling" appetites, activities, and fears. And increasingly, as I mentioned earlier, many mothers are enabled, socially and technologically, to control many aspects of pregnancy and labor. It will take far more listening than I have done to begin to articulate concepts of control adequate to a birthgiver's experience in particular medical and political circumstances. I would only suggest that the concepts of control in natal reflection and maternal thinking will be central, distinctive, and connected.

Finally, I imagine at the center of natal reflections, as at the center of mater-

19. Similarly, in *Maternal Thinking*, I try to *develop* a "welcoming" response to children's embodied willfulness, all the time aware that many nonsadistic good-enough mothers have punitive and fearful responses to children's bodies.

nal thinking, a distinctive construction of self and other. A birthgiver's self-care, motivated by her material entanglement with an emergent being, challenges physically as well as conceptually the distinction between self and other. Yet, though the boundary between self and other cannot be drawn, the aims of birth and maternal connection affirm separation and differentiation. To cite Irigaray again, "Prior to any representation we are two. . . . Let's leave one to them" (1985b, p. 216).[20] The natal connection of fetus and birthgiver cannot be assimilated to a mother's relation to the actual, unpredictable, increasingly complex embodied willfulness of her children. Yet both relationships may foster a capacity to "wonder," to marvel at—without possessing—one's own emergent and finally separate creation.[21] The natal connection foreshadows the maternal relation: both aim for a differentiation that does not deny, but rather is sustained by caring, careful dependence.

Now, let me admit that in looking for hints of natal reflection, I am not trying to look at birth plain and simple. Any woman's birthgiving is shaped and constrained by class, race, ethnicity, religious or secular rituals, gender politics, and prevailing medical resources, to mention only some obvious cultural determinants. It is not possible to look through these abstractions and find birth. Rather, I am trying to invent a metaphysical act of birthgiving—as earlier I invented the "human child"—while recognizing that each act of birth is socially constructed and individually unique. Such metaphysical enterprises are motivated by political purposes that become inscribed in the inventions they achieve.

I read both birthgiving and mothering with an explicitly feminist eye. I seek only representations of mothering that will undercut the subordination of women whether or not they are mothers and will enable those mothers who are women to take increasing control over and pleasure in their lives. Similarly, I will test emerging representations of birth by their ability to empower birthgivers. Just as determinant is my desire to chip away at militarist thinking and fantasy, and begin to build in their place nonviolent relationships and ways of knowing. I have articulated one deliberately antimilitarist version of maternal

20. Irigaray is speaking here not of birth but of the relation of two women lovers or perhaps of a woman to her (childhood) self. In "Ethics of Sexual Difference," "Questions to Emmanuel Levina" (in *Irigaray Reader,* 1991), and throughout her translated work, Irigaray is attempting to develop a nonviolative relation to the "other." Also throughout her writings she gives the mother-daughter relationship a central ethical and political importance. But on my reading, she speaks throughout *of* the mother from a daughter's point of view. See, e.g., "The Bodily Encounter with the Mother" in *Irigaray Reader.* Irigaray does not separate birthgiving from mothering but rather clearly links "the maternal" with women ("the mother in all women, the women in all mothers . . . We are always mothers once we are women" ["Bodily Encounter"]). Thus Irigaray does not encounter the problems I address in this chapter. On the other hand, she comes close to ruling out the gender-free, gender-full mothering I still long for. I have come to Irigaray's work belatedly and am puzzled, provoked, and fascinated by it; I am just beginning to appreciate how much can be learned.

21. See Irigaray, "The Ethics of Sexual Difference." She is drawing upon Descartes.

thinking and have scrutinized maternal practices and thinking for ideals of nonviolence. Now, in looking at birth, I see attitudes and capacities required for peacemaking: for example, active waiting, resistance to fantasies of perfect control or despairing passivity, and the capacity to wonder. As I mentioned earlier, I *look* for a conception of chosen pain that rejects heroism and sacrifice. Similarly I see both the natal and maternal relationships of self and other as prefiguring one ideal of connection that is central to nonviolent relationships (Ruddick, 1989). I believe that these ideas are "really" there, to be found, in the thinking of some birthgivers. But I discover them there because, when I look at birth, I am already preoccupied with peace. People who looked at mothering or birth with different aims would see them differently.

In a similar heuristic mode I conclude with an anticipatory utopian representation of the separate but connected activities of birthgiving and mothering. All human life begins in some woman's birthgiving but no woman's birthgiving is ever more than a beginning. The point of birth—the creation of an infant—is realized only in a potentially gender-full, gender-free practice of mothering. Recognizing that all mothering depends upon some particular woman's birthgiving labor, men and women mothers create policies and institutions that respect female bodily birthgiving. Moreover, as they face the daily challenges of their work, many of these mothers find themselves drawing upon the lessons they learned, the thinking they acquired, as birthgivers and attentive companions in birthgiving, lessons that they share and therefore extend in conversation with mothers whose relation to their children's birth is less direct. In these maternal conversations mothers represent to themselves and to the world their maternal commitment. Often, in these efforts of self-(re)presentation, they find themselves invoking the promise of birth: *this* body counts; each birthgiver's bodily labor, each new body she creates, is a testament of hope. To war against any body, to neglect, abandon, terrorize, or injure bodies, is to break birth's promise. To become a mother, whatever one's particular relation to individual acts of birth, is to welcome, shelter, protect, and nourish birth's bodies and thus to undertake a work of peace.

References

Bordo, S. (1993). *Unbearable weight: Feminism, Western culture, and the body.* Berkeley: University of California Press.

Braidotti, R. (1989). The politics of ontological differences. In T. Brennan (Ed.), *Between feminism and psychoanalysis.* New York: Routledge.

Carby, H. (1987). *Reconstructing womanhood: The emergence of the African American woman novelist.* New York and Oxford: Oxford University Press.

DiStephano, C. (1989). Rereading J. S. Mill: Interpolations from the (M)Otherworld. In M. Barr and R. Feldstein (Eds.), *Discontented discourses.* Chicago: University of Illinois Press.

Fraser, N. (1989). *Unruly practice.* Minneapolis: University of Minnesota Press.

Habermas, J. (1971). *Knowledge and human interests.* Boston: Beacon Press.

Held, V. (1989). Birth and death. *Ethics,* January.

Hirsch, M. (1989). *The mother/daughter plot.* Bloomington: Indiana University Press.

Homans, M. (1986). *Bearing the word.* Chicago: University of Chicago Press.

Huston, N. (1985). The matrix of war: Mothers and heroes. In S. Suleiman (Ed.), *The female body in Western culture.* Cambridge: Harvard University Press.

Irigaray, L. (1985a). *Speculum of the other woman* (Trans. G. Gill). Ithaca, N.Y.: Cornell University Press.

Irigaray, L. (1985b). *This sex which is not one* (Trans. C. Porter). Ithaca, N.Y.: Cornell University Press.

Irigaray, L. (1991). The ethics of sexual difference. In M. Whitford (Ed.), *The Irigaray reader.* Oxford: Blackwell.

Jardine, A. (1985). *Gynesis: Configurations of woman and modernity.* Ithaca, N.Y.: Cornell University Press.

Keller, E. F. (1985). *Reflections on gender and science.* New Haven: Yale University Press.

Lazarre, J. (1991). *Worlds beyond my control.* New York: Dutton/New American Library.

Lloyd, G. (1984). *Man of reason.* Minneapolis: University of Minnesota Press.

Martin, E. (1987). *The woman in the body.* Boston: Beacon Press.

O'Brien, M. (1983). *The politics of reproduction.* London: Routledge.

Plaza, M. (1982). The mother/the same: Hatred of the mother in psychoanalysis. *Feminist Issues,* Spring, 75–100.

Rodgers, C. (1979). *It is deep.* In R. P. Bell, B. J. Parker, & B. Guy-Sheftall (Eds.), *Sturdy black bridges. Visions of black women in literature.* New York: Anchor Books.

Rothman, B. K. (1989). *Recreating motherhood.* New York: Norton.

Ruddick, S. (1989). *Maternal thinking.* Boston: Beacon Press.

Ruddick, W. (1988). Are fetuses becoming children? In C. Nimrod and G. Griendler (Eds.), *Biomedical ethics and fetal therapy.* Calgary: Calgary Institute for Humanities, Wilfred Laurier University Press.

Sprengnether, M. (1990). *The spectral mother.* Ithaca, N.Y.: Cornell University Press.

Williams, P. (1991). *Alchemy of race and rights.* Cambridge, Mass.: Harvard University Press.

Winch, P. (1982). *Ethics and action.* London: Routledge.

Young, I. M. (1990). Pregnant embodiment: Subjectivity and alienation. In *Throwing like a girl and other essays in feminist philosophy and social theory.* Bloomington: Indiana University Press.

JANE LAZARRE

2 Fictions of Home

This is a world in which the first thing one sees is a woman writing. Ursula Le Guin, "A Woman Writing, or The Fisherwoman's Daughter"

A woman sat at her dining room table and stared across an empty notebook page, a pen held tightly in her fingers. Perhaps she would draw as she used to when she was a child, instead of write these words which turned dead as soon as the letters were framed. Worse than dead. They looked like meaningless patterns of sticks, or at best letters and language belonging to a list more than a story: referential, thin, insignificant.

A woman with a pen in her hand and a notebook before her sits at a table of unstained oak whose simplicity gives her a feeling of peace. She stares out a window at another window in which, every so often, another woman—first in a slip, then a blouse and skirt, then a coat—makes coffee, drinks it, places the cup in the sink. The pen remains still, although the woman in the apartment across the way, especially when she was in her slip, has the large breasts and wide hips that for a moment cause Julia to want to describe her. She moves around her kitchen with the air of unconsciousness one uses at home. She reaches for a cup without thinking: the cups are on the left shelf. The hand knows where the cup is. And while she pours hot coffee into a red mug, she absently turns on the hot water. She needn't look to see which tap is hot, which cold. Julia watches, a voyeur noticing details of a woman at home. But what if she goes on with the story? Julia wonders, tapping the table with her pen and closing her notebook. The moment she moves beyond description there will be trouble. She knows this from trouble in the past. All sorts of complexities will arise, causing headaches and confusion. Her own life will shadow the other woman's, making her notice things about herself she can do without. Another story may gradually intrude until it takes over the one she had meant to tell. Or the story might end up some place she hadn't planned, forcing into language an insight better left to the comfortable ambiguities of semiconsciousness. There was something about the woman's way of moving, for instance, that suggested efficiency and assertion to which Julia is already negatively comparing herself.

Her apartment is quiet and neat. The walls are a pleasing cream color, not exactly white. Around the room, in rugs and chairs and curtains, are the green and brown tones Julia loves. She looks at the colors, runs open palms across the unstained oak of the table, and watches the woman across the way as she buttons her coat while looking out her kitchen window, perhaps at Julia, then disappears.

She returns her notebook to the shelf above her desk and begins to dress for school. Outside, behind moving layers of various grays in a darkening sky, snow seems to gather and threaten. If there is a storm tonight, Julia thinks, she will be even more resistant than she already is to going to the homeless shelter with Anthony. And all through the day, while she teaches classes and counsels students on their writing projects, she ponders and regrets her commitment to her son. Then instantly she feels guilty. Of course she will go with him. Anthony is cornered lately by his contradictory impulses toward suffering. He is obsessed by it, wallpapers his room with posters against every injustice. He writes dozens of poems about starving African children, all in the first person. Yet he keeps his distance from action of any kind. "It upsets me," he tells her. "I can't sleep at night." So she had called a friend, an activist for the homeless, who suggested a small, carefully screened program in a synagogue in Gramercy Park—not too overwhelming—a good place to begin.

Both Bruce and Daniel will be gone overnight. She will have some time to relax, she thinks as she enters her apartment at the end of the day, before Anthony comes home. She retrieves her journal from the shelf and writes underneath the short description of herself preparing to describe the woman in the window across the way: *I am going to serve food to homeless people in a small shelter tonight. With Anthony.*

It is a cold night in the middle of the winter of 1987. Sleet is falling in a thick film and the streets are deserted. Anthony and Julia walk down Twenty-second Street between First and Second avenues and turn onto the tree-lined block called Gramercy Park East. Number 120, an old synagogue housing a small shelter for the homeless, faces a gated park that can be opened only with keys provided to tenants of the exclusive apartments on the square. It looks to her like a scene from a novel set in old London—moments before the start of a fancy ball or of a grisly murder. Instead, having found themselves to be the first volunteers to arrive, Julia and Anthony wait for a group of homeless people who have been carefully chosen by city shelter managers as being relatively sane and certainly not violent. They are aristocrats of the homeless, allowed to come to this pleasant, large room night after night, so that for a few weeks at a time the shelter offers one quality of ordinary homes: there every night, or at least for the allotted ten; predictable, stable.

The volunteers have been welcomed and given instructions by a distinguished-looking black man, the custodian of the synagogue to whom Anthony virtually bows when he says hello. Then they begin pulling out the cots and arranging them in four rows, placing one cotton sheet at the foot of each, one folded gray army blanket, one striped pillow, one cotton pillowcase. Next, they are led into the kitchen to prepare plates of cookies and doughnuts and to count out paper cups for coffee and tea. Soon, a bus pulls up at the door, and about twenty people, all carrying shopping bags packed with belongings, begin filing in like weary world travelers arrived at last at their hotel, having been crowded on the tour bus all afternoon. Julia reaches for Anthony's hand. From the beginning, when they were infants in her arms, or strapped in colorful corduroy carrying packs to her chest, or leading her (so it seemed at times) down the street in their carriages behind which she obediently pushed, she felt, in addition to whatever resentment of her chores, obligations, the endless attentions they demanded, a sense of safety too whenever she was with them. She was no longer horribly visible—alone in the world—and no longer frighteningly invisible. She was Daniel's, then Anthony's mother.

There are ten or twelve volunteers this night, more than enough hands to serve the coffee, bring out the few plates of sweets. When the small troop of homeless people walks into the room, the workers stand idly, arms laced uncomfortably across chests, ridiculous smiling hosts. Within moments, however, the roles are reversed and the workers are the guests, useless, even intrusive, as the others walk to their cots and begin fitting sheets over thin mattresses, spreading blankets, placing belongings on the floor below. "This isn't a spectator sport, you know," an old man shouts across the room as he tucks in perfect hospital corners.

Anthony turns swiftly on his heels and heads for the kitchen from where he returns a few minutes later armed with napkins and enough paper cups for a battalion. He begins laying napkins out, carefully folded as he has been taught to do but never does at home, each one placed precisely equidistant from the next. Julia watches him and feels a surge of tenderness. She has brought him here to avoid the trauma of a first experience in a huge armory, teeming with sick and desperate people, too much work for the volunteers to manage, hopelessness flattening any possible belief in his power and therefore his responsibility to affect the world. Now, here they are at the other extreme, feeling superfluous. She follows him, straightening the perfectly straight napkins he is arranging on the table. "Will you leave them alone please? They're fine," he says.

"They'll be sitting down soon," a more experienced volunteer tells them. "You serve them from the table, then sit down and talk."

"Why do we have to serve them?" asks Anthony. "It's not that I mind. I'm just curious." Julia had assumed it was just a form of graciousness, creating the illusion of a restaurant, of a better life. But the man says, "They aren't allowed to take food directly from the table. State health law. They can only touch what they have on their own plates. Might have picked up anything on the streets. Germs.

Viruses. You know. But don't worry. They know the rules. They'll just tell you what they want."

Anthony shakes his head back and forth so quickly Julia is afraid he might shake it off his shoulders. Were it not for him, she would hang back herself, perhaps leave altogether, mumbling about the absurdities of all social life, heading for her study, her books, with a determination born of falsely alleviated guilt. The world can go to hell, she might have muttered out loud as she flagged a cab uptown. But she is his mother. If she fails to set an example of fortitude, who will? So she nudges Anthony, leading him to a table where three people sit, hands folded before them. "Would you like cookies or doughnuts, coffee or tea?" she asks them, a born waiter.

"Both," answers the old white man who shouted at them for staring at the sheet-folding. His hands are rough and thick and clean. His eyes convey a burdensome clarity as he stares into the air before him. "Coffee for me, please. Tea for my wife." He lifts his chin in the direction of a bedraggled woman next to him. Her dyed, red hair is knotted and wispy, her skin caked with several layers of pink powder which cracks in places exposing narrow rivulets of tan flesh. "Tea," she repeats, her eyes fixed on a dusty ball of green yarn she clutches in her hands.

"Anthony, they would like cookies and doughnuts. This is my son, Anthony," Julia tells them.

Briefly, the man looks surprised, noticing, Julia knows, her son's dark skin. She is used to this double take when she introduces her children. Even when they were very young and exactly the same olive tan as she is, people always knew. Their eyes would dart back and forth in an instant of surprise followed by a hostile or an overly friendly greeting. Julia feels a moment of mean gratification that the homeless man is white and will be served by a young black boy. But the man recovers and shakes Anthony's hand, muttering, "McNeil."

She moves over to the next person, inquiring about menu, while Anthony gathers the food. Finally, they are all seated at the table—Mr. and Mrs. McNeil, Anthony and Julia, and a middle-aged black man who has ordered doughnuts and tea.

"My name is Julia," she says to him, "and this is my son, Anthony."

"Weber," he tells them. "Welcome."

Mrs. McNeil throws her soiled yarn onto the floor and calls, "cloudy, cloudy, cloudy." The yarn unravels for several feet and stops.

"Came up from Florida two years ago," her husband intones as if it is habitual—this tiresome need to explain his wife's behavior. "Sold everything down there." He holds out a plate, which Anthony instantly grabs and fills. "Had a cat up here named Cloudy."

"My cat's name is Pepper," Anthony says, and Julia is touched by his need, his effort to converse, but Mr. McNeil ignores him. Perhaps because he has to get the story out in order to avoid annoying questions, thinks Julia. She hopes it is not because Anthony is black.

"Then things got bad," he continues. "I lost my job. She needed an operation. We were evicted. Held onto Cloudy for a while on the streets, but in the end we lost her. Who knows? Maybe she found her way back to the apartment." He shrugs narrow rounded shoulders. "Cats do that." He turns his head slightly in the direction of his wife. "She thinks it's still here."

"That's terrible," says Anthony, sounding so alarmed that Mr. McNeil finally smiles at him and asks, "Where do you go to school, son?"

While Anthony begins describing his private school, trying to slide over the location in the tree-lined streets of Riverdale, the huge playing fields, although Mr. McNeil is clearly interested in sports and perks up at the mention of Anthony's participation on the teams, Julia turns to Mr. Weber. As if resigned that it is his turn to speak, as if she is an elementary school teacher welcoming a new class, he says, "I'm from D.C. originally. Lived in Brooklyn for a while." And although his tone is conversational and without any resentment, this time color makes her feel ashamed of herself, a white woman requiring an older, poorer black man to tell his story.

"I come here with my wife," he says, nodding in the direction of a small, dark woman still engaged in preparing her belongings for the night. She takes a blue bathrobe from her shopping bag, folds it in her lap, then pulls one out for her husband and lays it across the pillow, which she fluffs up before turning down the sheet. Carrying two white towels and a large plastic bag filled with soaps and creams, she walks out of the room as if she is alone and busy in her own home, as if there are not a dozen people seated at tables, many of them watching her intimate preparations for the night. As Julia, too, watches she thinks of her father, who died before Anthony was born, and who gave her one of her first lessons, she realizes now, in the uses of fiction.

"When you get old," he had told her one afternoon as they sat across from each other in his dingy kitchen eating herring on rye, "if you are living alone and not entirely happy"—he winked and smiled ironically—"always set the table when you eat. Make your bed every day. And change your sheets once a week. A nice meal. A made bed. Clean sheets. It helps you stay on the straight path," he had said, clicking his tongue, indicating significance.

Then she recalls the previous time she remembered his advice. When her children were small and the apartment was filled with unpredictable paraphernalia and useless items (once she found seven used-up Scotch tape dispensers taking up room in a kitchen drawer); when dusty pennies rolled under every piece of furniture and discarded clothing remained stuffed in shopping bags for years, shoved into teeming closets; during those many years of mothering boys when she often awoke in a panic fearful that her sanity would scatter before she could get them dressed, fed, and on their way to nursery school, herself to work and chores, especially then, she needed her old furniture precisely placed in a room, clean towels lined up on a rack for bath time, little shirts and jeans carefully folded in a drawer. Even a superficial orderliness had provided a bastion against the chaos threatening her self-control.

While Anthony begins including Mr. Weber in his discussion with Mr. McNeil about high school athletics, Mrs. Weber returns from her bath, a towel wrapped around her hair. She wears the blue robe, tied at the waist, furry slippers, and carries her clothing over her arm. She retrieves a book from her shopping bag and places it on her pillow, packs her folded clothing into the bag, and comes over to the table. Politely and firmly she instructs Anthony to bring her two doughnuts, four cookies, and one cup of hot tea with milk.

Julia goes to get her own cup of tea with milk, then returns to the table where she sits across from Mrs. Weber. But she cannot think of anything to say because she is overcome with an embarrassing fear. She is afraid that one day she too may be coming to a synagogue or church for shelter, left without a home when her children are grown and Bruce is who knows where. And she is embarrassed because here she is fearing for herself what has already happened to someone else. Anthony is only thirteen, but Daniel is in his last year of high school and will soon be gone. And it has always seemed, at times, a precarious fiction to her, this *family*—this being a mother—this sense of protection from the world and the coldness of its nights. She will always be a mother. She knows this. Until she is dead she will be a mother. Even after she is dead the motherness of her will remain in Daniel's and Anthony's minds. But being a mother of young children—that story is nearing its end, she thinks, watching Anthony, now completely engrossed in his conversation with Mr. Weber and Mr. McNeil. That true-to-life story, that collection of innumerable stories, is nearly finished, she thinks, and she pretends to have to go to the bathroom so no one will notice the tears in her eyes.

The bathroom is immaculate and smells of ammonia. Now that she's here she might as well pee, and when she's done she washes her hands. Standing over the sink, feeling the cool water on her wrists, she remembers how when she was a child she hated anyone to tell her what to do. Even sensible rules seemed offensive to her, so when her grandmother, who lived with them for some years, insisted that she wash her hands everytime she went to the bathroom, she would instead let water run into the sink in case her grandmother was listening, but she would not wash her hands. Then, once, when the boys were small and Bruce's mother, an extravagantly clean woman, was spending many evenings with them, she found herself doing the same thing—going to the bathroom to pee, then letting the water run without washing her hands, feeling the same edge of prideful independence she'd felt as a child. Homeless, the need for shelter would subject you to all sorts of rules, and for someone like her—Daniel, for instance—too many rules of any kind could drive you mad. She thinks about her cousin, a boy she'd been close to as a child, who had become a drug addict and eventually landed in jail. In one letter to her, he'd said that the only way he could break their rules was by constructing even more rigid ones for himself— waking at 5 A.M., for instance, instead of the required 6. And only in breaking their rules could he retain some sense of himself. Now, standing in the bathroom and feeling nearly sick from the ammonia smell, she feels as potentially alone as she has ever before felt, and the potential seems as painful as the fact might someday be. Or perhaps it is not loneliness she feels but what she imagines to be

Mrs. Weber's despair, which must surely lie beneath her stoical fictions involving habits of cleanliness and order. Or, Julia thinks while drying her hands on a rough paper towel, she is experiencing the more naked desperation of Mrs. McNeil. Yes, she is sure of it. She would fail to manage the small rescues devised by her father and Mrs. Weber. She would be unable to conjure up a belief that any of it mattered. Like Mrs. McNeil, she would go mad. But what if this is the self-indulgence black people and poor people often speak of, this presumption of knowledge, this insistence on imagining a suffering one has in fact always been spared? But no, she thinks, it is not the physical fact of homelessness and its implications she is claiming to feel. (Though she insists she can imagine that. Not that she can imagine any deprivation. But almost certainly this one.) It is the obvious fragility she suddenly perceives in all the stories she makes up and has made up about her life. The one, for instance, about how her children will never really leave her, even though they have (naturally) been slowly doing exactly that since the day they were born.

Once, years before, they had taken the boys south to visit Bruce's family. They stayed on a large farm, the only land owned by either side of the family, where they grew tobacco and corn, raised and smoked pigs. There were three houses on the land in which three generations of Courtney Joneses lived—the old grandfather, the father who lived in the big house and ran the farm, and one of the sons, about ten years younger than Bruce, a young man who was on his way up in the bank. The week Julia and her family were there, the dog had recently given birth to seven pups, just old enough to start tumbling and running around. Anthony, who had always loved animals (which is why they finally got him Pepper, although Bruce hates and fears cats), spent much of his time rolling around in the grass and mud with those puppies. He had always been a very active child, not really overactive in the clinical sense, the pediatrician told them, but almost. But here, he seemed normal, running all day and wrestling with puppies. There is a photograph framed on her bookcase at home—a large mountain of seven pups and Anthony climbing on top of each other, Anthony's face being licked by three pups at once. He seemed more at home on that southern farm he'd never before visited than he'd ever been in their city apartment where in moments, hours, of overactive energy, he crashed into walls, broke dishes, wrestled with Daniel until their giggles and screams, ordinary boyish shouting, nearly drove her mad. "Stop it!" she'd shout. "And right this minute!" So that when Daniel, with his fast talking, got older, he'd subject her to lectures on the normality of brothers wrestling, shouting, even punching each other until one of them began to cry. "It's an oppression to us," he'd told her when he was a five-foot-ten-inch twelve-year-old and Anthony a lanky, clumsy eight. "Your need for silence."

They'd launch their large frames onto beds, leaving broken springs in their wake. They broke chairs, closet doors hanging off admittedly sloppily constructed hinges. Once a window was shattered when Anthony threw a baseball at Daniel's head. And Daniel was right. It was the thundering sound of bodies rolling across the floor, the sudden screams, and not the marred furniture that pushed her to the edge. "We *are* boys, you know," Daniel would accuse, ceasing their play, obedient and furious. "Can't you ever leave us alone?"

Though he was only thirteen, Daniel drove a tractor across the roads of the farm. He leaned forward in the driver's seat, steering the huge machine down dirt lanes, swerving for dogs and pigs. She watched in horror, but Bruce, made brave and cruel by his extended kin, joined all the Courtney Joneses in laughing at her. "Nothing can happen," they chuckled. "Leave the boy alone." Eventually, not to subject herself to further humiliation by conforming so predictably to the expectations of her gender, she retreated to the kitchen where the women were snapping beans.

"Those tractors," Aunt Bernice crooned when Julia sat down at the gleaming white Formica table and grabbed a bowl of garden vegetables to cut. "My boys loved 'em too. Don't worry, honey," she said.

"Why shouldn't she worry?" said Bruce's cousin Laverne who had moved up to Washington and was down home for a visit, like Julia herself. "Courtney Junior crashed one once and broke his leg. Don't you remember?"

"Oh, most of the time nothing happens," said Bernice, and turned back to her sink.

The next morning, Daniel began calling Julia Mama in the southern way, and his inflection was so perfect she felt a stranger to the name whose echoes of security and slavery she'd come to bless and curse. "Hey, Mama," he'd shout, as the tractor swerved and tilted over dangerous hills. Anthony rushed over to her every so often and patted her back, saying, "Don't worry, Mom" (the name she knew), assuring her of her place before he bolted again.

"This is your home," she always told them periodically, but after they came home from the visit south she told them frequently for some time. "You can say anything you want here," she would repeat emphatically, drawing a contrast between home, the one created by her, and the world of schools (and southern farms) where a word like fuck, for instance, was forbidden, where children were expected to be polite rather than honest. This is what she thought she had to give—a tolerance for truth, for honest words. With the compulsion of religious faith in the literal word of God, she had believed in the power of language to control life and protect love. As if there were no danger beyond their walls an honest declaration of feeling could not neutralize. As if there were no experience on earth she did not have the obligation and the endurance to describe.

She checks her watch, nervous that Anthony might be wondering where she is and eager for it to be time to go home. When she returns to the dining area, Mrs. McNeil is again calling out for Cloudy. Anthony is deep in conversation with Mr. Weber about the possibility of a Yankee-Met world series, much as he might have been with Bruce. For another hour, Julia walks up and down the aisles, between tables, serving coffee and tea, speaking respectfully of superficial matters to as many people as she can. Then the volunteers who are sleeping over night begin setting up their cots, and Anthony and Julia get ready to leave. Mrs. Weber, who has been stacking the paper plates as if they are bone china, puts a restraining hand on Julia's arm. "He's a good boy," she says. "Be thankful he's a good boy." Julia is not sure if Mrs. Weber is addressing her with a welcoming intimacy, as if Julia were black, or if she is instructing her about her son because she is white and might be too dumb to notice his nature. But she nods, feeling grateful and strangely relieved. Then Mrs. Weber turns to Anthony. "You keep being a good boy, hear?" she warns, managing to imply by her injunctions to them both the paradoxical belief that Julia has been blessed by fate in her son's essential goodness, and that he must continue to exert a determined will against badness lurking at every corner of the dangerous streets. As soon as the situation is named with such clarity, Julia knows it is how she has been feeling all along. Then, as if she were going home, Mrs. Weber shakes both their hands and returns to her readied cot and her book. She turns her back to them and they are gone.

In the taxi, Anthony remains silent. Sleet falls harshly against the window panes. The car has no shock absorbers, so they bump up and down, falling against each other continually. "I was just thinking," he says at last, then looks away from her, out the side window.

"What?"

"I was wishing I could find their cat for them. I would go to the old neighborhood and find the house. Their old apartment would be dark and empty but I'd hear the cat mewing, so I'd creep in, with a flashlight. Then I'd see Cloudy in a corner. They say cats can find their old homes, so she did. She was hungry and mangy. But she was still alive at least. I'd take her home and feed her until she was all well. Then I'd go back to the shelter one night and find Mr. and Mrs. Weber and give the cat back to them."

They enter the park road, twisting around curves. Passing headlights illuminate the angular structure of his face creating white streaks on his brown skin. "Anthony," she says to him, placing a tentative hand on his thigh. "The cat belonged to Mr. and Mrs. McNeil. Remember? It wasn't the Webers."

"I know," he says. "But I was thinking about finding Cloudy, and I really liked the Webers. Not that I didn't like Mr. McNeil, though she was pretty weird. But the Webers seemed so normal, like—like they could be my family. And I don't mean to hurt your feelings Mom, but I am black you know."

So here, as if she were writing a story, is the clarity she hadn't planned on. Besides the desire to help Anthony manage his empathy for the world, her own need to do something to help, she was constructing a story she could live by: about working in a homeless shelter, but also one about the closeness of a mother and a son, a story implying that no matter how separate they must learn to be they are still—well, *one* in a way, different yet the same. Here is the danger, and apparently it stalks her whether or not she writes the stories down. Because now she is silent in the taxi as Anthony relives aloud the details of the past three hours. "Did you see how Mrs. Weber acted as if she were in her own house? Did you hear how much Mr. Weber knew about sports? He was like a walking encyclopedia, Mom. It's incredible. How did that happen to them? I mean losing their home—" But as he goes on she hears only the timbre of his voice and behind the voice the rhythmic beat of sleet against the window, the whoosh of cars speeding by them. Then all the sounds meld into one low backup to the voice she hears in her head.

What color am I Mom?

Anthony was a lithe and slender child, and she ran admiring fingers across his narrow ribs, down his bumpy spine. His hair, brown like hers, caught gold and red in the light. Daniel was thick in the shoulders, like Bruce, but his thighs were slightly too short for his torso, like Julia's. His nose was small, like hers, and his mouth might have been a carefully designed replica of her mother's.

What color am I Mom?

Perhaps gold, or bronze, she thought, studying their flesh.

It is 1981, and Daniel is graduating from the sixth grade. Along with all the other parents, she sits in the auditorium, waving the program across her face to make the air move. Strains of music begin, a trill of scales, then the two chords she recalls from her own elementary school days which mean *Stand Up.* They stand, along with all the fifth, fourth, and third graders attending the ceremony. Now "Pomp and Circumstance" fills the room. A few fathers move into the aisle, kneeling, camera ready to snap when their child marches in. Girls in organdy and piqué. Boys in dark pants, white shirts, and red and blue ties around such thin and insubstantial necks. There are faces of pale tan and pink (what she used to call flesh color in her crayon drawings when she was a child), faces of olive brown, faces of tan with an ocher tint, in this neighborhood famous for its ethnic complexity. The line of girls passes down one aisle, boys down the other, all walking in time to the music, smiling, size places. Now, the tallest boys come down the aisle, the end of the line, and for the most part their faces are dark brown, a half dozen shades from burnt sienna to nearly black. The black boys are in the back of the line, most of them the tallest ones in the sixth grade. But there in their midst is Daniel, brown flesh sparkling, dark curls reaching around his shell-like ears.

"What color am I Mom? I mean what *color* am I? Not what color am I *really.* You know what I mean. What *color* am I? Really. Am I black? Like Daddy?"

"You are black like Daddy," she says.

And now, as he walks past her with the tallest boys, she sees that he is.

For weeks after that night, the walls of their apartment are permeable to the Webers and the McNeils. They worry about them in late night rain storms that before would have increased the warm comfort of their beds. Julia makes up stories for Anthony of happier endings so he can fall asleep, and somehow, although he knows they are not true, he feels temporarily comforted. Then she returns to her bed and unrestful sleep, dreaming of dangerous streets that mock her fictions of fairness and control. She finds she is unable to describe the shelter in her journal, but to record the memory of that night can manage only this: Speeding down the winding park road, surrounded by passing shadows that may be men and women huddled under plastic garbage bag tents, in the dark interior of the taxi I am stark white and visible.

PATRICIA HILL COLLINS

3 Shifting the Center:
Race, Class, and Feminist Theorizing
about Motherhood

I dread to see my children grow, I know not their fate. Where
the white boy has every opportunity and protection, mine will
have few opportunities and no protection. It does not matter
how good or wise my children may be, they are colored.
An anonymous African-American mother in 1904
(reported in Lerner, 1972, p. 158)

For Native American, African-American, Hispanic, and Asian-
American women, motherhood cannot be analyzed in isolation
from its context. Motherhood occurs in specific historical contexts framed by interlocking structures of race, class, and gender, contexts where the sons of white mothers have "every opportunity and protection," and the "colored" daughters and sons of
racial ethnic mothers "know not their fate." Racial domination
and economic exploitation profoundly shape the mothering
context not only for racial ethnic women in the United States but
for all women.[1]

    1. In this chapter, I use the terms *racial ethnic women* and *women of
color* interchangeably. Grounded in the experiences of groups who have
been the targets of racism, the term *racial ethnic* implies more soli-
darity with men involved in struggles against racism. In contrast, the
term *women of color* emerges from a feminist background where racial
ethnic women committed to feminist struggle aimed to distinguish
their history and issues from those of middle-class white women. Neither term captures the complexity of African-American, Native American, Asian-American, and Hispanic women's experiences.

Despite the significance of race and class, feminist theorizing routinely minimizes their importance. In this sense, feminist theorizing about motherhood has not been immune to the decontextualization in Western social thought overall.[2] Although many dimensions of motherhood's context are ignored, the exclusion of race and/or class from feminist theorizing generally and from feminist theorizing about motherhood specifically merits special attention (Spelman, 1988).[3]

Much feminist theorizing about motherhood assumes that male domination in the political economy and the household is the driving force in family life and that understanding the struggle for individual autonomy in the face of such domination is central to understanding motherhood (Eisenstein, 1983).[4] Several guiding principles frame such analyses. First, such theories posit a dichotomous split between the public sphere of economic and political discourse and the private sphere of family and household responsibilities. This juxtaposition of

2. Positivist social science exemplifies this type of decontextualization. In order to create scientific descriptions of reality, positivist researchers aim to produce ostensibly objective generalizations. But because researchers have widely differing values, experiences, and emotions, genuine science is thought to be unattainable unless all human characteristics except rationality are eliminated from the research process. By following strict methodological rules, scientists aim to distance themselves from the values, vested interests, and emotions generated by their class, race, sex, or unique situation. By decontextualizing themselves, they allegedly become detached observers and manipulators of nature. Moreover, this researcher decontextualization is paralleled by comparable efforts to remove the objects of study from their contexts (Jaggar, 1983).

3. Dominant theories are characterized by this decontextualization. Boyd's (1989) helpful survey of literature on the mother-daughter relationship reveals that though much work has been done on motherhood generally, and on the mother-daughter relationship, very little of it tests feminist theories of motherhood. Boyd identifies two prevailing theories—psychoanalytic theory and social learning theory—that she claims form the bulk of feminist theorizing. Both of these approaches minimize the importance of race and class in the context of motherhood. Boyd ignores Marxist-feminist theorizing about motherhood, mainly because very little of this work is concerned with the mother-daughter relationship. But Marxist-feminist analyses of motherhood provide another example of how decontextualization frames feminist theories of motherhood. See, e.g., Ann Ferguson's *Blood at the Root: Motherhood, Sexuality, and Male Dominance* (1989), an ambitious attempt to develop a universal theory of motherhood that is linked to the social construction of sexuality and male dominance. Ferguson's work stems from a feminist tradition that explores the relation between motherhood and sexuality by either bemoaning their putative incompatibility or romanticizing maternal sexuality.

4. Psychoanalytic feminist theorizing about motherhood, such as Nancy Chodorow's groundbreaking work *The Reproduction of Mothering* (1978), exemplifies how decontextualization of race and/or class can weaken what is otherwise strong feminist theorizing. Although I realize that other feminist approaches to motherhood exist—see, e.g., Eisenstein's (1983) summary—I have chosen to stress psychoanalytic feminist theory because the work of Chodorow and others has been highly influential in framing the predominant themes in feminist discourse.

a public political economy to a private, noneconomic, and apolitical domestic household allows work and family to be seen as separate institutions. Second, reserving the public sphere for men as a "male" domain leaves the private domestic sphere as a "female" domain. Gender roles become tied to the dichotomous constructions of these two basic societal institutions—men work and women take care of families. Third, the public/private dichotomy separating the family/household from the paid labor market shapes sex-segregated gender roles within the private sphere of the family. The archetypal white middle-class nuclear family divides family life into two oppositional spheres—the "male" sphere of economic providing and the "female" sphere of affective nurturing, mainly mothering. This normative family household ideally consists of a working father who earns enough to allow his spouse and dependent children to forgo participation in the paid labor force. Owing in large part to their superior earning power, men as workers and fathers exert power over women in the labor market and in families. Finally, the struggle for individual autonomy in the face of a controlling, oppressive "public" society or the father as patriarch constitutes the main human enterprise.[5] Successful adult males achieve this autonomy. Women, children, and less successful males—namely, those who are working class or from racial ethnic groups—are seen as dependent persons, as less autonomous, and therefore as fitting objects for elite male domination. Within the nuclear family, this struggle for autonomy takes the form of increasing opposition to the mother, the individual responsible for socializing children by these guiding principles (Chodorow, 1978; Flax, 1978).

Placing the experiences of women of color in the center of feminist theorizing about motherhood demonstrates how emphasizing the issue of father as patriarch in a decontextualized nuclear family distorts the experiences of women in alternative family structures with quite different political economies. While male domination certainly has been an important theme for racial ethnic women in the United States, gender inequality has long worked in tandem with racial domination and economic exploitation. Since work and family have rarely functioned as dichotomous spheres for women of color, examining racial ethnic women's experiences reveals how these two spheres actually are interwoven (Collins, 1990; Dill, 1988; Glenn, 1985).

For women of color, the subjective experience of mothering/motherhood is inextricably linked to the sociocultural concerns of racial ethnic communities—one does not exist without the other. Whether under conditions

---

5. The thesis of the atomized individual that underlies Western psychology is rooted in a much larger Western construction concerning the relation of the individual to the community (Hartsock, 1983). Theories of motherhood based on the assumption of the atomized human proceed to use this definition of the individual as the unit of analysis and then construct theory from this base. From this grow assumptions that the major process to examine is that between freely choosing rational individuals engaging in bargains (Hartsock, 1983).

of the labor exploitation of African-American women during slavery and the ensuing tenant farm system, the political conquest of Native American women during European acquisition of land, or exclusionary immigration policies applied to Asian-Americans and Latinos, women of color have performed motherwork that challenges social constructions of work and family as separate spheres, of male and female gender roles as similarly dichotomized, and of the search for autonomy as the guiding human quest. "Women's reproductive labor—that is, feeding, clothing, and psychologically supporting the male wage earner and nurturing and socializing the next generation—is seen as work on behalf of the family as a whole rather than as work benefiting men in particular," observes Asian-American sociologist Evelyn Nakano Glenn (1986, p. 192). The locus of conflict lies outside the household, as women and their families engage in collective effort to create and maintain family life in the face of forces that undermine family integrity. But this "reproductive labor" or "motherwork" goes beyond ensuring the survival of members of one's family. This type of motherwork recognizes that individual survival, empowerment, and identity require group survival, empowerment, and identity.

In describing her relationship with her grandmother, Marilou Awiakta, a Native American poet and feminist theorist, captures the essence of motherwork: "Putting my arms around the Grandmother, I lay my head on her shoulder. Through touch we exchange sorrow, despair that anything really changes." Awiakta senses the power of the Grandmother and of the motherwork that mothers and grandmothers do. "But from the presence of her arms I also feel the stern, beautiful power that flows from all the Grandmothers, as it flows from our mountains themselves. It says, 'Dry your tears. Get up. Do for yourselves or do without. Work for the day to come'" (1988, p. 127).

Awiakta's passage places women and motherwork squarely in the center of what are typically seen as disjunctures, the place between human and nature, between private and public, between oppression and liberation. I use the term *motherwork* to soften the dichotomies in feminist theorizing about motherhood that posit rigid distinctions between private and public, family and work, the individual and the collective, identity as individual autonomy and identity growing from the collective self-determination of one's group. Racial ethnic women's mothering and work experiences occur at the boundaries demarking these dualities. "Work for the day to come" is motherwork, whether it is on behalf of one's own biological children, children of one's racial ethnic community, or children who are yet unborn. Moreover, the space that this motherwork occupies promises to shift our thinking about motherhood itself.

Shifting the Center: Women of Color and Motherwork

What themes might emerge if issues of race and class generally, and understanding racial ethnic women's motherwork specifically, became central to feminist theorizing about motherhood? Centering feminist theorizing on the concerns of white middle-class women leads to two problematic assumptions. The first is that a relative degree of economic security exists for mothers and their children. A second is that all women enjoy the racial privilege that allows them to see themselves primarily as individuals in search of personal autonomy instead of members of racial ethnic groups struggling for power. These assumptions allow feminist theorists to concentrate on themes such as the connections among mothering, aggression, and death, the effects of maternal isolation on mother-child relationships within nuclear family households, maternal sexuality, relations among family members, all-powerful mothers as conduits for gender oppression, and the possibilities of an idealized motherhood freed from patriarchy (Chodorow & Contratto, 1982; Eisenstein, 1983).

Although these issues merit investigation, centering feminist theorizing about motherhood in the ideas and experiences of African-American, Native American, Hispanic, and Asian-American women might yield markedly different themes (Andersen, 1988; Brown, 1989). This stance is to be distinguished from adding racial ethnic women's experiences to preexisting feminist theories without considering how these experiences challenge those theories (Spelman, 1988). Involving much more than consulting existing social science sources, placing the ideas and experiences of women of color in the center of analysis requires invoking a different epistemology concerning what type of knowledge is valid. We must distinguish between what has been said about subordinated groups in the dominant discourse, and what such groups might say about themselves if given the opportunity. Personal narratives, autobiographical statements, poetry, fiction, and other personalized statements have all been used by women of color to express self-defined standpoints on mothering and motherhood. Such knowledge reflects the authentic standpoint of subordinated groups. Placing these sources in the center and supplementing them with statistics, historical material, and other knowledge produced to justify the interests of ruling elites should create new themes and angles of vision (Smith, 1990).[6]

6. The narrative tradition in the writings of women of color addresses this effort to recover the history of mothers. Works from African-American women's autobiographical tradition such as Ann Moody's *Coming of Age in Mississippi,* Maya Angelou's *I Know Why the Caged Bird Sings,* Linda Brent's *Incidents in the Life of a Slave Girl,* and Marita Golden's *The Heart of a Woman* contain the authentic voices of African-American women centered on experiences of motherhood. Works from African-American women's fiction include *This Child's Gonna Live,* Alice Walker's *Meridian,* and Toni Morrison's *Sula* and *Beloved.* Asian-American women's fiction, such as Amy Tan's *The Joy Luck Club* and Maxine Kingston's *Woman Warrior,* and autobiographies, such as Jean Wakatsuki Houston's *Farewell to Manzanar,* offer a parallel source of authentic voice. Connie Young Yu (1989) entitles her article on the history of Asian-American women "The World of Our Grandmothers" and re-creates Asian-American history with her grandmother as a central figure. Cherrie Moraga (1979) writes a letter to her mother as a way of coming to terms with the contradictions in her racial identity as a Chicana. In *Borderlands/La Frontera,* Gloria Anzaldua (1987) weaves autobiography, poetry, and philosophy together in her exploration of women and mothering.

Specifying the contours of racial ethnic women's motherwork promises to point the way toward richer feminist theorizing about motherhood. Issues of survival, power, and identity—these three themes form the bedrock of women of color's motherwork. The importance of working for the physical survival of children and community, the dialectical nature of power and powerlessness in structuring mothering patterns, and the significance of self-definition in constructing individual and collective racial identity comprise three core themes characterizing the experiences of Native American, African-American, Hispanic, and Asian-American women. Examining survival, power, and identity reveals how racial ethnic women in the United States encounter and fashion motherwork. But it also suggests how feminist theorizing about motherhood might be shifted if different voices became central in feminist discourse.

Motherwork and Physical Survival

When we are not physically starving we have the luxury to
realize psychic and emotional starvation.   (Moraga, 1979, p. 29)

Physical survival is assumed for children who are white and middle class. Thus, examining their psychic and emotional well-being and that of their mothers appears rational. The children of women of color, many of whom are "physically starving," have no such assurances. Racial ethnic children's lives have long been held in low regard. African-American children face an infant mortality rate twice that for white infants. Approximately one-third of Hispanic children and one-half of African-American children who survive infancy live in poverty. Racial ethnic children often live in harsh urban environments where drugs, crime, industrial pollutants, and violence threaten their survival. Children in rural environments often fare no better. Winona LaDuke reports that Native Americans on reservations frequently must use contaminated water. On the Pine Ridge Sioux Reservation in 1979, for example, 38 percent of all pregnancies resulted in miscarriages before the fifth month or in excessive hemorrhaging. Approximately 65 percent of the children who were born suffered breathing problems caused by underdeveloped lungs and jaundice (LaDuke, 1988, p. 63).

Struggles to foster the survival of Native American, Latino, Asian-American, and African-American families and communities by ensuring the survival of children are a fundamental dimension of racial ethnic women's motherwork. African-American women's fiction contains numerous stories of mothers fighting for the physical survival both of their own biological children and of those of the larger African-American community.[7] "Don't care how much death

---

7. Notable examples include Lutie Johnson's unsuccessful attempt to rescue her son from the harmful effects of an urban environment in Ann Petry's *The Street;* and Meridian's work on behalf of the children of a small southern town after she chooses to relinquish her own child, in Alice Walker's *Meridian.*

it is in the land, I got to make preparations for my baby to live!" proclaims Mariah Upshur, the African-American heroine of Sara Wright's 1986 novel *This Child's Gonna Live* (p. 143). The harsh climates that confront racial ethnic children require that their mothers, like Mariah Upshur, "make preparations for their babies to live" as a central feature of their motherwork.

Yet, like all deep cultural themes, the theme of motherwork for physical survival contains contradictory elements. On the one hand, racial ethnic women's motherwork for individuals and the community has been essential for their survival. On the other hand, this work often extracts a high cost for large numbers of women, such as loss of individual autonomy or the submersion of individual growth for the benefit of the group. Although this dimension of motherwork is essential, the question of whether women are doing more than their fair share of such work for community development merits consideration.

Histories of family-based labor have shaped racial ethnic women's motherwork for survival and the types of mothering relationships that ensue. African-American, Asian-American, Native American, and Hispanic women have all worked and contributed to family economic well-being (Dill, 1988; Glenn, 1985). Much of these women's experiences with motherwork stems from the work they performed as children. The commodification of children of color—from the enslavement of African children who were legally owned as property to the subsequent treatment of children as units of labor in agricultural work, family businesses, and industry—has been a major theme shaping motherhood for women of color. Beginning in slavery and continuing into the post–World War II period, African-American children were put to work at young ages in the fields of southern agriculture. Sara Brooks began full-time work in the fields at age eleven and remembers, "We never was lazy cause we used to really work. We used to work like mens. Oh, fight sometime, fuss sometime, but worked on" (Collins, 1990, p. 54). Black and Latino children in contemporary migrant farm families make similar contributions to their family's economy. "I musta been almost eight when I started following the crops," remembers Jessie de la Cruz, a Mexican-American mother with six grown children. "Every winter, up north. I was on the end of the row of prunes, taking care of my younger brother and sister. They would help me fill up the cans and put 'em in a box while the rest of the family was picking the whole row" (de la Cruz, 1980, p. 168). Asian-American children spent long hours working in family businesses, child labor practices that have earned Asian-Americans the dubious distinction of being "model minorities." More recently, the family-based labor of undocumented racial ethnic immigrants, often mother-child units doing piecework for the garment industry, recalls the sweatshop conditions confronting turn-of-the-century European immigrants.

A certain degree of maternal isolation from members of the dominant group characterizes the preceding mother-child units. For women of color working along with their children, such isolation is more appropriately seen as reflecting the placement of women of color and their children in racially and class-stratified labor systems than as resulting from patriarchal domination. The unit may be isolated, but the work performed by the mother-child unit closely ties the mothering experiences of women of color to wider political and economic issues. Children learn to see their work and that of their mother not as isolated from the wider society but as essential to their family's survival. Moreover, in the case of family agricultural labor or family businesses, women and children worked alongside men, often performing the same work. If isolation occurred, the family, not the mother-child unit, was the focus.

Children working in close proximity to their mothers received distinctive types of mothering. Asian-American children working in urban family businesses report long days filled almost exclusively with work and school. In contrast, the sons and daughters of African-American sharecroppers and migrant farm children of all backgrounds did not fare as well. Their placement in rural work settings meant that they had less access to educational opportunities. "I think the longest time I went to school was two months in one place," remembers Jessie de la Cruz. "I attended, I think, about forty-five schools. When my parents or my brothers didn't find any work, we wouldn't attend school because we weren't sure of staying there. So I missed a lot of school" (de la Cruz, 1980, pp. 167–168). It was only in the 1950s that southern school districts stopped the practice of closing segregated African-American schools during certain times of the year so that the children could work.

Work that separated women of color from their children also framed the mothering relationship. Until the 1960s, large numbers of African-American, Hispanic, and Asian-American women worked in domestic service. Even though women worked long hours to ensure their children's physical survival, that same work ironically denied the mothers access to their children. Different institutional arrangements emerged in African-American, Latino, and Asian-American communities to resolve the tension between maternal separation due to employment and the needs of dependent children. The extended family structure in African-American communities endured as a flexible institution that mitigated some of the effects of maternal separation. Grandmothers are highly revered in African-American communities, often because they function as primary caretakers of their daughters' and daughters-in-law's children (Collins, 1990). In contrast, exclusionary immigration policies that mitigated against intergenerational family units in the United States led Chinese-American and Japanese-American families to make other arrangements (Dill, 1988).

Some mothers are clearly defeated by this situation of incessant labor performed to ensure their children's survival. The magnitude of their motherwork overwhelms them. But others, even while appearing to be defeated, manage to pass on the meaning of motherwork for survival to their children. African-American feminist thinker June Jordan (1985) remembers her perceptions of her mother's work:

> As a child I noticed the sadness of my mother as she sat alone in the kitchen at night. . . . Her woman's work never won permanent victories of any kind. It never enlarged the universe of her imagination or her power

to influence what happened beyond the front door of our house. Her woman's work never tickled her to laugh or shout or dance. (p. 105)

But Jordan also sees her mother's work as being motherwork that is essential to individual and community survival.

But she did raise me to respect her way of offering love and to believe that hard work is often the irreducible factor for survival, not something to avoid. Her woman's work produced a reliable home base where I could pursue the privileges of books and music. Her woman's work invented the potential for a completely new kind of work for us, the next generation of Black women: huge, rewarding hard work demanded by the huge, different ambitions that her perfect confidence in us engendered. (p. 105)

Motherwork and Power

How can I write down how I felt when I was a little child and my grandmother used to cry with us 'cause she didn't have enough food to give us? Because my brother was going barefooted and he was cryin' because he wasn't used to going without shoes? How can I describe that? I can't describe when my little girl died because I didn't have money for a doctor. And never had any teaching on caring for sick babies. Living out in labor camps. How can I describe that?
(de la Cruz, 1980, p. 177).

Jessie de la Cruz, a Mexican-American woman who grew up as a migrant farm worker, experienced firsthand the struggle for empowerment facing racial ethnic women whose daily motherwork centers on issues of survival. A dialectical relation exists between efforts of racial orders to mold the institution of motherhood to serve the interests of elites, in this case, racial elites, and efforts on the part of subordinated groups to retain power over motherhood so that it serves the legitimate needs of their communities (Collins, 1990). African-American, Asian-American, Hispanic, and Native American women have long been preoccupied with patterns of maternal power and powerlessness because their mothering experiences have been profoundly affected by this dialectical process. But instead of emphasizing maternal power in dealing either with father as patriarch (Chodorow, 1978; Rich, 1986) or with male dominance (Ferguson, 1989), women of color are concerned with their power and powerlessness within an array of social institutions that frame their lives.

Racial ethnic women's struggles for maternal empowerment have revolved around three main themes. The struggle for control over their own bodies in order to preserve choice over whether to become mothers at all is one fundamental theme. The ambiguous politics of caring for unplanned children has long shaped African-American women's motherwork. For example, the widespread institutionalized rape of African-American women by white men both during slavery and in the segregated South created countless biracial children who had to be absorbed into African-American families and communities (Davis, 1981). The range of skin colors and hair textures in contemporary African-American communities bears mute testament to the powerlessness of African-American women in controlling this dimension of motherhood.

For many women of color, choosing to become a mother challenges institutional policies that encourage white middle-class women to reproduce and discourage low-income racial ethnic women from doing so, even penalizing them (Davis, 1981). Rita Silk-Nauni, an incarcerated Native American woman, writes of the difficulties she encountered in trying to have additional children. She loved her son so much that she left him only when she went to work. "I tried having more after him and couldn't," she observes. "I went to a specialist and he thought I had been fixed when I had my Son. He said I would have to have surgery in order to give birth again. The surgery was so expensive but I thought I could make a way even if I had to work 24 hours a day. Now that I'm here, I know I'll never have that chance" (Brant, 1988, p. 94). Like Silk-Nauni, Puerto Rican and African-American women have long had to struggle with issues of sterilization abuse (Davis, 1981). More recently, efforts to manipulate the fertility of poor women dependent on public assistance speaks to the continued salience of this issue in the lives of racial ethnic women.

A second dimension of racial ethnic women's struggles for maternal empowerment concerns getting to keep the children that are wanted, whether they were planned for or not. For racial ethnic mothers like Jessie de la Cruz whose "little girl died" because she "didn't have money for a doctor," maternal separation from one's children becomes a much more salient issue than maternal isolation with one's children within an allegedly private nuclear family. Physical or psychological separation of mothers and children designed to disempower racial ethnic individuals forms the basis of a systematic effort to disempower their communities.

For both Native American and African-American mothers, situations of conquest introduced this dimension of the struggle for maternal empowerment. In her fictional account of a Native American mother's loss of her children in 1890, Brant explores the pain of maternal separation. "It has been two days since they came and took the children away. My body is greatly chilled. All our blankets have been used to bring me warmth. The women keep the fire blazing. The men sit. They talk among themselves. We are frightened by this sudden child-stealing. We signed papers, the agent said. This gave them rights to take our babies. It is good for them, the agent said. It will make them civilized" (1988, p. 101). A legacy of conquest has meant that Native American mothers on so-called reservations confront intrusive government institutions such as the Bureau of Indian Affairs in deciding the fate of their children. For example, the long-standing policy of removing Native American children from their homes and housing them in reservation boarding schools can be seen as an effort to disempower their mothers. In the case of African-American women under slavery, owners controlled virtually all dimensions of their children's lives—they could be sold at will, whipped, even killed, all with no recourse by their mothers. In such a situation, simply keeping and rearing one's children becomes empowerment.

A third dimension of racial ethnic women's struggles for empowerment concerns the pervasive efforts by the dominant group to control their children's minds. In her short story "A Long Memory," Beth Brant juxtaposes the loss felt in 1890 by a Native American mother whose son and daughter were forcibly removed by white officials to the loss that Brant felt in 1978 when a hearing took away her custody of her daughter. "Why do they want our babies?" queries the turn-of-the-century mother. "They want our power. They take our children to remove the inside of them. Our power" (Brant, 1988, p. 105). This mother recognizes that the future of the Native American way of life lies in retaining the power to define that worldview through educating the children. By forbidding children to speak their native languages and in other ways encouraging them to assimilate into Anglo culture, external agencies challenge the power of mothers to raise their children as they see fit.

Schools controlled by the dominant group comprise one important location where this dimension of the struggle for maternal empowerment occurs. In contrast to white middle-class children, whose educational experiences affirm their mothers' middle-class values, culture, and authority, African-American, Latino, Asian-American and Native American children typically receive an education that derrogates their mothers' perspective. For example, the struggles over bilingual education in Latino communities are about much more than retaining Spanish as a second language. Speaking the language of one's childhood is a way of retaining the entire culture and honoring the mother teaching that culture (Anzaldua, 1987; Moraga, 1979).

Jenny Yamoto describes the stress of ongoing negotiations with schools regarding her part African-American and part Japanese sons. "I've noticed that depending on which parent, Black mom or Asian dad, goes to school open house, my oldest son's behavior is interpreted as disruptive and irreverent, or assertive and clever. . . . I resent their behavior being defined and even expected on the basis of racial biases their teachers may struggle with or hold. . . . I don't have the time or energy to constantly change and challenge their teachers' and friends' misperceptions. I only go after them when the children really seem to be seriously threatened" (1988, p. 24).

In confronting each of these three dimensions of their struggles for empowerment, racial ethnic women are not powerless in the face of racial and class oppression. Being grounded in a strong, dynamic, indigenous culture can be central in racial ethnic women's social constructions of motherhood. Depending on their access to traditional culture, women of color invoke alternative sources of power.[8] "Equality per se may have a different meaning for Indian women and Indian people," suggests Kate Shanley. "That difference begins with personal and tribal sovereignty—the right to be legally recognized as people empowered to determine our own destinies" (1988, p. 214). Personal sovereignty involves the struggle to promote the survival of a social structure whose organizational principles represent notions of family and motherhood different from those of the mainstream. "The nuclear family has little relevance to Indian women," observes Shanley. "In fact, in many ways, mainstream feminists now are striving to redefine family and community in a way that Indian women have long known" (p. 214).

African-American mothers can draw upon an Afrocentric tradition where motherhood of varying types, whether bloodmother, othermother, or community othermother, can be invoked as a symbol of power. Many African-American women receive respect and recognition within their local communities for innovative and practical approaches to mothering not only their own biological children but also the children in their extended family networks and in the community overall. Black women's involvement in fostering African-American community development forms the basis of this community-based power. In local African-American communities, community othermothers can become identified as powerful figures through furthering the community's well-being (Collins, 1990).

Despite policies of dominant institutions that place racial ethnic mothers in positions where they appear less powerful to their children, mothers and children empower themselves by understanding each other's position and relying on each other's strengths. In many cases, children, especially daughters, bond with their mothers instead of railing against them as symbols of patriarchal power. Cherrie Moraga describes the impact that her mother had on her. Because she was repeatedly removed from school in order to work, Moraga's mother would be considered largely illiterate by prevailing standards. But her mother was also a fine storyteller and found ways to empower herself within dominant institutions. "I would go with my mother to fill out job applications for her, or write checks for her at the supermarket," Moraga recounts. "We would have the scenario all worked out ahead of time. My mother would sign the check before we'd get to the store. Then, as we'd approach the checkstand, she would say—within earshot of the cashier—'oh honey, you go 'head and make out the check,'

8. Noticeably absent from feminist theories of motherhood is a comprehensive theory of power and an account of how power relations shape any theories actually developed. Firmly rooted in an exchange-based marketplace with its accompanying assumptions of rational economic decision making and white male control of the marketplace, this model of community stresses the rights of individuals, including feminist theorists, to make decisions in their own interest, regardless of the impact on larger society. Composed of a collection of unequal individuals who compete for greater shares of money as the medium of exchange, this model of community legitimates relations of domination either by denying they exist or by treating them as inevitable but unimportant (Hartsock, 1983).

as if she couldn't be bothered with such an insignificant detail" (1979, p. 28). Like Cherrie Moraga and her mother, racial ethnic women's motherwork involves collaborating to empower mothers and children within oppressive structures.

Motherwork and Identity

Please help me find out who I am. My mother was Indian, but we were taken from her and put in foster homes. They were white and didn't want to tell us about our mother. I have a name and maybe a place of birth. Do you think you can help me?   (Brant, 1988, p. 9)

Like this excerpt from a letter to an editor, the theme of loss of racial ethnic identity and the struggle to maintain a sense of self and community pervade the remaining stories, poetry, and narratives in Beth Brant's volume, *A Gathering of Spirit*. Carol Lee Sanchez offers another view of the impact of the loss of self. "Radicals look at reservation Indians and get very upset about their poverty conditions," observes Sanchez. "But poverty to us is not the same thing as poverty is to you. Our poverty is that we can't be who we are. We can't hunt or fish or grow our food because our basic resources and the right to use them in traditional ways are denied us" (Brant, 1988, p. 165). Racial ethnic women's motherwork reflects the tensions inherent in trying to foster a meaningful racial identity in children within a society that denigrates people of color. The racial privilege enjoyed by white middle-class women makes unnecessary this complicated dimension of the mothering tradition of women of color. Although white children can be prepared to fight racial oppression, their survival does not depend on gaining these skills. Their racial identity is validated by their schools, the media, and other social institutions. White children are socialized into their rightful place in systems of racial privilege. Racial ethnic women have no such guarantees for their children. Their children must first be taught to survive in systems that would oppress them. Moreover, this survival must not come at the expense of self-esteem. Thus, a dialectical relation exists between systems of racial oppression designed to strip subordinated groups of a sense of personal identity and a sense of collective peoplehood, and the cultures of resistance to that oppression extant in various racial ethnic groups. For women of color, motherwork for identity occurs at this critical juncture (Collins, 1990).

"Through our mothers, the culture gave us mixed messages," observes Mexican-American poet Gloria Anzaldua. "Which was it to be—strong or submissive, rebellious or conforming?" (1987, p. 18). Thus women of color's motherwork requires reconciling two contradictory needs concerning identity. First, preparing children to cope with and survive within systems of racial oppression is essential. The pressures for these children to assimilate are pervasive. In order to compel women of color to participate in their children's assimilation, dominant institutions promulgate ideologies that belittle people of color. Negative controlling images infuse the worlds of their male and female children (Collins, 1990; Green, 1990; Tajima, 1989). Native American girls are encouraged to see themselves as "Pocahontases" and "squaws"; Asian-American girls as "geisha girls" and "Suzy Wongs"; Hispanic girls as "Madonnas" and "hot-blooded whores"; and African-American girls as "mammies," "matriarchs," and "prostitutes." Girls of all groups are told that their lives cannot be complete without a male partner and that their educational and career aspirations must always be subordinated to their family obligations.

This push toward assimilation is part of a larger effort to socialize racial ethnic children into their proper subordinate places in systems of racial and class oppression. But despite pressures to assimilate, since children of color can never be white, assimilation by becoming white is impossible. Thus, a second dimension of this mothering tradition involves equipping children with skills to challenge the systems of racial oppression. Girls who become women believing that they are capable only of being maids and prostitutes cannot contribute to racial ethnic women's motherwork. Mothers make varying choices in preparing their children to fit into, yet resist, systems of racial domination. Some mothers remain powerless in the face of external forces that foster their children's assimilation and subsequent alienation from their families and communities. Through fiction, Native American author Beth Brant (1988) explores the grief felt by a mother whose children had been taken away to live among whites. A letter arrives giving news of her missing son and daughter:

> This letter is from two strangers with the names Martha and Daniel. They say they are learning civilized ways. Daniel works in the fields, growing food for the school. Martha is being taught to sew aprons. She will be going to live with the schoolmaster's wife. She will be a live-in girl. What is live-in girl? I shake my head. The words sound the same to me. I am afraid of Martha and Daniel. These strangers who know my name. (pp. 102–103)

Other mothers become unwitting conduits of the dominant ideology. "How many times have I heard mothers and mothers-in-law tell their sons to beat their wives for not obeying them, for being *hociconas* (big mouths), for being *callajeras* (going to visit and gossip with neighbors), for expecting their husbands to help with the rearing of children and the housework, for wanting to be something other than housewives," asks Gloria Anzaldua (1987, p. 16).

Some mothers encourage their children to fit in for reasons of survival. "My mother, nursed in the folds of a town that once christened its black babies Lee, after Robert E., and Jackson, after Stonewall, raised me on a dangerous generation's old belief," remembers African-American author Marita Golden. "Because of my dark brown complexion, she warned me against wearing browns or yellow and reds . . . and every summer I was admonished not to play in the sun 'cause you gonna have to get a light husband anyway, for the sake of your children' " (1983, p. 24). To Cherrie Moraga's mother, "on a basic economic level, being Chicana meant being 'less.' It was through my mother's desire to protect her children from poverty and illiteracy that we became 'anglocized'; the more effectively we could pass in the white world, the better guaranteed our future" (1979, p. 28). Despite their mothers' good intentions, the costs to children taught to submit to racist and sexist ideologies can be high. Raven, a Native American woman, looks back on her childhood: "I've been raised in white man's world and was forbade more or less to converse with Indian people. As my mother wanted me to be educated and live a good life, free from poverty. I lived a life of loneliness. Today I am desperate to know my people" (Brant, 1988, p. 221). Raven's mother did what she thought best to help her daughter avoid poverty. But ultimately, Raven experienced the poverty of not being able to be who she was.

Still other mothers transmit sophisticated skills to their children of how one can appear to submit to yet simultaneously challenge oppression. Willi Coleman's mother used a Saturday-night hair-combing ritual to impart an African-American women's standpoint to her daughters:

> Except for special occasions mama came home from work early on Saturdays. She spent six days a week mopping, waxing and dusting other women's houses and keeping out of reach of other women's husbands. Saturday nights were reserved for "taking care of them girls" hair and the telling of stories. Some of which included a recitation of what she had endured and how she had triumphed over "folks that were lower than dirt" and "no-good snakes in the grass." She combed, patted, twisted and talked, saying things which would have embarrassed or shamed her at other times. (Coleman, 1987, p. 34)

Historian Elsa Barkley Brown captures the delicate balance that racial ethnic mothers must achieve. Brown points out that her mother's behavior demonstrated the "need to teach me to live my life one way and, at the same time, to provide all the tools I would need to live it quite differently" (1989, p. 929).

For women of color, the struggle to maintain an independent racial identity has taken many forms, all revealing varying solutions to the dialectical relation between institutions that would deny their children their humanity and their children's right to exist as self-defined people. Like Willi Coleman's mother, African-American women draw upon a long-standing Afrocentric feminist worldview emphasizing the importance of self-definition and self-reliance, and the necessity of demanding respect from others (Collins, 1990; Terborg-Penn, 1986).

Poet and essayist Gloria Anzaldua challenges many of the ideas in Latino cultures concerning women: "Though I'll defend my race and culture when they are attacked by non-mexicanos, . . . I abhor some of my culture's ways, how it cripples its women, *como burras*, our strengths used against us" (1987, p. 21). Anzaldua offers a trenchant analysis of the ways in which the Spanish conquest of Native Americans fragmented women's identity and produced three symbolic "mothers." *La Virgen de Guadalupe,* perhaps the single most potent religious, political, and cultural image of the Chicano people, represents the virgin mother who cares for and nurtures an oppressed people. *La Chingada (Malinche)* represents the raped mother, all but abandoned. A combination of the first two, *La Llorona*, symbolizes the mother who seeks her lost children. "Ambiguity surrounds the symbols of these three 'Our Mothers,'" claims Anzaldua. "In part, the true identity of all three has been subverted—*Guadalupe* to make us docile and enduring, *la Chingada* to make us ashamed of our Indian side, and *la Llorona* to make us a long-suffering people" (1987, p. 31). For Anzaldua, the Spanish conquest that brought racism and economic subordination to Indian people and created a new mixed-race Latino people simultaneously devalued women:

> No, I do not buy all the myths of the tribe into which I was born. I can understand why the more tinged with Anglo blood, the more adamantly my colored and colorless sisters glorify their colored culture's values—to offset the extreme devaluation of it by the white culture. It's a legitimate reaction. But I will not glorify those aspects of my culture which have injured me and which have injured me in the name of protecting me. (1987, p. 22)

Latino mothers face the complicated task of shepherding their children through the racism of the dominant society and the reactions to that racism framing cultural beliefs internal to Hispanic communities. Many Asian-American mothers stress conformity and fitting in as a way to challenge the system. "Our parents are painted as hard workers who were socially uncomfortable and had difficulty expressing even the smallest opinion," observes Japanese-American Kesaya Noda in her autobiographical essay "Growing Up Asian in America" (1989, p. 246). Noda questioned this seeming capitulation on the part of her parents: "'Why did you go into those camps,' I raged at my parents, frightened by my own inner silence and timidity. 'Why didn't you do anything to resist?'" But Noda later discovers a compelling explanation as to why Asian-Americans are so often portrayed as conforming: "I had not been able to imagine before what it must have felt like to be an American—to know absolutely that one is an American—and yet to have almost everyone else deny it. Not only deny it, but challenge that identity with machine guns and troops of white American soldiers. In those circumstances it was difficult to say, 'I'm a Japanese American.' 'American' had to do" (1989, p. 247).

Native American women can draw upon a tradition of motherhood and woman's power inherent in Native American cultures (Allen 1986; Awaikta 1988). In such philosophies, "water, land, and life are basic to the natural order," says Winona LaDuke. "All else has been created by the use and misuse of technology. It is only natural that in our respective struggles for survival, the native peoples are waging a war to protect the land, the water, and life, while the consumer culture strives to protect its technological lifeblood" (1988, p. 65). Marilou Awiakta offers a powerful summary of the symbolic meaning of motherhood in Native American cultures: "I feel the Grandmother's power. She sings of harmony, not dominance. And her song rises from a culture that repeats the wise balance of nature: the gender capable of bearing life is not separated from the power to sustain it" (1988, p. 126). A culture that sees the connectedness between the earth and human survival, and that sees motherhood as symbolic of the earth itself holds motherhood as an institution in high regard.

Concluding Remarks

Survival, power, and identity shape motherhood for all women. But these themes remain muted when the mothering experiences of women of color are marginalized in feminist theorizing about motherhood. The theories reflect a lack of attention to the connection between ideas and the contexts in which they emerge. Although such decontextualization aims to generate universal theories of human behavior, in actuality the theories routinely distort or omit huge categories of human experience.

Placing racial ethnic women's motherwork in the center of analysis recontextualizes motherhood. Whereas the significance of race and class in shaping the context in which motherhood occurs is virtually invisible when white, middle-class women's experiences are the theoretical norm, the effects of race and class stand out in stark relief when women of color are accorded theoretical primacy. Highlighting racial ethnic mothers' struggles concerning their children's right to exist focuses attention on the importance of survival. Exploring the dialectical nature of racial ethnic women's empowerment in structures of racial domination and economic exploitation demonstrates the need to broaden the definition of maternal power. Emphasizing how the quest for self-definition is mediated by membership in different racial and social class groups reveals how the issue of identity is crucial to all motherwork.

Existing feminist theories of motherhood have emerged in specific intellectual and political contexts. By assuming that social theory will be applicable regardless of social context, feminist scholars fail to realize that they themselves are rooted in specific locations, and that the contexts in which they are located provide the thought-models of how they interpret the world. Their theories may appear to be universal and objective, but they actually are only partial perspectives reflecting the white middle-class context in which their creators live. Large segments of experience, those of women who are not white and middle class, have been excluded (Spelman, 1988). Feminist theories of motherhood thus cannot be seen as *theories* of motherhood generalizable to all women. The resulting patterns of partiality inherent in existing theories—for example, the emphasis placed on all-powerful mothers as conduits for gender oppression—reflect feminist theorists' positions in structures of power. Such theorists are themselves participants in a system of privilege that rewards them for not seeing race and class privilege as important. Their theories can ignore the workings of class and race as systems of privilege because their creators often benefit from that privilege, taking it as a given and not as something to be contested.

Theorizing about motherhood will not be helped, however, by supplanting one group's theory with that of another—for example, by claiming that women of color's experiences are more valid than those of white middle-class women. Just as varying placement in systems of privilege, whether race, class, sexuality, or age, generates divergent experiences with motherhood, examining motherhood and mother-as-subject from multiple perspectives should uncover rich textures of difference. Shifting the center to accommodate this diversity promises to recontextualize motherhood and point us toward feminist theorizing that embraces difference as an essential part of commonality.

References

Allen, P. G. (1986). *The sacred hoop: Recovering the feminine in American Indian traditions*. Boston: Beacon Press.

Andersen, M. (1988). Moving our minds: Studying women of color and reconstructing sociology. *Teaching Sociology,* 16(2), 123–32.

Anzaldua, G. (1987). *Borderlands/La Frontera: The new Mestiza*. San Francisco: Spinsters.

Awiakta, M. (1988). Amazons in Appalachia. In B. Brant (Ed.), *A gathering of spirit* (125–30). Ithaca, N.Y.: Firebrand.

Boyd, C. J. (1989). Mothers and daughters: A discussion of theory and research. *Journal of Marriage and the Family,* 51, 291–301.

Brant, B. (Ed.) (1988). *A gathering of spirit: A collection by North American Indian women*. Ithaca, N.Y.: Firebrand.

Brown, E. B. (1989). African-American women's quilting: A framework for conceptualizing and teaching African-American women's history. *Signs,* 14(4), 921–29.

Chodorow, N. (1978). *The reproduction of mothering*. Berkeley: University of California Press.

Chodorow, N., & Contratto, S. (1982). The fantasy of the perfect mother. In B. Thorne & M. Yalom (Eds.), *Rethinking the family: Some feminist questions* (54–75). New York: Longman.

Coleman, W. (1987). Closets and keepsakes. *Sage: A Scholarly Journal on Black Women,* 4(2), 34–35.

Collins, P. H. (1990). *Black feminist thought: Knowledge, consciousness and the politics of empowerment*. New York: Routledge.

Davis, A. Y. (1981). *Women, race, and class*. New York: Random House.

de la Cruz, J. (1980). Interview. In S. Terkel (Ed.), *American dreams: Lost and found*. New York: Ballantine.

Dill, B. T. (1988). Our mothers' grief: Racial ethnic women and the maintenance of families. *Journal of Family History,* 13(4), 415–31.

Eisenstein, H. (1983). *Contemporary feminist thought*. Boston: G. K. Hall.

Ferguson, A. (1989). *Blood at the root: Motherhood, sexuality, and male dominance*. New York: Unwin Hyman/Routledge.

Flax, J. (1978). The conflict between nurturance and autonomy in mother-daughter relationships and within feminism. *Feminist Studies,* 4(2), 171–89.

Glenn, E. N. (1985). Racial ethnic women's labor: The intersection of race, gender and class oppression. *Review of Radical Political Economics,* 17(3), 86–108.

Glenn, E. N. (1986). *Issei, Nisei, war bride: Three generations of Japanese American women in domestic service.* Philadelphia: Temple University Press.

Golden, M. (1983). *Migrations of the heart.* New York: Ballantine.

Green, R. (1990). The Pocahontas perplex: The image of Indian women in American culture. In E. C. DuBois & V. Ruiz (Eds.), *Unequal sisters* (15–21). New York: Routledge.

Hartsock, N. (1983). *Money, sex and power.* Boston: Northeastern University Press.

Jaggar, A. (1983). *Feminist politics and human nature.* Totawa, N.J.: Rowman & Allanheld.

Jordan, J. (1985). *On call.* Boston: South End Press.

LaDuke, W. (1988). They always come back. In B. Brant (Ed.), *A gathering of spirit* (62–67). Ithaca, N.Y.: Firebrand.

Lerner, G. (Ed.). (1972). *Black women in white america: A documentary history.* New York: Vintage.

Moraga, C. (1979). La Guera. In C. Moraga & G. Anzaldua (Eds.), *This bridge called my back: Writings by radical women of color* (27–34). Watertown, Mass.: Persephone Press.

Noda, R. E. (1989). Growing up Asian in America. In Asian Women United of California (Eds.), *Making waves: An anthology of writings by and about Asian American women* (243–50). Boston: Beacon Press.

Rich, A. (1986). *Of woman born: Motherhood as institution and experience.* New York: Norton.

Shanley, K. (1988). Thoughts on Indian feminism. In B. Brant (Ed.), *A gathering of spirit* (213–215). Ithaca, N.Y.: Firebrand.

Smith, D. E. (1990). *The conceptual practices of power: A feminist sociology of knowledge.* Boston: Northeastern University Press.

Spelman, E. V. (1988). *Inessential woman: Problems of exclusion in feminist thought.* Boston: Beacon Press.

Tajima, R. E. (1989). Lotus blossoms don't bleed: Images of Asian women. In Asian Women United of California (Eds.), *Making waves: An anthology of writings by and about Asian American women* (308–17). Boston: Beacon Press.

Terborg-Penn, R. (1986). Black women in resistance: A cross-cultural perspective. In G. Y. Okhiro (Ed.), *In resistance: Studies in African, Caribbean and Afro-American history* (188–209). Amherst: University of Massachusetts Press.

Wright, S. (1986). *This child's gonna live.* Old Westbury, N.Y.: Feminist Press.

Yamoto, J. (1988). Mixed bloods, half breeds, mongrels, hybrids. In J. W. Cochran, D. Langston, & C. Woodward (Eds.), *Changing our power: An introduction to women's studies* (22–24). Dubuque, Iowa: Kendall/Hunt.

Yu, C. Y. (1989). The world of our grandmothers. In Asian Women United of California (Eds.), *Making waves: An anthology of writings by and about Asian American women* (33–41). Boston: Beacon Press.

JEAN BETHKE ELSHTAIN

4 The Mothers of the Disappeared: Passion and Protest in Maternal Action

All right, my esteemed ladies, the time has come to show you
my words were true. Some of you have thought and even said
that what this captain wants is for us to give up worrying
about this matter so he can gain a little time. That's what
you've said and thought. I'm going to prove to you it wasn't
so. The Supreme Government has become interested in every
one of you, in every single mother of this generous land we
have the honor of living in together. And that's because, for the
nation's army, there is nothing more sacred than woman and
nothing greater than motherhood. It is in defense of that
woman and of the values of the home which she seeks to
preserve above all else that we have always acted. That women
is the sweetheart, the wife, the mother of the
fatherland.   Ariel Dorfman, *Widows*

We are what is real, you and I, the mothers. We are so real that
the men who may even now be looking down on us and
making jokes about the Crazy Ones are afraid. Think of that!
They disdain us publicly, have their toadies call us crazy in
their papers, but they are afraid of a bunch of women and two
men who have the courage to hold signs and walk in the heat
of the midday sun.   Lawrence Thornton, *Imagining
Argentina*

This is the story of a nightmare. There is no happy ending. The
ingredients are the stuff of a tragic political trauma: terror and
triumph, despair and hope. I knew little of the nightmare until
after the worst had already happened. The bare bones of the story

go like this: March 1976, a military coup in Argentina, which, for the first time in Argentine history, creates direct control by the military of all government branches and functions. The coup was justified as a response to the pitiful charade of the government of María Estela (Isabel) Martinez de Perón and to terrorist activity that had by then claimed some eight hundred lives. The leading terrorist groups were the ERP (Marxist-Leninist People's Revolutionary Army) and Montoneros, their far more ferocious Peronist cousins. Government and police officials were the main targets of left-wing terrorism, although civilians also got caught in the crossfire. Right-wing terrorist bands had begun their own assassination campaigns in turn. The terrorist campaign had lost steam around 1975. But people remained apprehensive, yearning for order.

Into this situation, one ripe for such intervention, moved the military. Argentina was to be governed for the next eight years by three successive juntas. This was not a standard Argentine scenario, one in which the military lurked in the background calling the shots. No, the "Process of National Reorganization," the *proceso,* inaugurated by junta leader Jorge Rafael Videla in 1976, gave birth to a period of naked control and state terrorism that claimed an estimated 10,000 lives (Mignone, 1987). The tortured and killed were disproportionately young: 69 percent were between the ages of sixteen and thirty, and 147 were children. No one knows how many babies were born to mothers in captivity. Estimates run to 400–500. No one knows how many of those babies were killed and how many were "adopted" by military families.

It is terrible but true that the deaths of children may enrage mothers and compel them to engage the powerful, in this case, the symbolic fathers in uniform who killed their children. While most, male and female, mothers and fathers, shrunk back, paralyzed with fear, convinced nothing could be done, or tacitly collaborated with the self-anointed bringers-of-order, a group of intrepid Mothers said: No More. This is their story as I struggled to comprehend, to make their nightmares my own, only to find myself faltering as I tried to tell the tale, flaying myself for my inability to get it right, to do justice to what I had seen and heard. Their story escaped my "poor powers to add or detract."

Intimations of Something Worse Yet to Come

In October 1982, I was in Buenos Aires at the invitation of a center for the study of women in culture and society. The center's work was psychoanalytically driven, and many of the key players in its activities were a group of brilliant, tireless female psychoanalysts. Our sessions were long—one ran for an entire day with a short breather for a quick bite of lunch, a very Protestant schedule, I thought. But there were a few free mornings and one clear, bright, nippy October afternoon opened up. I decided to wander the streets. It was a rather unsettled time politically. The reigning junta spearheaded by General Leopoldo Fortunato Galtieri had been thoroughly discredited by the debacle in the Malvinas/Falkland War; pressure from human rights groups, including "some

Mothers" had gained international attention; the economy was in tatters; and Argentines were restless for a change.

My meandering took me past glittering shops stocked with attractive goods, especially chic women's attire. I happened on the Calle Florida, the heart of the city's European-style definition of itself—confiterias, more posh shops, wine bars, respectable old structures culminating with a duck's row of banks and government buildings designating this place, the heart of the city, the Plaza de Mayo, a great public square. There, walking in a silent circle around a monument in the heart of the Plaza, were hundreds of women wearing white scarves, some well dressed and middle class, others in rougher, more rustic attire, their faces a bold contrast to the whiteness of their covered heads. I noticed embroidered names and dates on the backs of the scarves and visible around the necks of these women were photographs of young men or women, some couples, some children. Beneath the photos were printed names and dates. They wore necklaces of despair and grief as others might wear peals or brooches.

I hurried across the street into the Plaza and joined a small crowd of onlookers. Some passersby clustered for a moment and moved on. Others stood, arms folded, watching. A few mothers whispered into the ears of their stroller-bound children and pointed in the direction of the eerily hushed processional. Some men and women took the sun on nearby benches, munching on empañadas and churros, uninterested in, or unaware of, the slowly moving display of human grief and courage and rage taking place just a few feet away. A tumble of young women, giggling, animated, hair tossing in the breeze, snaked through the tangle of humanity. They were followed by a group of energetic young men, handsome, decked out in the stylish uniform of an elite school, or so I surmised.

"Who are these women?" I asked my hosts. They were Mothers, a sorority bound by loss, the most terrible imaginable. Their children had been "disappeared," the noun turned into a verb. To be disappeared, to be sucked off the street, grabbed in one's apartment or from one's school, often never to be seen again. One sucked up into this nether world of violence joined with involuntary ranks of the disappeared, acquiring a new identity as a *desaparecido*. But I also detected great reticence to speak of the matter. Voices grew softer and suddenly hesitant. Heads shook and lowered. One psychoanalyst, a powerful professional woman, very much immersed in feminist questions having to do with the Symbolic Father and how the female is culturally constructed and how and in what ways all this should be defused or transformed, told me that she and many other professional women felt "ambivalent" about these Mothers of the Disappeared. She claimed they strategically used the Symbolic Mother as *mater dolorosa* and, in this process, wound up deepening and legitimating the mourning mother as the ideal-typical female identity. This "negative critique," to use the fancy but ubiquitous currency of social criticism, went something like that.

Besides, another woman told me, something had to be done about the *terrorista*, the *subversivo*. Certainly no one expected the *proceso* and the excesses of *la guerra sucia*, the "dirty war," but I must keep in mind the context. Now all anybody wanted was an end to fanatical politics of any brand, left or right. And the Mothers, I sensed, had become a bit of an embarrassment with their incessant demand for the disappeared to reappear alive, *aparicion con vida.* Shortly before I left the city, the *Buenos Aires Herald,* an English-language paper that has been published continually for over one hundred years, printed an item headlined "Mothers visit unmarked graves." It read, in part:

> Members of the Mothers of the Plaza de Mayo prayed yesterday over unmarked graves at the cemetery where they believe 400 persons thought to have disappeared may be buried.
>
> The Mothers, who for six years have been unsuccessful in their efforts to obtain information on what happened to thousands of people who disappeared during the military's so-called "dirty war" on terrorism, rushed to the municipal cemetery a day after learning that one of the missing was buried there.
>
> The Permanent Assembly for Human Rights (APDH) said on Friday that as many as 400 of the estimated 6,000 to 20,000 who disappeared between 1976 and the present may be buried in 88 unmarked graves in the Grand Bourg cemetery in San Miguel, 25 kilometers west of Buenos Aires.
>
> Cemetery officials and neighbors have said that security officers driving Army trucks brought "six or seven" bodies to bury in the cemetery about once a week while the anti-terrorism campaign was going on. (Sunday, October 24, 1982, p. 13)

I was to learn later that the disappeared, tortured, and murdered went into the ground (if they were buried at all rather than being dumped out of military transport planes into the Rio de la Plata) as N.N., "No Name." The Mothers bore the particular, irreplaceable, concrete names of their children around their necks, framed with the accusatory question: *Donde esta . . . ?* (Where is . . . ?). No Name. It was insupportable.

Has Anything Been Written?

A standard text on Argentine history told me that "the interested observer of Argentine affairs can predict that the armed forces will continue for several years and perhaps for several decades to exert the predominant political role in Argentina and to act as an authority above civilian government" (Scobie, 1971, p. 231). But the text trailed off before the terrible events that gave birth to Las Madres. Amnesty International's 1981 workbook on "disappearances" documented in stark detail the cold mechanics of this ever-more-popular political phenomenon, one not exclusive to Argentina. But the Mothers remained in the shadows, haunting and haunted images, their scarves blurred after-images, the photos round their necks fading stigmata. At times I wanted to forget I had ever seen them; at others I wanted to return, to march with them, to understand why and how—how they managed to go on when all I could conjure up as I thought of the torture-murder of a child was a life prostrate with grief and corroded with rage.

I discovered a book by anthropologist J. M. Taylor (1979) on *Eva Perón: The Myths of a Woman*, which helped me to put one piece of the vast Argentine political puzzle into place. My curiosity had been piqued by the phenomenon of the many impressive, powerful career women—nearly all of them mothers—I had met during my stint in Buenos Aires. (Having live-in Paraguayan maids certainly helped these women to work flat-out and full-time but did not explain the imperatives that drove them into the professions in the first place.) This didn't seem to fit with North American chatter about the horrors of machismo. Nor, for that matter, did the image of the Mothers defying arrest, imprisonment, torture, even death, to march in the Plaza de Mayo.

I learned from Taylor's work that Argentina has long harbored powerful women in its gallery of great ones. Focusing on the strange and many-sided myth of Eva Perón, Taylor showed the political and class dimensions of constructions of Perón, variously, as the Lady of Hope, the Woman of the Black Myth, and Eva the Revolutionary giving birth to revolutionary sons and daughters who proclaimed that whenever they were discouraged, Eva gave them strength. They fought because of her and for her. The vitality of the myths of Evita were such that decades after her death she continued to spark political longing and loathing. Even as revolutionaries still fought under her banner, defenders of the status quo claimed her sanction for their activities in behalf of traditional authority. Various brands of Peronism vied with and against one another even as they pitted themselves against those for whom Evita embodied the worst of womanhood, the bad woman, a whore, who seduced and controlled her husband, Juan. Those who celebrated Eva as the saintly mother had no trouble reconciling her own childlessness with their sanctimonious embrace. No, "she was the mother of the nation as a whole, particularly to the common people and the poor and needy of Argentina" (Taylor, 1979, p. 75). She was the "Spiritual Mother of All Argentinean Children" by popular acclamation and political fiat. Eva, concludes Taylor, was a woman who used "culturally defined, characteristically female attributes as a basis for power in a role accessible to both males and females," and she was able to do this because Argentine culture, in common with many others, links "images of feminine nature with certain types of mystical power," even "with revolutionary roles" (pp. 144–145).

Do not expect a tidy picture. What one finds consistently linked in the many and even antipodal Eva images is a vision of femininity, of "mystical or spirtual power, and revolutionary leadership," and all these elements put "a person or a group at the margins of established society and at the limits of institutionalized authority" (p. 147). The most powerful woman in Argentine history, a spellbinding rhetorician who cried out to rapt assemblies of tens of thousands, held no office. Beyond or outside of institutional arrangements, she was paradoxically free to inhabit many roles, to play many parts, and to be imagined by others in fantastically at-odd ways. This freedom, of course, had built-in limits; she always claimed she was but the poor mouthpiece of Perón: "I do not have in these moments more than one ambition, a single and great personal ambition: that of me it shall be said . . . that there was at the side of Perón a woman who dedicated herself to carrying the hopes of the people to the President, and that people affectionately called this woman 'Evita.' That is what I want to be" (pp. 144–145).

She later added that her "permanent vow" was to place herself "entirely at the service of the *descamisados,* who are the humble and the workers" (pp. 144–145). The humble and the workers gave her great latitude and cherished her memory even as others excoriated her base influence, her evil seductions, her cruel treatment of any who stood in her way. She was the intermediary between the people and her powerful husband who claimed that she was "an instrument of my creation." Her work was extraordinary, he added. God himself operated through her; hers were tasks assigned by Providence. Evita did not object (p. 55).

Taylor speculates that the personalized and familial style of leadership wildly successful in the case of the Peróns was knowingly crafted by them to appeal to points of stability (family authority) in an otherwise often disordered political environment. This cultural context gave rise not to images of submissive females but to problematic and very powerful public women. The "gender ideology" of Latin America in general, Argentina in particular, was perhaps more flexible than similar ideology in North America. After all, one encounters large numbers of important women outside the domestic realm and a rich variety of mythic images to portray such women. Argentina regularly sent forth more women into the professions as lawyers and doctors than did the United States. Machismo, it seemed, wasn't nearly so clear-cut a case of dominant fathers versus doleful mothers as culturally parochial, North American polemicizing repeatedly claimed.

This helped a bit, for it reminded me of the continuing force of familial imagery in Argentina in contrast to the United States. Strangely, Taylor spilled few words on Catholicism in her treatment of Evita. Surely, I mused, a religion that includes a Holy Mother as an object of veneration, devotion, prayer, and yearning offers a much more potent symbolism as part of its repertoire than do religions that have been stripped systematically of any such imagery. Had not Martin Luther chastised the "papists" for putting "that noble child Mary right into the place of Christ"? They would have us rely more on "Mary the Mother of Jesus and the Saints," Luther insisted, than on *the* Incarnate Word (Todd, 1982, pp. 142, 162). With a lively company of female saints, plus the Madonna, the symbolic and spiritual force of Catholic motherhood seemed assured (whatever the political fallout and however one evaluated it) by comparison to symbolically beggared Protestantism, especially in its ever-more watery North American varieties. There had been a distinctly, indeed overwhelmingly, ritualistic cast to the silent march of Las Madres that October day in the Plaza, an eerie and unsettling fusion of the living and the dead.

In April 1982, six months before my initial foray into Argentine life, my essay "Antigone's Daughters" had appeared in what turned out to be a short-lived publication called *democracy,* a journal aimed at the independent, democratic left. In that essay I advanced a "note of caution," arguing that "feminists should approach the modern bureaucratic state from a standpoint of skepticism that keeps alive critical distance between feminism and statism, between female self-identity and a social identity tied to a public-political world revolving around the structures, institutions, values, and ends of the state." I took on those brands of feminism that "presumed the superiority of a particular sort of public identity over a private one," a public identity that "would require . . . the final suppression of traditional female social roles." In other words, I argued against the new woman as a variant on the old man.

Drawing upon *The Antigone* as a prototypical tale pitting a woman representing the unwritten imperatives of familial obligation and traditional duty against a king urging that *raison d'état* must override all other obligations, I elaborated a modest morality play for consideration by contemporary feminists. At the essay's conclusion, I drew on Sara Ruddick's construction of maternal thinking as a way of seeing and acting that places the preservation of fragile human life above the instrumentalities of technocratic power (Ruddick, 1989). I concluded with these words, "Maternal thinking, like Antigone's protest, is a rejection of amoral statecraft and an affirmation of the dignity of the human person" (1982, p. 59). And I lodged a query: how can one hold on to a social location for contemporary daughters of Antigone without insisting that women accept traditional terms of political quiescence? After all, Antigone fuses tradition *and* radical challenge in her agnostic clash with Creon who frets insistently that he will not be bested by a mere woman.[1]

Had not mere women in Argentina shown not so much that the emperor had no clothes but that the junta had bloody hands? Does the continual force and fury of the Antigone story help us to sort this out, to come to grips with the phenomenon of Mothers acting *out* in the public sphere, in the open, and claiming full responsibility for their words and deed-doing? It seemed so to me, and the Mothers took on the classical grandeur of Antigone in my mind. Was not George Steiner right that "men and women re-enact, more or less consciously, the major gestures, the exemplary symbolic motions, set before them by antique imaginings and formulations" (1984, p. 108)? Did not important novelists— Ariel Dorfman and Carlos Martinez Morena, among others—knowingly and powerfully play off the Antigone story in portraying women pitted against dictatorial power? Dorfman notes that the missing are deprived of more than their homes, even their lives. "They are also deprived of their graves"; they are N.N. (1984, p. v). And women are the symbolic, at times politicized, keepers of those graves. In his novel, *El Infierno,* Carlos Martinez Morena depicts the bloody business of the Tupamaro guerrillas in Uruguay and the even more bloody state terror that repressed them and took a huge human toll. He offers the terrible image of a hooded prisoner being pitched from the top of a stadium and, in the aftermath, "his wife battling like Antigone for his body" (1988, p. 262).

---

1. I will not delve into the firestorm of protest this essay elicited upon publication, as this would offer only a footnote to what seems to me now the perfervid politics of feminism at one stage in its recent history.

Return to Buenos Aires: The Voices This Time

This matter is of no concern to us. These women are mad.

Spokesman for the junta, June 1977

In 1986 I returned to Argentina, having been invited by two friends to lecture. I was officially an academic specialist and I was due in Argentina August 3 for a ten-day stint.

I put in a request: Could interviews please be arranged for me with members of Las Madres? And perhaps, with Adolfo Pérez Esquivel, the 1980 Nobel laureate and an apostle of militant nonviolence, who worked out of his center, Servicio Paz y Justicia en América Latina in the Calle México?

As my airplane, having taxied away from its gate, sat on the tarmac at JFK for half an hour, then an hour, then nearly two, waiting out a terrible thunderstorm in the early August New York mugginess, I read the only book in English I could find with the Mothers in the title. It was a disappointment, featuring the Mothers in but one chapter—this despite the title *The Disappeared and the Mothers of the Plaza,* by two journalists, John Simpson and Jana Bennett. But I did learn some facts, gained a bit of additional background, and became familiar with a few names. I was reminded of what I already knew: three juntas; ten thousand to thirty thousand disappeared. It was April 13, 1977, a Saturday, when the Founding Mothers, fourteen intrepid women, arrived at the Plaza de Mayo and entered it tentatively, in full view of the presidential palace (Casa Rosada) and wandered ("nervously," said the book) for a few minutes. This group of fourteen encouraged others to join them. Their leader was Mrs. Azucena DeVicenti who was herself disappeared along with two French nuns in December 1977 and never heard from again. The Mothers were dubbed *Las Locas de la Plaza,* "The Mad Women of the Plaza," by the authorities in an attempt to discredit them.

I read of betrayals, the worst being the story of one charming young man who joined the Mothers claiming his brother had been disappeared; he turned out to be one Captain Alfredo Astiz, implicated in several disappearances, later charged but released and pardoned. The Mothers believe he is responsible for the disappearances of Founding Mother Mrs. DeVicenti as well as the nuns. The Mothers "always resisted any temptation to become a secret society, everything they did was open, including the meetings at which they discussed their strategy" (Simpson & Bennett, 1985, p. 161). Their numbers grew. Through harassment and arrests, the Mothers succeeded with only occasional lapses in keeping up their weekly vigil in the Plaza. At one point the violence was so great they gathered in churches. But they recouped, gained international attention, and on every Thursday at 3:30 in the afternoon, they continue to this day to gather in the Plaza. They say they will stay until all the disappeared are accounted for and their tormentors brought to justice.

In the most dramatic way possible, the Mothers entered the Plaza de Mayo and made it their own. Interviewing several of the key players in Las Madres, Simpson and Bennett found similar stories, shared concerns, even obsessions.

The Mothers succeeded in placing an ad listing the names of 237 desaparecidos in the newspaper *La Prensa* on October 5, 1977. This was a public gesture and was followed by the delivery of petitions with over 24,000 signatures to Congress, calling for an accounting of the disappearances. But little changed. Two hundred of the Mothers delivering petitions had been arrested but were released within a few hours. Many of their fellow citizens refused to see the full extent of the horror and clung to the soothing belief that those who were disappeared *must* have done something to warrant arrest and torture: *Debe ser por algo,* "it must be for something."

Now, as I returned to Buenos Aires, tree years had passed since the restoration of civilian rule. The state of siege was suspended officially on October 29, 1983, and President Raul Alfonsin took office December 10, 1983. The disappearances had stopped and a presidential commission, appointed by President Alfonsin, had produced copious documentation of Argentina's nightmare. Published in Argentina in late 1984, *Nunca Mas* immediately became a best-seller—300,000 copies were scooped up in a few months. The commission's report, calling to mind Nuremberg war trial testimony, is a descent into hell. Ernesto Sabato, one of Argentina's most respected novelists, introducing the gruesome testimony, trying to account for the why and how of the proceso, spoke of Argentine history, the scourage of terrorism, right and left, and the peculiar ethos that dominated the Argentine military—its grand, salvific view of itself as the only thing that stood between communistic chaos and decay, on one hand, and protection of authentic Argentinean identity, *argentinidad,* on the other. In their hermetically sealed world of enemies, plots, conspiracies, and subversion, it was not enough to cut the branches off tainted trees, no, the tree of subversion must be uprooted utterly and all its offshoots, from revolutionary armed organizations to progressive Catholicism to Masons to Zionists had to be destroyed, literally uprooted. Against such a vast conspiracy, the Ford Falcons with unmarked license plates roaming the streets and preying on the young were a necessary defense, a prophylactic against a spreading disease. Absolute brutality, utter caprice; this was the dirty war and the voices of the victims were heard at last. Thousands of detailed stories, each a tragedy rippling out and joining the ripples of other stories, each heartbreaking, each unbelievable. My airplane sleep was even more disturbed than usual.

Telling the Story

> They knew I was pregnant. It hadn't occurred to me that they would torture me while we were traveling. They did it during the whole trip: the electric prod on my abdomen because they knew about the pregnancy. . . . One, two, three, four. . . . Each shock brought that terrible fear of miscarriage . . . and that pain, my pain, my baby's pain. (Partnoy, 1986, pp. 53–54)

> A new cry makes its way through the shadows fighting above the trailer. Graciela has just given birth. A prisoner child has been born. While

the killers' hands welcome into the world, the shadow of life leaves the scene, half a winner, half a loser: on her shoulders she wears a poncho of injustice. Who knows how many children are born every day at the Little School? (Partnoy, 1986, p. 121)

I fretted that "merely" communicating the Mothers' despair would cheapen their grief and their political presence, would somehow falsify their voices by situating them in too straightened a framework, too academic a genre. Just as certain *features* of institutionalized Holocaust studies had become problematic to many because of a pervasive encoding of the bathos of mass victimization, I hoped to avoid seeing the Mothers through a prism that reified their loss, freezing them in a posture of permanent grief and requiring, in order that they might continue to serve *my* purposes or the purposes of others, that they remain forever a fixed tableau of maters dolorosa.

In talking to others about the Mothers, I surrounded their words, those voices that told of terror and hope, with as little conceptual and theoretical material as possible. It seemed important not to categorize nor to capture what they had gone through, what they had done, and what the aftermath of it all might be, too quickly. Following our participation on a panel on women, war, and violence, I shared my interview transcripts with my friend, Sara Ruddick, who made good use of the words of one Mother in a chapter in her book, *Maternal Thinking* (1989). But whenever I decided the time had come to "tell the story" I shied away with a tightening in my chest and an experience of rising anxiety. The words of Czeslaw Milosz haunted me. His poetry, he writes, "has always been a means of checking on myself. Through it I could ascertain the limit beyond which falseness of style testifies to the falseness of the artist's position; and I have tried not to cross this line. The war years taught that a man could not take a pen in his hands merely to communicate to others his own despair and defeat. This is too cheap a commodity; it takes too little effort to produce it for a man to pride himself on having done so" (1990, p. 216).

Perhaps my fear about getting it right was its own form of pridefulness at the presumption that I might be able to do justice to such terrible and moving events as torture, loss, grief, and public courage. That, surely, was beyond anyone's powers. As well, matters had grown more complicated because I was by now close to several of the Mothers. One, to whom I gave a copy of "Antigone's Daughters," was a friend and correspondent. That unavoidably dramatized the situation: I needed to do right by Renée who had lost all three of her children to the tortures—she was a face, a voice, an ongoing presence. Her children—Luis, Claudio, Lila—were real victims with real names. Unable to write about the Mothers myself, I turned to the experts. What did political science have to offer?

Normal or mainstream social science misses the mark, especially accounts that excise "the political" from "the ethical," a real trick indeed when what one is dealing with is torture, murder, and disappearances. The richest social science account is one that finds a way to characterize the politics of terror *institutionally* and politically, unpacking the inner workings of bureaucratic, authoritarian states. Although not concerned explicitly with Las Madres, Argentine political scientist Guillermo O'Donnell (1986), reflecting on the Argentine experience, looks at the converging forces that made authoritarianism not only possible but well-nigh irresistible: economic crisis, waves of mass popular mobilization (the Perón era), widespread top-down politicization of all arenas of human life, and the turn toward violence as a political means and end. In a climate of "pervasive fear and uncertainty," most voices are silenced, although in some cases the "vertical voice," the ability to address the rulers, usually as supplicant, remains as a limited option.[2] But another type of voice—essential to any political life—is wiped out, a voice O'Donnell calls "the horizontal voice." By that he means the "right to address others, without fear of sanctions, on the basis of the belief that those others are 'like me' in some dimension that at least I consider relevant." Only the operation of this horizontal voice makes possible the creation of "we"—a group political identity. Indeed, horizontal voice is a necessary condition of group formation.

Hoping to find a sharp "opposition to the regime that we supposed many concealed behind a very privatized life," O'Donnell and his wife, Cecilia Galli, investigated the fears Argentines had of falling victim to the junta. In the midst of "pervasive and chaotic violence," what they found was a few occasionally addressing the rulers but rarely, if ever, daring to "use horizontal voice." One had to avoid "the dangerous world of public affairs" (O'Donnell, 1986, p. 7). The logic of *divide et impera* worked, as any and all "attempts to extend mutual recognition as opponents to the regime" faded and nearly disappeared (p. 15). Indeed, the "obliteration of horizontal voice means that those social sectors whose mode of voicing cannot but be collective are condemned to silence" (p. 14). That is, the vast majority were not those who usually address or have access to vertical channels. People took refuge in private life and then later denied the refuge they had taken. For in responding after the restoration of constitutional government to a new set of interviews (O'Donnell and his wife claimed the first interview data had been lost), their respondents *claimed* a political identity that had, in fact, been obliterated earlier. They recalled their own thoughts and deeds in a much more favorable light.

Remarkably, the Mothers defied each of O'Donnell's conclusions. They deployed the vertical voice, loudly and incessantly, and that having failed, they did what he argues is nearly impossible—they created a "we," they forged a group political identity on the basis of their shared experience. Condemned to silence, they repudiated the sentence of the regime, took to the Plaza, and voiced their grief and their outrage. They rejected what it meant to be a "good Argentine." They embraced the forbidden—"the dialogical structure entailed by horizontal voice" (O'Donnell, 1986, p. 13). Having lived an atomized life of grief, they found strength and political identity by deprivatizing their mourning. In light of the overwhelming evidence O'Donnell amassed on privatization, silence, depoliti-

2. O'Donnell's argument is based on the concepts of Albert O. Hirschman in his book *Exit, Voice, and Loyalty* and appears in an essay by O'Donnell (1986).

cization, fear, the story of the Mothers becomes, if anything, *more* difficult to understand. Why didn't they succumb? Why did they defy all the social science expectations and conclusions on individual and group behavior in a chaotic, terror-ridden, and punitive surround?

The explanation from a human rights standpoint offers a partial understanding of the Mothers' talk and action, that astonishing dialogue the public appearance of the Mothers generated. Human rights entered into and became constitutive of the political group identity of Las Madres. Political theorist James Tully claims that human rights is "the only bulwark, however fragile, against the brutalization of everyday life in many parts of the world" (1983, p. 15). The notion of human rights, one of the great achievements of Western political culture, is one "part of the normative culture of every country and is advanced by international institutions"; it follows that "the resistance to oppression will tend to take the form of a struggle for the establishment of liberty in its rights form" (p. 15). Tully goes on to argue that dissident groups must practice what they preach inside their own organizations *if* the discourse of human rights is to be politically authentic rather than merely fashionable or cagily strategic.

At least some of the Mothers understood, and understand, rights-talk in its fullest amplification as setting boundaries to their own politics even as it served as a weapon against their tormentors. Countering the cult of death with the language of life and maternal suffering came naturally, so to speak, being deeply encoded in the maternal symbolism and identity of the West, especially in Catholic societies. But human rights language, with its juridical features and its privileging of legal limits to what can or should be done to anyone for any reason, political or not, is scarcely so ancient as a maternal language of mourning and loss. Women came late, relatively speaking, to the juridical identity of official rights-bearing subjects in the West. Many women today, especially mothers in rights-rampant societies such as the United States, are wary of excessive chatter about personal freedom to the exclusion of social responsibility. But that was not the case for the Argentine Mothers. Human rights was, for them, a way to express the timeless *immunities* of persons from the depredations of their governments rather than a vehicle for entitlements. It was a way to say "Stop!" not "Gimme." Rights gave political form and shape to their disobedience, linking them to an international network of associations and watchdog societies, particularly Amnesty International and Americas Watch. Thus the rights discourse of the Mothers never descended into the narrowly individualistic or numbingly legalistic (Schirmer, 1988). Armed with grief and rights, the Mothers took to the streets and created a space for antirepressive politics.

In this matter no vast interpretive armature is needed, for the rights-based self-understanding of the Mothers comes through loud and clear in interviews and in their written documents. In a way, rights talk afforded the Mothers a framework within which to canalize their grief, to make it do political work. And those mothers who seemed to me to be coping best were those who had been able to somewhat transcend the vortex of personal devastation in order to make common cause through human rights efforts both within Argentina and internationally. Thus María Adela Antokoletz:

On the first day there were only fourteen Mothers, in 1977. Since then we have been going to the Plaza uninterruptedly and after a time we started to travel to Europe, to go anywhere we could, to speak to many people, to the media, to spread the word about what was happening. Our struggle has always had a very clear moral purpose; we have always been non-violent; and we have carried out our struggle with dignity. Despite this the costs have been very high. We have been humiliated and offended and mistreated and threatened and blood has been shed. Three Mothers were disappeared as were two French nuns. One of the three mothers was the one who founded the group. I, myself, have never been arrested, though my sister was but she was later released. We never had a narrow political agenda. Ours was a moral protest about political abuse, about how and why people disappeared.

At this point Renée Epelbaum, the mother of three desaparecidos whom I alluded to earlier, in response to my question about what the punishment should be for those who tortured people, kidnapped people, murdered people, said:

I was asked the same question at the end of a film about Las Madres. My answer was: it's a very painful subject for me. My daughter was thrown into the sea. The man or people who did it are as criminal as those who gave the orders. Both must be punished. We don't believe in such a thing as "due obedience." Human beings are not robots. Human beings are responsible for what they do. They destroyed the rights, the lives, of other human beings. People ought to realize they were committing crimes; they were murdering helpless people. Sometimes I give an example. A man makes a robbery. There is someone who plans the whole thing. Maybe he stays at home. And then some go into the bank and do it. Maybe one kills. He is guilty but I ask you, you must involve all of them. We do not believe in the death penalty. We do not want to torture the torturers. We want justice, not vengeance.

María Adela added, "When justice is not fulfilled, when rights are not cherished, those who killed and tortured will do it again because they got away with it. The military has such a hatred. They cannot believe the judgments against them. They wanted to eliminate an entire generation and then make everyone forget what happened." Renée, sadly and musingly, continued, "You know, we understand that not everyone responsible can be punished—that's utopian. But we must do more than judge the high-ranking ones. This leaves all the rest and they will get restless, those men who were so brave to kidnap people who couldn't defend themselves and are afraid to face judgment."

Moving to a sore point—it was clear nobody much wanted to talk about a split that had by then occurred in the Mothers that cold, damp August of 1986—I asked: "What's the difference between your group and other Mothers?"[3] Renée's answer was a classic recognition that human rights discourse imposes responsibilities on its advocates for how they conduct their own affairs as well as for how they apprehend the wider world of political life. Her words, in full, went like this:

> Renée: You know, when we began our struggle, we demanded to know the fate of our children. I lost three; Mariá lost a son; Lydia a son; Marta a daughter and a son-in-law and perhaps a baby because she thinks her daughter was pregnant. We didn't ask the mothers if their children were politically committed. We didn't ask about political beliefs or religious beliefs or social class. It was a pluralist movement. We only demanded truth and justice. We are afraid that some of the leaders of the other group are turning the movement into a class movement. We took a different course, not because of social class but because we want to support all demands towards human rights— including the right to free speech, to have a home, to be educated. We support the Declaration of Human Rights. We don't want the Mothers movement changed into a class movement. Also, there is a question of style. We criticize the policy adopted by the Alfonsin government as too timid. We demand justice strongly. But we know that the current government is not a continuation of the junta. That is just not true. It is not the Alfonsin government which kidnapped, tortured, and killed our children. They are not doing all they should to investigate, to bring justice. But it is not the same thing. We call our line the "foundation line." It is very hard to explain all of this to you. It is a very hard thing. In our group we are all equal. We have differences; we discuss. But Hebe Bonafini, if you didn't think the same as her, accused others of treason.[4] She was bringing the organization to authoritarian ways—giving orders and commands. We had a meeting of the board and we decided in a democratic way what we were going to do. That didn't please her. For a while we went along because we didn't want to show divisions. But now we are living in a democracy and we should not run our own affairs in ways that are against democracy.

> Mariá Adela: We have good reasons for going our own way. It has to do with an enormous difference over internal democracy. If we keep quiet and accept a bad situation we become accomplices. And that is not good for the movement. In my opinion, to have several trends is not necessarily bad; it might give us more strength because you get other options and consult and exchange ideas.

3. Although there is a difference between the two Mothers groups that emerged after the schism, the Linea Fundadora is more solidly grounded in human rights discourse, in both its political orientation and its internal structure. The Bonafini-dominated Mothers downplayed human rights by comparison to a more conspiratorial and accusatory language of militance, as I note further on.

4. Hebe Bonafini is the powerful, initially self-appointed president of Las Madres from whom the Linea Fundadora group of the original Mothers separated in early 1986.

Renée: They don't want to discuss the problem. They want to give orders. That is hopeless. It is very sad.

Mariá Adela: Some people have come to us and say we should be unified once again but we have different positions. I emphasize that we believe in moral protest, in democracy.

JBE: Do you expect to go on indefinitely?

Mariá Adela: What we want and think is that the Mothers of the Plaza de Mayo must endure forever, much more than in our own lifetimes. It has to do with having a guardian position on society in order to watch so this will not happen again—not here or not anywhere else in the world.

Renée: To watch and to denounce. Perhaps it won't be necessary to go to the Plaza if here we have transformation and the guilty are punished. But we want to associate, to witness, to denounce every violation. Because you know at the beginning we only wanted our children. But, as time passed, we got a different comprehension of what was going on in the world. Today I was listening to the radio and there was somebody who sings very well who was singing about babies starving. This is also a violation of human rights. Perhaps there is not much that we can do. I repeat something that Lord Acton said, he knew a lot, he said that people for human rights and humanity must realize justice where they can. They must have a sense of hope *and* reality. I explain so many times that when people who are interested in our fight, in human rights, that we find friends and supporters everywhere. And we say to everyone; be very alert. We never imagined such a thing could happen here. We were the Europeans of Latin America, a civilized country, not a banana republic. But, you see . . . there are always very dangerous things.

Renée's words are reflected in the January 1989 "Project Proposal of Madres de La Plaza de Mayo—Linea Fundadora," a statement of purpose and a search for international support. "We are certain that our actions contribute to the strengthening of democracy. . . . We are also certain that history has given us the role of being the Memory, so that NEVER AGAIN will there be repression in our country, and the children of our nation could grow and mature in freedom." Specific demands included, among others, continued investigations into the fate of each and every disappeared person plus trials of those accused of disappearances; abolition of Law 23.492 of "full stop" (*punto finale,* or statute of limitations), which ended trials against human rights violators; and abolition of Law 23.521 ("due obedience"), which freed accused violators of criminal charges, declaring their crimes null and void.

But, most important, these Mothers encoded democracy in its specifically liberal understandings—grounded in human rights construed as immunities and duties—into their political self-definition. Through their actions and deeds, the ethical force of an argument from human rights helped to animate quiescent sectors of a moribund and demoralized civil society. Whatever Argentina's future fate, these Mothers would say, human rights can never again be trampled upon with such impunity. That is their wager—one to which they have devoted their lives in the name of the lost lives of their children.

Christmas Day, 1988. An early telephone call. I thought it was probably my mother but it was Renée, calling to wish me a Merry Christmas, and asking after my husband and children, and my parents, too. She especially wanted to know of rites of passage—any graduations, engagements, marriages—all those special moments in the life cycle torn from her, denied observance in her own life, with her own children. I assured her that I had not put the story of the Mothers out of my mind, that I cited her and Mariá Adela in the paper on "The Power and Powerlessness of Women" delivered at the University of Leiden, September 1987, tying their politics to that of Vaclav Havel, then jailed dissident, now, remarkably, president of a democratic Czech Republic.

And I was writing yet another essay, drawing upon something she had said about being a daughter of Antigone. She thanked me and called me her friend. Truth to tell, I was having a lot more difficulty "incorporating material" from my Argentine experience and the politics of Las Madres than I let on to Renée. But I've already done enough hand-wringing on this issue. One does what one can. The story isn't over. Not by any means. But this much can be said. The Mothers remained faithful to the dominant image of the mother of their society. Yet they politicized this tradition against a repressive state, both as a form of protection—the state should fulfill its rhetorical claims to defend motherhood—and as a newfound identity—mothers looking for their children, mothers for human rights. By confronting a repressive state and forcing this issue into the streets and the Plaza de Mayo, the iconography of Motherhood in Argentine society was forever altered: from weeping woman to defiant witness. Determined as they are not to have their individual tragedies dismissed as private dramas, the Mothers held and hold to the conviction that if a society censors its memory and denies the past to its children and its grandchildren, hope for a more just social order must always be tinged with desperation, perpetually forlorn.

These are bits of a collage in an un-still life, a world taking shape, struggling to be born, open to the stubborn reality of the everyday and to the "miracle," as Hannah Arendt put it, of new beginnings. A politics of corpses or a politics of "hope and reality"? They jury is out.

> We *are* your daughters of Antigone. I did not get to bury my children, as Antigone buried her brother. But I have risked my life to make public their suffering. Now, somehow, I must find the strength to go on living. I can do this because if I do not my children will have died twice, once at the hands of their tormentors and a second time from my silence. Thrown into the sea, tossed like garbage into mass graves, where are my children? I cannot bring flowers, nor pray, nor visit their final resting places. Like the Mothers, the Disappeared are everywhere, wherever a single person is abducted, tortured, killed unjustly. Like Antigone, we will endure beyond our lifetimes. This is what we recognize. This is our hope. (Elshtain, 1989, p. 235)

References

Dorfman, A. (1984). *Widows.* New York: Aventura.

Elshtain, J. B. (April, 1982). Antigone's daughters. *democracy,* 2(2), 46–59.

Elshtain, J. B. (1989). Antigone's daughters reconsidered. In S. K. White (Ed.), *Life-world and politics: Between modernity and postmodernity.* Notre Dame: University of Notre Dame Press.

Martinez Morena, C. (1988). *El Infierno.* London: Readers International.

Mignone, E. F. (1987). The military: What is to be done? *Report on the Americas,* 21(4), 18.

Milosz, C. (1990). *The captive mind.* New York: Random House.

Nunca Mas: The report of the Argentine national commission of the disappeared (1986). New York: Farrar, Straus and Giroux.

O'Donnell, G. (1986). On the fruitful convergences of Hirschman's *Exit, voice and loyalty,* and *Shifting involvements: Reflections from the recent Argentine experience.* Notre Dame: Notre Dame University, Kellogg Institute, Working Paper no. 58.

Partnoy, A. (1986). *The little school: Tales of disappearance and survival in Argentina.* San Francisco: Cleis Press.

Ruddick, S. (1989). *Maternal thinking.* New York: Beacon Press.

Schirmer, J. G. (1988) "Those who die for life cannot be called dead": Women and human rights protest in Latin America. *Harvard Human Rights Yearbook.* Vol. 1, 41–76.

Scobie, J. R. (1971). *Argentina.* New York: Oxford University Press.

Simpson, J., and Bennett, J. (1985). *The disappeared and the mothers of the Plaza.* New York: St. Martin's.

Steiner, G. (1984). *Antigones.* New York: Oxford University Press.

Taylor, J. M. (1979). *Eva Perón: The myths of a woman.* Chicago: University of Chicago Press.

Thornton, L. (1988). *Imagining Argentina.* New York: Bantam.

Todd, J. M. (1982). *Luther: A life.* New York: Crossroad.

Tully, J. H. (Ed.). (1983). *John Locke: A letter concerning toleration.* Indianapolis: Hackett.

MARIANNE HIRSCH

5 Maternity and Rememory:
Toni Morrison's *Beloved*

Under these arrangements the customary lexis of sexuality,
including "reproduction," "motherhood," "pleasure," and
"desire," are thrown into unrelieved crisis.   Hortense
Spillers (1987)

Memory, prehistoric memory, has no time.   Toni Morrison
(1987)

In 1928, Virginia Woolf suggested that "we think back through
our mothers if we are women" (Woolf, 1957, p. 79). Although in *A
Room of One's Own,* Woolf connects this act of thinking back and
through the mother with the woman writer's relation to a female
literary tradition, she also brings this form of thought back to
her own personal motivation for writing. In her memoir, *Moments of Being,* Woolf reveals that every day from the age of
thirteen, when her mother died, to the age of forty-four, when
she wrote *To the Lighthouse,* she was haunted by her mother's
ghost (1985, p. 80). Completing the novel enabled her to exorcise
the ghost and to cease thinking about her mother. Informed by
childhood desire and nostalgia, Woolf's composition of this
novel follows an expected generational sequence. The thirty-year
distance between the mother's death and the daughter's ability
to write it is itself a literary and a psychological factor that
explains the quality of maternal representation in many women's

I would like to thank the editors of this volume as well as Elizabeth
Abel, Mary Childers, Carla Freccero, Lynn Higgins, Gail Reimer, Brenda
Silver, Valerie Smith, Leo Spitzer, and Mary Helen Washington for their
suggestions on earlier drafts of this chapter and Toni Morrison for her
encouragement. This chapter was completed in the fall of 1990.

narratives: the distancing and objectification of mothers, the nostalgia that surrounds them, the tone of celebration and mystification, and the inverse degradation with which they are shaped.[1]

How much more unusual to have the opposite sequence—a maternal narrative haunted by the ghost of a child. Through such a violent and disturbing reversal of generational continuity, Toni Morrison's *Beloved* allows us to look at women's writing from the different perspective of *maternal* subjectivity (Morrison, 1987).[2]

I undertake this exploration of maternity at a moment of crucial urgency for feminist inquiry. At a moment when science and the legal system are engaged in the process of charting definitions and rights of families, children, fathers, and mothers—in debates around choice, reproductive technologies, custody, adoption, enforced sterilization, child care, AIDS, and so on—it is crucial for feminists to understand the terms through which we want to enter these debates. At a moment when the popular women's movement is rallying around a "family agenda," it is necessary for academic feminists to focus on "family" as rigorously as possible. And yet Morrison's novel can also help to define how difficult it is to do so in an ideological climate dominated by a hegemonic familial mythos that continues to perpetuate itself even as it ceases, more and more, to correspond to the realities of most of our lives. The nuclear patriarchal oedipal family, which grants authority to the father, fragility and the future to the children, and the total care of that fragility, the devoted nurturing of that future, to the mother, persists in the unconscious of contemporary United States culture—even throughout its subcultures. Although it has outlived its viability, the oedipal family romance remains a cultural master narrative and reference point against which other arrangements are measured, structuring feeling and thinking, theories and narratives, about family and about mothers most especially, even among feminists.

How can feminists, how can mothers, claim a discourse that more and more speaks *for us?* Although it is unlikely that feminists will ever reach a comfortable consensus on these issues, it is crucial that we understand the terms of the argument, and to do so we must try to scrutinize motherhood from personal, subjective, legal, psychological, biological, economic, historical, and technological vantage points. Yet we are virtually prevented from doing so by a mythos of the nuclear family that is founded on maternal objectification and erasure. Jocasta, the silent and virtually absent *mother* in the narrative of Oedipus, serves as an emblem for the way in which the psychological story of subject-formation focuses on the child and leaves out the mother. If the notion of the individual *subject* is defined in such a way that its very formation and development, that subjectivity itself, needs to take place either against or in relation to the background of an *object*—a silent maternal figure—how can maternity be studied

---

1. I trace the shape of these representations more fully in *The Mother/Daughter Plot: Narrative Psychoanalysis, Feminism* (1989).

2. Subsequent page numbers in the text refer to this edition.

from the perspectives of mothers? Are there such perspectives if our theories insist on defining subjectivity from the point of view of the developing child?[3] Are there such perspectives if our theories persist in conceiving the symbolic in relation to a presymbolic dominated by a maternal figure who never emerges beyond it *as mother?* Are there such perspectives if mothers are mythified, mystified, objectified, abjected, othered, in the process of subject-formation as we tend to conceive it, and in the theories that conceive it in this way?

In my work on maternity, I have been trying to imagine what model or definition of subjectivity might be derived from a theory that began with mothers rather than with children. I have been wondering whether we could envision development other than as a process of separation from a self-effacing "holding" background. If we started our study of the subject with mothers, mothers who are always already double—both child and adult, both daughter and mother—rather than with children, what different formulations of subjectivity might emerge? In what ways might such a study enable us to combine a grammatical/psychological conception of the subject, in the sense of "developing person" and "subject of discourse," with the social/political notion of a subject who is "subjected to" and "interpellated by" certain structures of power, certain hegemonic ideologies and institutions?[4] In trying to arrive at a notion of maternal subjectivity, I see the mother as doubly "subjected": she is "subject to" the institutions of family and maternity as defined by the hegemonic culture, and those institutions in turn "subject" her to the needs, demands, and desires both of the culture itself and of the child whom she rears to become subject to that culture in his or her own right. Thus, the mother is the "object" to the child's "subjectivity" in that other sense of "the subject" as the ego or the "I"— the subject of discourse, of consciousness, of identity. The term *subject* remains useful, then, precisely because of its ambiguity and multivalence. Unlike such other humanist terms as *self* or *identity* and *individuality,* which imply an undivided sense of self-ownership, *subject* combines the divisions, contradictions, and erasures theorized in poststructuralism, psychoanalysis and neo-Marxism with the sense of uniqueness and singularity that, although a leftover from humanism, continues to be powerful in the constitution of personhood as our culture conceives it.[5] Furthermore, the notion of "subject" also includes a definition of "subjectivity" as "interiority" and depth. It is precisely the notion of "subject" and "subjectivity" that enables us to ask what happens, in the process of the work of maternity and in the process of the child's "subject formation," to the maternal "I," to maternal self-consciousness, identity, and selfhood. It en-

3. For more extensive discussions of the child-centered bias of psychoanalytic and feminist theories, see Suleiman (1985, 1988) and Chodorow and Contratto (1989).

4. For a useful discussion of the term *subject* and the various theoretical appropriations of that term, see Paul Smith (1988).

5. For a feminist critique of the postmodernist dismantling of the humanist subject, see Miller (1988). See also Owens (1983) and Jardine (1985).

ables us to attempt to describe and to theorize maternal "subjectivity" in this complicated and contradictory sense.

As a text for this exploration, *Beloved* tests in very particular ways the familial ideologies that have controlled maternal representations. Morrison's Sethe is a slave mother, and, as such, she participates in a different familial and maternal mythos and has a different relation to any conception of "selfhood," "individuality," or "subjectivity." The slave mother is interpellated first and primarily into the institution of slavery: family and maternity therefore have different meanings for her. And she is "subjected" less subtly with the whip and the chain; her very body marks her as a slave. Slavery heightens and intensifies the experience of family and of motherhood, of connection and separation. It raises questions about what it means to have a self, and to give that self away. It raises questions about what family means, and about the ways in which nuclear configurations (dominant in the master culture and in that culture's master narrative) prevail as points of reference even in economies in which they are thoroughly displaced and disrupted.[6]

Since the infamous Moynihan report in 1965, Americans have come to see the African-American family as a matriarchy in which mothers rather than fathers have power and presence (Moynihan, 1965). But we have also been taught that children need to be dispossessed of a maternal power deemed illegitimate and harmful. Moynihan and later Bill Moyers in his 1986 television documentary on "The Vanishing Black Family: Crisis in Black America," as well as other analysts of what we are told is "the crisis of the black family," see the history of slavery with which mothers mark their children as the root of familial structures that are dysfunctional, especially for sons.[7] In recent years, African-American writers, feminist scholars, and cultural critics have unveiled the racist assumptions that underlie these representations, as they have confronted with one another the divergent ideologies of gender that shape black femininity and masculinity, on the one hand, and white femininity and masculinity, on the other. They have insisted, as Patricia Hill Collins (1990) does most recently, that the maternal practices of African-American mothers can provide models for a critique of hegemonic familial structures dominated by patriarchy and capitalism and therefore oppressive to women and children.

Beloved reveals these divergences: it tests the notion of matriarchal power and its effects on children by allowing an African-American mother herself to speak, to assert and to probe, however tentatively, a maternal *subjectivity,* the

6. The figure of the slave mother appears in a number of recent discussions both of maternity and of slavery, perhaps because the violation of maternal love can be useful in defining both the extent of the inhumanity of slavery and the power of that love. For example, Chesler (1987) uses Harriet Jacobs as a paradigm of the socially powerless mother. See also Williams's novel (1986) about maternity under slavery.

7. See Moyers (1986). For an excellent summary and analysis of the twenty-five-year history of media representations of the black family, see Gresham and Wilkerson (1989).

voice of both mother and subject. I would like to offer this maternal voice as a paradigm, more broadly useful, for a different, a feminist, way of thinking about families and about mothers.[8] Freud used the family of Oedipus—a family that transgresses against the most basic definitions of convention and norm to the point of constituting, rather, a counterfamily—as a model for the emotions that structured his vision of Family. Similarly, we might use, in *Beloved,* a family constituted under a slave economy that violates the most basic definitions of humanity and individuality, as a paradigm for and a critique of the emotions and the patterns that structure both the hegemonic master narrative of Family, and its fantasies about other models—Moynihan's black matriarchy, for example. This is an attempt, then, to respond to Hortense Spillers's blunt question— "Does the Freudian text translate in short? . . . Is the Freudian landscape an applicable text (say nothing of appropriate) to social and historical situations that do not replicate moments of its own cultural origins and involvements?"— by demonstrating that the particular historical situation of United States slavery foregrounds the need to historicize psychoanalytic and literary paradigms (Spillers, 1989, pp. 160–168). Slave mothers, because they "own" neither themselves nor their children, pose the question of maternal discourse with particular emphasis. As the maternal subject in Morrison's novel becomes the repository for the most repressed, the most unspeakable cultural memories and narratives, the novel scrutinizes its potential to represent a resistant, even an oppositional cultural voice. It may seem surprising, even counterintuitive, to identify maternal discourse as oppositional: mothers, after all, are usually seen as the conservers of value and tradition. Yet the peculiar maternal memory defined in Toni Morrison's novel as *rememory* serves as a ground of resistance and opposition. Rememory is neither memory nor forgetting, but memory combined with (the threat of) repetition; it is neither noun nor verb, but both combined. Rememory is Morrison's attempt to re-conceive the memory of slavery, finding a way to re-member, and to do so *differently,* what an entire culture has been trying to repress.

Teresa de Lauretis has recently suggested that "feminist theory came into its own in a post-colonial mode," that "a feminist critical theory as such begins when the feminist critique of socio-cultural formations (discourses, forms of representation, ideologies) becomes conscious of itself and turns inward . . . in pursuit of consciousness—to question its own relation to or possible complicity with those ideologies, its own heterogeneous body of writing and interpretations, their basic assumptions and terms, and the practices which they enable and from which they emerge" (1990, pp. 137–138). Looking at family from the perspective of maternity is such an inherently demystifying act. Moving toward

---

8. I use the term *feminist* here without qualifying it as either black or white because I hope to be able to cut across the divergent familial ideologies the novel reveals without, however, erasing the differences between them. A feminist discussion of maternity, as I see it, is precisely a discussion that takes differences that are due to race, class, ethnicity, and historical specificity into account, even while allowing points of convergence to emerge.

Family from the oblique perspective of counterfamilies, feminist theory can come to a consciousness about its terms and conceptions, about their multiplicities and divergences. We can perform the act of "translation" suggested by Spillers and attempt to cut across what she defines as the parallel and presumably nonintersecting lines that "the African-American text" draws in relation to "a Eurocentric psychomythology" (Spillers, 1989, p. 175). Translation needs to be performed in multiple directions, however, as the oedipal patriarchal mythos of Family is confronted with alternative models. Scrutinizing familial definitions and narratives in heightened and intensified form, we can perhaps unmask the master narrative of Family as no more than the master's narrative.

Elsewhere I have suggested that Toni Morrison's Sethe, the maternal protagonist of her novel *Beloved,* is a revision of Sophocles' silent Jocasta or of the powerful mythic figure of Demeter (Hirsch, 1989, pp. 5–8). Like the Oedipus story, Morrison's novel is about the murdered/abandoned child, here a daughter, returning from the other side to question the mother, and, like the story of Demeter and Persephone, it is about a temporary, perhaps a cyclical, reunion between the mother and the daughter she lost. Like those two texts, *Beloved* is a ghost story about a child who returns to reestablish connection, a deep bodily and emotional connection with the mother who was responsible for her death. *Beloved* is not only about the child's longing for a lost maternal object but about the immense loss experienced by a mother who is unable to keep her children alive and to rear them: It is about maternal fantasies of reparation and recovery. It is about the embodiment of maternal memory and about the material and erotic confrontation with a past that, paradoxically, is represented and embodied by the child. Yet Morrison's novel, unlike the Oedipus story, *begins* with the mother, and allows *her* to *tell* her tale, to attempt to explain her incomprehensible act.

The novel begins in 1873, eight years after the end of the Civil War, in Cincinnati and returns through flashbacks to the Mississippi slave plantation ironically called Sweet Home. There the owner, Mr. Garner, who believed in treating his slaves humanely, created an atmosphere of relative comfort: Sethe and Halle could "marry," Halle could buy his mother's freedom, the Sweet Home slaves were "men," and not "boys." When Garner dies and his brother-in-law, referred to as Schoolteacher, arrives with his nephews to run the plantation, the slaves come to know both the material and the psychological humiliations of their condition. Schoolteacher uses them to prove the animality of the black race by measuring their heads and keeping tables about them.

When life becomes intolerable, Sethe and the Sweet Home men undertake a nightmarish escape plan; most are killed or disappear, including Halle, but Sethe and Paul D. separately make it to "freedom." For Sethe this is hardly a triumphant escape: she sends her three children ahead, and in the final stages of her fourth pregnancy, she is brutally raped of her breast milk by Schoolteacher's nephews and then badly beaten and scarred when she complains to her mistress. In this wounded condition, she rushes on across the Ohio to bring her milk to the baby she sent ahead, but on the way she gives birth to Denver with the help of a "whitegirl," Amy. There is a brief respite when she reaches 124 Bluestone Road and her mother-in-law, Baby Suggs, who nurses her back to health. But all too soon, her freedom and her children's is threatened by the arrival of School-teacher who comes to claim them under the Fugitive Slave Act. As Sethe sees them arrive, she "tries to put her babies where they'd be safe": she kills the baby girl and would have killed her two boys and herself too if there had been time. Her infanticide does buy her and the children a form of "freedom." Eventually released from jail, Sethe lives a life of guilt and abandonment: Baby Suggs, broken by her grief, dies, and the two boys, afraid of their mother, run off.

Only Sethe, Denver, and the ghost of the baby girl are left eighteen years later, when Paul D. arrives to tell his part of the story of escape and liberation: the death of Sixo, one of the Sweet Home men, who was roasted alive singing after trying to escape; Halle's smearing his face with butter after watching the nephews' assault on Sethe; and the indignities Paul D. himself suffered when he was forced to wear a bit in his mouth, and when he worked on a chain gang and escaped, chained to a group of other men. He also tells how he dealt with these memories until seeing Sethe: by sealing them and the emotions they evoked off into a tin tobacco box which he wore inside his chest.

The mother-daughter narrative in Morrison's *Beloved* depends on male inter-vention for its inception. In this it seems to confirm not only a pattern set in the Demeter story—there is no story before Hades abducts Persephone—but also psychoanalytic patterns described by Freud and Lacan, who identify the sym-bolic space of narrative with the paternal third term, the name of the father. Paul D.'s sudden appearance disrupts the uneasy household in which Sethe and Denver have coexisted with the baby ghost. His presence makes it possible for Sethe to find a way to tell the story of motherhood under slavery, a story by which she has been obsessed for the eighteen years following her escape. His presence also dispels the ghost, evoking instead the appearance of the mysterious female figure who turns out to be the murdered baby Beloved returned from the dead to make contact with the mother she has been longing for on the other side.

Familial structures in this novel are necessarily shaped by the institution of slavery. Freud (1908) insists in his essay "Family Romances" that once children understand reproduction, the mother is "certissima," whereas the father is "semper incertus," and he builds an entire theory of childhood desire and nostalgia around this difference. But Sethe spoke to her own mother only once. When she saw her mother hanged one morning, Sethe was not allowed to check for the mark under her breast by means of which she might have been able to recognize her definitively as her mother. When Sethe's mother showed Sethe the mark that branded them both as descendants of a maternal lineage of enslavement, she rewrote the slave owner's inscription as her own subversive maternal language.[9] With this maternal act, Morrison's narrative aptly qualifies the ahistoricity of psychoanalytic certainties. Sethe is permanently separated from her husband, Halle, and separates herself from her own children when she

9. This is the illuminating point made by Goldman (1990).

sends them ahead to freedom. In this economy in which even one's own body is not one's property, the white masters can rob Sethe of everything, including her mother's milk. Her maternal labor is supposed to be theirs, not hers or her children's; she needs to devise a discourse of resistance to assert her own maternal knowledge: "All I knew was I had to get my milk to my baby girl. Nobody was going to nurse her like me" (p. 16).

It is no surprise, then, that the inhabitants of 124 Bluestone Road do not constitute a nuclear family that might fit Freudian paradigms. Morrison underscores this incongruity when she writes the ambiguous "124," which opens the novel: (Oedipal) triangles are repeatedly broken and displaced, as a *fourth* term either supplements or replaces the third. Sethe, her daughter Denver, and the grandmother, Baby Suggs, are joined by the ghost; after the grandmother's death, Sethe, Denver, and the ghost are joined by Paul D; and after the ghost is chased off, Sethe, Denver, and Paul D., whose shadows on the road do form a triangle, are quickly joined by the ghostly Beloved who thoroughly disrupts any possible nuclear configuration. When Paul D. leaves and the three women are left in the house, their hermetic interaction is unbearable and the three need again to be disrupted, first by Denver's departure, then by the community women's return, and, eventually, by the exorcism of the ghost and the return of Paul D. This sequence of rupture and dislocation confronts us with the novel's first words and shapes the novel as a whole. Morrison herself explains this choice of beginning: "The reader is snatched, yanked, thrown into an environment completely foreign, and I want it as the first stroke of the shared experience that might be possible between the reader and the novel's population. Snatched just as the slaves were from one place to another, from any place to another, without preparation and without defense" (Morrison, 1989). She underscores the difficulty of the "124"—numbers seen, difficult to read and pronounce: is it one twenty-four or one, two, four? And what, when we read "124 was spiteful," is "124"—a number, a character, a house?

Sweet Home itself already functions as a distorted family: the Garners substitute the slaves for their children, and when Mr. Garner dies, a trio arrives made up of Schoolteacher and his two nephews. The fact that the white families in the novel—the Garners, the Bodwins, Amy Denver—are all childless and motherless serves to heighten the symbolic import of the theft of Sethe's milk and clears the space for an exploration of the black mother, a figure Morrison reclaims from prevailing stereotypes. Under slavery, where mothers cannot "own" their children, they experience separation and loss all the more intensely. Possessives dominate in this novel as the characters problematically insist that they own each other: "you are mine." Yet at the end of the novel, Sethe is tentatively able to allow a maternal voice and subjectivity to emerge, to question the hierarchy of motherhood over selfhood on which her life had rested until that moment, for, reversing the prevalent sequence, Sethe was a *mother* before she became a *subject*. This does not mean, of course, that Sethe does not have an interior subjective life at Sweet Home or in Cincinnati; she certainly does to the point of resistance, escape, and murder. It does mean that because of her status in the "peculiar institution," she was personally and legally not an "I," not a subject, until after she freed herself, and she did not free herself until after she was already a mother. For this reason, Sethe's subjectivity is not in fact "born" until the very end of the novel when she both recognizes Beloved as her child and begins to recognize herself as "Me? Me?"

Here is the moment in which maternal subjectivity is born. It echoes another moment in an earlier Morrison novel, Nel's self-recognition as subject in *Sula:* "I'm me. I'm not their daughter. I'm not Nel. I'm me. Me" (Morrison, 1973, p. 24). We need, however, to assess the difference between this sort of daughterly subjectivity and the maternal subjectivity we find in *Beloved.* We need to examine what makes Sethe's moment of birth into maternal subjectivity possible and what its implications are at the present moment of feminist consciousness and social thinking about maternity.

Birth is an important theme in Morrison's novel, and Sethe's "Me? Me?" gains in significance as we place it in the context of other birth moments. The birth of Denver, in particular, occurs at a crucially symbolic juncture in the text, one to which many of the characters return. Denver is born during Sethe's flight to freedom in a boat, just before the crossing of the Ohio into freedom. Sethe repeats to all who marvel at her ability to make it under these circumstances that she gave birth not alone but with the help of a "whitegirl," Amy Denver. Several things occur at the same time, then: the birth of a new child, Denver; Sethe's emergence into freedom and reunification with her other children; her birth as a free subject; and the sisterhood, the collaboration of a white women and a black woman, united by their gender, their poverty, their subordinate social status, and by their stories of cruel masters, absent mothers, unknown fathers—yet forever separated by the absolute reality of slavery. In a privileged moment of connection around a work they share, privileged because they are allowed to have a space separate from any social framework ("no patroller came and no preacher"), Sethe and Amy can talk for a few brief hours, Amy can rub Sethe's feet and wrap Sethe's baby in her undergarment. Significantly, as well, she takes the place not only of the other black women who would have acted as midwives in such a birth but also of the black father whose power to name the child she occupies by "giving" the baby the name Denver.

What is significant in this privileged moment in the novel is how it narrates and ultimately mythifies birth, maternal creation, subject-formation, and future hope. This process of mythification, and its ultimate demystification by the events of the novel, sets up the structure of narrative and counternarratives, memory/forgetting and rememory, on which the novel is structured.

Although Denver's birth is referred to on several occasions, the only full account of it occurs in a scene between Denver and Beloved, who, in Faulknerian fashion, reconstruct the scene together based on the stories Denver had heard her whole life from Sethe and from Baby Suggs. It is the interaction between the sisters that finally makes the story and Sethe's own role in it come alive for Denver: "Denver was seeing it now and feeling it—through Beloved. Feeling what it must have felt to her mother. Seeing how it must have looked" (p. 78). In her adoration of Beloved, Denver gives her the most precious thing she owns, the story of her own origin, and through that act of giving, the story grows and is enriched, uniting the sisters, keeping one interested in the other. More than a sister, Denver becomes a "mother" who feeds stories to her "child."

In the sisters' daughterly reconstruction, the narrative of birth acquires mythic proportions: not only does it occur outside of time (it is late afternoon, the sun is still shining, but the stars are already out), outside the social, between slavery and freedom, on the edge of the river (the river Lethe?), but in celebrating the power of maternal creation against immeasurable odds, it becomes a glorious tale of mythic maternal heroism—a mythic birth of a hero. This is the child's search for her origins; this is the mediated memory of slavery held by a generation that is already born into freedom. But the daughter cannot tell that story without heroizing and mythifying it.

Throughout her painful journey and labor, Sethe, who feels the pain, and Amy, who watches it, both wonder "what God had in mind." Just after the baby is born, "the wet sticky women clambered ashore to see what, indeed, God had in mind." They face a fantastic landscape that archetypically repeats the birth they have just enacted: "Spores of bluefern growing in the hollows along the riverbank float toward the water in silver-blue lines hard to see unless you are in or near them, lying right at the river's edge when the sun-shots are low and drained. Often they are mistook for insects—but they are seeds in which the whole generation sleeps confident of a future. And for a moment it is easy to believe each has one—will become all of what is contained in the spore: will live out its days as planned. This moment of certainty lasts no longer than that; longer perhaps than the spore itself" (p. 84). Under the shower of bluefern, we have a story of maternal creation and survival that, unlike the rest of the novel, *is* "a story to pass on," a story that does get passed on, that is hopeful and forward-looking and therefore understandable to the empathic, but ultimately self-interested, daughters. It is a story of sisterhood and hope with which daughters can identify, out of which memories and inspirations for the future are made. In allowing them to heroize this tale, Morrison allows the daughters to find themselves in the mother's story so that Denver might develop into the mature, self-reliant, caring, and community-oriented woman she becomes at the end of the novel.

This account of Denver's birth corresponds to Sara Ruddick's recent discussion of the philosophical preconceptions of the birth process: "Birth is a beginning whose end and shape can be neither predicted, nor controlled. . . . To engage in giving birth is an expression of trust in others and a determination to become trustworthy. It is an expression of hopefulness in oneself and in 'nature,' one's own and that of the child to whom one has given birth" (1989, pp. 209–210). As the novel articulates that hope here, it can use it as a critique of the culture of slavery in which mothers give birth neither to hope nor to individuals nor to a future, but to property.

The story of Denver's birth is embedded in and materially marked by another story that the daughters can only begin to understand and that is also inscribed on the mother's body—the story of slavery and escape, which qualifies and transforms the story of individual and cultural birth and rebirth. This is the story Denver hates, the story she wants to silence, and from which Sethe tries to protect her: "To Sethe, the future was a matter of keeping the past at bay" (p. 42). "Denver hated the stories her mother told that did not concern herself, which is why Amy was all she ever asked about. The rest was a gleaming powerful world made more so by Denver's absence from it" (p. 62). But that story is there nevertheless, inflecting and informing the other. Thus the blood is not just the blood of birth but the blood on Sethe's back where she was beaten, the blood on her feet on which she had to run. The milk is not just the milk she developed for this new baby but the milk she was carrying for the baby girl she had to send ahead, the milk taken by the masters at Sweet Home provoking her escape. Sethe's body, the birthing maternal body, is marked by the narrative of slavery, just as her own mother's body was marked by a circle and cross under her breast. In this novel, the mother's body is not merely a vehicle for the child's birth and creation: it has a narrative of its own. It is not merely the vehicle of a birth into freedom: it must itself be (re)created and cared for in the transition between slavery and freedom. Sethe cannot be freed; she cannot begin to be born into subjectivity without a "mother" of her own, and in the novel that mother is Baby Suggs. But *this* birth constitutes one in a series of counternarratives to the other.

Our introduction to Baby Suggs and to the scene of Sethe's arrival at 124 Bluestone Road occurs by way of Baby Suggs's work as an "unchurched preacher" in the clearing, where she gathers the freed slaves and teaches them to love themselves, to love, nurture, and celebrate every part of the bodies that had been despised and tortured by the white masters: "we flesh," she insists, "flesh that needs to be loved" (p. 88). When Sethe arrives, Baby Suggs does just that— she washes Sethe in sections, wraps her body as though in swaddling clothes, and sews her a new dress. She soaks her feet, rubs her nipples, greases her wounded back, washes the blood that has inscribed on the sheets the narrative of Sethe's suffering. It is thus that Sethe can literally be born again.

Baby Suggs, the freed mother who has lost all of her own children, can offer Sethe an alternate to the maternal care she could have from her own mother. In her only moment of meaningful contact with her mother, Sethe was shown the mark under her mother's breast and was slapped when she wanted to be marked as well. She *is* marked by her mother, of course, not only by the bodily scars of slavery, but by her mother's history of infanticide which she ends up repeating. Baby Suggs, the alternate mother, the mother-in-law, in contrast, tries to erase the marks as she washes Sethe. In Baby Suggs's house, she can be nurtured differently than she had been by Nan who had nursed her and told her, in a language she no longer remembers or understands, that she was special, that she was the only one her mother had not thrown away. And Sethe herself can perhaps mother differently from Baby Suggs who, in order to be free, had to separate herself from her only remaining child, and who could now barely remember how her children looked or what they were like.

Sethe's negative memories—she does *not* speak her mother tongue, she was *not* marked, she had *not* been thrown away, she could *not* properly recognize the mother who had been hanged, her mother had *not* done her hair—had to be replaced by Baby Suggs's positive love of her flesh, by the spit the baby girl drooled on her face, by the "real-talk" with new neighbors. And through that love, Baby Suggs herself hopes to repair some of her own losses. Together, perhaps, they could invent a new and different form of mother-daughter relation and transmission. As Sethe explains to Paul D. eighteen years later, "Freeing yourself was one thing; claiming ownership of that freed self was another" (p. 95).

The self that Sethe learned to claim with the help of Baby Suggs and the community during the short twenty-eight days of her rebirth process is not entirely hers to own; if Baby Suggs puts her together, it is not just for herself. As she rushes to get her milk to her baby, interrupted only by the birth of another child, Sethe constructs herself as the object of her children's needs. Sethe's is a *maternal* self, connected to the new baby she has just given birth to, to "the crawling-already baby girl" she is still nursing, and to the two boys who used her body as their toy. It is connected to the memories of Halle and Sweet Home and the past, and that past is part of any future life she can possibly build with her children and her mother-in-law. Again, Sethe explains these connections to Paul D.: "I did it. . . . I birthed them and I got them out and it wasn't no accident. . . . It was a kind of selfishness I never knew nothing about before. It felt good. Good and right. I was big, Paul D., and deep and wide and when I stretched out my arms all my children could get in between. I was *that* wide" (p. 162). As she emerges from captivity at 124 Bluestone Road, as she emerges in body and in soul, Sethe conceives of herself in and through these affiliations.

These multiple connections are ever more pressing and confusing when this rebirth scene is repeated at the end of the novel, this time with Paul D. in the maternal nurturing role. After losing her daughter for the second time, Sethe retreated to Baby Suggs's bed with "no plans at all," ready to die. Again her body has to be restored to her, for she has lost it: "If he bathes her in sections will the parts hold together?" she wonders. But in this scene the birthing and nurturing is mutual and multiple. Through the memory of Sixo and the Thirty-Mile Woman, Paul D. realizes what Sethe can do for him: "She is a friend of my mind. She gather me, man. The pieces I am, she gather them and give them back to me in the right order" (pp. 272, 273).

And, as he holds her hand with one of his hands and her face with the other, he can help her to realize that it was not her child who was her best thing: "You your best thing, Sethe. You are." He can help her get to the point of asking, "Me? Me?" With this double question, this double assertion of herself not in the affirmative as Nel had done in *Sula* but in the interrogative, not in the subject and object position "I'm me" but in the object position alone, the maternal subject appears. It is a subject constructed in question and in relation. After all the threes and fours, we have a two here; after Denver's heroic birth into individuality and after Sethe's repeated birth into family and community, we have a birth into a couple here, a couple with one child, Denver, who returns only during the day. We might ask whether this is a reversion to oedipal mediations and triangulations, to the heterosexual adulthood Freud dictates for women, to a story that is always already read. We might ask why Sethe's moment of self-realization is located in the plot of heterosexual romance. It is obvious that Sethe and Paul D. do not correspond to the heterosexual couple that is the cornerstone of the oedipal family: Paul D. is not the father, he has no authority, he has been walking for eighteen years and comes to Sethe to put his story next to hers, not to exercise patriarchal privilege. Sethe and Paul D., the couple attempting to give birth to "some kind of tomorrow," are not alone in that room. With them are their rememories—Baby Suggs, the children who have gone, the community women who have returned, Sixo and the Thirty-Mile Woman, Halle, the other Pauls. Their story is not single, but multiple: they have put their stories next to each other, next to the stories of all the others. Sethe's maternal subjectivity is still affiliative; it cannot be born without the physical intercon-nection of "his holding fingers" which are "holding hers." And no adult maternal subjectivity can be voiced, even tentatively and questioningly, without the haunting rememories of slavery inscribed on their bodies—Sethe's chokecherry tree that marks her back but that she will never see or feel, Paul D.'s continued consciousness of the bit in his mouth and the collar around his neck—and embodied in the murdered third child, Beloved. It is here, in the act of re-memory, that we can find the differences between the freed person, the freed mother, that Sethe was when she first arrived at 124 and the maternal subject who says "Me? Me?" at the end of the novel.

Two other more obscure scenes of birth and origin serve to throw light on this evolution. The first, more straightforward one is the uncanny scene of Beloved's arrival out of the water, her thirst, and Sethe's simultaneous seemingly endless urination, equated with "water breaking from a breaking womb" (p. 51). Sethe speculates that this literal rebirth of the baby's/young woman's ghost "in the flesh" must have occurred with the help, on the other side, of Baby Suggs. Later that ghost's own rememories, however, place this particular "birth" moment into a series of other infinitely more disturbing ones.

There is no account of the baby girl's birth at Sweet Home; there is only a very brief account of her death, of the truth Sethe calls "simple" and believes she will no longer have to remember: "I stopped him. . . . I took and put my babies where they'd be safe." This is the end of hope and trust, the opposition of the outlook of birth described by Ruddick. Yet, as impossible as that may be to absorb, it is a maternal act of, to borrow another term from Sara Ruddick, preservation: Sethe wants to make sure her baby will be *safe* from the dehuman-ization of slavery.[10] This moment is, of course, the most problematic of the novel, and, as such, it takes the text out of the pattern of narrative and counter-narrative, to the point of antinarrative. Sethe's act of infanticide is simply not

---

10. Ruddick, *Maternal Thinking;* see especially the chapter entitled "Preservative Love."

told: It is read about in the newspaper clipping by Paul D.; it is circled around by Sethe; it is barely touched on by Beloved. "Sethe knew that the circle she was making around the room, him, the subject, would remain one. That she could never close in, pin it down for anybody who had to ask. If they didn't get it right off—she could never explain" (p. 163).

To Beloved herself that moment when her head is hit and her throat is cut seems not to feel like violence, as it appeared to the terrified surviving children who could not sleep for years. She complains instead of abandonment: "Beloved accused her of leaving her behind. Of not being nice to her, not smiling at her. She said they were the same, had the same face, how could she have left her?" (p. 241). The "hot things" she is obsessed with, the milk her mother carried for her from Sweet Home and the blood that separated her from that milk forever, both constitute the strange combination of connection and separation she has come back to tell about.

What Beloved remembers as a point of origin offers a devastating counternarrative to the story of Denver's birth and even to the narratives of Sethe's repeated rebirths. Beloved's is a composite personal and cultural memory that boldly equates the womb with the tomb with the slaveship, the crouching in the Middle Passage with the fetal position, the sea with uterine fluid, milk with blood. In *this* memory, Sethe and Beloved are together, "she is my face smiling at me doing it at last a hot thing now we can join a hot thing" (p. 213). Here Sethe, Denver, and Beloved merge, as personal pronouns cease to differentiate between their voices and positions: "Will we smile at me?" And Sethe, Denver, and Beloved insert themselves into a long line of female transmission where maternal love, maternal pain, and maternal violence are dangerously indistinguishable. Beloved's chapter stands alone in the novel. Her voice is fragmented yet continuous, unpunctuated yet ruptured, particular yet sweeping. This is Beloved's narrative, but, again, neither she nor anyone can tell it because Beloved actually *embodies* that narrative.[11] Beloved *is* memory itself; she is the story of slavery, the memory of slavery come back to confront the community whose future, until that point, had been to "keep the past at bay," the community that had been trying not to remember. The embodiment of that past, Beloved threatens to take possession of their present lives. Paul D. disquietingly insists: "She reminds me of something. Something, look like, I'm supposed to remember" (p. 234). As Valerie Smith (1989) suggests, when he has sex with Beloved, he has to face the *bodily* memory of slavery, because memory is always in the flesh.

11. In my discussion of Beloved as "embodiment" of the story of slavery, I do not mean to suggest that her appearance is that of a "symptom," particularly as Sethe's symptom, as Spillers has brilliantly, though to my mind problematically, argued in her paper "Toni Morrison's *Beloved:* Managing Memory." I find problematic such a psychologizing of the figure of Beloved, although I do believe that the novel represents a psychoanalytic process of healing. The term *embodiment* is broader than *symptom* and is meant to suggest the far-reaching nature of Beloved's intervention and disturbance of the communal "managing" of memory.

But when she becomes pregnant and her body grows to unmanageable proportions, she threatens to perpetuate the pain of memory to the lethal point where
she has to be stopped. As the embodiment of her story, Beloved offers a model of
subjectivity different from the daughterly subjectivity of the differentiated Denver or the maternal subjectivity of Sethe, and it is the confrontation with Beloved's desperate, destructive, and cannibalistic confusion of boundaries that
allows Sethe ultimately to define her own subjectivity as "Me? Me?"

Sethe, when she realizes who has returned, believes she can now cease to
remember her pain; she believes she can explain and reconcile. She believes
that, like Woolf's maternal ghost, the child ghost can be exorcised, put aside, laid
to rest. But she is wrong. It is her maternal rememory combined with Paul's
return and Denver's longing that has made the return of Beloved and of the story
she embodies possible. But that story's emergence cannot again lead to forgetting: Sethe cannot become Lethe. The merging, undifferentiated, engulfing,
collective voice that emerges from Beloved's memories threatens to kill. As Amy
had asserted in relation to Sethe's aching feet, "Anything dead coming back to
life hurts" (p. 35). Contrary to Denver's heroic birth and emergence into freedom, Beloved incarnates the terrifying equation of birth and death, past and
future, mother and child, loss and reparation, retribution and forgiveness, rage
and reconciliation. She is the past that persists in the present. "All of it is now it
is always now." As Sethe insists to Denver, Sweet Home, slavery, the past, is never
gone. It retains its material presence "even though it's all over—over and done
with—it's going to always be there waiting for you. . . . Places, places are still
there. If a house burns down, it's gone, but the place—the picture of it—stays,
and not just in my rememory, but out there in the world" (p. 36).

Sethe can know this, she can be the privileged and dangerous ground for
rememory, because she is a mother. Memories of children may seem to fade, but
like the chokecherry tree, they are always there, even when we don't feel their
pain. As mother, Sethe has known the connection with her children, both at
Sweet Home and, differently, at 124. She has lived the loss of her baby girl for
eighteen years. And, now, after Beloved's return, she is almost, but not quite,
reengulfed by the relation not only with Beloved but with all the other children,
all the other mothers whose rememories the figure of Beloved represents.

In the terms of Hortense Spillers (1987), "we might well ask if this phenomenon of marking and branding actually 'transfers' from one generation to another, finding its various *symbolic substitutions* in an efficacy of meanings that
repeat the initiating moments?" As though in response to such a question,
Morrison casts the black mother as the holder of meaning and rememory whose
mark does extend across generations in the service of her community's self-
recognition. Thus she becomes the voice of resistance in a society that managed
to find a way to survive through repression. Through Sethe's, the mother's,
rememory the inhabitants of Bluestone Road are forced to confront Beloved,
beautiful and seductive, yet devastating and terrifying like Sweet Home. She *is*
the rememory of slavery, the story of a past that is still there, out there in the
world for everyone to bump into like a burned down house. Beloved comes forth

to tell the story that Paul D. had locked up in a metal tin, the story that Sethe had never told Denver, the story of the past that Ella believed should not be allowed to take over the present, the story that Stamp believed he had already paid for. And what she tells threatens, in her beautifully pregnant body, to engulf and transform. What she tells can be neither reconciled nor integrated, neither forgotten nor remembered.

When the community women return to help Sethe send Beloved back to the other side, Sethe is born once again: "the voices of women searched for the right combination, the key, the code, the sound that broke the back of words. Building voice upon voice until they found it, and when they did it was a wave of sound wide enough to sound deep water and knock the pods off chestnut trees. It broke over Sethe and she trembled like the baptized in its wash" (p. 261). Denver has been feeding her, and Paul D. has helped her say "Me? Me?" As though as a consequence and a precondition, the novel's last chapter repeatedly asserts that Beloved is now again gone and forgotten. Even as the novel had convinced us that nothing ever dies, the novel also has to end; like all ghost stories, it must find a way to send the ghost back and to recover from the disruption it caused. This, seemingly, is what happens here, enabling a look toward "some kind of tomorrow" after having confronted the yesterday the characters so fully share. "They forgot her like a bad dream . . . all trace is gone" (pp. 274–275).

Yet Beloved's story, the suppressed narrative of slavery and of maternity, cannot find closure.[12] In *Beloved,* time is neither linear nor cyclical; memory and forgetting are replaced by the strange third option Morrison calls re-memory: repetition + memory, not simply a recollection of the past but its return, its re-presentation, its re-incarnation, and thereby the re-vision of memory itself. Through the rememory of Beloved, the past again becomes present but its presence does not re-engulf, it does not kill. It can be survived. "Down by the stream in back of 124 her footprints come and go, come and go. They are so familiar. Should a child, an adult place his feet in them, they will fit. Take them out and they disappear again as though nobody ever walked there" (p. 275). It is Sethe, the mother, who is the agent of this reincarnation and of the survival it can tolerate. At the end of the novel, Sethe is the maternal subject who in saying "Me? Me?" has offered her own self both for herself to contemplate as a proposition and for connection with Paul D., her children, her community. The connections she establishes, however, are different from the undifferentiated mirrorings experienced by Beloved on the other side; they are different from Sethe's own wide all-encompassing body that could contain all the love she felt for her children when she was first freed and that is reflected back to her by Beloved's falsely pregnant body. By daring to voice her "Me? Me?" first, she can understand perhaps the false possessiveness of "mine" and the "too thick love" that enabled her to kill her child. And she can live with the unending pain of that

12. Gayle Greene cites a conversation with Toni Morrison in which she claimed that the novel's ending was not intended as an ending but as a transition to another section; it was declared an ending by the book's editors and not by its author. See Greene (1991).

understanding. She can experience the separation involved in voicing a singular first person pronoun, and it is this knowledge that enables her to accept the connection of Paul D., his story next to hers, and the story of the others as well. Thus Sethe can undertake and perpetuate the act of rememory which, in this novel, has no end and no beginning, and she can do so and not be destroyed by it.

Linear and cyclical narratives of family are replaced, in Morrison's novel, by another shape, constructed like rememory, made possible by the 124, the gap in the sequence that opens up spaces of difference, upsets binaries, erases distinctions, reverses sequences. The trace is there and it is gone. The house burned down but it still exists, "out there." Sethe and Beloved have the same face. Beloved and Amy (Aimée), Amy Denver and Denver, have the same name. The Pauls have the same name. The grandmother is baby, Baby *Suggs*. Sethe is the mother; Beloved is the child. Sethe is the child; Beloved, pregnant, combs her hair, counts her teeth, beats her up. Sethe diminishes; Beloved grows. Mr. Bodwin is Schoolteacher. Mrs. Bodwin teaches Denver. Slave life is like free life in Ella's thoughts, "every day was a test and a trial" (p. 256). This sameness need not destroy: it can illuminate.

The novel's early reflections on maternal memory—never good enough to remember the good (Baby Suggs agonizes about all the details about her eight children she cannot remember) and never bad enough to forget the pain—are replaced later on with maternal rememory which is like weather. It is always there, "not the breath of the disremembered to be accounted for, but wind in the eaves, or spring ice thawing too quickly. Just weather." Maternal rememory, once Sethe fully experiences it in the novel, may indeed be capable of performing a task deemed impossible in the beginning of the novel—to remember the beautiful trees of Sweet Home *and* the bodies hanging from them. As the story of the past embodied in Beloved emerges, such distinctions and separations vanish and no one position remains comfortably distinguishable, categorizable in schoolteacher-style into separate characteristics. A series of counternarratives, of counterfamilies, offers a metonymic escape route out of the master narrative of Family—the master's narrative.

Emerging from that master story we can begin to adumbrate another tale— the shape of maternal subjectivity that can replace the oedipal configuration with a multiply interconnected embodied subject, one who is both multiply "subjected" and a resisting agent in her own plot, one who is "wide enough" to contain all the memories of the past—all the pain, the guilt, the love, the knowledge, the power of the experience of maternity—yet clear enough to offer her "Me? Me?" to others who can then put it next to theirs. The maternal emerges out of these interconnections as a critique of the individuality and possession that made slavery possible in the first place. No longer a fixed place in a stable structure, it becomes a shifting function in a plural process.

Sethe and Beloved are rendered paralyzed when they claim to own each other to the point of killing each other. That sense of ownership is a repetition of a slave system supported by such conceptions of individuality, autonomy, and self-possession. Sethe is happier, more hopeful, when she accepts Paul D.'s holding fingers and his story next to hers. The act of putting their stories and their subjectivities next to each other, an act that issues from maternal experience but that Morrison locates not between mothers and children but in the adult hetero-sexual couple of Sethe and Paul D., suggests a relation from subject to subject that can reconceive the objectification of slavery and of patriarchy. The individual subjects of Morrison's novel are shattered subjects who yearn for wholeness and wonder what will hold them together and who might help them to become whole. By putting these shattered subjects and their stories next to each other, the novel suggests how unspeakable memories might in fact be spoken, how a story that should not be passed on can in fact be transmitted. This act of transmission is a peculiarly maternal one.

References

Chesler, P. (1987). *Mothers on trial: The battle for children and custody.* Seattle, Wash.: Seal Press.

Chodorow, N., & Contratto, S. (1989). The fantasy of the perfect mother. In N. Chodorow, *Feminism and psychoanalytic theory.* New Haven: Yale University Press.

Collins, P. H. (1990). *Black feminist thought: Knowledge, consciousness, and the politics of empowerment.* New York: Unwin Hyman.

de Lauretis, T. (1990). Eccentric subjects: Feminist theory and historical consciousness. In *Feminist Studies,* 16, 1.

Freud, S. (1908). Family romances. In *Standard Edition.* Vol. 9, 237–41. London: Hogarth Press, 1953.

Goldman, A. (1990). "I Made the Ink": (Literary) production and reproduction in *Dessa Rose* and *Beloved.* In *Feminist Studies,* 16(2), 325.

Greene, G. (1991). Feminist fiction and the uses of memory. *Signs,* 16(2), 318.

Gresham, J. H., & Wilkerson, M. B. (Eds.) (1989). Scapegoating the black family: Black women speak. *Nation,* July 24/31.

Hirsch, M. (1989). *The mother/daughter plot: Narrative psychoanalysis, feminism.* Bloomington: Indiana University Press.

Jardine, A. (1985). *Gynesis.* Ithaca, N.Y.: Cornell University Press.

Miller, N. K. (1988). *Subject to change: Reading feminist writing.* New York: Columbia University Press.

Morrison, T. (1973). *Sula.* New York: New American Library.

Morrison, T. (1987). *Beloved.* New York: Knopf.

Morrison, T. (1989). Unspeakable things unspoken: The Afro-American presence in American literature. In *Michigan Quarterly Review,* 28(1), 32.

Moyers, B. (1986). *The vanishing black family: Crisis in black America.* CBS Special Report, January 25.

Moynihan, D. P. (1965). *The Negro family: The case for national action.* Washington, D.C.: U.S. Government Printing Office.

Owens, C. (1983). The discourse of Others: Feminists and post-modernism. In

H. Foster (Ed.), *The anti-aesthetic: Essays on post-modern culture*. Port Townsend, Wash.: Bay Press.

Ruddick, S. (1989). *Maternal thinking*. Boston: Beacon Press.

Smith, P. (1988). *Discerning the subject*. Minneapolis: University of Minnesota Press.

Smith, V. (1989). "Circling the Subject": History and memory in Toni Morrison's *Beloved*. Paper delivered at the 1989 English Institute Conference.

Spillers, H. (1987). Mama's baby, Papa's maybe: An American grammar book. *Diacritics* 17(2), 67.

Spillers, H. (1989). The permanent obliquity of in(phal)llibility straight: In the time of the daughter and the fathers. In L. E. Boose & B. S. Flowers (Eds.), *Daughters and fathers*. Baltimore: Johns Hopkins University Press.

Spillers, H. (1990). Toni Morrison's *Beloved:* Managing memory. Paper delivered at the School of Criticism and Theory.

Suleiman, S. (1985). Writing and motherhood. In S. N. Garner, C. Kahane, & M. Sprengnether (Eds.), *The (M)Other tongue: Essays in psychoanalytic feminist interpretation*. Ithaca, N.Y.: Cornell University Press.

Suleiman, S. (1988). The "Other Mother": On maternal splitting (a propos of Mary Gordon's *Men and Angels*). *Signs* 14(1), 25–41.

Williams, S. A. (1986). *Dessa Rose*. New York: William Morrow.

Woolf, V. (1957). *A room of one's own*. New York: Harcourt Brace Jovanovich.

Woolf, V. (1985). *Moments of being* (2nd ed.; Ed. J. Schulkind). New York: Harcourt Brace Jovanovich.

Part II The Paradoxical
Nature of the Maternal Position

JANINE CHASSEGUET-SMIRGEL

6 Being a Mother and Being a Psychoanalyst: Two Impossible Professions

Femininity arouses in everyone deep conflicts with the first woman in our lives, with our mother, and our own identification with her, regardless of our sex. It was at the time of the publication of my article "Feminine Guilt and the Oedipus Complex" (1964) that I first came to reflect on this. In speaking before an audience of the Psychoanalytical Society regarding the main points advanced in my article, a colleague took issue with my arguments concerning an unconscious knowledge of the existence of feminine sexual organs. This was a central question for Freud. Until she reaches puberty, the girl supposedly ignores, even on the unconscious level, that she has a vagina. Such ignorance accounts for the intensity of penis envy. Correspondingly, the boy ignores the existence of the girl's internal genital organs.

My arguments in favor of an unconscious knowledge of female sexual organs were compared by this colleague to those in the story of the leaking copper kettle that Freud (1905a) related on a totally different subject: A borrowed copper kettle is returned to its owner with a hole in it. The owner demands an explanation. The borrower replies successively that he never borrowed the copper kettle, that he returned it intact, and finally that it already leaked when he borrowed it. In addition to indicating that I should return to my pots and pans, this culinary metaphor revealed this man's interesting representation of the feminine body—a copper kettle with a hole in it.

Now, some twenty years later, it has been suggested by feminist psychoanalysts that my work accords too much importance to the father.[1] Take, for example, a passage from an interesting interview with Jessica Benjamin in the book *Women Analyze Women* (Baruch & Serrano, 1988). Benjamin says:

> The antagonism to feminism has a number of roots. I think on the one hand it reflects an infantocentric point of view, that psychoanalysts really still want mother locked up and being there for the child. . . . And I think the other side of it is that there is this tremendous idealization of the father. Recently when Chasseguet-Smirgel was here, she gave this talk that said, outright, all the things that are stated only implicitly in her other papers. How it's the paternal law that brings the child to the truth, to the reality principle; that it was Freud's reconciliation with his father that really made him understand that you have to take responsibility for your own drives and for knowing the truth. . . . So it's really the father that saves us.
>
> I said to her that it seemed to me that this was an extremely one-sided viewpoint, that only the father brings the child to the reality principle. What about all the child rearing that the mother does, in which she really is socializing the child? And so then she said, "well, of course, I am not talking about reality. I am just talking about the unconscious with its image of the archaic mother."
>
> . . . She is juxtaposing two ego states that are really quite different; it's really the idea that there is a historic battle within the child between the two ego states, the pre-Oedipal ego state and the Oedipal one. And in her view, the Oedipal ego state is exclusively associated with the father and the pre-Oedipal with the mother. I think her reading reveals the underlying thought structure of psychoanalysis which is normally left implicit. (pp. 321–322)

There is a most unfortunate confusion here between the mother as an internal object (imago) and the mother as a real external object, between the conscious and the unconscious, primary processes and secondary processes, the child inside the adult and the adult. A similar confusion of levels can sometimes be found in Freud's descriptions of women. This is true of the arguments he advanced in "The Taboo of Virginity" (1917). The male's fear of defloration is not ascribed to his imago of women (not therefore to his projections) but to the *reality* of the woman's castration wishes owing to her penis envy. The topic of femininity is probably the sole instance in which Freud can be put at fault and accused of inconsistency.

In a program on British television in which Juliet Mitchell and I took part,

---

1. This is not the case for Nancy Chodorow. Her book *The Reproduction of Mothering* (1978) faithfully retraces my views, as they then stood in 1964. On fundamental points my ideas have not varied. Rather, I have enlarged on the ideas advanced in particular in my 1975 article, "Freud and Female Sexuality: The Consideration of Some Blind Spots in the Exploration of the 'Dark Continent.'"

Jean Baker Miller spoke out against representations of the mother as a dangerous, devouring figure. I pointed out that these were unconscious representations, to which she replied that they have to be changed.[2] By all means. But for those who believe in the unconscious, we know that no decree can ever bring about such a change.

At this point it may be appropriate to recall that the imago is a kind of stereotyped mental picture that forms in the unconscious, reflecting not only real experiences with the object, the mother, but also all sorts of early experiences that, given the relative lack of differentiation between the subject and the mother and between the mother and the world in general, are experienced as having been caused by the mother. Illness in infancy, for example, creates the imago of a bad mother regardless of her true nature. Additionally, the infant's own drives—for instance, the wish to devour—contribute to the dangerous maternal imago. I believe that the premature condition in which the young of the human species are born and the fact that the infant continues for a considerable period of time after birth to be totally dependent for survival on the mother or her substitutes is one of the principal explanations for the creation of an all-powerful and invading maternal imago. In individual analysis, dreams and nightmares are especially informative as to the nature of imagos, whereas on the collective level they appear in myths and religions and fairy tales. A relatively good external mother is as liable to generate a terrifying maternal imago as is an objectively frustrating and harmful mother—for instance, when she falls sick shortly after the birth of her child, causing the infant to feel abandoned, or in cases where the infant suffers physical pain or is constitutionally endowed with an exceptional appetite.

On thinking more about this whole subject, I now see that what I experienced as a misinterpretation of my own ideas simply duplicates the misunderstanding of which the mother and maternity are victims. Because I cannot hope to deal with so vast a subject in any detail, I shall begin by outlining those representations of the mother and maternity that follow from our conflicts and are related to human beings' premature and helpless condition—the fact that we are "sent into the world in a less finished state" than most animals (Freud, 1926a). Obviously, the real mother (or father) contributes to establishing one or another of these imagos in the psychic organization of a given individual, but she is not alone in this. We are already at the heart of the question and the potential misunderstanding.

These representations can be divided into three categories depending on the degree to which the subject is able to accept the reality of his condition, namely that at birth he is separated from his mother.[3] This argument is advanced for the

2. It should be noted that Jean Baker Miller is not an analyst.
3. I have given various other definitions of reality, in particular the following: reality resides in the differences of sex and generation; and (in line with Freud) I have also stated that the father represents reality. Far from being contradictory, these definitions view the problem from different angles.

purposes of exposition; in actuality these representations coexist in the same subject and may become dominant one after the other.[4]

First, we have apocalyptic representations with the mother divested of her ability to bear children. Next come what I call "Marian" representations (in reference to the Virgin Mary) that reflect a compromise with reality. The mother's childbearing capacity is recognized, even idealized, whereas the father's role in this is denied. The third category of representations implies a fear, conscious or unconscious, of the mother. That part of reality in which the maternal imago exerts an appeal is ignored. Within this representation there is recognition, even idealization of the father's role. These are representations that I think of as involving a "fatal attraction." This psychic constellation is the most frequent in both sexes and the one most often mobilized. It is likely that this series of representations is the principal factor determining the condition of women. I shall only briefly mention the palliative measures society can and does provide against the impact of these representations.

Apocalyptic Representations

Following Ferenczi's ideas, Bela Grunberger (1971) has constructed a theory of narcissism based on the human wish to return to the prenatal state, a prototype of Lost Paradise, the absolute state of bliss in which desires are satisfied before even being recognized as such. The fetus (not only the father) is the model of Almighty God.

I have been able to pinpoint in the material of mainly borderline patients a wish to unite with the mother again, a wish that entails destroying whatever obstacles prevent the subject from returning inside the mother's body. Certain dreams and apocalyptic fantasies stage great disasters in which the world might become a desert or return to the ice age, followed by a feeling of great bliss. The subject finds himself alone or one of a small group of the "elect," as in the Revelation of St. John or in certain utopian writings.

In one such dream a prepsychotic patient who had repetitive dreams in which he was bombing cities, often dropping atomic bombs, dreamed he was looking at a picture of palm trees in a desert. Then, taking a brush, he carefully painted over the palm trees with paint the color of the sand until only the desert remained. He felt highly elated. He associated to his father, brother, and sister who lived far away. His father and mother were separated and he wondered if he would return to live with her again; perhaps he (the patient) would visit her during the holidays. Then he told the analyst he had just moved. At the end of the session he gave the analyst his new address, which turned out to be in the very building in which the analyst lived, but across the courtyard in the back![5]

4. Since our main concern is pathology I shall not deal with representations of the genital, procreative mother.

5. This is not one of my own cases.

Another prepsychotic patient, a woman this time, became very confused when I told her I was to move shortly. She spoke disjointedly of my husband and my children, imagining that I was moving because termites were eating away the woodwork (her fragmented aggressive thoughts entering me to take possession and control my body). She came to the next session with the following dream: "I am standing in the middle of a large common. Behind me there are dozens of dead kittens" (in French, *petits chats*). "Chats . . . Chasseguet," she added. "In front of me the common is just bare land, all the green grass has gone. I'm the only one on the common. It's a lovely feeling."

In my view, the desert and the bare common in these two dreams represent the mother who has been made sterile; nothing grows, the palm trees have disappeared along with the green grass (my husband, "Grun" = "green"; the patient frequently associated green with his name). The kittens are my children. The palm trees represent the brother and sister of the patient who "atomizes" the contents of Mother Earth. The obstacles to union with the mother, represented by what grows inside her, deposited by the father, have been destroyed in both cases.

In another register we can find the apocalyptic fantasies of a famed and very sick man:

> If today, for example, the surface of the earth were upset by some tectonic event and a new Himalaya rose from the ocean floods, by one single cruel catastrophe the culture of humanity would be destroyed. No state would exist any longer, the bands of all order would be dissolved, the documents of millennial development would be shattered—a single great field of corpses covered by water and mud. But if from this chaos of horror even a few men of a certain race capable of culture had been preserved, the earth, upon settling, if only after thousands of years, would again get proofs of human creative power. (Hitler, 1925, p. 356)

The earth is ravaged but not flattened, as is usually the case. Nevertheless, we probably have here the same process of taking possession of the earth, and I think that we can say that the towering rocky peak that stands where the earth, before the disaster, had been peopled with living creatures figures the subject's ego.

Reality is the fact that the world is teeming with life, just as, thanks to the father's act and his penis, the mother's body is peopled with children. After birth the mother's body becomes inaccessible. The father represents reality by reason of his very existence, not because of any one specific "objective" characteristic.

These three examples present us with representations of the mother (Mother Earth in fact) that call to mind T. S. Eliot's (1922) poem "The Waste Land." They come from subjects who are unable to renounce absolute possession of the mother—that is, who are unable to cope with loss, mourning, and separation.[6]

---

6. At least this is true of the two patients in analysis. With Hitler one can only make suppositions. He cannot be compared to those patients who only dream or fantasize the apocalypse—he set out to achieve it.

The central problem here is an inability to accept the primal scene, which implies the existence of three terms: mother, father, and child. Without acceptance of these three terms, the subject will remain in chaos and confusion. Unless impressions are classified, the mental apparatus cannot function. Classification rests on a ternary system. Therefore, for thought to exist, integration of the father is essential not because of any specific virtue of his but because he stands in the way of primal fusion.

Marian Representations

Another category of maternal representations implies not merely acceptance but the celebration of fecundity, at least where manifest content is concerned. Here we find the ancient rites of fertility, the cult of the mother goddess and, on the individual level, the love of nature. It can be supposed that in this case there is a reconciliation with the father, his derivatives (the penis and children), and the primal scene. Such is often the case. But at times love of nature, especially when it takes the form of a cult, comes close to the previous category of representations. Nature (or the earth) produces fruit, harvests to be reaped, springs that come gushing from its depths, and lofty trees soaring upward. But nature's productions must seem to be completely spontaneous—a parthenogenetic process, so to speak. When humans intervene, as they inevitably will, they must never disturb the "natural" order of things. This is Heidegger's (1954) position. His hatred of technique, as I interpret it, masks a fantasy of Mother Earth, which corresponds to the concept the Virgin Mary symbolizes in the Catholic religion—a mother united with her son without any paternal intervention, a mother who is both chaste and fertile. For example:

> The birch tree never grows beyond the line of its possible. The colony of bees lives in its possible. Only will power, enlisting technique in every direction, shakes the earth and starts the cycle of great fatigues, wearing it away and imposing the variations of the artificial. It forces the earth to break the circle of its possible, such as it has developed about it, and pushes it into what is no longer the possible and which is therefore the impossible. The fact that by its plans and measures technique succeeds in many an invention and produces an uninterrupted procession of novelties is no proof that its victories can make even the impossible possible. . . . Simply making the most of the earth is one thing. It is quite another matter to receive the earth's benediction and to gradually come to feel at home in the law of this conception, in order to protect the secret of being and to preserve the *inviolability* of the possible. (Heidegger, 1954, pp. 113–114; emphasis added)[7]

7. An English rendering of this passage based on the French translation by André Preau.

The earth is sanctified. "The earth is the serving bearer, blossoming and fruiting, spreading out in rock and water, rising up into plant and animal" (Heidegger, 1975, p. 149). Hence an interminable celebration of bridges because "the bridge lets the stream run its course" (p. 152). Hence a dithyramb in honor of the pitcher and "outpouring": "In the gift of the outpouring earth and sky, divinities and mortals dwell together all at once" (p. 173).[8]

This same love for earth or nature that remains intact, or with the slightest of inflections, brought about, so to speak, as the result of a fervent prayer to the Virgin Mary, is characteristic of romanticism. The description of Julia's garden in Jean-Jacques Rousseau's *La nouvelle Heloise* (1761) shows what I mean:

> After having admired the effect produced by the vigilant care of the most respected and orderly of housewives, I visited the place to which she retreated for what had become her favorite walk, a remote spot she called her Elysium. This spot, very close to the house, can in no way be perceived; a covered wall completely hides all sight of it. The thick surrounding foliage will allow no eye to penetrate it and it is always kept carefully locked. I was hardly inside before the door was hidden by the branches of alder and hazel which left only two narrow passageways on each side. When I turned round I could no longer see where I had entered, and perceiving no door, I felt as if I had fallen from the sky. On entering this would-be orchard I was overcome by an agreeable sensation of freshness, of dark leafy shade, of verdant luxuriance, of scattered flowers all about, the gurgling of running water and the song of a thousand birds which was as appealing to the imagination as it was to the senses; but I had before me, I thought at the same time, the wildest, most solitary spot in nature, and my impression was: that I was the first mortal to ever penetrate this wilderness. Surprised, captivated, transported by such an unforeseen spectacle, I stood awhile, motionless. (p. 353)[9]

"What do you think has been the cost to make it thus?" Julia asks Saint-Preux, who replies: " 'Well, nothing more than negligence. True, the place is charming but rustic and left to run wild; I see no trace of human labour. You locked it; the water came I know not how; nature has done the rest.' 'That is so,' she said, 'nature has done everything, but under my guidance.' . . . I began to wander, enraptured, in this grove where such a metamorphosis had come about" (pp. 353–354).

8. Concerning this last line, the translator of the French edition adds the following comment: "Outpouring preserves. At the precise moment of outpouring the pitcher retains and preserves. It preserves because it leads what it has received to its destination. This is the way it accomplishes its being." Also note the religious tonality of both Heidegger and his translator.

9. Since the translator of this article has been unable to find an English translation of Rousseau's book, this is her rough rendering of the original French.

This passage sings the praises of the landscape garden, as opposed to the formal garden "a la française" where man, in intervening, has "spoiled the works of nature"; in fact the whole of this letter from Saint-Preux is a hymn to the English garden. We also know that Rousseau's mother died at his birth and that he retained a deep nostalgia for maternal love, as his life and writings show, while at the same time being impelled to repeat this separation by abandoning his own children, proof of his great ambivalence with regard to maternity. He withdrew his children from the care of Therese Levasseur, his companion.[10]

Whereas, for centuries, Western iconography has been dominated by the idea of a sacred Virgin Mary united with her son (the Christian "solution" of rejecting the paternal universe, which also results in the suppression of feminine sexuality), the work of Joel Peter Witkin (1989), a contemporary photographer, expresses a barely transposed hatred and envy of maternity. His photographs portray faces encased in masks, mouths distorted by dental plates or closed by a zipper or a bird's beak, breasts in which needles or nails have been planted or pierced through with iron stakes, breasts nursing a monkey or an eel, a hermaphrodite giving the breast to a fetus, gravid, obscene bellies, and tortured, deformed, degraded, and putrifying bodies of obese women. Overshadowing all this is the recurrent theme of the cross, as if the Christian "solution," accompanied by centuries of idealization, has now suddenly revealed its black underside.

The Fatal Attraction

A third category of representations of maternity includes terrifying images of the witch, apparitions of Death, and so on. As these are dealt with in other sections of this book, I shall simply advance a few hypotheses as to the relation that exists between Freud's notion of female sexuality and his fear of a return to origins—the womb. I shall deal at some length with Freud's fears of merging with the archaic mother, reactivated at the time his cancer was diagnosed. Two essays, "The Infantile Genital Organization" (1923) and "Some Psychical Consequences of the Anatomical Distinction between the Sexes" (1925), are clearly connected by Freud with the death threat hovering over him:

10. Romanticism is, of course, a collective movement, but Rousseau was one of its principal precursors in France. The English landscape garden, which started to become fashionable in the eighteenth century with the Enlightenment, also heralds romanticism. Can it not be considered that the great cultural movements represent the solution of one given period to the intrapsychic problems of human beings at that time (for reasons of overdetermination)? For instance, the prevalent maternal representation in this is a Marian figure projected into external space—Nature left to follow its own course— whereas the formal garden of the seventeenth century, with its arrangement of paths bordered by clipped hedges, is the projection of a maternal body controlled by man (the father).

Formerly I was not one of those who are unable to hold back what seems to me a new discovery until it has been either confirmed or corrected. My *Interpretation of Dreams* (1909) and my *Fragment of Analysis of Hysteria* (1905) . . . were suppressed by me—if not for the nine years enjoined by Horace—at all events for four or five years . . . But in those days I had unlimited time before me, "oceans of time." . . . But everything has changed. The time before me is limited. . . . If I see something new, I am uncertain whether I can wait for it to be confirmed. And, further, everything that is to be seen upon the surface has already been exhausted, what remains has to be slowly and laboriously dragged up from the depths. (1925, p. 248)

As early as the *Three Essays* (1905b) the depth of femininity seemed to be "veiled in an impenetrable obscurity." But from around 1925, metaphors evoking darkness, disquiet, the uncanny, become increasingly numerous. In "The Question of Lay Analysis" (1926b) Freud refers to the "dark continent"; in "Femininity" (1933) he evokes "the riddle of femininity." In a 1931 paper he asserts the importance of the preoedipal phase for the girl (but not for the boy). The affect that accompanies his discovery irresistibly evokes "the uncanny," which he had connected with "what ought to have remained secret and hidden but has to come to light" (1919). It is also known that Freud's interpretation of the uncanny is that it is "the mother's genitals or her body." In the 1931 papers he says: "Our insight into this early, pre-Oedipus phase in girls comes to us as a surprise like the discovery, in another field, of the Minoan-Mycenean civilization behind the civilization of Greece" (p. 226).

This fear of identification with women culminates in this same paper when he pretends that women analysts are in a better position than he to perceive certain facts connected with femininity owing to the *maternal* transference that is bestowed upon them. This fear of understanding women, of identifying with them (behind which one may suppose the fear of being engulfed into the womb and into death), is summed up in Freud's question to Marie Bonaparte: "What does a woman want?"

In *Civilization and Its Discontents* (1930) Freud states: "I cannot think of any need in childhood as strong as the need of father's protection." In my 1964 paper, I was already struck by the fact that in Freudian theory the father, both in the positive and negative Oedipus complex, is finally more the object of the boy than of the girl. This does not fail to be paradoxical, but it is more comprehensible if the father's function consists in protecting the son against an engulfing and deadly, omnipotent, archaic mother. This obviously leads the boy to a certain homosexual fixation on the father and his penis. It is striking, for example, that Freud never mentions the son's *castration* wishes toward the father.

The wish for the father's death is certainly central in the Freudian conception of the boy's Oedipus complex; but Freud does not mention the wish to castrate the father in men, a wish that is only attributed to the girl in connection with penis envy. We can certainly not believe Freud when he pretends that he has never experienced the oceanic feeling, when the inspiration underlying his writings implies the (momentary) ability to lose the ego's limits. But one can assume that illness (his cancer) has built up a wall within him against merger with the archaic mother, and the shadow of this wall is projected onto his writings on female sexuality. This listing of certain representations of femininity and appending affects in Freud's work would be of limited interest if they were not shared by both men and women.

In my first paper on female sexuality (1964) I stressed female guilt in connection with the interdiction to identify with the imago of the omnipotent mother who is relayed by the anal mother. Such an interdiction is not only external; it is above all internal and connected with the idealization of the father, especially when the relationship with the mother has been bad. For the little girl—even more than for the boy whose penis helps him free himself from her—the father is the one to whom one turns, the one who protects against the archaic mother.

The father is looked upon as a savior when the child grapples with representations such as these. Of course, such representations are full of the child's own aggressive wishes against the mother. And the maternal imago will be the more dangerous when the child's own pregenital drives have not been integrated.

The fact that the archaic and the terrifying are generally stored in the unconscious under the heading "mother," while clarity and the daylight that dispels the terrors of night are attributed to the father, follows from our need to "classify" our impressions, as Freud says (1918). He describes this as an inborn need and refers to "hereditary schemas" (personally I would prefer to say that they are structurally inherent in the mental apparatus), and cites the Oedipus complex as the best known example of such schemas. Freud points out that the danger of castration is usually attributed to the father even though the threat may come from the mother or her substitutes. This convinces us, he says, of the victory of the schema over events of personal history. The victory of this schema is necessary, one understands, to deliver the subject from chaos, confusion, and terror.

In the Kleinian (1946, 1957) system, the mechanism acquired during the paranoid-schizoid phase of splitting the object into a "good" and a "bad" part has the same positive function, provided it does not become rigid and absolute. Prior to splitting into father and mother (breast and penis), aspects of the mother, or rather the breast, are divided in this way. Then, when it becomes inoperative, this splitting concerns two different objects. Just as, according to Freud, the castration threat is "foisted off" on the father, so I believe (on the basis of my understanding of clinical work) that the obscure, the "uncanny," and the archaic are "foisted off" on the mother, while the father is vested with the power to save the child from the maternal depths. This must not, however, be described as the Oedipus complex.[11]

11. For Lacan, the father's appearance on the scene to end the continuum between mother and child—the child taking the place of the phallus she lacks, the object of her desire—*is* the Oedipus complex.

I have not been explicit enough about this in the past (1964). Therefore I want to make it quite clear that there is no oedipal situation without *ambivalence*. The daughter fears and hates her mother but also loves her. If the daughter turns to the father only to be protected, if she brings into play only mechanisms of counteridentification with the mother, then she will never be able to integrate her own femininity or the Oedipus complex in its evolved form. As for the boy, he will retain a permanent homosexual fixation on the father. This double configuration is extremely common in fact. For the boy, a certain dose of homosexuality, of attachment to the father's penis, is a means of resisting the attraction of incest and its prototype—fusion with the mother. It is a way to preserve his identity.

The myth of Ulysses ordering his men to bind him to the mast of his ship so that he will not be lured to destruction by the singing Sirens is a perfect representation of the "struggle to resist" the attraction of the maternal depths. The fact that in the unconscious the father and his penis represent a protection against chaos, confusion, and the mists clouding the mind is also marvelously portrayed in William Golding's book *The Lord of the Flies* (1954). The return to Nature, to the Mother, absolute freedom, the absence of limits and laws, soon turns into a nightmare.[12] Murder and the founding of a pagan cult testify to the disappearance of the paternal dimension.[13] At the end, a British officer arrives, bringing order and salvation. The scene in the screen version of this book in which the young hero, Ralph, lying on the ground where he has fallen, grabs the leg of the officer, clutching onto the cloth of the officer's white trousers as if it were a life buoy, is particularly eloquent. Here again, we find an opposition between the father in the role of savior, with his phallus (the leg covered by the brilliant white cloth of the trousers), and the hell of Nature (Mother Nature's hell), which is rank with the vilest of pregenital orgies.

In fact this is the juxtaposition not, as Jessica Benjamin supposes, of a preoedipal mother and an oedipal father but, in accordance with the laws governing the unconscious, of a dangerous and persecutory archaic mother and an idealized father.[14] Only the genital father (and his penis) is totally differentiated

12. The frequent theme of the island in literature and myths can be taken to represent the maternal uterus where abundant beauty, happiness, purity, and tranquility reign. But the island may also become a trap that closes in on its prey as in the legend of Circe, Count Zarhoff's hunting expeditions, Agatha Christie's *Ten Little Indians*, etc. The island with its dual meaning shows the extent to which the longing to return to the uterus is accompanied by fear. In Golding's novel, which is set on a tropical island, the island is initially a place of bliss but turns into a fatal trap, lending the story a strikingly paranoid tone.

13. The cult practices adoration of a pig's head, "The Lord of the Flies," i.e., Baal-Zebub in Hebrew, the pagan god lusting for human sacrifice and later known as the Devil, once monotheism became established.

14. Here I am principally referring to the fascination and the struggle to resist this wish to return to the maternal body insofar as it menaces the autonomy, the identity, and the very existence of the subject. Elsewhere (1975/1986) I have described the effects of prematuration and the child's dependency on the formation of an omnipotent maternal imago and the accompanying wish to free oneself from it. I shall not return to this now.

from the mother. When pregenital "paternal" representations reign in the un-conscious, these are "foisted off" on the mother to preserve the integrity of the mental apparatus. Such foisting off may be impossible when the real parents have too pervasive a presence—an alcoholic father, say, and a weak, complaisant, or absent mother—in which case splitting of the parental imagos becomes impossible and the subject sinks into a state of psychotic confusion affecting all the thought processes.

The father's essential function is not defensive as in the case of the subject who turns to the father to allay the fears mobilized by the wish to fuse with the mother. On the contrary, it is a decisive step toward becoming a civilized human being. It permits creation, the process of symbolization and sublimation, and paves the way for a moral standard of conduct. For both sexes, when development is satisfactory, genitalized representations finally supersede the dangerous, omnipotent mother.

At the end of a lecture I gave on the "Analytic Situation" (1989), I felt it necessary to conclude by saying:

> To dissipate any possible misunderstanding, in speaking of the father as a separation principle and as representing reality, I do not mean that men are closer to reality than women (I even wrote the opposite, 1984). I am speaking of a *function* that the presence of an obstacle between mother and infant fulfills, this being of fundamental importance in the early development of the human mind. It has nothing to do with whether men are superior to women or not, and does not imply that women are not rational human beings. Should I think this, I, being a woman, would give up any endeavor to understand the human mind. Nonetheless, the unconscious knowledge of the process of development of the mind might increase some prejudice against women. It is my hope that by rendering people more aware of this, prejudice may be reduced; a stupid father plays at an early stage the role of obstacle in the same way as a Nobel Prize winner, or even an outstanding analysts does.

The difficulties I have met in attempting to differentiate the father's and mother's respective *functions* from the actual reality of the parents in a subjects' individual history, however, are almost identical to those the mother faces in reality when, at times of danger and critical moments in a lifetime, the archaic maternal imago is reactivated. The best of mothers may be (re)transformed into a witch, a Fury, or a Gorgon.

As we have seen, my supposition is that Freud's fear of death affected his representations of femininity. Another frequent example is that of the woman in her menopause. Physically unable to bear children, she finds herself back in the condition of the girl who has not yet reached puberty. But whereas the girl may hope to acquire maternal capacities and to become a mother, a woman who has passed the childbearing age finds herself struggling with a terrifying maternal imago that ensures her final victory over her daughter by definitively making her sterile. (Of course, such states of anxiety are not shared by everyone). This is also the case for young women deprived through illness of the generative capacity.

Jean Baker Miller would say that the poor mothers cannot be reproached with the fate of their poor daughters, and she would be right. But how can one convince the unconscious of this, other than by embarking on the long, arduous work of analysis?

Additionally, the most megalomanic, the most sadistic men identify not with the father but with the imago of the archaic mother who is still very present. The Nazi regime, the S.S. and Hitler himself, lacked the paternal dimension. They "actualized" the archaic mother. Their pseudo-virile gear (the whip, boots, and black uniform) was nothing more than a pregenital (anal-sadistic) imitation of the father's genital penis, available moreover to both sexes. The Nazi regime reestablished the cult of the Goddess Mother (the Nation, Mother Earth, Nature) Astarte, thirsting for human sacrifice. This universe resembled that of *The Lord of the Flies*—in all probability Golding's intention was to portray a return to barbarity such as we in the twentieth century have witnessed.

The mother's all-powerful presence in the unconscious and the splitting of the mother and father to which this leads—a state to which subjects readily regress—make the position of mothers, and hence women, particularly difficult. The relationship with the primitive maternal imago is reflected in administrative and social institutions, and although there has been progress in the Western world, the fact remains that maternity—the fantastic *power* of bearing and bringing children into the world—is reversed and becomes an *obligation* in many countries. In certain cultures, feminine activities never exceed the biological order, which is experienced by men (and even women on a certain level) as a crushing force placed in the hands of women.[15]

Where individuals are concerned, psychoanalysis sets out to interpret imagos and hence to break them down into elements, with the aim of allowing the analysand to integrate into the ego that part of the imago that is made up of the subject's own drives. Other parts of the imago, related to the frustration provoked by infantile helplessness and also to early painful experiences that at the time were attributed to the mother, become, in principle, obsolete. Ideally, all that remains is a relatively realistic representation of the mother. To guard against overoptimism, however, allowance must be made for the fact that, as clinical practice shows, painful events reactivate primitive imagos, the trace left

15. In Muslim countries—even in Morocco, a developed and relatively democratic country that has not yet become fundamentalist—a woman wishing to travel abroad for even the shortest of stays must obtain the written permission of her husband, her father, or, failing this, her son, however young he may be. Thus a forty-year-old woman may be dependent on her eight-year-old son simply because he is a male. Examples such as this seem extravagant to us but are abundant in Muslim countries. They give some idea of the fragility of the male citizen's virile identity. A possible explanation could be the relatively late age at which circumcision takes place in this country (between the ages of four and eight).

by these in the unconscious seeming to seize greedily on all later experiences capable of giving it renewed life.

Although imagos may be partly independent of the reality of external objects, this does not alter the fact that too frustrating or too lax an attitude on the part of the parents, especially the mother, may have a profound effect on the nature of the imagos. The education a child receives from his or her parents and the relationship between the two parents are of capital importance, even though the degree to which the maternal imago is more or less satisfactorily integrated does not exclusively depend on these factors.

On the collective level, the problem is to determine the extent to which organized society is capable of correcting the effects produced in the unconscious by these representations of the mother and maternity, and also the accompanying sadistic and/or destructive wishes.

How can we reconcile the wish to regain the mother's body without this resulting in an apocalypse or psychosis? In fact, religion and the belief in a return to Paradise have always provided an outlet for this wish, in the fantasy that life on earth is a more or less lengthy period of exile from the maternal matrix to which we will return after death.

In the West, the decline of religion and the failure of the ideologies that took its place now leave the young more unarmed than before. On a more modest scale, however, people try to create enclaves where it is possible to fuse temporarily and partially with a substitute for the mother or the lost matrix: in love, of course, but also by means of what we most appropriately call the family "circle" (albeit an increasingly distended family) and the "circle" of friends.

On a still more modest scale, we engage in leisure pursuits that allow us to immerse our bodies in the sea, to slide over snowy slopes, or to walk deep in the heart of nature for a certain period of time, these being so many ways of regressing to the mother's bosom—and as essential as our daily night's sleep.

These matrix-like enclaves may be gardens (each garden is a small paradise; the biblical Paradise is the Garden of Eden), "gastronomic temples," or concert halls. A country's standard of living and its educational level play an important role in helping its citizens benefit from these enclaves, which act as safety valves against the emergence of apocalyptic wishes. Increased comfort and greater security help keep the dangerous maternal imago at bay, whereas famine and fear, on the other hand, awaken this imago.[16]

The condition of women has in fact improved in developed countries. This is not only because culture, when it becomes widespread, leads to a higher level of thinking on the collective scale but also because the spread of culture comes from a general well-being, meaning therefore that witches can stay shut away in the pages of children's fairy-tale books.

16. It is certainly no mere chance that at the time Saddam Hussein was amassing huge supplies of conventional arms, chemical weapons, and gas, he passed a law giving any man who suspected his wife, mother, sister, or daughter of committing adultery the right to kill her.

References

Baruch, E., & Serrano, L. (1988). *Women analyze women.* New York: New York University Press.

Chasseguet-Smirgel, J. (1964). Feminine guilt and the Oedipus complex. In J. Chasseguet-Smirgel (Ed.), *Female sexuality: New psychoanalytic views.* Ann Arbor: University of Michigan Press, 1970; London: Karnac Books, 1985.

Chasseguet-Smirgel, J. (1975). Freud and female sexuality: The consideration of some blind spots in the exploration of the "Dark Continent." In *Sexuality and mind.* New York: New York University Press, 1986.

Chasseguet-Smirgel, J. (1989). Some thoughts on the analytic situation. To be published in *Journal of the American Psychoanalytic Association.*

Chodorow, N. (1978). *The reproduction of mothering.* Berkeley: University of California Press.

Eliot, T. S. (1922). The waste land. In *Collected poems.* New York: Harcourt Brace, 1952.

Freud, S. (1900). The interpretation of dreams. In *Standard Edition.* Vols. 4–5. London: Hogarth Press, 1953.

Freud, S. (1905a). Jokes and their relation to the unconscious. In *Standard Edition.* Vol. 8. London: Hogarth Press, 1953.

Freud, S. (1905b). Three essays on the theory of sexuality. In *Standard Edition.* Vol. 7, 125–243. London: Hogarth Press, 1953.

Freud, S. (1917). The taboo of virginity. In *Standard Edition.* Vol. 11, 193–208. London: Hogarth Press, 1955.

Freud, S. (1918). From the history of an infantile neurosis. In *Standard Edition.* Vol. 17, 7–122. London: Hogarth Press, 1955.

Freud, S. (1919). The "uncanny." In *Standard Edition.* Vol. 17, 219–252. London: Hogarth Press, 1955.

Freud, S. (1923). The infantile genital organization: An interpolation into the theory of sexuality. In *Standard Edition.* Vol. 19, 141–148. London: Hogarth Press, 1961.

Freud, S. (1925). Some psychical consequences of the anatomical distinction between the sexes. In *Standard Edition.* Vol. 19, 243–258. London: Hogarth Press, 1961.

Freud, S. (1926a). Inhibitions, symptoms and anxiety. In *Standard Edition.* Vol. 20, 77–175. London: Hogarth Press, 1959.

Freud, S. (1926b). The question of lay analysis: An introduction to psycho-analysis. In *Standard Edition.* Vol. 20, 177–250. London: Hogarth Press, 1959.

Freud, S. (1930). Civilization and its discontents. In *Standard Edition.* Vol. 21, 57–145. London: Hogarth Press, 1961.

Freud, S. (1931). Female sexuality. In *Standard Edition.* Vol. 21, 223–246. London: Hogarth Press, 1961.

Freud, S. (1933). Femininity. In *Standard Edition.* Vol. 22, 112–135. London: Hogarth Press, 1964.

Golding, W. (1954). *The lord of the flies.* New York: Coward McCann.

Grunberger, B. (1971). *Narcissism: Psychoanalytic essays.* New York: International Universities Press.

Heidegger, M. (1954). *Essais et conferences.* (Trans. A. Preau). Paris: Gallimard, 1988.

Heidegger, M. (1975). *Poetry, language, thought.* (Trans. A. Hofstadter). New York: Harper and Row.

Hitler, A. (1925). *Mein Kampf.* (Trans. R. Manheim). London: Hutchinson, 1969.

Klein, M. (1946). Notes on some schizoid mechanisms. In *Developments in psychoanalysis.* London: Hogarth Press, 1952.

Klein, M. (1957). Envy and gratitude. In *Our adult world.* London: Hogarth Press, 1963.

Rousseau, J. J. (1761). *Julie ou la nouvelle Heloise: Lettres de deux amants habitants d'une petite ville au pied des Alpes.* Paris: Garnier-Flammarion, 1967.

Witkin, J. P. (1989). *Joel Peter Witkin.* Catalog prepared for the exhibition of his work organized by the Spanish Ministry of Culture. Centre National de Photographie, Palais de Tokyo, Paris.

JESSICA BENJAMIN

7 The Omnipotent Mother: A Psychoanalytic Study of Fantasy and Reality

Karen Horney (1932) began her classic essay on "The Dread of Woman" with Schiller's poem about "The Diver," whose search for the woman doomed him to the perils of the engulfing deep. In her remarks, Horney suggested that man's longing for woman is always coupled with "the dread that through her he might die and be undone." This fear may be concealed either by contempt or by adoration: while contempt for woman repairs the blow to masculine self-esteem, adoration covers dread with awe and mystery. Regarding the origin of these feelings, Horney declares, "If the grown man continues to regard woman as a great mystery, in whom is a secret he cannot divine, this feeling of his can only relate ultimately to one thing in her: the mystery of motherhood" (p. 135). Modern disenchantment has no doubt worked to diminish the mystique surrounding procreation and motherhood. But of course, the fading of this immediate sense of mystery has hardly been enough to alleviate the dread of maternal power; it has only banished it to the darkness beyond the portals of enlightenment. There it remains alive, in the unconscious if you will, ready to serve diverse (divers) fantastic purposes.

Freud (1930), in a more indirect way, addressed the same themes of mystery and motherhood when he quoted the Schiller poem in his remarks on "the oceanic feeling" in *Civilization and Its Discontents:* "I am moved to exclaim in the words of Schiller's diver: 'He may rejoice, who breathes in the roseate light'" (p. 73). Freud allowed that the ego's earliest, primordial feelings are those of oneness with the world—"the oceanic feeling"—like that of the infant at the breast who does not yet distinguish the world from itself. But Freud rejected Romain Roland's contention that this feeling constitutes the foundation of religion, that is to say, of culture. Instead, Freud insisted that religious feeling centers on the need for rescue by the father from primary helplessness. Reading between the lines, we see that this helplessness is nothing other than dependency on the mother.

The notion that the child begins in helpless dependency upon a mother from whom he must separate has guided psychoanalytic thinking ever since Freud's formulations. The implications of this image of the mother and the child's relation to her are far-reaching. Simply put, this notion has repeatedly led to the proposition that men have to denigrate or dominate women because men are actually dependent on and envious of the mother who can give birth and nurture the young. Because it is necessary for men to separate from mother and give up their original identification with her, the pull to her is felt as a threat to their independent identity (for example, Marcuse, 1962; Stoller, 1975). This argument underlies the most common psychoanalytic explanations for male dominance; it has been elaborated by psychoanalysts sympathetic to feminism like Robert Stoller (1975) as well as the feminist theorist Dorothy Dinnerstein (1976). In an important contribution, the French analyst Janine Chasseguet-Smirgel (1976) challenges Freud's notion that the vagina is unknown to children, suggesting that unconscious knowledge of this organ is actually a source of fear for the little boy. She points out that the boy's conscious image of the little girl as inferior and lacking an organ is the exact opposite of his unconscious image of the mother as omnipotent and overwhelming. The theory of phallic monism, which maintains that children know only about the penis, reflects the child's effort to repair a narcissistic wound, the sense of helplessness and dependency on the omnipotent mother. This primary helplessness later takes the form, in the boy's case, of the oedipal realization that he is too small to satisfy or complete mother. The original threat is not castration by the father but narcissistic injury in relation to the mother. Indeed, the admired and powerful phallic father actually saves the child from helplessness at the hands of the mother. The "natural scorn" for women that Freud often noted and the transfer of power to the father actually conceal and assuage terror of the omnipotent mother. Chasseguet-Smirgel, like many diverse psychoanalytic thinkers before her— Fromm and Lacan, for example—accepts the transfer of power to the father as the only means by which the child can free himself or herself from the helpless subjection to the omnipotent mother and enter the realty of the wider world.

Dinnerstein (1976), of course, sketches a similar relationship between early dependency on the omnipotent mother and paternal rescue as an escape from unfreedom. But she considers this constellation of mother and father to be not inevitable; rather, it is the source of all our cultural sickness. Inevitably, the infant projects omnipotence upon the first person who cares for her or him, and this projection is countered by conferring authority onto the father. Dinnerstein believes this process can be defused or modified only by setting up a different caretaking situation so that the child projects the earliest, undifferentiated feelings onto both parents. If men also nurtured children in infancy, if men also embodied the dangerous, enchanting thrall of early intimacy, we could no longer split off all the envy, greed, dread, and rage and apply it to women.[1] But, alas, the wish for omnipotence and the projection of it onto more powerful others are an inevitable result of dependency for which there is no antidote.

The difficulty with this analysis is that it provides only an external social solution to a psychological problem, the problem of omnipotence. It does not recognize any intrinsic psychic force that would oppose the tendency to project omnipotence onto the parental figure. Omnipotence can be distributed more equitably, but it cannot be countered or dissolved. Although Dinnerstein's vision exposes the fantasies about the mother more exhaustively than any other writer's, her argument assumes the omnipotence of the mother as a kind of psychic bedrock, whose consequences can at best be socially modified.

Chodorow (1978), despite her critique of Dinnerstein's assumptions, does wind up making a similar appeal to changing parenting arrangements. This makes more sense for Chodorow, since she sees the social basis as more determining than the psychological basis. She does not make the mother's psychic function into the prime motive of historical events, does not see maternal omnipotence and the reaction against it as a primary psychological fact underlying the social reality of gender domination. Together with Contratto (1982), she criticizes Dinnerstein for assuming that the fantasy of maternal omnipotence springs from the real dependence on the mother, and also for her equating woman with mother. Women are much more than just mothers, and their active subjectivity encompasses more than fantasies about mothers (Chodorow, 1979). Consistent with this position, Chodorow ascribes to the psyche an ability to recognize the mother's subjectivity, to see her as like subject and not just needed object. Hence there is a psychic force of differentiation that counterbalances omnipotence.

To postulate female mothering as an original universal cause of the human malaise as Dinnerstein does seems too omnipotent indeed. But Chodorow's suggestion that we counter that fantasy with so-called secondary-process knowledge of mothers as people (Chodorow & Contratto, 1982) inadequately describes how we really come to such recognition even as it too quickly forecloses an elaboration of the way omnipotence works. If psychic dread of the mother's power fuels and justifies men's social subjugation of women, it would be helpful to understand more deeply the fantasies that nourish it and the psychological force that might counteract it. I am not trying to postulate historical or psychic origins of that cycle, to invent an ultimate cause. But I do think that to intervene in or subvert that cycle now requires an understanding of the psychic forces that prevent or encourage such intervention.

1. A questionable aspect of this argument is the assumption that there is no gender difference apart from parenting, which, however convenient, seems untenable because it leaves out cultural representation and the pervasiveness of gendering.

If we assume that children do have the capacity to recognize the mother's subjectivity, to perceive her as human rather than as omnipotent, the question is, why don't they? This question has preoccupied me for some time. We cannot simply attribute the persistence of omnipotence fantasies to the child's early dependency upon the mother's care, to events in the preoedipal phase. That argument assumes, rather than explains, a paranoid reaction against dependency. Furthermore, we have had time enough to observe that dependency upon two parents eliminates neither the dread of woman nor the problem of omnipotence. Probably, as Chodorow (1979) and I (1988) have suggested, the decisive moment at which the mother becomes dreaded and repudiated is the oedipal phase, in which the male turns the table on the female and the reversal of power relations becomes enmeshed with male cultural hegemony. I intend to elaborate this insight and to suggest how the process of gender differentiation as we know it actually stalemates the potential recognition of subjectivity in the mother-child relationship. The deeply rooted cultural bifurcation of all experience under the poles of gender perpetuates the fantasy of omnipotence. By unpacking the relation between reality and fantasy in light of current theorizing about psychic development, we can clarify the association between omnipotence and gender.

I have been developing a point of view that encompasses the doubleness of psychic life (Benjamin, 1990), both the fantasy of maternal omnipotence and the capacity to recognize the mother as another subject. For our purposes, we can align two contrasting moments of psychic life—a mode of intersubjective reality (by this I mean a relationship between two or more different subjects sharing certain feelings or perceptions) and a mode of fantasy as the unshared property of an isolated subject—with the capacity to recognize the mother as another subject and the fantasy of maternal omnipotence, respectively. Ideally these distinct tendencies of our psychic organization constitute a tension rather than a contradiction, an "either-or" as has often been supposed. In the best of circumstances, we do not get rid of dangerous fantasies; rather the fantasies exist in tension with reality. The fantasy world of the unconscious in which self and objects can be omnipotent is balanced by the relational world in which we recognize, empathize, and grasp the subjectivity of real others. This tension is roughly equivalent to that between the depressive and schizoid positions in Kleinian theory, which are no longer understood as successive but as dialectically alternating or complementary (Ogden, 1986). It is the *breakdown* of the tension between these two modes, and not the existence of fantasy (omnipotence) per se, that is detrimental to the recognition of other subjects.

This breakdown consists, in effect, of moving from the state in which I know my fantasy to be a result of my feeling—something even a child of three can at times realize—to a state in which I externalize, I project my feeling onto someone else. Here Horney's (1932) remarks on male dread of woman are once again prescient: "'It is not,' he says, 'that I dread her; it is that *she* herself *is* malignant, capable of any crime, a beast of prey, a vampire, a witch, insatiable in her desires. *She is* the very personification of what is sinister'" (p. 135). The usage of "she is" is an important key to the whole matter. It signifies a collapse of reality and fantasy. All that is bad and dreaded is projectively placed on the other; all the anxiety is seen as the product of external attack rather than one's own subjective state. The issue, then, is not simply that male children disidentify with and then repudiate the mother. It is also that this repudiation involves the psyche in precisely those projective processes—"she *is* that thing I feel"—and these intensify the fear of the other's omnipotence and the need to retaliate with assertion of one's own omnipotence.

Before I go on to discuss the way this world historical power struggle gets anchored in the psyche, let me say a few words about the idea of a counterforce in the psyche that pushes for recognizing the mother and for intersubjective reality in general. This is a relatively new idea (see Chodorow, 1979). For most of its history, psychoanalytic theory itself has reflected the imbalance between intersubjective reality and the intrapsychic. It has failed to conceptualize the mother as a separate subject outside the child. However, as I have discussed elsewhere (Benjamin, 1988, 1990), recent developments in psychoanalytic theory and infancy research are more consonant with a view of early development as a process that involves mutual recognition between mother and child.

Infancy theorists have argued that the metaphor of the mirror is not appropriate to represent early mothering (Beebe & Lachmann, 1988; Stern, 1985), that even at four months an attuned mother is not undifferentiated, does not create the illusion of perfect oneness and is not perfectly attuned. In her play she stimulates an incipient recognition of otherness, difference, discrepancy, and this pleases the infant, who likes the excitement that a brush with otherness brings. Later, at about nine months, the infant begins to be aware of the fact that, as Daniel Stern (1985) described it, separate minds can share similar states. Commonality, attunement, shared feeling can unite separate persons. At this point, the child is able to realize that another shares her or his excitement or intention and enjoys that fact. Likewise, the mother is aware of her child's capacity to share feeling and now takes pleasure in contacting her or his mind. Thus the infant's sense of the other develops incrementally through a tension between sameness and difference, union and disjunction.

We might say that the original psychoanalytic theory or ideal of a mother who offers a perfect oceanic symbiosis hardly captures the multiplicity and complexity of the infant's actual experience of life with mother. Yet this supposed state of oneness has been adduced to explain the fear of regression that is the basis of the dread of mother and of woman: the fear of being drawn back into the limitless ocean of maternal union. Of course, both women and men project the dangerous longing for a return to amniotic life onto mother, but how did this one partial image come to stand for the whole and so become the trope for the entire theory of infancy?

The new perspective on infant perception of the mother is, of course, not just a product of adhering to empirical observation; to assume that would be naive. Not surprisingly, scientific development can here be seen to reflect the changes in women's status and the ideology of motherhood as well as to help organize those changes. But this perspective on infancy suggests that the simple existence of dependency in infancy is, in itself, an insufficient explanation for man's infantile stance regarding his fantasy of the mother. Once our representation of the psyche includes the aspect of intersubjectivity, the capacity to differentiate and recognize other subjects—the "counterforce"—it is possible to see this working in counterpoint to omnipotence fantasies. How does an appreciation of a shared reality with the other person mitigate a fantasy that we, or they, are omnipotent? How does it open up a space in which fantasy can be expressed symbolically rather than concretely? And what impedes the evolution of inter-subjective space, of the ability to see the other's subjectivity and to take our fearful projections back into ourselves?

I have suggested that the fantasy of omnipotence is not an originary state but is a reaction to confronting the other.[2] It probably begins in the first crisis of recognizing the other, the first conscious encounter with the mother's indepen-dence, during the separation-individuation phase. Margaret Mahler (Mahler, Pine, & Bergman, 1975), whose observations of separation-individuation have been so influential in current psychoanalytic thinking, called this crisis "rap-prochement." In rapprochement a conflict emerges between the infant's grandi-ose aspirations and the perceived reality of her or his limitations and depen-dency. When the child begins to be aware that reality will not always bend to her or his will, that thought cannot always be translated into action, a pitched battle of wills can ensue, "a struggle to the death for recognition." Expressed in terms of intersubjectivity: the tension between asserting self and recognizing the other breaks down and is manifested as a conflict between self and other. The paradox of recognition is that we must recognize the other in return, else their recognition means little to us. In the very moment of realizing our own indepen-dence, we are dependent upon another to recognize it. At the very moment we come to understand the meaning of I, myself, we are forced to see the limitations of that self. At the moment when we understand that separate minds can share similar feelings, we begin to find out that these minds can also disagree. What if the other does not do as I wish, recognize my intent? There is a new sense of vulnerability: I can move away from mother—but mother can also move away from me.

It is no accident that the observational studies of this period focused on mother's leaving. For mother's departure (to work, to go out) confronts the child with mother's independent aims—a point usually ignored. This is therefore not just a matter of separation anxiety, as it is frequently portrayed, but of recogni-tion: recognize my will, do as I want! Or rather, separation consists not so much

2. The fantasy of omnipotence is more than simply the original inability to differenti-ate thoughts from reality that is typical of infancy; it is a defensive reaction to disappoint-ment. The wish says, in effect, I wish I could control everything as I once did (thought I did) when mother did everything I wanted; or, if only mother would make everything perfect, which she could do if she wished. Once the cognitive capacity for distinguishing wish and reality begins to develop, mental omnipotence is a dynamic psychic matter, not a simply inability to differentiate.

of losing mother's presence as losing control of her coming and going. This conflict also confronts the mother with the problem of her own separate existence and so with conflict; she may experience the child's demands now as threatening, as tyrannical, irrational, willful. The child is different from *her* fantasy of the perfect child, who would want what she wants. In her mind, the child and she may switch places, the child now becoming the repository of omnipotent aspirations she once attributed to herself in the persona of the all-giving mother. The mother, as I shall discuss in a while, also has to be willing to relinquish her fantasy that she can be perfect and provide a perfect world for her child; she has to accept that injuring the child's sense of complete control over her is a step on the road to recognition.

This formulation of the process might make it seem that the mother bears sole responsibility for her own recognition by the child. I shall modify this notion of responsibility later on, but for now let us assume that at an individual level the mother often passes on her own solutions to the dilemma of omnipotence. If the mother is unable both to set a clear boundary for the child and to recognize the child's intentions and will, to insist on her own separateness and respect that of the child, the child does not really "get" that mother is also a person, a subject in her own right. Instead, the child continues to see her as all-powerful, either omnipotently controlling or engulfingly weak. Whether the child attributes the omnipotence to the mother or attributes it to herself or himself, the process of mutual recognition has not been furthered.

The paradox of recognition cannot be resolved. The "ideal" is for it to continue as a *constant tension* between recognizing the other and asserting the self. This crisis point poses a new and taxing demand to recognize outside reality, and so the tension between recognition and assertion breaks down and must be created anew, at a more sophisticated level. In Mahler's theory, however, the rapprochement conflict appears to be resolved through internalization, what is called object constancy. This means the child takes the mother in and is able to separate from her because her existence as an internal object is not dependent on her being there on the outside and, more specifically, on her gratifying the child. In this picture, the child has only to accept mother's being disappointing; there is no need to shift her or his center of gravity to recognize that mother does this because she is a person in her own right.

How would we go about conceptualizing the way that a child begins to make this shift? What we are tracking here is how a person comes to have a sense of shared reality and appreciate the subjectivity of the other versus what reinforces the sense of omnipotence. The point here is not to dismiss or denigrate fantasy, play, and the narcissism of Her or His Majesty the baby, but to acknowledge the necessity of a struggle between two important, but conflicting tendencies.

The British object relations theorist D. W. Winnicott, who was also a pediatrician, offered a way to think about the struggle that the child engages in to come to terms with the necessity of recognizing the other. Winnicott (1971) came up with the idea that in the course of development we do a rather paradoxical thing: we try to destroy the other person in order to discover that they survive. By destroying the other, he did not mean literally trying to annihilate them, but rather denying or negating their independent existence, refusing to recognize them. In fact, what he meant was to absolutely assert our right to have it our way and to make the other person subject to our fantasy, do our will. His idea was that by wiping out the person inside our mind (he calls it the sphere of our "omnipotence") we actually have the effect of placing the other outside our mind (outside "omnipotence"). Because, it is hoped, the other does not actually get destroyed, we discover the other to be outside our mental powers. By engaging in a fantasied act of maximum control, by negating the other's separate existence, we discover the outside reality.

Of course, this works only if the other actually does survive, which means that the person continues to be an effective, responsive, and nonthreatening presence. Winnicott (1964) specifically talks of how the baby has a terrible fit of rage and feels that he has destroyed everyone and everything around him, but as he calms down, he notices that everyone is just as before—still loving and still there. This allows the baby to distinguish between what he imagines and what is real, between inside and outside. When the destructiveness damages neither the parent nor the self, external reality comes into view as a sharp, distinct contrast to the inner fantasy world.

So in this model, fantasy and reality become differentiated, rather than one canceling out the other. And the way this happens is not that we suppress our omnipotence, deny our fantasy that the other can perfectly meet our wishes, but that we acknowledge them as fantasy and tolerate their distance from reality. The problem that so often occurs on this path to recognizing the other is that if the other retaliates, or caves in and withdraws, we don't really experience the other as outside us, but rather they seem to be just like our persecutory fantasy; they do not survive and become real. In this case, a power struggle is inaugurated, and the outcome is a reversible cycle of doer and done to. If the mother does not survive, a pattern is established in which there is no real other subject, no real feeling for the other. Let us imagine a mother who gives in to the child and never leaves. The child, feeling he or she has succeeded in controlling Mommy, now feels "Mommy is still my fantasy; Mommy is also afraid, and I can never leave Mommy without great anxiety either." Thus, even as the child loses contact with the real independent mother, the omnipotent fantasy mother, who is powerful in her need as well, fills the space. Now the child is no longer able to encompass the feeling "I am full of anxiety," but rather feels mother to be the source of the solution to anxiety. Alternatively, let us imagine that mother leaves and returns and they share a happy reunion. Now what the child feels is that the bad feeling about mother leaving and the projection of that anger onto mother, which would return as punishment or abandonment, is not true, was only a fantasy.

The flip side of Winnicott's analysis would be that when aggression is not worked through in this way, it continues to fuel fantasies of revenge and retaliation attributed to both self and other. The whole experience shifts from the domain of intersubjective reality into the unconscious domain of fantasy, from a feeling we can own to a projection onto the object. Where do we put the bad feeling? We keep it inside, projected onto the figure of a frightening, dreaded other. All real experience is also elaborated in fantasy, of course, but when the other does not survive and aggression is not dissipated, experience becomes almost exclusively fantastic. It is the loss of balance between omnipotence and recognition, between fantasy and reality, that is the problem (Benjamin, 1990).

Ideally, a child's negotiation of conflict with the other (mother) allows the infant's original fascination with and love of what is outside her or his appreciation of what is different and challenging to continue under more complex conditions. This appreciation gives to separation an element of affection, rather than merely hostility: love of the world, not just leaving or distance from mother. To the extent that mother herself is placed outside, she can be loved: "I'll cut you in a hundred pieces!" says the little pirate waving a sword. At bedtime he snuggles up and reminisces fondly, "Remember I said I'm gonna cut you in a hundred pieces?" Now separation is truly the other side of connection to the other. This appreciation of the other completes the picture of separation and explains what lies beyond internalization—the establishment of shared reality.

Elsa First (1988), a psychoanalyst who has worked with children, has provided some germane observations of how the toddler begins to establish shared reality, using fantasy and identification with mother to deal with mother's leaving in the third year of life. She observed the symbolic play in which mother's leaving for work was represented by the child. There was an evolution in the toddler play, first enacting an aggressive, retaliatory reaction and then moving into identification with the one who is leaving, putting the self in the place of the other based on understanding (once again) similarities of inner experience. The two-year-old's initial role-playing imitation of the departing mother is characterized by the spirit of pure retaliation and reversal: "I'll do to you what you do to me." But gradually the child begins to identify with the mother's subjective experience and realizes that "I could miss you as you miss me," and, therefore, that "I know that you could wish to have your own life as I wish to have mine." First shows how, by recognizing such shared experience, the child actually moves from a retaliatory world of control to a world of mutual understanding and shared feeling. Her analysis shows how the child comes to recognize that the leaving mother is not *bad* but *independent*, "a person like me."

We can sum up the problem of holding onto both shared reality and omnipotent fantasy. The initial response to the discovery of the difference between my will and your will is a breakdown of recognition between self and other: I insist on my way, I refuse to recognize you, I begin to try to coerce you; and therefore I experience your refusal as a reversal: you are coercing me. The capacity for mutual recognition must stretch to accommodate the tension of difference, to reach beyond coercion, and it does this through identification, expressed in communicative play that gives the pleasure of shared understanding. In this light, the early play at retaliatory reversal may be a kind of empowerment, where the child feels "I can do to you what you do to me." A necessary step, the ability to play with omnipotence fantasies, gives the child a certain freedom and it tests survival. But then the play expands to include the emotional identification with the other's position and becomes reflexive, so that, as First puts it, "I know you know what I feel." This advance in differentiation means, "We can share feelings without my fearing that my feelings are simply your feelings." There is now a space between the mother and child that allows differentiation of self and other, fantasy and reality.

The child who can imaginatively entertain his own and his mother's part— leaving and being left—has attained a space that symbolically contains negative feelings so that they need not be projected onto the object ("she *is* dreadful") or turned back upon the self ("I am destructive").[3] The mother has survived, has helped the child to contain and share these feelings, has provided a space in which they can be safely understood as fantasy. Now the child can use this space to begin to transcend the complementary form of the mother-child relationship. When the child is able to identify with the mother, the movement out of the world of complementary power relations into the world of mutual understanding means that power is not shifted back and forth like a hot potato but (momentarily, at least) dissolved.

The complementary structure dictates a reversible relationship, which allows one to switch roles but not to alter them or hold them simultaneously. One person soothes, the other is soothed; one person is recognized, the other negated; one subject, the other object. This complementarity does not dissolve power but keeps its positions, keeps it moving from one partner to the other; domination can be reversed but not undone. There are only two possible positions, with no space in between them to allow for difference. When the tension of mutual recognition breaks down—something that we see in the culture writ large—the absence of a real other creates a kind of void that has to be filled with fantasy, usually the kind of fantasy in which the other is threatening and must be subjugated. The cycle of destroying the reality of the other and replacing it with the fantasy of a feared and denigrated object, one who must be controlled for fear of retaliation, characterizes all relations of domination.

Ordinarily, I think, each child is exposed to both possible solutions to the problem of omnipotence—complementarity and mutuality. The paradox of recognition is not resolved once and for all in the second year of life but remains an organizing issue throughout life, becoming intense with each struggle for independence and each confrontation with difference. Ordinarily there is a necessary tension between complementarity and mutuality in the mother-infant relation. It is thus not my intention to suggest that maternal failure is responsible for the prevalence of omnipotence fantasies, of complementary structures, the persistence of domination. But how shall we even formulate the question of what keeps the complementary structures in place?

The question for psychoanalytic theory is how cycles of domination can be

---

3. Of course, I am simplifying matters. Another way to describe this is that projection continues in the paranoid position, but the self occupies that position only at times; it is able much of the time to be in the position of taking back the projection and experiencing fantasy as such.

broken into rather than merely reversed. Obviously, the fantasy of maternal omnipotence would be sustained even were male domination reversed in favor of women, a point often lost on antipsychoanalytic feminists. But by and large psychoanalytic theory has not even begun to conceptualize a way out of complementarity; it has tacitly accepted the existence of domination. Psychoanalytic theory has understood domination in terms of narcissism, the subjective position that underpins it: the inability to recognize the other and confront difference without surrendering to or controlling the other. The theory did not envision the overcoming of narcissism, the possibility of recognition and mutuality occurring within the dyad, which it conceived exclusively in the complementary metaphor of subject and object. In various ways, it insisted that only the intervention of a third figure, the father, could bring the child out of fantasy and into reality by giving up the mother. The assumption was that recognition of the other could not evolve within the relationship to the primary other, that two subjects alone could never confront each other without merging, one being subordinated and assimilated by the other.

One side of the coin was attribution of regressive traits to mother for holding the child back from civilization; the other side was the notion that only the father's intervention could break up the mother's omnipotence. Mother's failure, father's justification; mother's disparagement, father's idealization—these went together like a horse and carriage. The only alternatives were for the child to retain omnipotence for himself (I say "him" advisedly), remaining stuck in narcissism, or to displace the fantasied power on to the father.[4] The later oedipal solution, in which the father is "the third term" who creates space between mother and child, who creates symbolic capacity, is accepted in Lacanian feminist accounts as the only path to break up narcissism, "the Imaginary" (for example, Mitchell, 1982; Ragland-Sullivan, 1986).

So let us try a reversal here. In light of our present conception of the mother-child relationship, we can say that in the oedipal phase the boy is wrested away from the very possibility of establishing mutuality through identification. The boy displaces the mother's envied power onto father and then identifies with it rather than finding a way out of that power struggle. The oedipal theory inadvertently expresses the problem, but not its solution; the Oedipus complex does not

---

4. Some examples of this way of formulating the father's role can be found among influential psychoanalytic writers such as Loewald (1980) and, of course, Chasseguet-Smirgel (1985). I realize that the Oedipus complex is not always interpreted in such a way as to stress the father-son relationship as one between subjects, and the mother-son relationship as an objectifying one. Certainly, it has sometimes been crudely understood as love of mother and hatred of father. But such hatred, as analysis consistently reveals, is a particular way of identifying with father. Even when oedipal theory stresses not the boy's identification with father but his rivalry or murderous impulses, we know that rivalry represents a kind of struggle to the death for recognition between subjects; indeed, in Hegel's description of the struggle it epitomizes it. And rivalry is a way in which to identify with someone while remaining opposed to him.

dissolve narcissism; it displaces it. The seldom recognized effect of the oedipal phase is to shift the form of omnipotence. Whereas the child in the preoedipal phase is overinclusive (Fast, 1984) and wishes to be "everything"—that is, to polymorphously incorporate the organs and abilities of both sexes—the oedipal child repudiates all that is other and insists that what he (or she) has is "the only thing" (Benjamin, 1991–92). Thus the theory of phallic monism reflects the contempt for mother's organs and her value in general that is essential to the oedipal boy's move to deal with envy and difference: Everything I can't have is (worth) nothing. Traditional oedipal theorizing states that the boy realizes he cannot have mother, accepts the limit that father sets, and so gives up omnipotent control over the primary object. But at another level, omnipotence is restored through the repudiation of the mother, whereby that which he gives up is turned into nothing, and indeed, father now has "everything," the phallus.[5]

Thus, though the oedipal achievement of complementarity is supposed by the theory to represent mature acceptance of limits, being only the one or the other, it actually conceals the unconscious narcissistic omnipotence of being "the one and only." Having recognized the finesse in this maneuver, the point is still not to disavow or get rid of the oedipal structure, which is in any event no more possible than to get rid of the fantasy of omnipotence. The point might be to envision a next step, which partially dissolves this form of omnipotence and restores the balance of mutuality. Psychoanalytic theory, as Bassin (1991) has pointed out, has the potential to envision something beyond the oedipal organization of sexuality, a phase beyond the phallic have/have not that encompasses bisexuality, and this project will doubtless be part of the feminist revisioning of sexuality.

For the time being, however, the prevalent structure of male gender dominance can be understood as the oedipal complementarity writ large. The principal reaction to giving up identification with the opposite sex, or shall we say, to the discovery of exclusive difference in the oedipal phase is a reassertion of omnipotence in a new form. The new form, found in girls as well as boys, is chauvinism, based on repudiation: I must be the One, not the Other. I agree with Chodorow (1979) that men have been able to make their chauvinism hegemonic because of their position of power, not because only males are chauvinistic. We might argue that the disruption of identification brought about by the oedipal male repudiation of mother actually undoes mutuality and makes the complementary structure of doer and done-to the dominant residue of infancy. The model of complementary power relations has prevailed in the male orientation stance toward women, producing a formal fit between complementary subject-object relations and male-female relations. Dynamically, the omnipotent

5. Lacan, who emphasized the role of the phallus as the ultimate signifier, inadvertently gives a good example of the oedipal move from loss of the object's love to devaluation of the object. He mistranslates (1966) the famous phrase uttered by Herr K. in the Dora case, "I get nothing from my wife" (an accurate rendering of the German), as "My wife is nothing to me."

mother of this dyad becomes the basis for the dread and retaliation that subsequently inform men's exercise of power over women. The adult relation between men and women becomes the locus of the great reversal, turning the tables on the omnipotent mother of infancy.

This reversal works because the rigid complementarity and male repudiation of femininity produces a foreclosure of the intersubjective space of identification with the mother. This has several consequences: first, the mother is no longer recognized as a subject like the self, something I've said before; second, the omnipotence attributed to the mother cannot be defused by the identificatory fantasies and communicative interaction described earlier; third, the omnipotence of the overinclusive position cannot be integrated and so finds a more destructive expression in the chauvinism of being the one sex; fourth, the father is defensively idealized and becomes the final embodiment of this omnipotent oneness, which cannot be broken up in interaction with a real other subject; and finally, all the feelings of envy, guilt, and destructiveness cannot be symbolically contained as felt properties of the self but must be projected out as properties of the object: "She *is* dangerous, a goddess, a temptress."

It is not necessary that the fantasy of maternal omnipotence be dispelled, only that it be modified by the existence of another dimension—that of intersubjectivity. This dimension evolves, as we saw in the toddler's identification with the leaving mother, through the symbolic space of communicative interaction and fantasy play in the dyad. With the closing of this space, the projective power of the fantasy becomes more virulent: "she is that thing I feel." Segal (1957), a psychoanalyst in the Kleinian school, called this a symbolic equation, a function prior to symbolization in which the symbol does not stand for something; it is that thing. In the symbolic equation (she *is* that thing) the verb *to be* forecloses the space in between (Ogden, 1986), a space opened by the verbs *seem* or *feel*, by the action of play and just-pretend. The attenuation of intersubjectivity can be conceptualized as an assimilation of the subject to the object (Horkheimer & Adorno, 1947), as the lack of the space in between subjects.

As the analyst Thomas Ogden (1986) has noted, the existence of potential space between mother and child allows the establishment of the distinction between the symbol and the symbolized. The subject who can begin to make this distinction now has access to a triangular field—symbol, symbolized, and the interpreting subject. The space between self and other can exist and facilitate the distinction, let us say, between the real mother and the fantasy mother (who is symbolized). This can happen in the early dyad without an intervening third person (Trevarthen, 1980), although in it the place of a third is generated.[6]

The dread of the mother, with which I began this inquiry, reflects the foreclosure of that intersubjective space between mother and child in which omnip-

6. It may be that this symbolic function then becomes equated symbolically with the father as third person—as when the theory imagines that the father brings this function into being, rather than that under certain conditions the father as a symbol represents this function.

otence is transformed through use of symbolic processes. Accordingly, the structural role of the oedipal father would then be not to create, as in genesis, a symbolic order out of an absence of symbolism. In reverse, it might be tempting to say that the father as symbol, or better yet, symbolic equation ("the paternal order") often substitutes an authority structure for the symbolic intersubjective process of the maternal dyad. This paternal symbolic structure is rooted in the intrapsychic situation of subject-object complementarity; it retroactively re-defines the mutual intersubjectivity of mother and child as a threat to masculinity or a regressive flight from reality. But in fact, the imposition of a paternal order is no solution (or only an imaginary one) to the problem of recognizing the other subject; it is a theoretical fantasy. In reality, the structures of early intersubjectivity, "the maternal order," remain available to men as well as women and are no more the essential prerogative of mother than of father.

Indeed, any such opposing of a "maternal order" to theories of paternal order, even for the sake of argument, justifiably deserves to be considered a counter-idealization (Kristeva, 1981). Therefore, I wish to counter the preceding argument immediately with yet another reversal. I want to consider the difficulty that the fantasy of omnipotence poses for the mother herself. In seeking to define a space within the dyad, a symbolic potential that does not rely on a powerful idealized father of separation, feminist theorists have often been tempted to re-create a mirror image of the father—a perfect, ideal mother in whom the old wish for omnipotence is revived. In the current wave of feminism we have seen an outpouring of women's writing that seeks to restore a lost maternal or feminine order in writing, on the margins of culture, in the private spaces of play, creativity, and erotic life, in the nonverbal representations of mutuality—a different kind of symbolic space founded in intersubjectivity. In fact, to an astonishing degree the notion of finding one's own desire has been articulated through the image of woman as writer. Yet even as this search has appealed to the maternal image, it has had to contend with the constant companion of the maternal ideal, a deep fear of destroying one's mother or child by separating.

Given the centrality in current feminist thought of the figure of the woman writer (rather than, say, the woman politician—though this may be changing even as we speak), the conflict between woman's subjectivity and mothering responsibilities is formulated in terms of the desire for the inner, not the outer world. This effort to reclaim subjectivity presents the difficulty, or shall I say temptation, of the search for "the perfect mother" (Chodorow & Contratto, 1982). The perfect mother of fantasy is the one who is always there, ready to sacrifice herself—and the child is not conscious of how strongly such a fantasy mother makes him or her feel controlled, guilty, envious, or unable to go away. The child simply remains terrified of her leaving or of destroying her by becoming separate. In turn, the mother feels terrified of destroying her child with her own separation. Thus separation and guilt often emerge as the axis of conflict for contemporary women writers. When the dangers of separation that inspire guilt are seen as real rather than fantasized, space is foreclosed and the mother-child relationship becomes a zero-sum game: The mother's child "is" the obstacle to her self-expression and her self-expression "is" a threat to her child (again, the symbolic equation of the verb *to be*).

A kind of evolution of this problematic can be seen in the reflections of the feminist critic Susan Suleiman. Musing on the fear of separation, she offers for scrutiny her fantastic conviction, "With every word I write, with every act of genuine creation, I hurt my child" (1985). Subsequently, in a discussion of Mary Gordon's *Men and Angels,* Suleiman (1988) shows the outcome of this fantastic conviction to be a foreclosure of the space between reality and fantasy. She grapples with that foreclosure in Gordon's story, which reaffirms the zero-sum stakes of a mother's choice by depicting how a mother who chooses to pursue her own writing really does place her children at risk. Suleiman recognizes that this portrayal is inspired by the woman's unconscious clinging to an image of a perfect mother, and not merely by the social reality that mothers are almost exclusively responsible for their children. And Suleiman continues to inquire how to escape that equation in which the mother *is* to blame. At a still later point, Suleiman (1990 and chap. 16 below) proposes that there is a mother who can play with her child and thus be recognized "most fully as a subject— autonomous and free . . . able to take the risk of 'infinite expansion' that goes with creativity," a mother who can open up the symbolic space of play.[7]

The difficult task this sets feminist consciousness is for a woman, as daughter or mother, to transform the space of inevitable separation and loss into a space of creation and play. Jane Lazarre, whose account of a stormy young motherhood, *The Mother Knot,* conveyed the inability to conceive of separation without destruction, has sought to deconstruct the formula in which the mother must sacrifice her children or her self. Her new book, *Worlds beyond My Control* (1991 and chap. 2 above), takes its title from Sara Ruddick's *Maternal Thinking* (1989): "To give birth is to create a life that cannot be kept safe, whose unfolding cannot be controlled, and whose eventual death is certain. . . . In a world beyond one's control to be humble is to have a profound sense of the limits of one's actions and of the predictability of the consequences of one's work" (p. 72). Recognizing the illusion of the daughter who blames the mother and is determined to outdo her when she becomes a mother, Lazarre struggles to accept this condition.

Lazarre's character no longer constructs her children as obstacles to her writing, or her writing as obstacles to her mothering. She realizes, instead, that her obstacle is the dream of perfect symmetry, her own wish to be completely

7. Suleiman's second statement is part of a commentary on Gordon's *Men and Angels* that lucidly articulates the problem of splitting in the novel between a "good mother" and an "other mother," the alternate caretaker who takes on the badness (indifference, selfishness, even hostility) not acceptable in a good mother. And in her discussion of the mother playing (1990) she offers a vision of "boys (later to be men) who actually enjoy seeing their mother move instead of sitting motionless, a peaceful center around which the child weaves his play [Barthes]; of girls (later to be women) who learn that they do not have to grow up to be motionless mothers" (p. 180).

recognized, completely responded to, the fantasy of perfect self-expression in a perfect world. Her dilemma is, how can she continue to write, to love, to seek recognition, in the absence of the fantasy mother who would constitute that world? She comes to recognize that she cannot re-recreate that mother either in her writing or in her efforts to protect her children from the world. Rather, her character has to find a way to contain, through writing, the loss of an illusion that was common to both the "pristine beginning" of her writing and her "newborn's unscarred flesh": the illusion that she would achieve "the perfect reparation."

It seems to me that the early phase of feminist revival, the phase of redis-covering the mother, was characterized by this wish for perfect reparation. As is characteristic for such a wish, it reflected a needed effort to formulate what had been missing or lost, as well as a kind of manic denial of loss and a celebration of identity. The latter, a celebration of the sisterhood of all women, could be seen as a euphoric "return" to the earliest phase of mother-child mutuality: "You and I are feeling the same feeling."[8] No doubt, this excess lent credence to the critique of feminism, which contended that the banishing of the symbolic oedipal father invariably leads to such denial of difference. But this was an oversimplification of both the intentions and the aims of feminism. Further, as I have been proposing, that denial of difference simply adopts the preexisting positions of complemen-tarity; it reflects a foreclosure of space for which the idealized father was the original model. The fantasy of the redeeming mother represented a kind of reversal, a substitution for the ideal father. Ultimately, though, whether it is a maternal or a paternal ideal, the fantasy of an omnipotent figure, in and with whom we are redeemed, condemns us to a life of denial of loss and to a world in which complementary power relations triumph over mutual understanding.

But the deconstruction of this fantasy should not be equated with the bitter disillusionment that turns us against ourselves, chastising ourselves as victims of false hope, of a childish longing for redemption. Nor does disillusionment alone constitute a real base for the knowledge of difference. By itself, it reflects only the disparagement of what was once loved, the countering of mania with depression, the refusal to grieve concealed by a repudiation of all longing. The real alternative to a defensive fantasy of omnipotence is the labor of mourning (Santner, 1990). And mourning gives rise to acts of reparation, which need not be perfect in order to restore the expressive space of connection to an under-standing other. As I have suggested before, it is good enough for us to counter-balance fantasy with that real connection, which transforms in turn our rela-tionship to fantasy, enabling us to own it as ours. This, in turn, allows the

8. This phase was superseded by another reversal, one that denied sameness of feeling in favor of difference. In this simple negation, however, the principle of identity was preserved, this time sequestered in particular groups that opposed any universal feminine identity. Should we speculate that the historical dialectic will go according to plan, so that these might be followed by a phase of restoring the tension between sameness and difference, particular and universal?

acceptance of loss to ameliorate the aggression that fuels omnipotence. Historically, the sedimenting of the omnipotence fantasy in our cultural life is too great to overcome except by adding this new layer of recognition and awareness of loss. So it is good enough—in fact it is better—not to disown all fantasy but simply to recognize that the other is not that thing I dread or that god I adore. Accepting that the other is outside our fantasy allows us to take our fantasy back into ourselves and begin to play. The intersubjective space of understanding can help contain the inevitable experience of leaving and losing the other, even of death. In the space of creativity and communication, the self can play, even with adoration and dread, can find consolation for the inevitable disappointment of not being, or having, everything.

References

Bassin, D. (1991). The true genital phase. Paper delivered at spring 1991 meetings of Division 39, Psychoanalytic Psychology, New York.

Beebe, B., & Lachmann, F. (1988). Mother-infant mutual influence and precursors of psychic structure. In A. Goldberg (Ed.), *Frontiers of self psychology* (Vol. 3, 3–25). Hillsdale, N.J.: Analytic Press.

Benjamin, J. (1988). *The bonds of love: Psychoanalysis, feminism and the problem of domination.* New York: Pantheon.

Benjamin, J. (1990). An outline of intersubjectivity. *Psychoanalytic Psychology,* 7, Supp., 33–46.

Benjamin, J. (1991–92). Like subjects and love objects: Identificatory love and gender development. Paper delivered at Psychoanalytic Association clinical workshop, New York and San Francisco. Forthcoming in *Like subjects and love objects.* New Haven: Yale University Press, 1994.

Chasseguet-Smirgel, J. (1976). Freud and female sexuality. *International Journal of Psychoanalysis,* 57, 275–87.

Chasseguet-Smirgel, J. (1985). *The ego ideal: A psychoanalytic essay on the malady of the ideal.* New York: Norton.

Chodorow, N. (1978). *The reproduction of mothering.* Berkeley: University of California Press.

Chodorow, N. (1979). Gender, relations and difference in psychoanalytic perspective. In *Feminism and psychoanalytic theory.* New Haven: Yale University Press, 1989.

Chodorow, N., & Contratto, S. (1982). The fantasy of the perfect mother. In B. Thorne (Ed.), *Rethinking the family: Some feminist questions.* New York: Longman.

Dinnerstein, D. (1976). *The mermaid and the minotaur: Sexual arrangements and human malaise.* New York: Harper and Row.

First, E. (1988). The leaving game: I'll play you and you'll play me. In A. Slade & D. Wolfe (Eds.), *Modes of meaning: Clinical and developmental approaches to symbolic play* (132–60). New York: Oxford University Press.

Freud, S. (1930). Civilization and its discontents. In *Standard Edition*. Vol. 23. London: Hogarth Press, 1953; New York: Norton, 1967.

Horkheimer, M., & Adorno, T. (1947). *Dialectic of enlightenment*. New York: Seabury Press, 1972.

Horney, K. (1932). The dread of woman. In *Feminine psychology*. New York: Norton, 1973.

Kristeva, J. (1981). Women's time. *Signs*, 7, 13–35.

Lacan, J. (1966). Intervention in the transference. In J. Mitchell and J. Rose (Eds.), *Feminine sexuality: Jacques Lacan and the école freudienne*. New York: Norton, 1982.

Lazarre, J. (1991). *Worlds beyond my control*. New York: Viking.

Loewald, H. (1980). Ego and reality. In *Papers on psychoanalysis*. New Haven: Yale University Press, 1989.

Mahler, M., Pine, F., & Bergman, A. (1975). *The psychological birth of the human infant*. New York: Basic Books.

Marcuse, H. (1962). *Eros and civilization*. New York: Vintage.

Mitchell, J. (1982). Introduction I to J. Mitchell & J. Rose (Eds.), *Feminine sexuality: Jacques Lacan and the école freudienne*. New York: Norton.

Ogden, T. (1986). *The matrix of the mind: Object relations and the psychoanalytic dialogues*. New York: Jason Aronson.

Ragland-Sullivan, E. (1986). *Jacques Lacan and the philosophy of psychoanalysis*. Urbana: University of Illinois Press.

Ruddick, S. (1989). *Maternal thinking*. Boston: Beacon Press.

Santner, E. (1990). *Stranded objects*. Ithaca, N.Y.: Cornell University Press.

Segal, H. (1957). Notes on symbol formation. *International Journal of Psychoanalysis*, 38, 391–97.

Stern, D. (1985). *The interpersonal world of the infant*. New York: Basic Books.

Stoller, R. (1975). *Perversion: The erotic form of hatred*. New York: Pantheon.

Suleiman, S. (1985). Writing and motherhood. In C. Kahane, S. Garner, & M. Sprengnether (Eds.), *The (M)Other tongue* (352–77). Ithaca, N.Y.: Cornell University Press.

Suleiman, S. (1988). On maternal splitting: A propos of Mary Gordon's *Men and Angels. Signs*, 14, 25–41.

Suleiman, S. (1990). Feminist intertextuality and the laugh of the mother. In *Subversive intent*. Cambridge, Mass.: Harvard University Press.

Trevarthen, C. (1980). The foundations of intersubjectivity: Development of interpersonal and cooperative understanding in infants. In D. R. Olson (Ed.), *The social foundations of language and thought*. New York: Norton.

Winnicott, D. W. (1964). *The child, the family and the outside world*. Harmondsworth, England: Penguin.

Winnicott, D. W. (1971). The use of an object and relating through identifications. In *Playing and reality*. London: Tavistock.

ELSA FIRST

8 Mothering, Hate, and Winnicott

Mother has to be able to tolerate hating her baby
without doing anything about it. She cannot express it
to him. If, for fear of what she may do, she cannot hate
appropriately, when hurt by her child, she must fall
back on masochism, and I think it is this that gives rise
to the false theory of a natural masochism in
women.   D. W. Winnicott (1947, p. 202)

Mothering, like most work traditionally assigned to women, has
been simultaneously idealized and devalued by being considered
merely natural and so taken for granted. Part of the feminist
enterprise has been to rescue mothering from idealizations and
to reconsider it as a body of sophisticated skills and a form of
disciplined and thoughtful work.[1]

Winnicott, who coined the phrases "the ordinary devoted
mother" and "good-enough mothering," has been presumed to
belong with the idealizers. I would like to present an alternative
reading of Winnicott's work and suggest that he be considered an
ally in the project of valorizing maternal practice and someone
who added a new dimension to our consideration of maternal
subjectivity.

Winnicott's abiding interest was in the constitution of selfhood, and his focus was on what we might now call the two-
person situation—that is, how the provision of maternal care
facilitates or impedes the emergence of selfhood in the young
child. In regard to psychoanalytic technique, his concern was
how the implicit provisions of the analytic situation (such as
reliability and safety) also help or impede selfhood in the borderline patient. In addition, he was interested in how the man-

1. See, e.g., philosopher Sara Ruddick's book *Maternal Thinking*
(1989).

ner and timing of the analyst's contributions affect the patient's developing sense of self, a process he compared with the effects of early mother-child interactions.[2] Winnicott was a pediatrician before he was an analyst, and he continued a clinic practice as a pediatric psychiatrist throughout his analytic career.

The mothering situation and the analytic situation were both equally substantial to him and equally worthy of observation, study, and reflection. He examined problems in terms of analogies between what mothers do and what analysts do, or more accurately, in terms of analogies between the nursing couple and the analytic couple. The analogy was always between one dyad and another. He was not saying that analysts are mothers, or patients babies, but that at a certain level of work, the analyst tries to repair what mothers try to develop.

In this chapter I want to try a new project, which is to trace and study Winnicott's use of these analogies throughout his work. It is a tribute to Winnicott's throwaway, low-key style that the analogies per se have not attracted critical attention, although they are so central in his work. My concern here is to highlight the analogies as a way of rediscovering some of Winnicott's ideas of mothercraft.

Within psychoanalysis Winnicott's analogies have usually been read in one direction, with mothering assumed to be the familiar domain that he used to illumine hitherto unnoticed aspects of the analytic situation. We can also choose to read his analogies in the other direction, taking the analytic example as the familiar one and using it to widen our consideration of what mothers do. Winnicott's rhetoric sometimes worked in this way: He would begin by alluding to some moment or turning point in analytic work as if it were a common reference, and he might move from there to a point in early development or to an aspect of maternal care. From the detail of mothering he might then weave back to an aspect of treatment that in fact had not been salient before. Meanwhile, the reader's sense of the substance and significance of what mothers do would have been greatly enriched. The most fruitful reading is, therefore, to let the analogy play back and forth. Here I will consider the play of the analogy in four key papers (Winnicott, 1941, 1947, 1958, 1971), starting with the first appearance of the analogy.

Reaching for It

Winnicott's (1941) paper, "The Observation of Infants in a Set Situation," describes an experiment he liked to do routinely as part of a pediatric consultation. A shiny spatula was placed within reach of the baby, and Winnicott would ask the

2. Although not with the specificity of current observational infant research. Some of the interactional nature of early communication is elided in his idea of the "environment mother."

mother to hold the infant without any intervention, either to encourage or to discourage it. The babies had to be between five and thirteen months, because earlier they could not reliably reach for something they wanted, and later their range of interest had widened too much. Typically, the baby would reach for the shiny object and then undergo a moment of hesitation. If allowed to take its time, the infant would work through the hesitation and reach for the object in a more intentional way, proceeding to mouth it and to use it for play, perhaps pretending to feed mother or the observer.

Winnicott spoke of what took place during that moment of considered initiative as "accepting the reality of desire" (1941, p. 54). The entire paper is a complex psychoanalytic speculation on what that moment of hesitation meant. In this early paper, Winnicott was already interested in the interplay between the mother's ability to hold the baby calmly and allow it to have its own experience and the baby's ability to make desire a part of itself and to experience initiative, which he later described in "The Capacity to Be Alone" (1958) as a function of a relaxed state. We can see here the first adumbration of the idea of the *holding environment* and of the idea of the capacity for *the use of the object.*

At the end of the paper, almost casually, Winnicott suggests that analysts might consider their interpretations as glittering objects and note how the patient reaches for them. He thereby shifts the focus from content to process— to the patient's ability or inability to grasp the interpretation and play with it. In shifting the focus from content (what does the interpretation say?) to process (how does the patient respond to an attractive offering?), he causes our attention to dwell on the interchange between analyst and patient. And, in so doing, he draws the camera back and shows us the analysis as a two-person situation in which all possible difficulties in giving and in taking are played out. Here is what Winnicott writes:

> In the intuitive management of an infant, a mother naturally allows the full course of the various experiences, keeping this up until the infant is old enough to understand her point of view. She hates to break into such experiences of feeding and sleeping and defecating. In my observations [with the spatula] I artificially give the baby the right to complete an experience. . . .
>
> In psychoanalysis . . . there is something similar. . . . The analyst lets the patient set the pace. . . . Psychoanalysis differs from this work with infants in that the analyst is always groping . . . , trying to find out what, at the moment, is the shape and form of the thing that he has to offer the patient, that which he calls the interpretation. Sometimes the analyst will find it of value to look behind all the multitude of details and to see how far the analysis he is conducting could be thought of in the same terms as those in which one can think of the relatively simple set situation I have described. Each interpretation is a glittering object which excites the patient's greed. (1941, p. 67)

If we unfold the analogy, we can see that Winnicott portrays the mother as the one who presents the objective world to the baby.[3] If she does it so that she allows him to make his own relation to it, the baby (patient) will be able to grasp the toy (interpretation), play with it, and use it as a medium of communication. Similarly, there needs to be some equanimity in the way the analyst offers an interpretation that genuinely allows the patient to take it or leave it. No doubt such equanimity is predicated on the hard-won belief of the analyst that it really is up to the patient which interpretations are usable by her or him. Winnicott shows us how crucial it is to the infant's ability to make use of the world to be allowed to take its own time while being securely held. Here, the maternal skill is presented as though it were common knowledge, though Winnicott's articulation of it is actually new and it brings us to an unfamiliar view of analysis.

Being with Yourself

"The Capacity to Be Alone" (1958), a little paper once considered eccentric, offers an important view of the function of the "holding environment." The paper is based on the back-and-forth play of an analogy between the analytic situation and the mothering one. Here the specific analogy is between the psychoanalytic patient who is able, "perhaps for the first time," to fall silent on the couch, and an infant or small child contentedly playing "alone in the presence of its mother" (1958, pp. 29–30).

The image of the patient able to fall silent comes first. It refers to a relatively sophisticated adult experience, one that requires a skillful and informed forbearance on the part of the analyst. Winnicott writes: "In almost all of our psychoanalytic treatments there come times when the ability to be alone is important to the patient. Clinically this may be represented by a silent phase or a silent session, and this silence, far from being evidence of resistance, turns out to be an achievement on the part of the patient. Perhaps it is here that the patient has been able to be alone for the first time" (1958, p. 29).

Because Winnicott wants to predicate and imagine the *earliest* experiential form of this capacity for positive aloneness, infancy is brought in next. His main point is that a positive solitude, aloneness without withdrawal or fear, is a capacity that is grounded in relatedness and therefore can best be understood in a two-person context.[4]

Winnicott remarks that this sort of positive aloneness might correlate with various accepted concepts in psychoanalytic theory, such as Melanie Klein's (1940) internalization of the good object or with the so-called oedipal resolution, but he wants us to think of an experience that might be present from

3. Winnicott does have the idea here that the world of objects is symbolically the realm of the father and that in offering a thing, mother is offering father's thing.

4. He gives as an example contented aloneness along with another "after satisfactory intercourse."

earliest life, even before there are internal objects, and that might take sophisti-cated forms in adulthood.[5] There is a kinship between Winnicott's "holding" mother, who allows the baby initiative, and Stern's mother who allows the baby to terminate and initiate contact—separateness and relatedness are both pres-ent, in oscillation, from the start (Stern, 1971). As Winnicott summarizes:

> The main point of this contribution can now be stated. Although many types of experience go to the establishment of the capacity to be alone, there is one that is basic, and without a sufficiency of it the capacity to be alone does not come about; *this experience is that of being alone as an infant and small child in the presence of mother.* Thus the basis of the capacity to be alone is a paradox; it is the experience of being alone while someone else is present.
>
> Here is implied a rather special type of relationship, that between the infant or small child who is alone and the mother or mother-substitute who is in fact reliably present even if represented for the moment by a cot or a pram or the general atmosphere of the immediate environment. (1958, p. 30).

We may be rightly suspicious of representations of motherhood that call for unobtrusive reliability as a virtue. But there's an implied analogy here with the analyst, with whom the patient can first experience a safe solitude. This analogy allows us to begin to think about mother's ability to let baby be alone as much more than self-effacingness or the provision of a reliable setting; rather, we can think of it as a thoughtful skill—a nurturant letting-be—based on judgment and requiring confidence in the child's potential. Just as most analysts could say something about how they decide to let a patient stay silent, so most mothers could talk about how they decide a child is best left playing on its own, enjoying its own world. Mothers know when their own wish to play with the child might undermine the child's capacity to be alone rather than helpfully stimulate it. Winnicott's awareness of such sensitively calibrated judgments brings into focus the kind of thoughtful maternal work that mothers do. Like analysts, mothers have to be able to tolerate uncertainty about such technical choices and be alert for corrective feedback.

The capacity to be alone, then, is a capacity to be apart from others—not actively relating, though neither withdrawn nor craving, simply relaxed, as-if-held. In Winnicott's view this is the basis of initiative and meaningful activity:

5. Oedipal resolution would bring with it a kind of capacity for aloneness in the sense of independence and, in Winnicott's view, the capacity to tolerate the excited relation of parents to each other without being crippled by feelings of exclusion or crippling one's own sexuality, e.g., inhibiting childhood masturbation. Melanie Klein's establishment of the internal good object is roughly equivalent to object constancy: the abiding inner sense of an ongoing loving relation with an internal good mother, untroubled by too much anxiety/aggressiveness.

When alone in the sense that I am using the term, and only when alone, the infant is able to do the equivalent of what in an adult, would be called relaxing. The infant is able to become unintegrated, to flounder, to be in a state where there is no orientation, to be able to exist for a time without either being a reactor to an external impingement or an active person with a direction of interest or movement. The stage is set for an id impulse. . . . In the course of time there arrives a sensation or an impulse. In this setting the sensation or impulse will feel real and be truly a personal experience. (1958, p. 34)

When dealing with this letting-be aspect of the holding environment, Winnicott does not inquire into mothers' subjective experience. The image of the baby playing in its crib may serve to evoke contented preoccupation in the infant. But the crib is not what gives security. It is the mother's ability to hang-out contentedly preoccupied alongside her baby, while going-on-being her own alive self, and without necessarily engaging the baby. Mothers would, however, need to be able to imagine their babies at rest as selves with their own subjectivity, in order to leave them appropriately alone.

Allowing for Hate

The paper that opens the door and invites us to explore the subjectivity of mothers is "Hate in the Counter-Transference" (1947). The title retains the mildly shocking, supremely sensible tone it must have had at the time, proposing two taboo topics at once. This paper was written as a plea for acknowledging the naturalness and pervasiveness of the analyst's struggle with hatred toward the patient. Winnicott gathered all negative feelings from mild annoyance to murderousness under the name hatred to dignify them by putting them on an equal footing with love. The paper also includes a plea for "unsentimental" child rearing, by which he means acknowledging the naturalness and inevitability of parental ambivalence toward the child. Winnicott suggests that only with a mother who can acknowledge her own hatred can a child come to terms with its own aggression and use it in a healthy way. It also, notably, contains a list of everyday reasons why an ordinary mother "hates her baby."

Written in the immediate postwar period, the paper was shaped by the odd—or not so odd—conjunction of two issues of the time: the psychiatric abuse of electroshock and psychosurgery (leucotomy), which Winnicott saw as a form of violence against psychotic patients done out of *unacknowledged* "hate and fear"; and the resentimentalizing of housework and motherhood attending the postwar shift of women from the industrial work force back to the home. Here is what Winnicott writes:

Sentimentality is useless for parents, as it contains a denial of hate, and sentimentality in a mother is no good at all from the infant's point of view. It seems to me doubtful whether a human child as he develops is capable of tolerating the full extent of his own hate in a sentimental environment. He needs hate to hate.

If this is true, a psychotic patient in analysis cannot be expected to tolerate his hate of the analyst unless the analyst can hate him (e.g., experience and acknowledge this hatred within himself).

If all this is accepted there remains the question of the interpretation of the analyst's hate to the patient. (1947, p. 202)

This quote is a good example of the rapidity of the intercutting between the analytic and mothering situations, and of the depth of what Winnicott is trying to articulate.

Winnicott uses considerable tact to introduce the idea of the normalcy of countertransferential hatred. Moving from the hate that might be evoked by a violent psychotic patient, Winnicott goes on to speak of a normal baseline hatred felt in "ordinary analyses"—a "latent hatred" that is "ordinarily unfelt as such" because it is counterbalanced by the personal rewards of the work. The nature of the analyst's baseline hate is here for the reader to recognize in Winnicott's famous remark: "Moreover, as an analyst I have ways of expressing hate. Hate is expressed by the existence of the end of the hour. This is true even when there is no difficulty whatsoever and the patient is pleased to go" (1947, p. 197).

What hate is this? This is a hate that is almost indistinguishable from self-respect, a hate that says, "I have my limits, and the fact that I am able to set limits to your use of me is expressed by the fixed end of the session." So a mother's need for an "end of the hour" would understandably exist even in a good mother-child relationship. The end of the hour signifies that we will not be abused. Abuse begins when analyst or mother deals with stress by masochistic compliance (for example, being temporarily paralyzed by defensiveness or guilt). The *existence of the end of the hour* means "I can stay connected with you during a stressful situation because of your special needs at the moment, but also because I know there is an end in sight."

Winnicott also uses the infant-patient analogy to argue that patients, especially very disturbed ones, are stressful to the degree that they cannot relate to the other as a whole person with whom they can identify. Similarly, the wear and tear on mothers has to do with the degree to which the child can see the mother's point of view.[6]

The analyst's struggle with his potential "unfelt" hatred is central to the maintenance of "neutrality" in the analytic stance. As the analyst has to maintain a kind of optimal on-the-job mental availability and flexibility, so an important part of the job of mothering is to maintain the capacity for a nurturant

---

6. The infant-patient analogy is also part of his argument for allowing therapeutic regression within the treatment without trying to interpret the patient out of it prematurely: "An analyst has to display all the patience and tolerance and reliability of a mother devoted to her infant; has to recognize the patient's wishes as needs . . . and has to seem to want to give what is really only given because of the patient's needs" (1947, p. 202).

"neutrality" and emotional availability, rather than an incapacitating degree of guilt, envy, rivalry, or hurt. Winnicott also alerts us to the risk of a masochistic solution to the task of being hurt by the baby without retaliating: this is the martyr mother who lives "for" or "through" the child. Winnicott also recognizes, however, that the analytic framework and the analyst's social position protect the analyst from stresses that frequently debilitate mothers, particularly the stress of economic insecurity.

Winnicott lists the analyst's everyday rewards, unsystematically, as:

Analysis is my chosen job, the way I feel I will best deal with my own guilt, the way I can express myself in a constructive way.

I get paid, or I am in training to gain a place in society by psychoanalytic work.

I am discovering things.

I get immediate rewards through identification with the patient, who is making progress, and I can see still greater rewards some way ahead, after the end of the treatment.

Moreover, as an analyst I have ways of expressing hate. Hate is expressed by the existence of the end of the hour. (1947, p. 196)

A list of why even a devoted mother hates her baby is invoked by Winnicott to show that sometimes hatred is fairly innocent, not pathological or incompetent or wicked. If a nursing mother is allowed to dislike it when her baby "makes her doubt herself," then the analyst is allowed to dislike a patient's accusations or disregard (p. 201).

Here is Winnicott's unsystematic list of "reasons why an ordinary mother hates her baby":

The baby is not her own (mental) conception.
    The baby is not the one of childhood play, father's child, brother's, etc.
    The baby is not magically produced.[7]
    The baby is a danger to her body in pregnancy and at birth.
    The baby is an interference with her private life, a challenge to preoccupation.[8]
    To a greater or lesser extent a mother feels that her own mother demands a baby, so that the baby is produced to placate her mother.
    The baby hurts her nipples even by suckling, which is at first a chewing activity.
    He is ruthless, treats her as scum, an unpaid servant, a slave.
    She has to love him, excretions and all, at any rate at the beginning, till he has doubts about himself.

7. We could summarize these as the baby is a real baby, not an ideal one and not the imaginary dream baby of various childhood love situations. For Winnicott this is a legitimate disappointment that mothers have to deal with.

8. As I write this, three girls are playing a game of hide and seek that consists of seeing who can creep up behind my chair unnoticed.

He tries to hurt her, periodically bites her, all in love.

He shows disillusionment about her.

His excited love is cupboard love, so that having got what he wants he throws her away like orange peel.

The baby must at first dominate, he must be protected from coincidences, life must unfold at the baby's rate, and all this needs his mother's continuous and detailed study. For instance, she must not be anxious when holding him, etc.

At first he does not know at all what she does or what she sacrifices for him. Especially he cannot allow for her hate.

He is suspicious, refuses her good food, and makes her doubt herself, but eats well with his aunt.

After an awful morning with him she goes out, and he smiles at a stranger, who says, "Isn't he sweet?"

If she fails him at the start she knows he will pay her out forever.

He excites her but frustrates—she mustn't eat him or trade in sex with him. (p. 201)

This list, with its heaping up of the tragic and the trivial, is so endearing it appears almost sentimental. It is still, of course, based on Winnicott's image of an ordinary devoted mother whose main and perhaps sole devotion at this time of her life is to the baby and to doing a good job with it. Mother's other work, interests, desires, needs, and pleasures appear only as "preoccupations," which the infant "challenges." The tone, however, is collegial: mother is a whole person on a job, perhaps on a job with some sense of vocation, as much as is the analyst whose job satisfactions are listed earlier. Both jobs involve the satisfaction of profound wishes (to repair damage, to help develop, and so on) and dirty work. "She has to love him, excretions and all," is a temporary job requirement only, not a requirement of infinite benevolence.

The most searching and original question raised in "Hate" is whether and when it might be helpful for the patient to realize the analyst's responsive hate. Winnicott's initial example here is of the foster child who, once he has gained hope, tests the foster parents to see if they are genuinely enough attached to him to feel "hate." Winnicott moves from this example to the assertion that "in certain stages of certain analyses, the analyst's hate is actually sought by the patient, and what is then needed is hate that is objective. If the patient seeks objective or justified hate, he must be able to reach it, else he cannot feel he can reach objective love" (1947, p. 199).

In summarizing an analytic case, the clinician often finds that a consideration of negative countertransference is a revealing organizer of key issues. Similarly, in studying the tasks of mothering or in working with mothers, one may find that an exploration of the stresses involved in containing what might be considered the negative countertransference could be a helpful organizer for the mother's self-reporting and reflection. The question for a mother would not be "what's wrong with you that you are angry?" but "let's notice what makes you angry in order to locate what parts of this job you are finding difficult and how it could be made less stressful."

Maternal Resilience

Winnicott's thinking about the containment of hatred was extended in his paper "The Use of the Object" (1971). "Hate" (1947) is about the importance of the analyst's or the mother's ability to acknowledge and accept the legitimate hatred felt toward the one dependent on his or her care. "Use" is about the importance of the analyst's or the mother's "survival" of the patient's or infant's "attacks," by which Winnicott means attacks on their ability to be a competent analyst or mother. His most original idea here—set out, again, by analogies between the analytic process and mothering—is that it is the analyst's or mother's "survival" that enables certain patients and children to arrive at appreciating and respecting other people as separate individuals. In the case of the infant, it is the discovery that mother is not destroyed by the "ruthlessness" of the baby's passions that shows that mother is "out there" and "usable."

The territory covered in both "Hate" and "Use" is hate in a two-person relationship: how it is communicated, received, contained, or acted out, and how it may be modulated or transmuted by the way the other person deals with it. Remember that in "Hate" Winnicott suggests that sometimes the child or patient needs to know that he or she has been able to have an effect on the mother or analyst—has been able to stir hatred—in order to know that the other person cares.[9] The mother or analyst who acts as if she or he cannot be touched by anything the child or patient feels creates an unreal, useless situation. But the mother or analyst who reacts as if she or he felt personally threatened or damaged by the pain or anger of the child or patient also creates a useless situation in which no growth can occur.

A clarification of terminology is called for here, because Winnicott's definition of "use" in this paper is opposite to ordinary parlance.[10] Making good use of another person, in Winnicott's sense, involves acknowledging the individual's separate otherness, appreciating what the person has to offer and acknowledging that you are getting something from outside yourself. Not being able to use could mean wasting what the other has to offer (Winnicott, 1989).[11] Not being

---

9. Knowing you can stir hatred does not have to be the same as soliciting a beating, however. The sadomasochistic situation, it should be clarified, is the opposite of what Winnicott had in mind. In the sadomasochistic situation, pain is inflicted and accepted as a token substitute for caring, in a context of imaginary or real indifference and anonymity.

10. He contrasts making good "use" of an object with merely "relating" to an object. Usually we mean the opposite: by using someone, we mean exploiting, abusing an object; relating to someone has a positive connotation.

11. It could be a way of using the analyst to waste (ignore, reject) what she has to offer for some time, and experience her ability to tolerate and survive being wasted—e.g., that her need to be appreciated and effective is not overriding (Winnicott, 1971, p. 233). This applies in parenting also.

able to "use," in the terms of contemporary psychopathology, would refer to borderline or narcissistic states in which there is an "omnipotent" denial of any meaningful dependency or interdependency. Before the acceptance of otherness and difference the analyst's interpretations may evoke wholesale compliance or rejection rather than real give and take.

According to Winnicott there is a particular turning point in the psycho-analytic process when a patient shifts into being able to "use" the analyst: "With certain patients, there comes a moment or a place in the analysis when one can say that whereas up to now the patient has in some sense not used the analyst, now and from now on the patient is using the analyst. Something has happened in the patient which makes this change of language right" (1989, pp. 233–234).

In "Use," Winnicott characterizes the turning point at which the patient becomes able to use the analyst as the point at which one can begin to see the end of treatment. If a child is able to make good use of what her parents have to offer, we are similarly able to feel confident about her growing up to indepen-dence. Winnicott also notes that the patient who has reached this turning point finds that others in his everyday life are now able to make good use of him: "Closely following this there is the corresponding alteration in the experience of the patient, who now finds himself or herself being used. This can give great satisfaction to the patient and can be a reward for the years of blind groping which analysis can seem to be" (1989, p. 234).

This marker could be thought of as the reverse side of what Klein (1957) meant by a capacity for gratitude—a capacity to give based on a sense of personal worthwhileness. Again, we can look for this in early mother-child interactions and throughout growing up. Can the parent "use" what the child has to offer? And, likewise, can the child "use" what the parent has to offer?

Winnicott reflected that he could write "Use" only because of a shift in his own analytic technique in the direction of less interpretive intervention and more attention to the patient's own development within the analytic process. His position is summed up in an often quoted remark: "I think I interpret mainly to let the patient know the limits of my understanding" (1989, p. 86). In this newer clinical stance, Winnicott came to feel that what really brought the patient out of a self-enclosed world was the repeated demonstration that the analyst could remain himself or herself through the patient's storms. This meant not withdrawing and not striking back; this was the analyst's "survival": "In psychoanalytic practice, the positive changes that come about in this area [being able to appreciate otherness and to make good use of others] can be profound. They do not depend on interpretive work. They depend on the an-alyst's survival of the attacks, which involves and includes the absence of a quality change to [toward] retaliation" (Winnicott, 1971, p. 91).

The whole paper is a meditation on what attack and survival might mean in the analytic situation and in the early mothering situation, using each to illumi-nate the other. This survival is not the minimal survival of the victim, but implies resilience—that the mother or analyst has not been damaged in her ability to be a person. For both analyst and mother "not to survive, . . . also means to suffer change in quality, in attitude" (p. 93).

By "attacks" he does not mean simply criticism or denigration or threats.[12] "Attacks" refer to whatever makes it difficult for the analyst to remain fully "alive" and himself, as a working analyst, in the session. "Attacks" might be attempts to subvert the analyst's integrity or to impair his attentiveness, capacity for responsiveness, and ability to think.

Similarly, he hypothesizes it is the mother's "survival" that carries the infant over to the perception of the object as an external phenomenon, the recognition of it as an entity in its own right. In his own clinical practice, Winnicott observed that some mothers are better able than others to carry their babies over into a realm of reciprocity. The babies who have been "seen well" through this phase are more assertive and more able to use their aggression constructively.

Winnicott dramatizes the earliest moment of this in an imaginary metaphysical dialogue: "The subject says to the object: 'I destroyed you,' and the object is there to receive the communication. From now on the subject says: 'Hullo object!' 'I destroyed you.' 'I love you. You have value for me because of your survival of my destruction of you.' 'While I am loving you I am all the time destroying you in (unconscious) *fantasy.*'"

But what then is the destruction "in unconscious fantasy" (elsewhere the "backcloth of destruction") that he says from then on enhances the reality of the object? This is the most obscure point in the argument. It requires our intuitive assent and needs to be given specific content on the basis of our clinical experience of patients' anxieties about their own destructiveness. Something like: "I imagine that if I use you I am using you up, exhausting you, obliterating you." Also: "If I assert myself there will be no room for you." Perhaps also: "I wish to have all of you, all to myself"; or, "I might have destroyed you in my exuberance. You were blotted out for me, but I see you remain."

Winnicott confesses to having the idea that he is suggesting a major revision of the theory of aggression. I think it fair to say that he is moving toward a two-person account of aggression: that a child's aggression (and aggressive fantasies) contains within it at any point something of how it was received and responded to by the object: "*There is no anger* in the destruction of the object to which I am referring, though there could be said to be joy at the object's survival. From this moment, or arising out of this phase, the object is *in fantasy* always being destroyed. This quality of 'always being destroyed' makes the reality of the surviving object felt as such, strengthens the feeling tone, and contributes to object constancy. The object can now be used" (1971, p. 93).

This is mythology—a story of origins. But it is meaningful as an account of an aspect of the work that both mothers and analysts do. Winnicott's analysis helps us understand the patient's gradual appreciation of the survival of the analyst and the child's appreciation of the survival of the mother.

12. He mentions danger to the analyst's life as a limiting case—e.g. "where the patient carries a gun, the work cannot be done."

What makes for maternal resilience? What helps an analyst not be hurt is often the capacity to identify with the potentially wholesome or object-seeking knife edge of the aggression. Is the knife edge taken as an invitation to an old sadomasochistic game or as an effort at individuation? This is often the issue in treatment or in child rearing. Can we turn a tantrum into a communication without letting ourselves be hurt?[13]

One way we as analysts maintain neutrality under attack is to identify with the potentially constructive aspect of the aggression, even while the patient may still feel it as only destructive. Mothers under fire do this as well. So a mother would need to be on good terms with her own aggression, to feel where it has been constructive to her, to be able to identify with the child's aggression and play with it resiliently. This is an argument for helping mothers appreciate the reality and validity of their hate as well as of their love.

Resilience, analytic or maternal, requires acceptance of aggressivity and activity in oneself, as a part of one's own aliveness, rather than fearing that any assertion of one's own rights will be destructive to the other. A mother, to stay resilient, has to recognize potentially constructive energy in the attack and to identify with it and even, for the child's sake, to enjoy it while protecting herself. That is, a mother can relish the child's aggression without feeling she must accept being hurt and without feeling she has to present herself as devoid of a fighting spirit. The mother who feels she has rights is better able to defend them without retaliation.

A Wild Patience

Winnicott increasingly saw the therapeutic process as one in which the therapist's task is to find ways of continuing to *be with* the patient in the session— a "being with" that enables the patient to come more into contact with herself, thus facilitating the patient's growth and individuation. His insistence that the analyst's way of being in the session was of basic importance often took the form of a droll simplicity, as in his dictum that in doing analysis all he aimed at was "keeping alive, keeping well, keeping awake, . . . being myself and behaving myself" (1962, p. 166).

He thought about these matters by comparing them with what he observed mothers do that seemed to make it more or less possible for babies to go on being themselves and to use their endowment while "in the presence of" and in relationship with other people.

He also became increasingly aware of how challenging a task this seemingly simple going-on-being-oneself in the presence of the disturbed patient was. In

13. The overfamiliar and banalized example of this is the recognition of the positive aspect of rebellion in adolescence. Winnicott wrote this paper in 1968, the year of the student uprisings, although he began thinking about it several years earlier. The connection in his mind between resilience and rebellion is clear in a talk he gave to the British Student Health Service.

fact, for some patients at some times, challenging and attacking the analyst's aplomb or liveliness was their way of getting better. Discovering that someone else could stand them, they could begin to stand themselves.

Winnicott told Piggle, the little girl he treated until she was five years old, that he was glad she had finished using him because now he could return to being all the other Winnicotts he was instead of just the special-treatment Winnicott created by her (1977, p. 191).[14] Similarly, mothers need to be able to return to all the other selves they can be before the child is finished using them to grow up with.

Being a mother is in some ways even more difficult and perhaps in some ways easier—at least more directly gratifying—than Winnicott imagined. At times his vision of mothering is a little more strained or constrained than it need be, as in his depiction of the mother who has "to seem to want to give what is really only given because of the infant's needs" (1947, p. 203). The difficulties and complexities of going on being a mother while being other things as well (in and out of the presence of the child) are not addressed by Winnicott. On the other hand, his rich analogies between the two tasks help us realize how complex and substantial the work of mothering is, and how maintaining maternal resilience is central to this craft. And allowing the mother to be a person first is the key to maternal resilience.

Although Winnicott never thought through what maternal resilience might or would mean in terms of maternal subjectivity, it is clear that pure patience—the patience of the Madonna, angelic patience—is not what he had in mind. What Adrienne Rich (1981) called "a wild patience" is probably closer.

References

First, E. (1978). A good doctor. *New York Review of Books*. August 17.

Klein, M. (1957). Envy and gratitude. In *Envy and gratitude & other works, 1946–1963*. New York: Delta, 1977.

Klein, M. (1940). Mourning and its relation to manic-depressive states. In *Love, guilt and reparation*. New York: Delta, 1977.

Rich, A. (1981). *A wild patience has taken me this far*. New York: Norton.

Ruddick, S. (1989). *Maternal thinking*. Boston: Beacon Press.

Stern, D. N. (1971). A micro-analysis of the mother-infant interaction: Behaviors regulating social contact between a mother and her three-and-a-half-month-old twins. *Journal of American Academy of Child Psychiatry,* 10, 501–17.

Stern, D. N. (1985). *The interpersonal world of the infant*. New York: Basic Books.

Winnicott, D. W. (1941). The observation of infants in a set situation. In *Through pediatrics to psycho-analysis*. New York: Basic Books, 1975.

Winnicott, D. W. (1947). Hate in the counter-transference. In *Through pediatrics to psycho-analysis*. New York: Basic Books, 1975.

14. For more on Winnicott and *The Piggle,* see Elsa First (1978).

Winnicott, D. W. (1958). The capacity to be alone. In *The maturational process and the facilitating environment*. New York: International Universities Press, 1965.

Winnicott, D. W. (1962). The aims of psycho-analytical treatment. In *The maturational process and the facilitating environment*. New York: International Universities Press, 1965.

Winnicott, D. W. (1968). Adolescent immaturity. In *Home is where we start from*. New York: Norton.

Winnicott, D. W. (1968). The use of the word "use." In *Psycho-analytic explorations*. Cambridge, Mass.: Harvard University Press, 1989.

Winnicott, D. W. (1971). The use of an object and relating through identifications. In *Playing and reality*. New York: Basic Books.

Winnicott, D. W. (1977). *The piggle*. New York: International Universities Press.

Winnicott, D. W. (1989). *Psycho-analytic explorations*. Cambridge, Mass.: Harvard University Press.

DONNA BASSIN

9 Maternal Subjectivity in the Culture of Nostalgia: Mourning and Memory

. . . Memory speaks:
You cannot live on me alone
you cannot live without me
I'm nothing if I'm just a roll of film
stills from a vanished world . . .
left for another generation's
restoration and framing . . .
    Adrienne Rich (1991, p. 43)

Adrienne Rich's poem evokes a tension between memory as an animated and interactive process and memory as a collection of inert images and representations. Her imagery depicts what psychoanalysis attempts to cultivate, an opportunity for the self's engagement with the past. Through memory the self is provided with a sense of history and the potential for renewal. Rich metaphorically contrasts this dynamic quality of mind with the static image of a roll of film left for the next generation to frame and place outside itself. The fantasy of transforming the self through memory is dependent on an object outside the self, and the capacities that underlie transformation—agency and activity—are tied to a past that is sought and wistfully longed for in an array of objects of affection.

Other cultural commentators have written about America's preoccupation with its past and its great difficulty in recognizing the past other than in fossilized souvenirs and keepsakes (Hines, 1987). Stephen Drucker (1991) writes, "these days it is possible to feel nostalgic about just about everything." This general observation regarding contemporary culture's nostalgia preoccupation, specifically applied to the problem of maternal subjectivity, is the point of departure for this chapter. I shall discuss the passive character of this nostalgic relation to our childhood past as well as its potential to develop into a psychologically dynamic memorial that underpins maternal activity, initiative, and agency.

The nostalgic relationship to childhood speaks to the difficulty of making internal and one's own the active transformative functions of the mothering other and represents a state of arrested mourning; the dynamics of nostalgia prevent a true identification with the transformational aspects of maternal practice.[1] This nostalgia relationship locks us into a sentimental and passive relationship to our earliest caretaker (initially mother). As Winnicott (1986) pointed out, the issue of memory is tied to recognition of the mother. He states: "Children grow up and become in turn fathers and mothers, but, on the whole, they do not grow up to know and acknowledge just what their mothers did for them at the start" (p. 124). Winnicott was not alluding to a lack of gratitude, but rather to a lack of recognition.

In her work on intersubjectivity, Jessica Benjamin (1988, 1990) has illuminated the need for recognition of the mother as children journey toward their own subjectivity. Recognition of the mother requires the ability to contain and tolerate difference, awareness of the separateness of the mother, and freedom from the wish that she had been different. Gaining this freedom requires access to and use of the dynamic memory states that are characteristic of the early relationship with the mother; and this in turn implies a process of remembering and recognizing a past that no longer exists in its original form (Odgen, 1990). This process enables us to be influenced by and to use our history and helps us cultivate good mental representations of significant others. Without recognition of our origins and our maternal history, parenting and other potentially generative work may become repetitious, nostalgic enactments.

Bollas (1987, 1989) contributes to a generative understanding of the maternal relationship in his amplification of the transformational object. According to Bollas, transformational object-seeking is an endless memorial search for something in the future that resides in the past and is associated with a transformation of the self. The transformational aspect of the mother is her dynamic activity—she is the mother who makes things happen. To the degree that the growing child identifies with her power and agency, the child will in turn develop

1. This phrase was suggested to me by Virginia Goldner in her discussion of an earlier draft of this essay presented at the 1992 spring meeting of the Division of Psychoanalysis, American Psychological Association. I am grateful to Dr. Goldner for her discussion, which led me to a much fuller understanding of my own work. I also wish to express my appreciation to my co-editors, Meryle Kaplan and Margaret Honey, and to Christopher Bollas, Pearl Ellen Gordon, and Daniel Hill for their support in the development of this chapter.

a sense of her or his own efficacy. It is the *metabolization* of this process of identification with the transformational mother that I believe facilitates and propels a regenerative cycle. The life cycle task of generativity, in the tradition of Erikson (1950), encompasses hope and a belief in change through the next generation and in one's own creations.

The current nostalgia among baby boomers for their fifties childhood is evidenced by the increased seeking and collecting of retro artifacts and the surging increase of flea markets and vintage stores. The fifties was itself an era built on nostalgia for better times, and illusions of transformation and utopian possibilities were promoted after the deprivations of wartime. Collectors of nostalgia, however, are doing more than just recycling, collecting, and hoarding these fossilized objects; they are attempting to collect material reminders of a utopian past. This activity is closely related to the means and procedures of transformation that originate in the mother-infant matrix and that, when internalized within the self, contribute to the development of subjectivity. The fantasies surrounding nostalgic activities can be appreciated as a reflection of powerful affects and anxieties that guard against dependency, fragmentation, unresolved narcissism, and powerlessness. I would also suggest, however, that these fantasies represent an attempt, thwarted, but an attempt nevertheless, at mourning play.[2] I define mourning play in a nostalgic relationship as an activity of the ego that both mourns the loss of difference and celebrates, playfully, the possibility of oneness regained.[3] Attempts to refind the mother and rehabilitate a maternal sensibility require passage through this difficult and most resisted process of mourning.

What Is "The Fifties"?

In the fifties plastic plants were manufactured on a large scale—they looked amazingly real and needed no tending. Plastic contact paper was invented—any surface could look like something it wasn't, marble, wood, even bricks with ivy growing over them. Paint-by-number kits were introduced—anyone could be an artist. Frozen T.V. dinners first appeared in the market—a cook could turn out a meal of turkey, sweet potatoes, and peas in under half an hour. Kitchen utensils and household items were toylike, seemingly freeing mom for leisure pursuits

---

2. I have borrowed the term *mourning play* from Eric Santner's brilliant analysis of mourning and memory in postwar Germany. Mourning play is a variant of Walter Benjamin's analysis of *Trauerspiel,* which literally means "mourning play" and refers to the German baroque dramas. Santner suggests that "the postmodernist appropriates the Benjaminian analysis of *mourning* play as one of mourning *play"* (1990, p. 12).

3. This definition of *mourning play* is how Loewald (1988) describes the activity of sublimation. Loewald has advanced the traditional and limited psychoanalytic understanding of sublimation as a defense, albeit a good defense, to a state of ego development. Loewald's expansion fleshes out the proactive use of symbolism in this oscillation of subject/object. Here differences are not transcended or ignored but played with.

and hobbies. Credit cards increased Americans' financial power—the possibilities were unlimited. Girls were girls and glamorous, like Marilyn Monroe, and boys were just boys.

Actually, the fifties as lived, and not ironed out by time, was a mixed era and constructed in part by the media's exploitation of its own economic considerations. As well, the fifties is only the most contemporary cultural attempt at realizing utopian transformative fantasies. For example, Susan Buck-Morss argues that beginning in the late 1880s, the world's fairs aspired to provide the utopian fairyland for the masses by demonstrating how the Industrial Revolution would bring material realization of paradise (1989). The "Age of Populuxe," Thomas Hines's designation for the fifties American celebration of the big breast, is another historical moment with a subculture of illusion and promise of transformation.

For the baby boomers, the voices of the fifties provided a maternal sound. The home and the objects within it provided the maternal body. There is, however, a shame that we—the daughters of the Donna Reed and Harriet Nelson generation—feel, and a disgrace that academics feel in relation to the culture of the fifties. This culture served to filter out the toxicity of the cold war, the Korean War, the Alger Hiss case, the perfecting of the H-bomb, the turmoil over the integration of Little Rock schools, and Senator Joseph McCarthy's red-baiting. The repressed emerged in a projected form in our experience of the noxious "reds," "aliens from other plants," or nature out of control.

Stuart Ross underlined both the missionary task and the anxiety that many intellectuals in the postwar period felt concerning mass culture as a profitable opiate used for social control. This reductive view has since been modified to include an awareness of how culture "re-articulates desires that have a deep resonance in people's daily lives" (1989, p. 52).

The subculture of the "retro fifties"—as distinct from the actual fifties historical era—offers a productive analogy for the process of transformational object-seeking. Images cherished and perpetuated in the nostalgic subculture are a manifestation of the problematics and pleasures of the fantasy of the transformational mother. The fifties celebration of America as the all-providing magical breast and the fantasy of utopian transformation is associated with a metamorphosis of the self. The culture of the actual fifties was partly created out of a nostalgia for better times and out of a belief in the progress afforded by science and technology.

In short, as a country recovering from the deprivations of the wartime years, America was full of itself and its possibilities. Mothers "freed" from their obligation to serve the war effort were shuttled back to the home front to tend to their families once again. After the war the craving for all that Americans had been deprived of, including the lost mom and a sense of security, could be symbolically realized. Consumers recovering from wartime deprivations wanted it all and were led to believe they could have it all. Manufacturers utilized new materials created during the war to fashion products never before available on a mass-market scale. The desire for these objects was exploited materially by postwar industries' eagerness to create markets for the newfound materials. Objects like the newly designed electric blender with buttons promised quicker and more efficient work, although in actuality the buttons were no more efficient than the rheostat dial they replaced.

Clinical Commentary

I shall explore the meaning of the nostalgic use of memory by presenting the case material of two middle-aged patients who displayed a compelling interest in flea markets, garage sales, and fifties-vintage objects. Resistance to mourning tied these two women to an endless search for keepsakes that would provide them with transformational experiences and capacity. For these women and others scouring the flea market "field of dreams," souvenirs from a childhood past became vehicles for a relationship with a generative transformational mother.

Mrs. B, a child during the fifties, experienced great anxiety around what she perceived to be unresolvable conflicts about mothering and her professional life. At work, she suffered from panic attacks regarding the safety of her child, poignantly remarking that having a child was like "having your heart live outside your body." Her increasing anger and frustration was often displaced to her husband, whom she viewed as able to separate from their child without psychic pain. Mrs. B struggled to make decisions that she experienced as requiring her to choose between herself and her child. Despite her intellectual understanding of her need to take care of herself, she felt herself to be her daughter's object. Mrs. B was an ardent collector. She rummaged around in the yard sales and the bric-a-brac of flea markets. The objects she sought satisfied her need for control and stimulated the excitement of getting a bargain, something for nothing. Mrs. B was looking for something she called "comfortness from the past." She depended on the clutter of objects she had accumulated while disavowing any larger meaning they might hold for her.

What was she actually shopping for? What was the fifties dream she remembered as she tried to recollect herself through these weekly siftings and browsings? She was looking not just for comfort but for generative aesthetics, sensuous and fun. The objects she found—lunch boxes imprinted with pictures of early superheroes, old radios giving off the sound of crackling tubes, brightly colored kitchen clocks with loud ticks—represented more than just possessions. Someone else's clutter and castaways offered her renewal: an object was recycled from valued possibility to discarded possession and back to valued possibility. Possibility for what? She wasn't sure. There was a pleasure in seeking and finding that sometimes led to the discovery of something momentarily satisfying. These objects were never quite right, however, and her search would begin again. There was a fifties dream here, she thought, tied to her mother and her own relentless preoccupation with finding a better place to live. She craved a move to the suburbs on one register, hoping to refind there a mother who could mother her daughter and herself in a way she could not.

Another patient, Miss A, was a shopkeeper specializing in vintage clothing and retro artifacts. She spoke of the glamour of the object, of getting the "real thing." She discussed the thrill of acquiring a dress that was just like one she had had as a child. She didn't remember much about kindergarten—it was all locked up in a plaid taffeta dress with a dotted Swiss collar. She had lost memories; she said that she didn't have a "good sense of history" and so she collected to remember. What she wanted to know and remember was not clear. But it was clear that she was trying to make sense of her own activities, to gather some understanding of what she was doing. She was aware that she was involved in something other than buying, collecting, and selling.

She walked with her head down "looking for stuff." She didn't know precisely what she was looking for; if she did, she said, she wouldn't be in the vintage store business. She knew immediately, however, what it was when she found it: "I found the genuine Dale Evans mug; my fingers grasped the handle; it fit exactly; the price was right; I knew it was mine." She opted to go with the pleasure of seeking, which would inevitably lead to the discovery of something. Despite her economic needs, an object could not be sold until another more satisfying one entered her shop.

Her own mother, a major collector since the forties, had filled Miss A's childhood home with the bric-a-brac and kitsch of the fifties. Miss A's attempt to extinguish the clutter and to order her life brought her to move to a stark loft space during her treatment. After some time, she felt that something was missing in her new home, and she created what she called her "homey altar." This altar was constructed out of pieces of her baby blanket, china roosters, figures from her mother's kitchen, and other more recent keepsakes from her life. These keepsakes were more than a collection of souvenirs; she claimed they provided an internal space in which she could continue to renew herself and establish a sense of place.

Despite the fact that both patients reported active and competent mothers, neither spoke much about them. But the "transformational mother" was remarkably present for both women, appearing for Miss A as her next "major find" for her shop or her "homey altar," and for Mrs. B in the longed-for home in the suburbs or in her relationship with her daughter. Eventually, as the transference developed, the analysis itself took over as the ultimate transformational possibility. In the transference, both patients looked to me for the "big and pivotal interpretations" that might bring about change. They used interpretations, however, as they used nostalgic objects. Transformation was seen not as an interaction or as an identification of earlier ego change associated with the mother but as a property belonging to the analyst.

Despite disparate presentations of their complaints, these two patients shared a preoccupation with nostalgic activities and fantasies. For both, a never-experienced present, a never-arriving future, and a lack of generativity and agency related, at least in part, to the lack of a detailed sense of a dynamic past that was usable in the present. They had foreclosed mourning, focusing instead on some variant of a nostalgic object that resided safely away in an unclear past

and unattainable future. Both were, to varying degrees, eventually able to articulate their unconscious organizing fantasy of a transformational object and to
begin the mourning process that facilitated an identification with the transformational aspects of the mother. The analysis helped them see their nostalgic
preoccupations as nascent attempts to identify and recognize an internal maternal history.

Nostalgia

Nostalgia as exemplified in the experiences of these patients is an incomplete
mourning—an attempt to reenact reunion with the lost object. It is a bittersweet pleasure, tarnished with the adult knowledge of loss. Although the
nostalgic fantasy seeks metamorphosis and transformation, it is devoid of a
sense of internal agency and thus remains trapped in a process of endless
seeking. Susan Stewart (1984), in her reference to nostalgia as the "desire for
desire," captures the endless longing of the nostalgic state. The transformation
the nostalgic seeks is assumed to reside in a situation or an object rather than in
the self. The urge to hold onto the object that cannot be properly mourned
precludes investment in or libidinization of a new object. Thus, this pathology of
mourning—manifested in wistful nostalgic sentiment—is an obstacle to
growth beyond infantile wishes of mother.

Freud (1914), in his paper on remembering and repeating, pointed to a state
of mind in which "the patient does not remember anything of what he has
forgotten and repressed, but acts it out. He reproduces it not as a memory but as
an action; he repeats it, without, of course, knowing that he is repeating it" (p.
150). The pleasure of nostalgia resides in the search for the old object, and thus
the seeker avoids the awareness of loss. This leads to an indefinite quest for an
object that can never be found—a quest that temporarily fulfills desire. The
holding onto the nostalgic memory is one way of holding onto the lost mother.
In the nostalgic relationship the connection to the mother goes largely unrecognized. As a result, mourning for the mother or powerful transformative other is
resisted, and the nostalgic continually seeks to duplicate the transformational
relationship outside of the self, rather than re-create it anew within. In contrast,
mourning and subsequent identification with the active generative image of
mother enables a transformation from longing for the infantile good mother to
locating a dynamic maternal subject within.

I will return to the case material to examine an aspect of both patients'
activity that involves mourning play and points toward a cultural strategy that
makes use of transformational mother fantasies. Through acceptance and interpretation of transformational fantasies in which I, as the analyst, was alternately
a transformational object and the passive nostalgic ineffectual self, a new aspect
of each patient emerged.

Miss A began, albeit with a smile, to recognize her resistance to mourning.
She made a last-ditch effort to re-create me and the analysis as yet another

nostalgic state. Her difficulty in relinquishing the object tie to the transformational mother (among others) was apparent. Owing to avoidable financial difficulties, she orchestrated a situation wherein she could no longer pay her already low fee and thus once again would have to give up something she valued. Her fantasy was to leave treatment for a little while without actually terminating the relationship. In this way, she could imagine herself in treatment while simultaneously thinking about what she was missing. Her focus did change, however, as she gradually experienced her loss and her grief over what was missing for her and over my having (like her mother) disappointed her. These feelings surfaced, ushering in a welcome change. She was no longer compelled to leave the relationship in order to relish nostalgia's bittersweet pain.

Mrs. B was initially unable to resist her nostalgic longings for her own mother in her attempt to recollect her own internal transformational activity. She experienced herself only as an object—and a mothering object at that. Currently, rather than seeing herself merely as an object for her daughter, she is detecting glimmers of herself as a woman who has chosen to mother. Mrs. B's relationship to her objects has changed as well. Rather than focusing on ownership and control over someone else's discarded possessions, she is beginning to experience the objects she has collected as valued possibilities and as inspiration for transformation. For Mrs. B, recycling junk into possibility was an ideal metaphor for the psychic activity that was simultaneously occurring—the transition from an inert use of objects and things to a relational creative interplay with the self. Now that more and more of the world was invested with pieces of herself, she could allow new experiences to feel familiar and more homey. For example, she was able to let her child have a play date at someone else's house without undue fear. This shift represented the development of Mrs. B's identification with the transformative mother.

The objects that she appreciatively saw as reminders of transformational activity within herself, illusions notwithstanding, became symbols for possibility. This new appreciation is akin to the sentiment expressed in Anna Quinlan's (1988) essay "Tag Sale," in which she discusses preserving a relationship of possibility vis-à-vis the objects of her child's infancy. She describes her wish to leave the door of motherhood open, symbolized in her unwillingness to part with the "box of crib sheets, yellow with milk stains, yellowing just a bit with age. . . . I have a feeling of possibility within me that means too much to give away. I could use the closet space, but right now, it is something else I need much, much more" (p. 87). It is the feeling of possibility and the ability to use the transformational fantasy to renew and re-create that anchor motherhood in a truly generative place.

Mourning Play

Some of us played with dolls or plastic horses as children; we pretended we were good mothers who knew exactly how to take care of our babies. But eventually, the doll or the horse became just an inanimate object again and might have been tossed out, mutilated, or simply ignored.[4] If the displacement was not too great, the doll or horse was replaced with other objects and activities that encompassed transformation and animation.

These "babies," the individual objects or the collection as a whole, give material representation to the wished-for link between mother's and child's own insides, where interesting possibilities and transformations exist. The child is able to transform her connection to the mother into a new form of empower-ment through her capacity to represent absence and loss in manageable doses through substitute figures and play. The invisibility of the mother, when she disappears as object for the infant—either by her own actions or because of the infant's rageful "dismissal" of her—heralds the beginning of the child's use of substitute objects to comfort herself and to act as a holding environment until the return of the real mother. These transitional objects temporarily deaden the longing for the mother and simultaneously initiate the child's relationship with the world of others and her own subjectivity.

These same objects can also be seen as aids in mourning. The emphasis here is placed not on the object but on *objects used playfully.* Freud's description of his grandson's *fort/da* (gone/here) game illustrates the child's working through of the everyday losses of mother as she comes in and out of the child's view. By throwing and retrieving a spool the child reenacts the mother's coming and going. In the fort/da game, the child not only has the object under his control in order to mediate grief and re-creation but is able to transform his feeling state. Without the opportunity to play out her leaving, he would be left with only her loss. The playing gives him something else; it shifts the feelings of transforma-tion and agency to the self ("mother leaves and transforms me from a happy, contented, safe child to a frightened and lonely one" becomes "I can make things come and go and I can feel myself as an agent of change").[5]

First's (1988) observation of children's reactions to maternal departure sug-gests that the toddler "allows" the mother to leave as he identifies with her subjective experience of having her own life. He comes to realize, as Benjamin (1988, 1990) has articulated, that separation (object loss) is the other side of connection to the other. That is, through this process of identification one can imaginatively appropriate aspects of the other for the self. The process of "trans-formation" means not just that the substitute object is sought (again not just the archaic all-perfect, instinctual mother) but that through the process of substi-tuting one achieves a sense of agency and activity. An identification with the

4. See Judith Kestenberg's work on doll play and maternal experience (1956, p. 286).

5. It is not within the scope of this chapter to discuss the actual operative process of ego identification, which, as Meissner (1970) notes, was left rather vague in Freud's work, except to say that there can be an alternation in the ego before the object is lost, and there can be an identification with attributes or activities of the object. Thus through simul-taneous leave-taking and identification the child obtains a sense of her or his own power to change feeling states and becomes empowered as a transformer.

transformational activity of the lost mother is now part of the self, and it is this that allows us to be creative in our own lives. When the process of mourning and subsequent identification is forestalled, however, objects are amassed indiscriminately, and nostalgia takes the place of agency and generativity. The subject tries to use these objects as a substitute external mother but is never satisfied. Hence Miss A and Mrs. B's endless search to own, control, and keep all for themselves.

The Re-creation of the Maternal Image through Generativity

"I'm in the Milk and the Milk's in Me"[6]

In this chapter I have explored the mother-infant relationship as a metaphor or a symbol for our own subjectivity in an attempt to articulate the mind's symbolizing and generative processes. Identifications with the activity of transformation constitute an important aspect of maternal subjectivity within the mother as well. The subjectivity of the mother is not merely a function of her status in the eyes of the other (Chodorow, 1989). Rather, it rests on her own ability to symbolize and be aware of her own symbolic value. The attempt to cultivate this process in others—our children and our community, for example—encourages a regenerative circle that is in itself a living memorial to the mother.

As daughters, we need to be able to acknowledge our own subject-object status in the eyes of our mothers. For mother-as-subject, the work of mothering may not always be in the best interest of the child. In fact, maternal pleasure and selfhood may reside in investing a piece of the self in the other and in turn refinding echoes of that self through the other. The poet Anne Sexton (1960) wrote about her daughter, "I made you to find me" (p. 39). Maternal subjectivity, in this sense, is an ongoing recycling of the self in the production of meaningful relationships with others.

Erikson (1950, 1959) in his profound but undeveloped idea of generativity attempts to elucidate a sensibility of adulthood. This adult sensibility is not about the reproduction of parenting per se, although mothering and fathering may be a vehicle for it, but has to do with creative nurturance of the next generation. Erikson's model is based on the wish to rework the life cycle and to take part in it as a conscious, active contributor. The crucial note here is agency; without it adulthood would be stagnation. To be used, as mothers so often are, in the regeneration of another is not an obstacle to our own subjectivity but a moment of development and possibility.

Theresa Benedek (1959), who has examined the reparative function of parenting, argues that mothering changes not only the infant but the mother as well. Through the complexities of maternal practice, there is an opportunity to rework our own relationship with the mother.

6. This is a line from Maurice Sendak's wonderful children's book about mother and dreaming, entitled *In the Night Kitchen*.

As we have seen, repetition, rather than true remembering and identification of an early transformational relationship with the archaic mother, is one of the obstacles to maternal subjectivity. If motherhood is taken on for nostalgic reasons, in an attempt to redeem a self that has lost its awareness of an internal transformational space, the mother can experience herself only as an object. Libidinal investment in a new other cannot occur until the old object (the maternal fantasy) is effectively mourned. For daughters—now mothers—when mother can be mourned, investment in self can occur.

Paradoxically, retro culture can be seen as both an interruption of the process of mourning the transformational mother and an attempt to capture the lost and longed-for mother who makes things happen. If, in collecting objects of the past, we are only quoting, then we are caught in nostalgia. But if, as co-partners with these objects, we are co-creators, then we are clearly occupying the space of subjectivity. The task for the mother-as-subject is to take forward into the present the old fantasies and feelings from the original dyad with an awareness of their origin.

There are other things that belonged to Mrs. B's child: tiny T-shirts covered with pictures of Batman, Ghost-Busters, and Mutant Ninja Turtles. They can't be discarded. These tiny T-shirts might be trash in the future, but now, in her mind, they represent the possibility of her child's retro collection, started in earnest by a mother. She is hoping that they will be used to recall the play between them, just as she recalls, through her collections, the generative possibilities of her own maternal ties.

References

Benedek, T. (1959). Parenthood as a development stage. *Journal of the American Psychoanalytic Association,* 7, 389–410.

Benjamin, J. (1988). *Bonds of love.* New York: Pantheon.

Benjamin, J. (1990). An outline of intersubjectivity: The development of recognition. *Psychoanalytic Psychology,* 7, 33–46.

Bollas, C. (1987). *The shadow of the object.* New York: Columbia University Press.

Bollas, C. (1989). *Forces of destiny.* London: Free Association Books.

Buck-Morss, S. (1989). *The dialectics of seeing: Walter Benjamin and the Arcades project.* Cambridge, Mass.: MIT Press.

Chodorow, N. (1989). *Feminism and psychoanalytic theory.* New Haven: Yale University Press.

Drucker, S. (1991). Billboards: Yesterday's pollutants, today's nostalgia. *New York Times,* September 29.

Erikson, E. (1950). *Childhood and society.* New York: Norton.

Erikson, E. (1959). *Identity and the life cycle.* New York: Norton.

First, E. (1988). The leaving game: I'll play you and you play me: The emergence of dramatic role play in two-year olds. In A. Slade and D. Wolfe (Eds.), *Modes of meaning: Clinical and developmental approaches to symbolic play.* New York: Oxford University Press.

Freud, S. (1914). Remembering, repeating and working-through: Further recommendations on the technique of psychoanalysis II. In *Standard Edition.* Vol. 12, 147–56. London: Hogarth Press.

Hines, T. (1987). *Populuxe.* New York: Knopf.

Kestenberg, J. (1956). On the development of maternal feeling in early childhood. *Psychoanalytic Study of the Child,* 11, 286.

Loewald, H. (1988). *Sublimation: Inquiries into theoretical psychoanalysis.* New Haven: Yale University Press.

Meissner, W. W. (1970). Notes on identification of origins in Freud. *Psychoanalytic Quarterly,* 39, 224–237.

Ogden T. (1990). *The matrix of the mind: Object relations and the psychoanalytic dialogue.* Northvale, N.J.: Jason Aronson.

Quinlan, A. (1988). *Living out loud.* New York: Ivy Books.

Rich, A. (1991). Eastern war time. In *An atlas of the difficult world.* New York: Norton.

Ross, S. (1989). *No respect: Intellectuals and popular culture.* New York: Routledge.

Santner, E. (1990). *Stranded objects.* Ithaca, N.Y.: Cornell University Press.

Sendak, M. (1970). *In the night kitchen.* New York: Harper and Row.

Sexton, A. (1960). For John, who begs me not to enquire further. In *The complete poems.* Boston: Houghton Mifflin.

Stewart, S. (1984). *On longings: Narratives of the miniature, the gigantic, the souvenir, the collection.* Baltimore: Johns Hopkins University Press.

Winnicott, D. W. (1986). *Home is where we start from.* New York: Norton.

MYRA GOLDBERG

10 Rosalind: A Family Romance

An Introduction to Our Heroine

Do you remember that painting, that Renoir, that beautiful woman of a certain age, that Madame Charpentier, sitting in a black velvet dress upon a sofa? With two little girls in lacy blue and white beside her. A dog somewhere, a poodle, perhaps, in Madame's lap. Lots of clothes, lots of textures, lots of skin tones. Well, in introducing Rosalind, our Rosalind Oliner Baumbach Twist, who is American and our contemporary, I want to make sure you remember this picture. Perhaps the publisher will put one in. French velvet sofas and the end of the nineteenth century, light falling lovingly on everyone, all those draperies behind them, that languidness that Madame C. assumes like a drapery—then picture our Rosalind:

A woman, more beautiful than Madame C., with pale skin, deep blue byes, snapping black hair, who is languid and decisive simultaneously. Her clothes, for example, are languid—gray blue silk pants and a gray silk shirt to her knees—and so is her pose, leaning against the sofa cushions, feet up. And on her lap, this little girl with strawberry curls and then this leggy almost teenager, standing tall beside her. Say the girls are wearing dresses. I mean, does anybody celebrate quotidian bourgeois beauty anymore—except the ads? But wait, this woman is rising, rushing off; she's got a job to go to, patients to see, a class to teach, the languidness gone as soon as the picture gets snapped. The girls go back to their sweatsuits and activities. It's the eighties, early on. May. Let's step back. To another look at this story. That spring. These lives.

Rosalind, Her History and Situation

For the first thirty-seven years of her life, Rosalind Oliner Baumbach Twist had been lucky. She'd been lucky in work, backing her way from a Ph.D. in sociology into a lucrative and rewarding practice as a psychotherapist. She'd been lucky in love (except for Baumbach, her first husband), and even he had left her something: a huge house in Brookline, Massachusetts, and a daughter whom she loved. She'd been lucky in small things—secondhand Volvos—and in large—neither her children nor her second husband, Henry, had problems inaccessible to goodwill, intelligence, or money, all of which she had. Moreover, Rosalind's brother and sister adored her; her parents placed her at the center of their family's earth. And if Rosalind considered her own character "impossible, a garden of neurosis," through psychotherapy, education, and experience she'd brought that garden into bloom: she was articulate about her failings, attuned to delicate distinctions among her feelings and complex formulations of relation and dismay.

Only her body eluded her. Sometimes merely plump, sometimes monumental, she hid her monument to what was fleshy like a crime. Beneath black tent dresses with romantic red roses strewn about, her thighs were large and soft, her breasts like Keat's autumn vegetables, her hips broad. Beneath her tents, she was still and statuelike. She walked slowly as if in pain and left dishes where she'd dirtied them on armchairs or the rug, as if, her children thought, they had offended her somehow. In fact she had, according to her brother, Lev, found the perfect profession in the practice of psychotherapy. For she could sit listening for long hours, her mind as active as her body was inert, participating for good in other people's lives. Or as Lev said, wrapping his knowledge and affection for his older sister in folk talk, like chewing gum in silver foil, "It's what you like to do anyway, Rosie. Sit and smoke cancer sticks and shoot the shit with folks."

Two weeks before her operation, she'd been sitting with her legs spread wide, her ankles thick above her rubber flip-flops on the front porch of a New Hampshire farmhouse, reading to her husband, Henry, from an article she'd been writing, "A jewish woman tells the following story." She'd paused beside "jewish." Something wrong with it. It needed caps. "A Jewish woman tells the following story. She was living near her mother in a city in Poland during Hitler's invasion." She felt a pain split her right shoulder, but went on reading. "With the German army coming closer, a Polish neighbor offered his attic for the mother and daughter to hide in, but the daughter refused." The pain was in her chest by now. "She couldn't stand the thought of living alone in an attic with her mouther for months or years perhaps." Ros stared at "mouther." "Mother," she said aloud. Then with her head bent over her legs, she murmured "heartburn" when Henry asked what was wrong. Then she straightened up. "Three months later, my patient got a chance to leave Poland alone. This time she refused because she couldn't leave her mother behind."

"Hold on," she told Henry. "I have to rest for a minute. But the piece gets better as it goes on." For she'd interpreted Henry's silence to mean that he disliked what she had written. She picked up the rimless glasses she'd set down on the porch and put them on for her last sentence. "My patient eventually left for this country where she prospered. Her mother, alone in Poland, perished in the camps."

She returned later that evening to Brookline from the farm she'd staged the summers of her sixties youth in, where life had been communal and a famous fugitive black man had spent a night. Then the pains had reappeared. And on Monday at Henry's insistence and because such pains were not endurable now that she'd endured them once, she'd gone to her internist in Cambridge.

Tests had been taken, blood had been drawn. Her friendly intelligent internist had cocked his head to rest his warm red ear against her breast and listen attentively, then hold his cold stethoscope to her flesh. Then more tests had been taken, more blood had been drawn. A few days later entering Dr. Kriegel's office, she met a friendly intelligent face that was in mourning for her. "I'm really sorry," he said in a voice that made her think he really was. "Indications, operation, mainstem clogged . . ." She'd heard. She hadn't heard. She'd driven home. She'd had Henry call his cardiologist uncle and she'd called her old friend Danny Kesselman, the holistic Berkeley internist, to find out what the West Coast thought.

Then hanging up, she'd gone on—called her brother, Lev, in Oakland, who'd called her sister, Lila, in New York, who'd volunteered to call their parents, then come for her children's sake to Boston. Then covering her most fragile patients with the empty hours of a psychiatrist friend, she'd informed them all that she was going to the hospital, packed her bags, and drove herself to Massachusetts General with her husband, Henry, beside her.

All of the above had been done briskly as if she were administering the affairs of someone else. A daughter, perhaps, in her early twenties, who had business in a country that was dusty, dry, and far from home. Or a patient, who needed clear, unemotional, practical direction.

At the hospital, Henry had listened again to her instructions about the children. "Check on Sophie to make sure she knows I haven't been buried in the basement of the hospital or some such story. Nana will be a help if you let her." He'd nodded, then held her, then left her, which was a relief for a moment, a chance to be alone. And it was only after pubic hair and arm hair and the tiny hairs on her nipples had been shaved that she began lying by the window in the hospital to feel alone for real, to feel afraid. But by then the little white cup of pills the nurse had brought had made her feel drowsy and her evening softened and slid away as more pills got brought to her and she was still sleeping the next morning when her body was rolled from her bed to a stretcher and from the stretcher to a table in the operating room and then her heart was frozen until it stopped and a machine in the corner took over and began to breathe for her while she was gone.

Later, with the stitches newly in, she lay in the recovery room and her heart stopped again—all on its own this time. Darkness and then a lake to stand by, toes in the freezing black water. "I can't leave the children," she heard a voice that was her own intone. Then her freezing toes pulled back. And so she lived (with the help of the hospital staff crowding around her bed).

She's Going Home. She's Trying to Stitch Her Life Together. She's Sitting . . .

Still as a statue, gazing at the noon-time sky, waiting for Henry who had driven her home from the hospital to open the door of the Volvo she was locked inside. I can always despair, she thought cheerfully, as if promising herself a treat. Sitting locked by the seat belt she couldn't remove, the car door she couldn't, with her muscles cut, push open, the cardiologist's sentence ringing inside her—he couldn't say what her chances were, he'd said, handing her (with pride) this snapshot of what her heart looked like before they'd closed it up. She'd refused to look. Stuffed the snapshot in her purse. Thought this man probably knew what her chances were, but wasn't—for fear of her reaction—telling. And then, that same instant, the car door was opened by Henry and she was removed, unlocked, then upright, standing on the gravel driveway, then before a yellow stucco house. Then figures began to move, small ones, larger, as she began to move herself. Sophie running with her arms held out. "Mommmmmeee." She flinched as a small body came toward her painful own, held her arms for protection to her chest. Said "Hello, darling," over Sophie's head, and found Nana waving casually beneath the maple with the sunlight shining on her golden head. Pounding in her chest (from happiness and fear) at the sight of all this life coming toward her. Then Sophie beneath her chest said, "Mommy," and Henry by her side said, "Careful" and her sister, Lila, appeared with tears in her eyes to say, "Ros," and an orchestra of voices were around her now, as she moved toward the house.

Growing things pulled at her like seaweed at the door, and she was desperate, exhausted, moving through the door, the hall, the dining room, where flowers and some dish that Nana'd cooked for her cried out for her attention!

"Look, Ma, what we made for you. The food. Your wedding china. Flowers."

Nana ushered her to the oak table, pulled the chair out, seated her. Pasta on the plate before her; must be cold. The wedding china set out. Love flooding her, for that handy bossy careful overseeing housekeeping little girl Nana. (Now twelve.) Glittering high-handed Nana who had everyone ranged around that table. Then everyone looking at Ros and saying Welcome Home. Welcome Home, Mom. Welcome Home, Ros. She felt the hard wood chair beneath her as her fork picked pasta up. Mouthed, it was a replica of that saltless, odorless, starchy hospital food.

"It's from this." Nana stood to wave a recipe book in front of her. THESE RECIPES SAVED MY LIFE, said the author on the back cover when Nana turned it over.

"Good," she said. "I certainly hope so." Cheerful, for irony was her meat and drink (when she wasn't eating cookies).

"It doesn't have to taste good," said Nana. "It's good for you." Her shining hair. Her health. Then Nana picked a rolled-up pasta piece from Rosalind's plate, tasted, and started to laugh. "Awful," she said.

"And look, Ma," Sophie pointed to the roses in the vase, adding (her precious darling) "Don't tell" to Nana.

"She stole them from the Rosenstock side of the fence," said Nana, matter-of-factly.

"But—no," said Sophie, in an awed and awful voice. That her sister was actually telling!

"Nobody knew," said Nana, munching and making a face; laying her fork down, like a sword turned into a ploughshare.

"They came over, really, the fence. Really. Hanging, sort of. They *grew* over the fence, Ma," said Sophie, with a worried fainting faintly nauseated look—oh the dramatic possibilities this child found!

"Sort of," said Nana, loving her understatement.

But now these children's faces upturned like flowers, waiting for Rosalind's interest and amusement to droppeth like the gentle rain upon them, and then, perhaps because they were calling on her, exhaustion overtook her, and she murmured, protesting, "I love all this, girls, I really do, but I must lie down, I must, to bed, I think, right now." She rose. (The girls behind her thought, But she always does that. Wait for the moment of happiness to arrive and then flee.) Then Henry took a year to get off his chair and come to her. Meanwhile the girls had risen, plus shining-faced younger sister Lila. Everyone threatened to follow. But Henry, taller than a crane or a stork, head brushing the chandelier, well Henry took her arm. "Come Rosalind." And she rose. And at the fullness of her name, the kids looked impressed, scared, hung back.

"Well, maybe you shouldn't be eating now," said Nana, preparing to clear and have the last word at the same time. As the grownups marched over to the stairway, Rosalind saw rug, saw stairs, a mountain of them, and then they climbed that stair mountain, and at the top by their bedroom, she looked down again and saw two figures who were small again, seen from upstairs. "I've missed you," she said softly to two small heads below, one blonde, one pale red. "I really love," as she turned away toward her bedroom. Feeling her voice had laid hands on them. And love had been a mystery until she'd found these children. Then she turned to Henry who would help undress her.

Picture it. You're lying in bed. The cessation of those ordinary sounds you and your body make while you are standing up, the squish of thighs, thump of feet, babble of your voice to someone else. It's afternoon. You've been driven through the town you drive through ordinarily.

You're—but listen now, to Rosalind, who is lying, listening to her heart while lying down. Thunk. Thunk. Thinking: Imperfect: like a phonograph record with dust on a groove whose needle will skitter away at any moment. Then life came back. After a moment of panic. Small sounds, a fly at the window screen, somebody's mower. Then children's voices—nothing particular, high, faint, louder, then fainter again. Nana's radio.

But with the return of all those noises, she had relaxed, she had fallen down a rabbit hole, she had heard, as from a distant country, some presence at the door, and then she'd slept and slept and slept.

The Mother Observed

That presence, that shadow, while she slept, was all of them: First Henry, looking down upon her face (how rich, how various, how new, she seemed to him—no longer the diminished and disappointing version of herself he'd picked up at the hospital). Still how displaced he felt, how far from her thoughts, as if some silent process had taken place during that marriage, whereby she'd kept silent watch over them, and now—

Nana, beside him, shouted, "Shhh, Ma's sleeping" to Sophie who'd moved into the corner by the door. Then Sophie was hissing, "Nana, come on, we'll go to the—"

"Shhhhhh," Nana shouted once more with her finger to her lips. Shouting Shhh was the kind of thing that annoyed Henry beyond all reason—that Nana should wake her mother by loudly calling for quiet. So he said, "Nana," loud and cold, then Nana said, "Henry," even louder. And Sophie said, "I didn't." And everyone looked to see who had awakened Rosalind, because that was what everyone wanted. That she should wake. But she slept. And slept. And slept.

He should have told me when he was going, thought Rosalind awakening the next morning. She meant Henry, of course, whom she knew from past experience had jumped from the bed they'd shared as from a fragile raft, pulled his pants on, and run downstairs to eat his breakfast. "The breakfast of champions," he joked about the white yogurt mound with the raisin in the center.

"But I'm it," she'd joked too. Protesting. "Le vrai chose. Woman. Why run for the symbolic?" Meaning a chat, perhaps, on the pillows about respective dream states. A little grope (but not lovemaking, although one without the other was impossible for Henry, which is why he always jumped up). Now wincing as she tried to straighten the pillow behind her and thinking: he should have touched me when he left today, told me he was going.

It had been different in the hospital. Buzzers brought nurses with breathing tubes, and in the morning, people fed her from a tray. And in the middle of the night, a hovering presence, a night light, a bell to ring, instead of awakening to find a wall of bone and muscle that was Henry's back turned toward her. She'd started, startled, wondered—can I keep going? Beating, boom through the darkness, then began, in that same darkness, chasing sleep, just before her, like a lover or a two-year-old. Just ahead, then catching up, then aahh. She'd found it. (She'd learned to do this during those years of getting up and down to tend to children.)

Now she looked up and found the rice-paper moon that hid the fixture on the ceiling, then left to where her grandparents lived mute within their plastic photo box. They'd been mute when living about the Poland they had run from. "I don't remember. There's nothing to say. Who wants to talk about such things? It stank, it smelled, of things, of blood." That heavy European contempt, that stolid European endurance.

"Where are they now?" Sophie had asked that winter. About her great grandparents.

"They're dead now," she'd answered. As if dead were a condition, a continuing tense.

Then her white-linened arm hit the drawer of the bed table.

"Oh shit." She pulled it open. Her life in little: a pack of cough drops, a pack of Merits, a pencil and notebook for dreams or ideas, a diaphragm, some jelly. And in the back, stuffed in by Henry yesterday, that awful photo.

She'd been gone for some episode, dead for a moment in the recovery room. But she was fine now; apparently, according to the doctors, all systems copacetic. A lot they knew. She knew them. (From teaching family therapy to medical idiots practicing psychiatry.) She thought of Henry jumping from their bed this morning. Then that table downstairs with roses yesterday as hands plucked at her to listen! Pay attention! Help! she thought, the way she used to, at the moment of pleasure, underneath the shower, with its warmth. And then a yawn. She looked at her lap. Then she plucked the least bent cigarette from the pack in the bed table drawer, then drew the matches from their place beneath the cellophane skin of the package. Lifted, lit, and puffed. Dizzy, nauseated, prepared for anything now, come get me life! she thought and rubbed the cigarette out against the cover of the cardboard pack, then dropped the pack in the drawer and left it open. Then she leaned back against the pillows and fell asleep.

She was awakening from a dream, a breathing tube that nourished her even as it consumed itself, when someone bent over to kiss her forehead.

The lips, as she awakened, became a voice. "Can I kiss you, Ma?" A face construed by her returning vision to be eyes, mouth, Sophie. "I had to come home from school, Mommy. I wasn't feeling too well."

"What's wrong with you?"

But Sophie, shrugging, indicated with her hand that Ros should make room on the bed for her to tell a story. "I met Birta Ogelthorpe this morning, Mommy. But then in language arts they said, 'Write what you did on this weekend in your notebook.' And I didn't feel like it and I couldn't. So I did nothing. Then itching came out all over." Scratching at her arms and chest. "And the nurse said, 'There's nothing wrong with you, Sophie, no temperature, but if you're feeling bad, go home. There's all kinds of chickenpox and everything around.' So Lila came and brought me home."

This wasn't a story made to be believable. Only pitiable. And believably false. This story says HELP! thought Rosalind, like—waving her hand. But it hurt to speak with hand signals, to say go on or stop, it's all the same, just stay here. Then she barely bothered to follow Sophie's version of Lila saying, "You know how fond of you I am," and Sophie answering, "I know you are, Lila," in a confident voice. "You bought me bubble gum shaped like a frankfurter in the minimart."

But a child's voice ran like a river beside her, and a tiny heart beat like a bird's. An adjunct to her body. Alternative. Young. "Well, if you're home, we might as well turn on the television and see what they'd got for us."

She breathed better as more voices and more people joined them on the screen; then a shadow passed across her eyes and settled on her shoulders.

"Sophie, would you peek in that open drawer, and get me a cigarette, like a darling?"

Puffing she could stand returning life. The fullness inside and outside her now. The pleasure she felt with her daughter beside her. The bone of my bone and the blood of my bone. But those couldn't be the words she wanted, flicking ashes into the top of the box.

Dreams and Realities of the Mothering Trade

"For unto us a child is born. For unto us a son is given." Since Ros had heard those words from *The Messiah* she'd wanted not a daughter but a child of unspecified gender, a son, perhaps. Or even, she thought afterward, a littler brother than Lev, a bird, a fish, a dog. Then at thirteen she'd gone to church on Christmas Eve and heard a red-robed chorus promise in unison that the rough places would be smoothed and the mountains made plain. The rough places smoothed. And the mountains made plain. She'd murmured going home round the corner, in the picturesque Christmas snow falling on Washington Square, its benches and branches. (It was the idea, at that time—this is me, Rosalind Oliner, walking home from church in Christmas snow that pleased her. Not the damp tickling her nose or her cold hands and feet, for she'd refused the gloves and boots her mother'd offered.) And something high, clean, purified, that chorus and snow had signified to her. Then entering their lobby with those words—made plain, made smooth—upon her tongue, she felt blessed and certain suddenly that what had been broken with her mother too long ago to name or date would be mended with the daughter she would have. She looked blank as the doorman wished her "Merry Christmas, Ros," for he was one of the cast of characters in her life she barely bothered to notice. Then she turned back to gush, "And you," remembering some inherited liberalism that went with her black stockings and Polish Jewish grandparents. Then she rode six flights up the elevator to glare at her mother, who hadn't wanted her to go to church. (You're Jewish, the reminder. As if she didn't know.)

Still later, after college, she saw that child who'd make things smooth and plain as someone to hold, cherish, educate. Someone at the heart of her life, which would be rich with love and work at its edges. Someone confident, stable, slender, bright. Not fat or stormy as she'd been, battling a mother she'd considered stupid, weak, and cold. (Brilliant, her mother called her, which felt like an insult, when all she had was insights, flashes in the pan of her essential ignorance.) She and her child would be intimate. She'd be empathic. Murmuring with this marvelous little girl around the edges of some dinner that someone else had made. Together they'd what? "We two form a multitude," it had said in *The Family of Man*.

At twenty-five, she'd had Nana. She'd waited at the hospital for Baumbach to come pick her up. Then she'd come home in a cab with the baby to find a note on the butcher block island in the middle of the kitchen: "I couldn't tell you this before. I'll be living with someone I met last year. We'll be in Burlington. I'll be in touch. P.S. I know you'll try to lay some trip on me about this, so I'm prepared."

Prepared by a lifetime of men she couldn't count on and by Baumbach in particular for this defection, she hadn't been prepared for Nana—the cries, the colic, the certainty, for the first time in her nonprofessional life, that what she was doing was necessary, but not necessarily up to snuff. She'd spent much of Nana's babyhood searching for sitters, money, and companionship, while Nana grew to be herself: practical, self-reliant, unintellectual, and mildly contemptuous of her harassed, intellectual mother. "Don't you realize there's no soap to wash the dishes with?" or "Don't wear that thing again. It looks funny." Or "Come on Mom. We'll be late. Can't you get organized?"

"Nana has the values of her peers," said Ros. "She'll be a real estate agent," said Henry. Respecting Nana and her right to be herself, Ros yearned at times for other women's daughters. For the rough places had become rougher instead of smoother with Nana, and she'd catch her daughter looking scornfully at her, as she'd looked at her own mother.

Sophie had been different. Ros had had a practice, a full-time housekeeper, a sense of herself, Henry's love, and Henry's help. And if breast-feeding still made her feel cowish and the shitwork, as she called it, went to Henry or the girl who cleaned for them, the reality of growing Sophie, her fears, her storms, her vivid imagination,were so engrossing that Ros's fearless, stormless, imaginary daughter died. And with her died the mother Ros had once imagined for her child. For as she watched her daughter grow, she watched herself. Comforting Sophie, as she hadn't been comforted, tender with Sophie's friends and feelings, engaged by Sophie's conversation, she loved doing with Sophie what she loved doing with everyone: talking, listening, making suggestions. Preferring at times her thoughts about Sophie to Sophie's actual presence, she avoided picnics, birthday parties, and the mothers of her daughter's friends. Ordinary life wasn't sufficiently something, she didn't know what exactly, she told Henry, to interest her. Then she'd chastise Henry, who didn't mind filling in for her, for taking Sophie roller skating. "She'll be bored. It's not stimulating enough. She needs something more related to people." She'd been grateful to the friend who'd pointed out that it was she who wouldn't like roller skating, not Sophie. And to Henry for not listening to her. For even with help, she knew she did things behind her back she'd disapprove of if she knew them. Still she counted on something: Was it touch, tone, feeling? Was it a fact that she could count on Sophie? To keep things close, to keep things humming between them? We two form a multitude. We too form a body.

Sophie, A Younger Daughter's View

The night her mother came home from the hospital, Sophie had gone to her little white bed and lay very still with a picture in her mind of those roses creeping over the garden fence. Then these pirates who put this woman and her baby in a zoo cage on an island. (Nana had told her this thing—that pirates had cut their mother's breast open. But that, said Nana afterward, was a joke.) But these pictures in her bed were Real—those real pirates and real mothers and real babies on a real island, near some war and Uncle Lev in rowboats. They had been rowing a boat across the ocean and then Henry met them in the Architecture Department after they got off the island. And real anything can happen in the world, thought Sophie wiggling her toes beneath her quilt, which was too hot. But maybe the father will come to rescue them. This was Sophie's idea. That someone in another boat could rescue them.

Then Sophie turned over and pressed her front parts to the mattress, which was hard beneath her body. And all that hardness made her brave, so she could open her eyes and turn over and throw her quilt on the floor Take That and get out of bed, then tiptoe through the darkness to the closet.

Pam, pam, pam were her feet cn the cold closet floor. Some dust. A broken toy—with wheels on it, that hurt and made more noises. Then the door—wide open like a mouth, or a breast pulled to open and shut. Then on her hands and feet in the closet, where her shoes were squirmy things, she touched a cardboard shoebox with a broken doll inside. This was the scariest thing in the world, worse than pirates. And inside the shoebox the dolly's head had fallen off and its arms had fallen off and its legs had fallen off and lost its body in the middle, because the rubber band that held it all together had snapped coming home from that farm on her mother's birthday. She had wanted the doll to see Everything going backward from that farm, so she'd twisted her dolly's head so hard that her head, legs, and arms had fallen off. And she'd screamed from her mouth before Henry could stop the car. And Henry said he'd leave her if she screamed like that again. She'd cause an accident. They'd all be broken.

Her mom said, Nonsense, Henry. You won't. But her mom was sick already, on that birthday, dying or lying in the back seat with Sophie, with her dirty bare feet on the front seat where Henry's shoulders were. Then Nana could help with the maps up front.

And now in that smelly closet darkness, Sophie lifted up the lid and bent to where that dolly's legs and head and arms were in a jumble and kissed what she prayed was the forehead of that doll. Tastes like plaster, something. Then she crawled out of darkness and raced with her heart pounding back to bed. Plop, plop, plop, her dirty dusty feet, like grit in your teeth up front.

Now it was morning and she was dressed in jeans. And Henry even taller in the kitchen, where all the pans hung down, after a flight of stairs where she skipped every other one, pam, pam, spooned the yogurt from his bowl. And as she watched, the same yogurt every morning went on disappearing down his throat. Then the bowl got empty and Henry was writing something with a pen. That tiny handwriting. Pinning what he'd written to the white refrigerator door with a magnet.

Dr. Kriegel. In case of *anything*.

491-2986.

She came up behind him.

She traced the numbers with her fingers. And anything, she thought, can happen in the world. Real pirates who cut off breasts. And real dolls with all their arms and legs cut off. Dirty feet on Henry's shoulders. And there was *anything* underlined on their refrigerator door full of Nana's soccer meets and "Henry remember!" in her mother's handwriting. "Pick up Sophie from school." He forgot sometimes.

"Is Ma going to die?" she asked suddenly.

She'd kept him there.

He stood.

Now he recognized and saw her. His blue eyes behind his glasses looking down, and at her. Now he saw her, heard her, kept his eyes on her. For she had learned at school: raise your hand and ask a question and you could stop things: like why wasn't America called by a Viking name if they discovered it? Why not? She'd asked and asked.

"No, I don't think so," he said, whispering from his tallness.

But then everything got confused and the air felt bad and stuffy because he left through the back door slam. And even though he'd already checked her pack for lunch money, glasses, and got your pencil box and all, he left before she left for school. And she left too, because on the sidewalk Birta Ogelthorpe was waiting for a real little girl with all her arms and legs attached. Her mommy. Then remembering spidery long-legged Henry, she pretended at the moment that she stepped outside that all his arms and legs were hers. And greeting Birta, with a waving hand, felt sure of everything for a moment.

"Hi Soph. We're late. Let's run."

Then she went to school and home again to see her mommy. And that bed, it was a raft, an island, with people's and television noises and the food she brought up for them and smoke—some hazy smoke—some dope, said Nana sniffing. Which was impossible, said Sophie, because its Mommy! Besides she's been sick.

She was a guardian angel going upstairs and down, like Mommy said. Be an angel Soph and get me some.

How these little winds blew from Mommy, these little sadnesses, that meant Sophie had to do this—get me some—anything. *What Mommy wants.* Little Mommy, she once called her, like a doll in that big bed, even if Nana on her way out to run made fun of her fat thighs under the covers. But Mommy was little, Sophie said, who didn't want to talk too loud because Mommy wouldn't like these thoughts or them discussing her. And couldn't explain how big could also be little. Then later, in the hot part of the afternoon, her mommy brought this photo out and said to Auntie Lila, "Take it downstairs," which Auntie Lila did and Sophie followed her down and Lila put the picture on top of the refrigerator, then went outside, and Sophie climbed up on the stepladder and looked. Saw blood in a pretty design. Knew it was something important. Felt sick, but couldn't not look.

"I could pretend this was an island," she said loud, climbing down from the stepladder, then up those stairs to Mommy's bedroom with her heart going boom. "I could be the raft that comes to rescue them." Up and down with stuff.

But sometimes (every night) she came right down again to say that Mommy is tired. She won't be down to supper. Then looked on top of the refrigerator for that picture, then went out again to the minimart for stuff.

Nana, the Eldest

Nana, swinging in the park, spotted Sophie. Long before Sophie spotted her. Way out on the edge of the park. And meanwhile, she, Nana, had been banished from that bedroom, no thanks, honey, coolly from her mom, but take care of things downstairs, make supper. But of course her mom was never down to eat it. And—well. There was that other thing, that certain sum of money that she'd asked for from her mom and now she was swinging and swinging in the baby park (she'd vowed to keep swinging!) until she came up with some other way to get it, pointing her toes toward that sum of money she had to get, to buy some sweats and running shoes. Because once her mother had banished her from that bedroom, why not, she'd run and run and run right around the high school track into that miracle, those high school girls, who asked could she join their relay team this summer and now she couldn't be on the relay team without the special shoes and sweats. And that card Mom had given her for the money machine at Coolidge Corner had had INSUFFICIENT FUNDS on it. Not that Mom hadn't been, "Sure, take the card, go get your sweats and shoes and stuff." That head sticking out of the covers. No haircut. Smelly arms. Those magazines and candy wrappers. Dope smells.

Sophie now with something brown and baggy in her arms was coming closer. Running right toward her without seeing her. Blind. That little sister chipmunk.

And Henry, that skunk, had said NO NO NO NO NO to her when she called him at Harvard. We haven't got the money for your running shoes and sweats. Your Mom's been sick. As if she didn't know. Or see Sophie in bed with Mom, who gave her money to get this trash at the minimart. Which would only make Mom sicker.

"Stop," she jumped off the swing to where Sophie with that bag ran right in front of her.

"Help! Nana!" Sophie shrieked. Looked down. Deciding to cry as Nana looked down too. Then up again at the package. In her paws. The package was long. Narrow. Brown baggy.

"Are those for Mom?"

The package tossed—wildly—like a football to the left side—and then quick, before Nana could swoop to pick it up, Sophie grabbed those Merits, good recovery! and ran, with Nana close behind. She caught her down the block near the house. Ripped the back of her jacket. Which was amazing. This little kid could run so fast. "I'm going to torture you." Hands on Sophie's neck above the rip. "I told you not to do it."

Then she held on to Sophie and pushed her back to the house, then down to the basement, where it smelled like a cave, and she took out a Merit cigarette and lit it.

Whoosh the match flared up.

"Okay Soph. You take a puff." She puffed first, coughed, handed the cigarette over. Sophie's eyes grew wide. A tiny gasp. She puffed, coughed, sputtered, gave the cigarette back. Then "come," said Nana gruffly. And Sophie followed her to the downstairs little toilet where Nana dropped the cigarette they'd puffed on into the bowl. They watched it together—drown. That brown stuff spilling out of its white cover.

"Pee on it, Soph. You do it."

"You first." But little Sophie was crying.

So Nana did it first. Cold toilet seat. Then Soph.

"Like dogs," said Soph, giggling. She'd had the seat warmed.

"Now you tell her. No more, Mom. Go on."

"I can't. You're older."

So Nana dragged her up from the basement and together they came to the bedroom. "Mom," said Nana. "The cigarettes are gone. There's no money. We don't want to get you any."

Their mother opened her mouth and things fell out. Resent, your business, ridiculous, appreciate concern, go away. "Goodbye," they both said, feeling terrible. Then Nana got her real idea, staring at the closet as she went out, of how to get her running suit and shoes.

"Mom's not coming down to supper," she let Sophie tell Henry, when they met on the stoop. "But we can make it. From stuff in the freezer. How's that, Pa."

It had been easy for Nana once she'd gotten her idea to carry it out. Easier having been so brave, standing up to that nut in the bed upstairs (her mom). Easy for her to stand inside her mother's bedroom closet, while her mother was asleep (my god! what luck), collecting clothes. (Her mother lay snoring and moaning.) And nobody bothered her as she'd stood inside her mother's closet picking out jackets and caftans and Mexican peasant blouses. Sweat smells, pocketbooks, dirty nightgowns. And dresses from Pakistan, Afghanistan, or whatever other country had a "stan" in it and poor babies with staring eyes on the hunger posters. Then she folded the stuff in the cardboard boxes she'd found in the basement in her closet. (Who'll get custody of Nana if Ros dies? in Henry's handwriting on notebook on his workbench. THINGS TO DO the page said. Which she refused to even think about. It was so dopey.) Folding clothes instead of stuffing them in boxes, so they'd be nice instead of wrinkled when she took them out. Then on Saturday morning. Baaam at six-thirty. The clock radio. The first box carried to the kitchen. Yes. But then in the yard, she'd spotted Lila and slipped back into the kitchen climbing the stepladder to temporarily store her clothing box on top of the refrigerator while she made up quick what she'd tell Lila if she came in. This was stuff for school, she'd say. The rummage sale for the single-mother kids who were divorced to play soccer in the after-school program. She had to be at the playground early to help set up. Or was it weird to put the box up there? So she got back on the stepladder to bring the box down and knocked some photo down.

Okay, okay, as she climbed down. Setting the box on the floor. Scooping the flash of a photo up into her hand, then her jean jacket pocket. Then braver and bolder, now that she had her story straight, she went out into the yard behind Lila, with her box.

This was the surprising part. Her heart beating, getting clothes from that closet, carrying them out behind Lila, but no panic, no speeding up, no grabbing at things the way she might have. Say she was still a kid like Sophie. Then she carried her box down the block to Coolidge Corner, where she left it at the Bagels And. "Please, I'll be back in a minute. Would you keep this for me, please?" The bald man behind the counter nodded at her. The golden smelly whitefish stared at her. She ran back home and got two other boxes. This time Lila noticed her, blinked, went back to drawing and Nana went back to the Bagels And with more clothes.

Four boxes got dropped at the Bagels And before the deli man said, "Girl, we need the room, the customers will trip."

She bought a pickle to make him happier. Then went outside and knelt on the sidewalk to spread the clothes on a blanket so that people could see them.

There were three customers before her now, reaching down as she reached up.

"Can I? Are you? How much?" And thank heaven for none of these kids or grown-ups being from the Runkle school or Browne Street or knew her mom. "Take as many dresses as you want," to a grown-up woman. "They're a dollar each if you take a lot."

The woman had a glint in her eye: "And this, maybe, at a dollar, why not?" And orange, pink, and red brown shawls got draped over people's shoulders and arms and sometimes Nana charged four dollars for everything, this sweatshirt and these old boots, and sometimes in her excitement, fifty cents.

"How come you never find such good things for men, secondhand. I mean, have you observed this phenomenon? That only women sell their clothes before they're wrecked." A handsome man like Uncle Lev with all his different kinds of language and golden hairs on his thick arms squatted beside her with his thick legs apart.

"Gee, I never," she said. So pleased to have him talking to her. "Maybe they don't wear out."

Then more people came and some dresses were too big for anyone except the pregnant girl with the skinny braid down her back who said she was from Chelsea. And the sun and Nana's stomach said Noon, so she paid a boy a dime to watch her things while she went to the Bagels And to buy a bagel and cream cheese chives with a cool pocketful of money she could touch when she reached in for it. And the shadows on the street and leafy trees and glints of mica on the sidewalk made her feel proud. For she belonged, with her pocketful of money, to the street and the world now. Felt her shadow stretching tall and skinny, wavering before her on the sidewalk as if it had substance.

We Back Up to Stella Oliner, Who Is Rosalind's Mother. What All This Mothering Was Like for Her.

Stella Oliner had had three children. Or rather Stella had had two children. Her youngest two. And a firstborn child, who was Rosalind and whom she'd felt was not a child exactly, but an adult who'd lived in a child's body, which was something else (and hard for her). There were other ways to look at this problem, of course. Perhaps Ros had been an ordinary child, but Stella had not, with her firstborn, become an ordinary mother yet. For by the time Lev had arrived four years after Rosalind, and Lila, four years after Lev, Stella had acquired a feel for motherhood, which meant she had a feel for childhood and for the bargains that children and their mothers strike.

Meanwhile, her temper had cooled from heat and noise to irony, and her despair at what was being asked from her was lightened by a knowledge of her limitations. For she had seen, by the time the last two came along, the limits on the harm she could do, as well as the limits on the good.

And so what, she thought, if Lev, her son, was somewhat silly and Lila was peculiar, or like the rest of the human race according to Stella, they were more likely to be foolish than be wise? She rested comfortably with her feeling that these two were dear to her, residing in that small backyard corner of the world where her loyalties were planted, like her husband, her sister, or her store. Stella was fierce about what belonged to her, but her younger children were equally fierce about their belief that family obligations were wrong, somehow. Or was it that any obligations were tacky? A belief that had flourished like roadside weeds along with other heresies in the late lamented sixties. And so they'd struck a bargain among the three of them. That if her children could decide to sidestep her wishes for their lives or move to California to avoid them, she'd avoid acknowledging their conviction, acquired in the world outside, that people were related if they *felt* like it. For families, Stella felt, as anyone not blinded by Ideas acknowledged, were made up of people who owned each other.

But Rosalind had been different. The first from the moment of birth. After a labor that made Stella question how her own mother, so brutally honest in other respects, could have failed to tell her what these pains would be like, she had handed her store over to her sister Julie and began staying home with her baby. Remembering two years later on an afternoon's visit to Julie that she hadn't always felt uncertain, fragmented, irritable, and bored, she'd returned against the advice of her friends quoting child psychologists to her place behind the counter. By then this creature, who cried at three A.M., developed rashes, grabbed cookies, other children's toys, or Stella's breasts, had become a sweet-natured, plump, acquisitive child. With a strong streak of willfulness: everyone had to play what Ros wanted them to, including Stella and Sidney. For if good-natured Sidney didn't mind stopping in the middle of "Geese and ducks and chicks gotta scurry" if Ros wanted him to, something, Stella felt, was being wrestled from her by this high-handed child—her motherhood, her adult authority, her God knows what.

Rosalind was a gangster of family life, Stella told Julie once, bending rules, other people's wishes, and life itself to her childish wishes, then revising family history so that she won not just the fealty of the household but their faith in the decisions she had made for them. Her gap-toothed sister grinned, reminded Stella that they already had a gangster in the family. An Uncle Nathan who'd sported a diamond on his pinkie and traded black-market sugar during the war and whiskey during Prohibition.

Stella was right as it turned out. For by the time Ros had reached the age of twelve, she ruled that uneducated Stella's contribution to her children was drudge work merely—serving lunches, nursing sicknesses, seeing to Sidney, who saw, in turn, to teeth. (He also made halfhearted forays during family fights into organizing truces that no one wanted.) And it was Ros, the eldest and the wisest, who organized day trips, saw to education, and offered her sister and brother spiritual guidance and advice. For who knew more about the world they were entering? Someone like Ros, who'd just come through these schools, piano lessons, romances? Or Stella, who'd spent her childhood in a grocery store upstate?

And now, in the midst of her Ros's own crisis, Stella felt superfluous, dismissed again. For she'd called and called and called her daughter's home and reached evasion and excuses in Boston. Ros was fine, everybody assured her. Only no one but them could see her. Her latest call had been different. Now Ros, according to Lila, was well enough to deal with patients, but couldn't speak to her mother on the phone.

"Do you think she's mad at me?" Stella had asked Sidney. "That I've offended her again somehow?"

"Not unless she's mad at both of us." Sidney, famous for his carpet-sweeper approach to family dirt, was convincing for the moment. For Ros liked her amiable father, even if her liking had a streak of contempt in it.

"But what if something dangerous is going on, only no one will have the decency to tell me?"

"You'll find out, dear. Soon enough."

"I can't," she wanted to say, "stand you sometimes." But it was Sidney's bargain with life she couldn't stand, not Sidney. For his good nature had been bought, she felt, by ignoring real dangers to his loved ones, had been paid for through passivity and at action's expense.

Stella Oliner at the Metropolitan Museum

Society woman. Stella Oliner fished the phrase up from her youth and pinned it on this woman who was standing, rich and unemployed, behind the Metropolitan Museum's information booth. "Thank you," for the brochure on rich paper she was given by that ringed hand, pointing out that Japanese ceramics were on the balcony, French drawings to the left of the marble staircase, American furniture near the Temple of Dendar.

Waiting in this hall for Lila, back from Boston, beneath a ceiling so vast it brought back that story from god knows when she'd read the kids: "and another little ant," said Scheherazade, "took another grain of sand away."

And how peculiar to be standing here with all these people/ants at noon, when in real life, usually, she was in the store. Or on her way to some garment manufacturer. Thaler and Magnus, yesterday, who now had their blouses sewn, she'd noticed yesterday, in Haiti. And her kids would complain: But those women stitching blouses in Haiti are going blind, Ma. Which might be true. And also it was true that maybe the money that came from selling those blouses had made her kids so compassionate and also late all time. But there was Lila, coming down a marble staircase that some countries in Europe were smaller than. Her long-legged daughter, red-haired in a blue and white striped not exactly clean, as Lila came closer, fisherman's shirt, and wide-legged British walking shorts. Hello, pantomimed across the hall. She was gratified by the outfit, the care in choosing, if not in laundromats.

Then after Lila bent to touch her cheek, they went on walking. Past Egyptian mummies with Lila chatting and Lila never chatted, Stella thought. And was she nervous? turning to touch Stella's arm, as they passed mummies, then examining her large hands as they sat down, chairs scraping, in the cafeteria. And then, "We ordered cappuccino. And two sandwiches. Has something happened?" Lila, who was getting tougher, asked the waiter, for they'd made it through some minutes without their orders being brought. Which wasn't bad, thought Stella, her standing up for them. Then conversation, which was harder, fell apart.

She doesn't like me, Stella felt, getting up to go to the bathroom for a break from all this. Then remembering that Lila liked everyone a little, and it was Ros who didn't like her and that she was in this place to ask: Could you come with us? With me and Ros to Arden, so Lila could keep them from getting on each other's nervous systems? She stood before the ladies' room mirror beside her daughter, who'd followed her in, peering into both their glass faces as steam heat left over from winter carried perfume and urine and hot water smells to her nose. And now she couldn't ask, for fear she'd be refused. Then wiping her hands with towels brown and rough and wet, she asked instead, what Lila was in this museum to see. And heard romance portraits, which turned out to be Roman. Like these towels, Lila said, wiping the wetness off her wrists. Rough and true like bags of cloves. You know what I'm saying? As if they smelled of something. Textures.

No, said Stella firmly, leading them out again into the hall. And knowing exactly what Lila meant, but why confuse the universe worse by saying these things aloud? Then back to their table, which now that Lila had said these things had coffee smells and something terrible about its white Formica top.

Lila at the Metropolitan Museum

Then Lila drowned her shyness in a glass of water, as her mother glancing around asked what besides Roman portraits she'd come to look at. And Lila started, after all these years, to tell the truth. "Touch base. As Ros would say. Are you sure you're interested? I'll show you upstairs, if you want, where when I was like seven or eight I used to wander because I thought: if we live in an apartment, we need an attic, so this would be my attic, like. While Ros and Lev would go, I don't know, to get a soda or something. Though sometimes Lev liked to get a rise out of me by coming in and telling me the mummies would climb out of their coffins, if we didn't run quick through that hall. So we ran and he made mummy sounds anyway. But mostly, it was the pictures upstairs, like that Brueghel thing which reminded me of Grandma, with all these folk people and the village she came from, didn't they have an inn? So I'd pretend I've lived inside the picture frame and could walk around the fields or lie around and fall asleep under the tree with the man with the beer mug. Like Lev and Ros did in the park."

"They did what? In Central Park?" said Stella.

"Of course, when I got to Music and Art, I found out that nobody else played Living in the Pictures. Or nobody talked about it. It isn't painterly, that's all, or sophisticated."

"You always were," Stella lifted the top slice of bread to examine the ham in her sandwich, "imaginative. But then this whole painting business, living alone like that and being so poor when you could do all kinds of things. I like paintings when I see them, but it's different," she smoothed her skirt, "for a life. You know, I wouldn't say this ordinarily, and I don't want you to take it the wrong way or be too sensitive, but I've always felt this painting business was something like that crush you got on Anthony What's-his-name when you were twelve and never got over."

"I think the same thing," said Lila. "I've waited all my life to have it over, which means, I guess, that I'll be someone else. But I never do. But I don't. But I feel drunk on this assertion or negative of an assertion," she said, she who never said in words what she was thinking. Then she got quiet and looked at the white pillar behind her mother's dark head, and the folds in the white blouse, and something in her mother's face that said: disquieting. Love. And the way the skin on her mother's arm was getting looser, but was still freckled, as if the language of language cut into things all the wrong way. No language of freckled flesh or even cotton blouses. Love. And Sunday boredom, she thought. No language of falling asleep on her velvet couch yesterday, drained of light the way the day was.

"What does Ros want from me?" her mother said suddenly. "And I was wondering also if you'd come up with us to Arden. I know how busy you are. But I can't imagine the two of us alone up there together."

But Lila narrowed her eyes to fix the shoulders of her mother's black padded narrow-shouldered jacket. And there was something absolute those Roman portraits captured: the way that spirit and the matter it assumed for life fit together. Which was the matter with death absolutely. "I can't come. I have to stay here." She let her eyes drop to the tabletop with coffee spills. "Ros is screwing up, and I don't know if she wants you to know, but she's making everybody nuts, by hanging around—"

Then she didn't want to tell on her sister, even if they were grown-ups now. That Ros was preferring to die, in order not, in despair (there was despair, yellow as nicotine, on Lila's own fingers now although she didn't smoke), to live differently with death in life. And Ros was preferring to die in order not to have to pay attention to what was wrong with her, absolutely. Or to be killed anyway, say she took her life in her hands. This thread drawn through the light behind her mother and words, here and there, strung like Christmas lights to keep them sane enough to sit there. "She's better now. But she, oh I expect she just wanted to get away. What she wants," looking at this woman so uneasy with her being, as if she'd come out wrong, "from you, I don't know," stirring her cappuccino, sugar in the bottom thick. Then seeing, as she stirred, those romance portraits, ordinary living dead people looking at her through eyes that might be Jewish from a thousand years ago, she looked at her mother's brown eyes and said, "I don't know how to say this. I mean, I told her to call you. But if I hadn't, she might have called anyway to, I don't know, keep up her quarrel with you, I mean, with life again. However you got mixed up with it. So things can be the same. Like before she got sick."

And things and people die. And other things go on and on. Had tumbled her over some edge now and made it legitimate, a life as real as any other, for her to spend her own time on earth trying to paint them all into living forever despite the way she knew it made them—everyone, herself included—nervous, uneasy, discomfortable, love.

She left the museum with her mother. Down the biggest front steps in the world she'd grown up with. Jugglers here on Sundays. And buses pulling up and stopping, and always wrong. To Thirty-fourth Street only. Or Eighth Street and Broadway. When they needed Eighth and Fifth. "Come on. Let's take that one." She did that. Took the not absolutely number thirty-three or whatever was the right one. Because it was fun, she told her mother, getting to walk from wherever the bus turned out to stop at the end.

A tree behind them with a tiny plot around it, as she stepped up to reach the bus. She felt the tree behind her, the tiny plot, as if it were a grave. Then she stepped up to reach the bus which rolled like a gigantic dice on rubber down Fifth Avenue. And mansions on her left, where people had lived in marble igloos with excrescences, or whatever you called them, once. This would all come right in her head, turn over into whatever they were called in the art history books, if she wanted. Renaissance palazzos. But she didn't want. For her sister's dance with death had freed her into riding free for once from wishing she were someone else. Then she stepped off the bus, toward a pyramid of granny smiths and oranges and purple cabbages that rose, extravagant and welcoming as royalty or prose, from the Korean vegetable market, and she was downtown, on the pavement, where she belonged.

Ros and Mother Stella in the Forest of Arden (At Last). Ros is Healed by . . . a Lot of Things, Mother Being One of Them

"But I—"

"But it's my refrigerator, Ros—"

"It's both of our refrigerators, mother. We're sharing this refrigerator even if the bungalow belongs to you." Stepping back, away from her mother, on the uneven kitchen linoleum. Glimpsing a bread knife on the counter.

"And I feel it needs defrosting."

"Great. Good. Only the frozen food will be ruined by the time the ice melts," said Ros calmly.

"If I waited until all the frozen food, my God, got eaten," Stella's white hands twisted, then clasped each other, "I would never defrost at all."

And my God, what were they arguing about? thought Ros, who'd disqualified herself as a housewife years ago to everybody's satisfaction. "There's ice cream in there, Ma. All kinds of things that will be ruined." Compassion in her voice for the food. "When the kids come up, we'll just have to run out and get more for them." Why was she reasoning with this crazy woman? "So why not wait until they eat us out of house and home? Then defrost." Joking, when the real joke was that she wanted to strangle this prissy critical person who was trying to run everything in sight.

"*You'll* eat the ice cream before they do, Ros." Her mother said calmly, her judgment absolute, but with a mournful and triumphant edge as if she'd been waiting all week to say this. "And while we're on the subject, what I really can't bear is your standing by the freezer peering in, as if God knows what were inside. You know how much that adds to the electric bill?"

But Ros began to laugh. To hold her sides.

"I pretend not to notice that I see you in there all the time," Stella went on. "Meanwhile, the ice is building up and the whole refrigerator will be lost because you're being so stubborn and irrational."

But Ros was laughing. Holding her stomach, her chest, the scar on her throat, then the oilcloth-covered table, as if her laughter had crippled her and she needed support. "I can't believe that we're arguing about this." Then laughter got throttled in her throat. Because even if this was funny, there was anxiety, animus, killing instincts in the air. Then something dawned about this competition. This almost-to-blows about this refrigerator that opened and closed with living stuff inside. "Is that what we're talking about?" Her hand on her mother's shoulder. "Who knows the most about my body? Who owns the goddamned thing?" Remembering with her own children: early morning sucking, diapers, shit, exhaustion, love.

But her mother looked bewildered. Moved away. Then dressed her face in with her eyes lowered and her Take Me Away from This Craziness look. "I haven't the faintest idea what you're talking about. Is this some psychological thing you learned at college or something?" Walking to the counter and leaning with her hand, as if exhausted, near the knife. "You always do that." A level accusation. "Bring up something—intellectual you know will make no sense to me."

"I don't know. I'm not sure. Do I? It feels right, absolutely, and also," shaking her head, "forget the interpretations. I just can't stand bossing you around. I had meant," trying to muster her dignity after that unpardonable slip, "being bossed. But never mind." Walking, to retrieve some dignity away from the table and that knife to outside, where the pines were, then thinking this (as the darkness and the tall trees came into view): a friend and an enemy, like Freud had. Always a friend and an enemy. Only I haven't seen my friend since when? Before the operation (loomed) and my enemy, always close to me: Henry, Stella, whoever's closest to my heart.

No sleep after that or sleep that somebody ripped open with the dawn (bird song).

Then something else, one afternoon, as seated outside in the Adirondack chair, she nodded. Something she couldn't capture about her own being captured by a big black net for certain purposes, nay (and that was the language of it) nay bread (that must be bred) for certain purposes and few of them were— doable. Or only a few of them were doable. Or some of them were done.

Then on her third sleepless night, she went with her flip-flops on and a raincoat over her nightgown to the beach. "Why me, why not Lev or even my mother?" she thought, sand and pebbles hitting her unprotected toes on her way down to the water. Kneeling by the water's edge to feel with her hand, how soft, how warm, how cold the lake was.

Then she went home again. "Well," she said to her mother at suppertime, "it's been a bitch this doing everything. I've wondered, off and on, could I have scaled back, somehow? Lived with more love in our lives, more pleasure, more ease, and even—more justly?" This was too general a remark for her mother, who disliked and feared and even hated abstractions. "Lived more simply. Worked less. Had a smaller house. Let Henry do more of the—take more of the responsibility, I guess."

"Do you think," asked her mother earnestly, "this has anything to do with your health?" Then the accusation beneath the question turned like a sword (Rosalind watched this) against herself and she began to weep. Gently. Inconsolably. Her mother was weeping and not Ros. "I should have . . . I always meant to say . . . but you, so sensitive . . . to criticism . . . way you people live."

How trite. (These wailings. She barely heard the words her mother said. But tears. Annoyed her until she joined them.) Then she shook her head. No, she said, and took a walk and thought a thought she'd thought before. (That was how it felt to her.) Which had something to do with the rain raining in the country and with—stop it, she thought. (About fleeing from her experience. Before, behind, anywhere but where she was.)

Pushing her life before her like a shopping cart full of unworn discarded clothes.

A howl in her throat the next night, when she came back down to the lake. A little earlier than the night before, but still in the dark. And each time she opened her mouth to the darkness of the water, a salt pool would soak through her skin and roll down her cheeks to her salty lips which she licked.

This is stupid, she thought. She thought. Licking the snot.

Her heart drawn out of her body. It went on walking on the midnight water across the lake.

This is scary.

Like a dog baying at the moon or a child sucking at its own salty hand, she wept. "I will never stop crying," she thought, scurrying back up the beach holding the sides of her flannel nightgown up to the steps, then the stone retaining wall, where she'd been first in a row of three children playing tightrope with their arms held out like poles. And her heart, thump, thump, now that she was away from the water came back to her. "I'm home," she thought, reaching the bungalow's front porch. Letting the screen door slam, despite the hour.

But her mother didn't awaken. So she ate a few things; she couldn't remember what later on and didn't want to.

It was fun the next evening, after supper, she sat on this stone wall, looking at the roped-off kiddy pool, white floats on a white plastic rope. Kicking her feet, happily in the water, letting go. Remembering: cherries, she'd eaten, one a rotten one. Then, "I am going to die," in her own unspoken voice. Quiet and screaming inside. A scream so impossibly quiet it could have been a scalpel cutting the I and the Going To and Die out so that the scream passed through her body but no sound came out. Or even registered as head or body talk. (It was still quiet and fun, in the place within where the cherries had been eaten.) Dusk over in the sky around gathered into fading pinkish next to dark. Then the center of pink began to fall like fireworks into the water. Or floated in the blue-black sky like cotton candy.

So what, came the answer. (On the dying question.) Lots of people will live on. This was from the pool in the center. They would be different from her. They would go on.

The thought seemed quiet. And humorous. Wicked in a way. Not to be devastated.

At home, afterward, in her iron bed, she dreamed the first dream she could remember since the operation. That her scar had opened up and her intestines had fallen out on the linoleum that her grandfather had glued down and were scurrying here and there like crabs for everyone to watch until they died.

Her mother was mending an ancient pair of jeans when she awakened from the dream and came out to the kitchen.

"Can I make you a cup of tea, Ma?"

Stella looked up, her blue eyes startled. Shyness and the offer had startled her. "No, thanks." Needle in her hand. The faded blue pants lifted up. Stella's left hand within one leg, while with the right, she sewed a patch on at the knee.

Stella still mended. Amazing. Who else did in this throwaway country?

"Do you remember, Ma?" as the teakettle's whistle blew. And she went walking toward its summons. "The night I was born, by any chance?" Sitting down backward, legs straddling a white wire ice-cream chair.

Clutching the back as if she were holding on to—a chair back, she told herself.

"Of course." Looking at her watch. "A little after four at the Astoria General Hospital. The war was just over and I was in the hall, there were no beds. We couldn't wait for things to really get started again. As if we'd been living in a nightmare instead of real life. But," shaking her head, "it's—this is you we're discussing. Lying in the hallway, you were dressed in rags. I was so upset I couldn't see how pretty you were until I got you home and dressed. And what I said when they brought you in to me?" Stella squinting, looked up from the jeans. Her face now young and flushed. "I was so excited. I'd been drugged of course. So I didn't see you born exactly. But then they brought you. In this raggy gown. And reaching out for you." She reached out with a needle in one hand pointed toward the space between them. Then shy again, she looked down at the pants in her lap. "I had to examine you everywhere to make sure you were all right. And then I said this funny thing. When I saw you had all your toes and fingers on. 'I have waited so long for you to join us, Rosalind.' Isn't that strange?"

"None of it sounds exactly like the person I know. Except for the examination. The clothes."

"I was young," said her mother shy again.

At noon the next day as the town whistle blew, Ros walked down the warm tar road in her flip-flops to the kiddy pond. Lay in the water, pushed off from the sand with her feet, swam a few strokes, came out of the water, and walked up the road to the bungalow. An old lady in a large straw hat trudged ahead of her. Her legs and arms shook as she walked along. She turned as Ros passed her. Smiled. False teeth in a dark wrinkled face. Glittery eyes. A Jewish trudger. At home, she and her mother ate cucumbers with sour cream. Greedily like girls.

"My mother had sisters to sew with. I am alone and buy ice cream." Rosalind's dream had been the night before. Now, in the afternoon back in the kiddy pond she lay sea-monster style, head up, and hands and belly on the sand below the water, feet kicking.

"Are you okay?" Her mother at the water's edge. "It's not too soon after your cold to go in again?"

"How would I know?" Kicking with her feet. Like a child learning to swim. "Don't worry so much about me, Stella."

"But who will worry about you if I don't?" Her mother's dress blowing.

"I will. I'm used to it, Ma."

And now her mother had turned from her and was trudging up the beach, skirt blowing, hair blowing, bending, reaching, looking for Popsicle sticks for the kids to build rafts with when they arrived.

"My mother had sisters to sew with. I am alone and buy ice cream." Her dream. Her feet kicking. Her body turned round, as she swam out.

Part III The Cultural Construction and Reconstruction of the Maternal Image

THERESE LICHTENSTEIN

11 Images of the Maternal:
An Interview with Barbara Kruger

Over the past decade Barbara Kruger's work, consisting of a montage of images and phrases, has produced an ironic social critique of sexuality and politics from a feminist point of view. By utilizing and manipulating mass media images (advertising, newspapers, billboards) Kruger creates ambiguous and powerful messages. Her work asks the viewer to reconsider the various societal roles of men and women by calling into question standard assumptions about masculinity and femininity.

Many of Kruger's works critically address the complex issues surrounding motherhood in relation to female subjectivity and empowerment. For example, her poster, "Your Body Is a Battleground," made for the march on Washington, Sunday, April 9, 1989, to support legal abortion, birth control, and women's rights, deals with the struggle between woman's control of her body and the law. These issues are often presented in Kruger's work by combining familiar images and texts from popular culture in a manner that interrupts and questions cultural stereotypes. Kruger exposes how conventional forms of representation construct our understandings of gender and sexuality and function in terms of power ideologies.

Therese Lichtenstein: How would you describe the kind of work you do?

Barbara Kruger: My interest is in dealing with the way pictures and words have the power to tell us who we can and cannot be—how they construct us as social beings. Because my focus is very much that of gender, it's obviously how women inhabit their bodies—how their bodies become figures into stereotypes—and then, how we can bring the body, the speaking body, into that

All illustrations in this chapter are by Barbara Kruger.

scenario and unmask the stereotype of that figure. I guess I'm more invested in the body's speaking than the figure's muteness, and my work contributes to altering those expectations of how women are and become.

TL: How does your work "Your Every Wish Is Our Command" challenge traditional conceptions of mothering and family in our culture?

BK: I think it is difficult to fix the meaning of my works, saying that they mean this or that. I'd say that some of the possible readings for that work could be a shifting speech. Who is speaking? Is it the child who is speaking and saying that it is in fact beholden to be the image of the perfection of that which created it, or is it the mother or father? But in this case the mother is saying, in fact, everything that you wish is something that I have to do, because it is my role in life not only to produce you biologically but to produce you socially, which means to comply with the norms that ask women to play certain roles in and around childbearing.

TL: These roles unfortunately are connected not only to a subservient placement of woman in our culture but often to a masochistic one as well, a position that is slowly changing.

BK: There have been incremental changes in the division of labor around domestic life in this country, obviously changes for the better that have to do with the empowerment of women. But there is no doubt that the positions still remain relatively fixed. In terms of the masochism involved I think it's a slow process of reeducating one's thoughts, one's subjectivity as to what can be allowed in the world and how much intervention one can make in certain authoritarian structures that tell us who we are. And again it's incremental, it's slow. It's not going to be a revolutionary break. It's rather a sequence of events that slowly chisel away at the constructions of power.

TL: It is disturbing and frightening to think how certain conceptions of motherhood and family today perpetrated and commodified by the Reagan era are a return to the values of the fifties—a neotraditionalism.

BK: One of the most disjunctive and radical accomplishments of the Reagan years was the substitution of an idyllic image of family life for the real-life material struggles of a dissolving American family. The number of single-parent families run by women, the number of absent fathers, of financially crippled social arrangements, is rising. I think that the hallucination of an ideal family is becoming more and more difficult to perpetrate. People can no longer believe it because they understand the lives they themselves are leading.

TL: I am curious about your thoughts on the diverse mass-media representations of the family and how they affect people's conceptions of their own lives and how they contribute to their "private" fantasies.

BK: Some of the most powerful examples of a conflation of negative critique and humor have been in the area of the depiction of the family. I'm not making a case for a serious theoretical rupture, but I can make a case for the

I am your

immaculate

conception

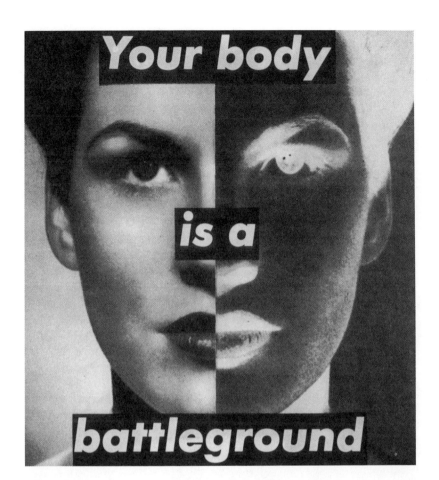

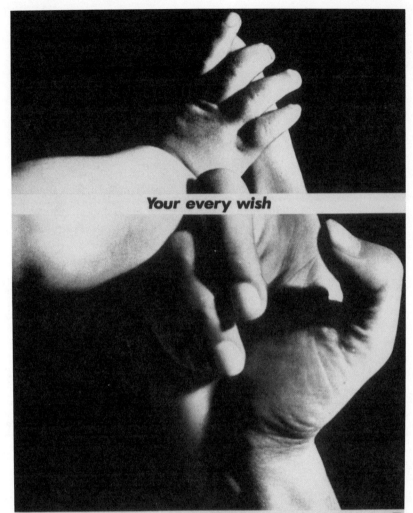

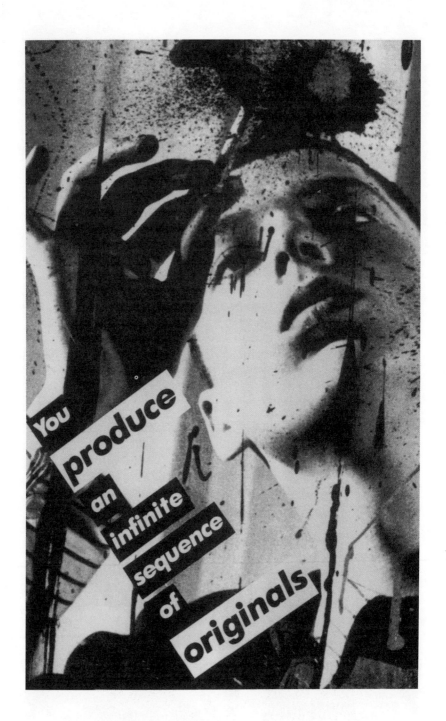

HELP!

We've finally sent the kids off to school. We're not getting any younger. I've got high blood pressure and arthritis. I just found out I'm pregnant. What should I do?

A Project of the Public Art Fund, Inc., New York City. Photo: Timothy P. Karr

notion of television shows like "Married with Children" and "The Simpsons" as entertaining legitimate negative critiques of what that fantasy was. Certainly, the idea of even mutual love between a husband and a wife and their children has been so rebuked in shows like "Married with Children," "Roseanne," and "The Simpsons." They are incredible examples of entertainment that enables us to laugh at ourselves and that creates the kind of negative mirror image of what the positive American family was like. And it's ironic that a Democratic party, which has until recently had such difficulty in constructing an effective electoral alternative to the Republican party, can still manage through the liberalism in Hollywood to construct very successful entertainment critiques of a political life. Everyone can build an empathetic audience through the ratings that verify the interest in this negativity around family life.

TL: In one of your images the words "Free Love" hang like a placard on the back of an infant who is held up between his mother's legs. The rest of the woman's body is absent. The connotation of "free love," a phrase culled from the 1960s in America, is pulverized and opens up to multiple meanings. Why do you invoke this phrase now and connect it to the infant?

BK: It refers to one aspect of motherhood, which might be a guarantee of an unconditional dependency and love which often helps women define themselves in a world that disallows definition in other areas. So it's sort of an impetus for that role. But there's another work I didn't submit (because it doesn't reproduce well)—a picture of a man's hand drawing a young child on a piece of paper. The work says, "Your Production Is Divine, Our Reproduction Is Human." Again, to me that brings back what the archetypal divisions have always been, the binary division between how men produce and create as opposed to the creative arena and the arena of production that women have been relegated to. But at times it has been a relegation of pleasure. There is no denying the incredible empowerment and pleasure that motherhood can offer. And this is not to dispute that, but just to make an allowance for choice, and an opening of that arena so that our definition can be done through all different kinds of production—not only by reproduction.

TL: I think that the term "free love" gets further complicated because it suggests sex as a utopian euphoria involving simultaneous or serial relationships in which pleasure and not necessarily a child is the result.

BK: I always felt that terms like "free love" were really rallying points and slogans for men rather than invitations for women. What was the sexual revolution? What exactly did women gain? I think they gained quite a bit. But we also saw a glaring incidence once again where the burden of birth control and the control of reproduction was on the shoulders, the buttocks, and the bodies of women. The promise of free love and open relationships was very often a catering to the pleasure of men and again to the control and confinement of women.

TL: Free love was really about physical pleasure and did not involve the complexities of emotional relationships or commitment, the relations between people and not bodies.

BK: Right. That's a really good point. I think that's probably true about the sixties, which was not a time that was very politically active for me mainly because I felt that there was this big revolution, you know, every one was doing his or her political thing, and guys were having their meetings, but the women were still there making coffee for them, baking bread, making tea, having their babies, and being their "old ladies." And, in fact, that politicized time did very little for an empowerment of women. Of course, the apotheosis of the back-to-the-land movement was the reactivation of the most traditional enslavement of women as the doyenne and prisoner of the interior.

TL: Another one of your works, "You Produce an Infinite Sequence of Originals," reminds me of Hans Namuth's film of Jackson Pollock making one of his poured, or drip paintings on glass. The "creative" cultural process of making art and procreation are equated in your piece. This image evokes a quality of passionless violence.

BK: Again, there are so many meanings that any picture and any work, not just my work, can establish. And, yes, I would say that the "infinite sequence of originals" could be read as a reproductive process. But it also could be a commentary on the act of creating original artworks, too. Just the silliness of the notion of the original around the art world is something that exists only to sustain a voracious and fickle marketplace.

TL: It continues the modernist myth of originality and the commodification of culture in late capitalism. In one of your works the words "You Are Getting What You Paid For" become a continuation of the drop of milk that begins to flow out of the nipple of a baby's bottle. The enlarged baby bottle head is thrust toward the viewer in an aggressive and ominous manner. In this image you utilize, as you often do in your other work, pronoun shifters, combining notions of nurturance with some kind of exchange, whether it be monetary or emotional.

BK: Yes, again there are quite a few readings possible in this work. And I don't like to fix the readings of the work, but, of course, it was at this point in my work that I was really trying to foreground the commodity status of the art object. So I did a number of works that did try to make the commodity speak, and in that way the commodity was speaking to perhaps an infantilized spectator or collector. I'd say that's a possibility.

TL: And by doing this, it raises the issue of the art object as a desirable commodity with power, reinvested with the aura that such status produces. Just as child rearing is not woman's individual responsibility alone, the question of developing and changing female subjectivities involves also the changing of male subjectivities—both men and women working together, in different communities, to make visible ideological changes that effect real people's lives. Deep emotional changes and the changes of codes are made possible through changes of behavior as well as understanding. Your recent installation at the Mary Boone gallery and your billboards and bus shelter posters interrupt familiar codes of viewing—from the position both of the spectator and of the images and texts you construct. Can you describe your bus shelter project?

BK: I try to visualize a site, a world where men are just as responsible for reproductive responsibility as women. So I've used three images of men—a construction worker, a high school student, and a young professional and his child—and try to invert the procedures of having these people get anecdotal about their lives and tell you that they just found out that they are pregnant. I am trying to deal with a serious topic in an anecdotal and comedic way, to engage viewers and make them laugh but also to rearrange their conceptions of what is possible. If men could have children, this sort of consideration of how one is empowered and how one is limited by biology would be a more discussed notion.

TH: Yes. These billboards are quite successful—especially in placing men in traditional female roles and what it would be like for them to bodily inhabit that space. It makes both men and women think of the enormous responsibility of the role of mothering and how it affects their lives.

RAYNA RAPP

12 The Power of "Positive" Diagnosis: Medical and Maternal Discourses on Amniocentesis

When we walked into the doctor's office, both my husband and I were crying. He looked up and said, "What's wrong? Why are you both in tears?" "It's our baby, our baby is going to die," I said. "That isn't a baby," he said firmly. "It's a collection of cells that made a mistake."   Leah Rubinstein, age thirty-nine

Late twentieth-century reproductive medicine offers both bene- fits and burdens. Its technologies are aimed at reducing mater- nal and infant mortality and helping assure normal, healthy outcomes. At the same time, however, it controls conditions of pregnancy, birth, and parenting in ways that scientize our most fundamental experiences. Being a woman, becoming a parent, experiencing birth, and sometimes confronting death are pro- cesses increasingly organized by reproductive medicine rather than by individuals, families, and communities. Indeed, many of the core experiences of sex, gender, and family formation are

I am deeply grateful to the many women who shared their amnio- centesis stories with me. All names and ages have been changed to protect confidentiality. I am also grateful to Dr. William K. Rashbaum, whose concern for his patients led him to recruit women to be inter- viewed for this study. I hope that he, and they, will find some of this material useful. Carole Browner, Michelle Fine, Susan Harding, Shirley Lindenbaum, and Emily Martin made suggestions and criticisms on an earlier draft of this chapter. And Karen Michaelson was a helpful editor. I thank them all and absolve them of any responsibility for the uses I've made of their good ideas.

now culturally defined by medical science. The access people have to reproductive medicine, as well as its respected or coercive quality, in part defines their experience of pregnancy.

Examining prenatal diagnosis, especially the use of amniocentesis, reveals a great deal about the changing definitions and controls of pregnancy and birth. On this frontier of reproductive technology, medical services are transforming the experience of pregnancy, personhood, and parenthood for the women and their families who use prenatal diagnosis. In offering a test for chromosome anomalies and some other inherited disabilities, amniocentesis holds out the possibility of choosing to carry or not to carry to term a pregnancy in which a fetus will become a child with a genetic disability. That choice is part of the medical definition of what constitutes an acceptable or an unacceptable child in American culture. The choices people make around amniocentesis also reveal the similarities and differences between medical and maternal perceptions of what it means to have a child with a disability.

Amniocentesis: Technology and Risks

The technology of amniocentesis is easily described. Pregnant women who choose the test are screened between the sixteenth and nineteenth weeks of their pregnancies. To help prepare parents, genetic counselors provide information about the risks and benefits of the test. A team of doctors and nurses uses ultrasound visualization of the fetus and placenta to guide the insertion of a thin, hollow needle into the amniotic sac, through which about three tablespoons of fluid are extracted. The liquid is cultured in a genetics laboratory, and sufficient fetal cells are usually available in three to four weeks for a diagnosis to be made. At that time, chromosome numbers, shapes, sizes, and bands can easily be read. About 98 percent of the women who have amniocentesis will receive the good news that their fetuses are free of the conditions for which they have been tested. The other 2 percent will have to confront the distressing news that their fetus has a disability. These women must weigh the stress and stigma of choosing a late abortion against the choice of having a disabled child.

Three groups of people are usually recommended for amniocentesis. One includes pregnant women and their partners whose families include someone with an inherited condition for which prenatal screening is now available. The second includes couples from ethnically specific populations in which certain autosomal recessive genetic diseases (for example, Tay-Sachs among Ashkenazi Jews; sickle cell anemia among African-Americans) are relatively frequent and for which both partners are known carriers. The third is "older" women, who are considered to be at elevated risk for several chromosomal abnormalities, of which Down's syndrome is the best known and most significant one. "Older" is, however, a social, not simply a biological construct. Although the incidence of Down's syndrome live-born babies steadily rises as women progress from their twenties to their forties, the cutoff age for the test has varied considerably. It was first recommended for women who were forty years of age or older. Then the recommendation dropped to thirty-eight and then thirty-five, and it is now moving toward the lower thirties.

The procedures used in amniocentesis are themselves not without risk, and thus the recommended age is identified by the intersection of two epidemiological patterns: One is the safety of the technology itself, and the other is the incidence of Down's syndrome in live-born babies of women in different age groups. Amniocentesis adds a small additional risk of miscarriage to the pregnancies of older women. Three more women per thousand who have had amniocentesis will miscarry than will women who have not had the test. The incidence of miscarriage with amniocentesis is thus $1/333$. This number approximates the incidence of fetuses with Down's syndrome born to pregnant women who are thirty-five, which is $1/360$ (Hook, 1981; Hook, Cross, & Schreinemachers, 1983; PDL, n.d.). If the technology improved so that it caused one less miscarriage per thousand, then the recommended age for its use would drop to match the incidence of fetuses with Downs' syndrome in that lower age group. We are thus witnessing the intersection of an increasingly routinized technology with the social pattern of delayed pregnancy in some parts of the U.S. population and not any absolute epidemiological threshold of risk.

The Sociology of Amniocentesis

The sociology of amniocentesis is more complex to describe. Initially recommended for relatively small numbers of older pregnant women, the test is rapidly becoming a pregnancy ritual for certain sectors of the highly educated urban middle class. Each year, scores of thousands of women use amniocentesis, but the test is very expensive and unevenly available.[1] Women living in major urban areas and/or near teaching hospitals and covered by comprehensive health insurance are most likely to use it. With the exception of a very few states that fund the procedure through Medicaid, amniocentesis remains the prerogative of the well-to-do. Several studies, however, indicate that low-income women would use the procedure if it were available to them for a minimal charge (Hsu, 1982; Joans, 1980; Marion et al., 1980; Sokal et al., 1980).

The discourse on amniocentesis is filled with the clamor of experts. Health economists tell us that it is cheaper to offer mass screening for Downs' syndrome than to support the services that disabled children require (Sadovnick & Baird, 1981). Geneticists assess the limits and future possibilities of their scientific field, hopeful of screening increased numbers of serious disabilities (Filkins & Russo, 1985; Harris, 1974; Lipkin & Rowley, 1974). Bioethicists comment on

1. Exact numbers of women using amniocentesis each year are unknown but seem to be growing rapidly. The President's Commission on Bioethics estimated 40,000 tests (1983) at the same time that the Center for Disease Control informally estimated 80,000, and the National Survey on Natality suggested 120,000. The lack of a "ballpark" estimate among government health-policy experts should alert us to the unregulated nature of a service that is available as part of the free-market economy of health care.

the eugenic implications of the technology (Hilton et al., 1973; Powledge & Fletcher, 1979). And feminists worry that the technique will be used for sex selection, discriminating against female fetuses (Corea, 1985; Hanmer, 1981). But when I entered the discourse as an anthropologist (and as a pregnant woman), the silence of the women and their families using or refusing the technology was deafening (Rothman, 1986). Yet it is precisely those voices that might describe the lived reality of a new reproductive technology that we must make audible if we are to understand its cultural and not simply its medical meaning, probing how the latter may be shaping the former.

A Pilot Study

This chapter reports on one aspect of the study of the social impact and cultural meaning of prenatal diagnosis: my initial pilot work with women and their families who received positive diagnoses—that is, the information that their fetuses had serious disabilities.[2] In interviews and letters, I asked people to recall the experience of getting a positive diagnosis, making a decision, and coping with its aftermath. My data come from forty women and their families, eleven of whom I interviewed in their homes, five of whom I interviewed by telephone, and twenty-four of whom entered into extensive correspondence with me. All but two ultimately chose to abort affected fetuses.

My sample was developed using medical and personal networks and responses to an article I published on amniocentesis in a nationally circulated women's magazine (Rapp, 1984). All respondents were self-selected, and the quality of information varied considerably, the telephone interviews yielding the most perfunctory information. Although the letters were written by women from all sections of the United States (in addition to two that came from abroad) recalling experiences with amniocentesis up to a decade ago, the home interviews were conducted with women who came from the metropolitan New York area and had received a positive diagnosis within the past twelve months.

My interview schedule probed for images of fetuses, disabilities, pregnancy, and family life. It asked for information about religious, ethnic, educational, and occupational backgrounds and queried the knowledge people had about the

2. I am currently doing fieldwork among scientists and support staff of a major genetics laboratory, observing genetic counselors at work with their patients, conducting home interviews with women and their families awaiting the results of amniocentesis, eliciting retrospective interviews with those who received positive diagnoses indicating serious genetic disabilities in their fetuses, participating in support groups for families whose children have the conditions (Down's syndrome, spina bifida) now diagnosable prenatally, and interviewing pregnant women who refused to use the new technology. This research is particularly concerned with differences of class, race, ethnicity, and religion in peoples' cultural construction of pregnancy and childhood disability. I hope it will result in a more complete picture of the social impact of amniocentesis than is given in this brief report of my pilot study.

disability diagnosed for their fetus prior to the time that they received their prenatal diagnosis. It contained questions concerning support and criticism from family and community members, experiences with the medical system, and steps toward resolution and recovery. It was sensitive to the use (or nonuse) of medical language in describing this perplexing experience and its aftermath. I include here many quotations from these interviews, changing only the names and ages to protect the women's privacy.

The Privatization of Experience

Although the pilot data are somewhat uneven, three themes appear consistently throughout. The first is the extreme privatization of the experience of reproductive choices—including abortions—which are considered to be personal matters in the contemporary United States, choices conventionally taken by an individual or a couple. Most of the women and their families told their immediate families about the positive diagnosis and, usually, about the subsequent abortion. Children of the family received age-appropriate information. Most also told a few close friends. But some told no one, because they lived in communities and in families where strong antiabortion sentiment was expressed. And virtually all referred to a "miscarriage" or "loss of a baby" in some contexts. The pain of reproductive loss is universal; the boundaries along which people fear they will incur judgment rather than support for a voluntary loss vary considerably. Privatization allows people some control over shaping that boundary between intimate friends who "deserved the truth" and public others who simply "needed some explanation." But privatization also reduces the quantity and quality of special support that an individual may receive for her grieving. No one with whom I spoke or corresponded had ever met another woman who had been through the same experience. This new form of intentional pregnancy loss occurs in unknown interpersonal territory. Technology here creates a traumatic experience that is so deeply medicalized and privatized that its social shape has yet to be excavated, and a cultural language to describe it is yet to be found.

The degree of isolation inherent in the experience of receiving a positive diagnosis is in part conditioned by the diagnosis itself. For the more than 80 percent of my respondents whose fetal diagnosis was Down's syndrome, some cultural knowledge was available. Everyone had an image of a child with Down's syndrome. Some had friends, family members, or community members whose children had the condition. Although their images of mentally retarded children, especially children with Down's syndrome, were often out of date, they still had a reference point for the diagnosis and felt competent to decide whether or not to end the affected pregnancy. In this pilot study, I had no cases of women continuing a pregnancy after a prenatal diagnosis of Down's syndrome. And medical statistics suggest an abortion rate of about 95 percent after this particular diagnosis (Hook, 1981).

Other, more arcane diagnoses were harder to understand and to judge. Two of my respondents received diagnoses of XYY syndrome, a sex-chromosome anomaly. The diagnosis of XYY includes possible mental retardation, anomalous sexual development, and putative aggressiveness. But the diagnosis is highly controversial and has sparked both technical and popular discussions of whether screening is appropriate or is an artifact of the abuse of minimal scientific information blown out of proportion (Hook, 1973). Both respondents who received this diagnosis spent whole days in a medical library trying to interpret the meaning of XYY syndrome before reaching their decisions. One family's fetus was identified as having a chromosomal tag so rare that a nationally known geneticist could point to just fifteen other reported cases and only vaguely predict its outcome. Another family received a diagnosis of organ damage and displacement so complete that they consulted with a battery of pediatric surgeons and neonatologists over the course of one month before they reached a decision. Two others didn't understand the language of the diagnosis and had to have it explained many times before they could make a choice. In such cases, unlike Down's syndrome, there is no collective fund of information available, and medical language necessarily dictates the shape of familial understanding.

The Language of Prenatal Diagnosis

The use of medical language in itself creates tensions in the discussion of prenatal diagnosis. This is the second theme that ran through all the interviews and letters. Medical language is not neutral; medical practices are often intentionally distancing, as the quotation that opens this chapter suggests. Some patients find this distance reassuring in its promise of rationality; others find it cold and denying of their experience. A war of words accompanied virtually all the stories I collected. *Cells, embryos,* and *fetuses* vied for center stage with *babies.* "Positive diagnoses" describe the medical discovery procedures, but they painfully reverse and mask the very negative experiences of parents who learn that their fetuses have disabilities. In some cases here, women literally assumed the burden of this impersonal language, speaking in total disconnection from their pregnant bodies: "So I was in labor for twenty-four hours and absolutely nothing happened. I mean nothing. A dead fetus, but it wouldn't come out. So I called Dr. X at eight A.M. and I guess I must have sounded crazy. 'Hello,' I said, 'I'm a demised fetus and a failed prostaglandin.' 'Oh no you're not, honey,' the nurse said. 'You're a lady that's losing a baby, and you'd better stop talking and start crying.'" (Sandra Larkin, age thirty-six).

Several families mentioned the struggles they had waged to see their dead fetuses or to retrieve them for burial. Usually, fetuses were sent to pathology to confirm a diagnosis. Legal and hospital procedures dictate this practice, which brings the reality of family mourning into conflict with medical protocols. Denied access to dead fetuses, some chose to bury or frame the sonogram visualizations that they had been given during amniocentesis. One family pasted the image into the family Bible. They thus created the emotional personification, albeit through technology, that family life required and medical procedures could not grant.[3]

The use of medical language and its accompanying procedures are purposive. As one respondent put it, "This late-abortion business is no picnic for the doctors and nurses." Medical discourse protects medical staff from the sad and disorienting experiences of their patients, allowing the routinization of services. But each women I interviewed had to perform a complex translation of the medical words she had been given into whatever her own experience of that pregnancy and its ending had been. Often only medical language seemed legitimate. Many women couldn't use the word *abortion,* yet hesitated over *termination,* the term used by medical professionals. Almost all switched from *fetus* to *baby* while describing their situations. Yet no one could recall the affected pregnancy without using medical descriptions of its length, dated from last menstrual period rather than by nausea, quickening, or some other intrabody sign. And, of course, the diagnosis itself was always discussed medically. Medical language here reinforces the privatization of the problem, for each woman is seen, and sees herself, as an individual patient rather than as a member of a larger group of women confronting a new technological possibility or coping with grief.

There is an awkward gap between medical and maternal discourses. Although some might argue that medical language neutralizes some of the anxiety associated with amniocentesis (Brewster, 1984), its function is actually more complex and powerful. Many scholars and activists have noted that medical discourses increasingly define pregnancy itself as a pathological (or potentially pathological) condition, thus justifying professional management and intervention (Rothman, 1982; Shaw, 1974; Wertz & Wertz, 1977). But pregnancy is also an embodied state and a time-framed activity about which a great deal of popular knowledge has been accumulated, often passed down from mothers to daughters, shared among friends, and held by ethnically specific communities (Oakley, 1979, 1980, 1981; Snow, Johnson, & Mayhew, 1978; Thompson, 1983). Thus, multiple discourses construct pregnancy as a whole, subdivided among specialists (for example, obstetricians and midwives may think and speak differently about their pregnant patients) and between specialists and pregnant women.

The same cannot be said for prenatal diagnosis, which is constructed as a specifically medical event. The experience itself exists only in relation to the technology, services, and personnel within which it is embedded. Unlike pregnancy, for which a woman has embodied experiences she can and does articulate and share with others (both pregnant and nonpregnant), the event of receiving a positive diagnosis bears no relation to either internal body cues or collective popular knowledge. There is no tradition to call upon in coping with the diagnosis. Acceptance of the test and its results implies a belief in epidemiological

---

3. Such technological personifications may be viewed as examples of cyborgs, science fiction chimeras interfacing people and machines, a late-twentieth-century cultural form insightfully analyzed by Haraway (1985).

statistics, an acknowledgement of risk factors, population parameters, and laboratory procedures all far removed from the individual or the collective sense of pregnancy itself. Those for whom a positive diagnosis is given are thus operating on an unknown terrain, far removed from pregnancy as they have experienced or learned about it. The stumbling words, the gaps of language, the silences surrounding this experience, are testimony to its totally medical construction. It is an experience removed from the maternal discourses by which pregnant women gradually become mothers, not simply medical cases.

The Ethics of Decision Making

A third generalization that emerged from these interviews is the ethical complexity and social embeddedness of the decision to abort (or in two cases, to keep) an affected pregnancy. Five respondents discussed their cases with religious advisers, and six saw psychological counselors in the course of making their decisions. But the majority did not seek nonmedical professional help. They retrospectively identified their decision as having been made at one of two times: it was made "on the day I decided to go for amniocentesis" (that is, with an almost-conscious knowledge that a diagnosis of any fetal genetic disability would be reason enough to choose abortion), or the decision was made "the minute we got the news" (in which case the couple, not the pregnant woman, was recalled as the decision-making unit, and their conversations were recalled verbatim). In the five cases for which anomalous diagnoses were given, decision making was protracted, involving several rounds of medical consultation and sometimes library research or home visits with families whose living children had the diagnosed condition. Yet even those couples who conducted research before making a decision reported strong leanings toward an abortion as soon as they knew that something was wrong.[4]

Reasons for the abortion decision were often phrased in terms of other family members:

> Some people say that abortion is hate. I say my abortion was an act of love. I've got three kids. I was forty-three when we accidentally got pregnant again. We decided there was enough love in our family to handle it, even though finances would be tight. But we also decided to have the test. A kid with a serious problem was more than we could handle. And when we got the bad news, I knew immediately what I had to do. At forty-three, you think about your own death. It would have been tough now, but think what would have happened to my other kids, especially my daughter. Oh, the

---

4. Anomalous diagnoses are compounded by the newness of the technology and fears—both accurate and exaggerated—of human and technical error in using it. And, as Emily Martin pointed out to me, many more women are told that something may be wrong owing to technical errors that are later corrected (e.g., maternal/fetal cell confusion in an amniotic sample) than will actually confront a "truly positive" diagnosis.

boys, Tommy and Alex, would have done okay. But Laura would have been the one who got stuck. It's always the girls. It would have been me, and then after I'm gone it would have been the big sister who took care of that child. Saving Laura from that burden was an act of love. (Mary Fruticci, age forty-four)

Many families with other children expressed similar concerns, citing the effects of a disabled sibling on prior children as the reason for choosing abortion. But over 60 percent of the respondents made an abortion decision during a first planned pregnancy. They had to take responsibility for the decision on the basis of their own needs, not adopt an altruistic stance toward dependent children. In these cases, ambivalence about parenting skills was sometimes expressed:

So he would have had this sex chromosome thing; he might have been slow, and he was going to be aggressive. I didn't know how to handle a kid like that. When he got rowdy and difficult, could I be a committed parent, or would I have thrown up my hands, thinking "It's in his genes"? [Q: What if you hadn't known through prenatal diagnosis?] I'm sure if it had just happened we would have handled it. But once you know, you're forced to make a decision. (David Kass, age thirty-five)

Concern for the marriage rather than the children was often identified as a reason for an abortion decision:

I talked with this couple who had a kid with Down's, and I thought they were terrific. The kid was nice, and they seemed like a fine family. But they'd been married almost twenty years when it happened, had raised three other kids, and were confident of their commitments. Stu and I have only been together for two years, and it's our first baby, and what if the strain were too great? What if we never got the chance to have a normal kid? What if we broke up over it? (Jane Butler, age thirty-five)

Altruism toward other household members was central to these descriptions. Yet two other themes were conspicuous in their absence. One was the fear of disability, a salient cultural theme for many Americans. The other was the limits of altruism, the admission that there are specific kinds of children that individual women would choose not to mother, given a choice. Both absent themes suggest a wealth of cultural attitudes concerning disability and maternity that medicalization of the experience masks. Of course, the standards for acceptable and unacceptable children and the meaning of specific disabilities are always culturally constructed. Some societies prescribe infanticide for those conditions they label socially inadmissible. In contemporary America, it is a medical procedure that appears to have become the cutting edge in defining the cultural construction of disability.[5]

5. Carole Browner and Shirley Lindenbaum both suggested that the cross-cultural evidence argues for universal constructions of acceptable and unacceptable disabilities.

To some degree the decision was diagnosis-specific: "When I heard my obstetrician's voice on the phone, I went numb. He told me it was Down's and said 'I think we should talk about it.' 'What's there to talk about?' I said. 'The decision comes with the disease'" (Leah Rubinstein, age thirty-nine).

Others had a harder time, depending on what they knew or could find out about their fetal diagnosis. Ultimately, however, all had to take responsibility for ending a pregnancy to which they had already felt a commitment: "The whole time I was getting ready, the tests, the visits, the hospital procedure, I kept thinking, 'this is awful, this is the most terrible thing.' I never, ever wanted to be here. But I am here, and it's my choice, and I'm the one who's making it. No one can explain this to me, not why it happened. No one. I have to stop looking for answers out there and trust myself" (Michelle Kansky, age thirty-eight). Like David Kass, who doubted his ability to parent a child with a sex chromosome anomaly once he had that information, Michelle Kansky was also expressing the burdens of individual choice. Informed consent is thought to lead to optimal individual decision making, which is deemed an absolute good in American legal and medical culture. Yet this commitment to individual decision making, while culturally appropriate, increases the burdens of privatization as well. It pushes people to rely on their own information and feelings rather than on any larger social grouping, as they confront the problems and possibilities a new reproductive technology offers.

All respondents described their painful decisions in terms of themselves, their marriages, their other children—in terms of individuals in nuclear families. Yet when we stepped back from these self-descriptions, it became apparent that other sociological facts weighed heavily in the decision to use amniocentesis and the responses to positive diagnosis. One was the role of occupation. In a small and totally self-selected sample, it is striking to find such a large number of helping professionals. Nine of the forty respondents were teachers, four were social workers, and nine out of the two groups worked with retarded children, retarded adults, or their families. How did their commitment to education and to working with disabled people and families shape their responses to parenting a potentially disabled child?

Even more striking is the importance of religious background in descriptions of the abortion decision. Nationally, women using abortion services are as likely to be Catholic as non-Catholic (Henshaw & Martire, 1982; Petchesky, 1984). But because we do not yet have a general picture of amniocentesis users, we cannot know if Catholic women and their families are as likely to use these prenatal services as non-Catholics. Nor do we know if they are as likely to abort if they receive a positive diagnosis. Yet six respondents identified themselves as Roman Catholics, four currently practicing and two reared as Catholics. For them, the choice was very hard and involved a personal exegesis on the meaning of abortion:

But our current cultural context is one of political struggle over the definitions of disability and social responses.

I was raised to take what you get in life, any life you get. If I had stayed at home in Granville, if I hadn't gone to college, if I hadn't married Joe [who is Jewish], I'd still feel that way. I do feel that way. But even though I was brought up Catholic to believe abortion is murder, I also believe in a woman's right to choose. In people's right to choose. And that choice is a big part of me now, just as big as my religion. (Terry Hanz, age thirty-four)

I think the hardest problem I faced was confession. I needed to have that abortion, but I also needed to confess, and I couldn't go to our parish priest, even though my mother and my mother-in-law knew. I just couldn't go to him. So I finally went to St. X, across town, where criminals and celebrities go to confess. And that helped a lot. Later, I was talking with the father of an old friend; he's an old man, very conservative, very Catholic. But he was saying how much he admired Geraldine Ferraro for her stand on abortion. "What does the pope know about these things? Let the women decide on this one, not old men, like me." That helped me, that really helped me, even though he didn't know my situation. Now I say, "Let anyone who'll judge me stand in my shoes first." I'm still a Catholic, but I say Catholics who judge women for having an abortion haven't lived through hard times. Only when you're going to live with the consequences do you get to judge the act. (Marie Mancini, age thirty-eight)

For the more than 30 percent of respondents who identified themselves as Jewish, the choice of abortion was philosophically simpler, if still personally painful. Many gave some variant of this account: "You ask why we chose to have amniocentesis and follow through with the abortion. I'll tell you this: If the technology is there, it's better to use it. Better to live with the benefits of modern science, cry over your loses, but use every means science gives you to have a better life" (Michelle Kansky, age thirty-eight).

And whatever their religious orientation, almost all felt the need to respond to the abortion controversy, which is currently central in American political and cultural life:

I share a lot of the feelings of the right-to-life movement. I've always been shocked by the number of abortion clinics, the number of abortions in this city. But when it was my turn I was grateful to find the right doctor. I sent him and his staff roses after it was all over. They helped me to protect my own life, and that's a life, too. (Mary Fruticci, age forty-four)

We baptized our little son [aborted after a diagnosis of trisomy 18]; we put the sonogram picture in the family Bible. No one can tell us we did the wrong thing, no matter how much they don't believe in abortion. He's gone now. But he was real. And abortion is real, and sometimes necessary. (Lena Jarowlski, age thirty-six)

There was no morally correct choice available. Abortion is a terrible choice. But so is the choice to bring a deeply damaged child into this world. People who are antiabortion can't imagine what this is like. (Carey Morgan, age thirty-six)

Amniocentesis and the Perception of Disability

The choice to abort after a positive diagnosis is made, in large part, because of the family's perception of what the child's disability will mean to them. The disability rights movement, however, has made a powerful case for the social rather than the biological nature of the problems that disabled people face. Whatever their individual medical problems and diagnoses, disabled children and adults—like pregnant women—are more than medical cases. They are people whose access to a high quality of life is limited by the social stigma and institutional barriers they confront. Prenatal diagnosis raises a complex of thorny issues about those prejudices. It is neither appropriate nor realistic to expect individual families to reexamine their attitudes toward disability at the moment that they are being informed that their fetus will have one. But as a society, we need to undertake that reexamination so that informed consent will include the social realities and not just the medical diagnosis of raising a child with a particular condition.

Many genetic counselors (especially if they work in pediatric, not only prenatal, service units) have information on services and support groups for children with genetic disabilities and their families. This information is rarely requested or volunteered during the crisis and decision making surrounding a positive diagnosis. Only two of the forty families requested visits with families whose live-born children had the conditions that had been diagnosed in their fetuses. In both cases the visit engendered more knowledge about the disability, lessening its mythic terror. Both couples went on to make an abortion decision. In the 80 percent of diagnoses involving Down's syndrome, all respondents could recall seeing children with the condition in their communities, and most had somewhere in their network friends, neighbors, or relatives with a child who had Down's syndrome. Some families were accepting, in principle, of children who are mentally retarded, but were grateful to avoid the reality in their own cases. Others expressed more shock, even revulsion, at the idea that their child would be retarded.

In almost all cases, the families' knowledge was outdated and did not usually include information about the accessibility of infant stimulation programs or the high level of function that many children with Down's syndrome now achieve (Garland et al., 1981; Pueschel, 1978). Nor did it include a realistic picture of what the emotional or financial costs of raising a child with both physical and mental disabilities were likely to be. This is not to suggest that the decisions were necessarily wrong ones or incorrectly made. I am only suggesting that at the present time, informed consent is a concept that focuses on individual medical knowledge, and that social knowledge about the real consequences of disabilities is often underdeveloped.

As long as disabled children (and adults) and their families remain segregated and stigmatized, the knowledge that potential parents might use to decide whether or not to abort a fetus with a diagnosis of disability will also remain unavailable. An individual rights focus is legally and medically appropriate to prenatal diagnosis and is consonant with deeply held American cultural beliefs. But it also masks the larger social attitudes on which knowledge, images, and insufficient services for disabled people are based. To enlarge the scope of informed consent, we must look beyond individual choice toward the sources of community knowledge and prejudice. And here, as with prenatal diagnosis, it is the voices and traditions of the disabled themselves, rather than only the medical and educational professionals, from which we need to learn.

Amniocentesis and the Language of Feminism

The language of individualism and prochoice feminism that was often used in describing the abortion decision after a positive diagnosis grows out of the transformation of work, gender relations, family life, and cultural politics that a generation of women in the United States has recently experienced.

> I've been a woman's movement activist for a million years; I've counseled abortions; I've helped to set up crisis hot lines for women. And this experience brought me as close to the right-to-life movement as I'll ever come. I'd felt the baby moving; it wasn't a fetus in my mind, it was our baby. Still I'm grateful to have had the choice. This was devastating; it permanently changed our lives, but then, so would the birth of a kid with Down's. I don't want the right-to-life movement changing my life. I have to do it myself. (Pat Gordon, age thirty-seven)

One informant cited Carol Gilligan's (1982) work to me: "Women are responsible for giving life, not for taking it. Women do have their own morality. Still, I've got to be responsible to myself, Stu, to our future kids, and those responsibilities come first" (Jane Butler, age thirty-five).

These women (and their male partners) were wrapped in the discourses of prolife-prochoice politics and mainstream feminism. This language of individual, even feminist, morality seems comfortable to middle-class women, unlike the awkwardness of the medical language, which constructs and constrains their experiences of positive diagnosis. The "second nature" of this discourse is no accident. Mainstream feminism now infuses large sectors of American culture despite its sometimes embattled, oppositional stance. The discourse of maternalism (even medicalized maternalism) is becoming more feminist, if by that we mean centered on the expansion of individual women's choices, whether we speak of choices in amniocentesis or styles of birthing babies.

But to examine the cultural imagery surrounding motherhood, it is necessary to shift our focus from the individual woman and her family to the larger community. Because the experience of prenatal diagnosis is so deeply privatized and medicalized, it is easy to miss the gender fault lines on which this new reproductive technology sits. The deeply internalized and socially pervasive imagery of motherhood in American culture is surely shifting. Women who have a choice, including the choice to abort genetically disabled fetuses, are less likely to see themselves or to be seen by others as "Madonnas"—long-suffering mothers whose nurturance is unconditional and ever-present. Although I would personally argue that freedom from such religiously referential, selfless images of maternity is, on the whole, liberating for women, I would also suggest that we cast a critical eye on the cultural imagery that may replace it—particularly if that imagery is defined in medical terms. The "new woman" of prenatal diagnosis may feel like an agent of quality control on the reproductive production line:

> I was hoping I'd never have to make this choice, to become responsible for choosing the kind of baby I'd get, the kind of baby we'd accept. But everyone—my doctor, my parents, my friends—everyone urged me to come for genetic counseling and have amniocentesis. Now I guess I am having a modern baby. And they all told me I'd feel more in control. But in many ways, I feel less in control. It's still my baby, but only if it's good enough to be our baby, if you see what I mean. (Nancy Smithers, age thirty-six)

Neither image—the selfless Madonna or the agent of quality control—is constructed by or for women's interests. Both are deeply embedded in patriarchal cultural discourses, the one traditional and religious, the other modern and medically technocratic. The future cultural conceptualization we hold of women as mothers in part depends on turning down the volume of expert voices so that the voices of women themselves may become part of the discourse of prenatal diagnosis.

References

Brewster, A. (1984). A patient's reaction to amniocentesis. *Obstetrics and Gynecology,* 64, 443–44.

Corea, G. (1985). *The mother machine.* New York: Harper and Row.

Filkins, K., & Russo, J. F. (1985). *Human prenatal diagnosis.* New York: Marcel Dekker.

Garland, C., et al. (1981). Early intervention for children with special needs and their families. WESTAR Series Paper no. 11. Chapel Hill: Frank Porter Graham Child Development Center, University of North Carolina.

Gilligan, C. (1982). *In a different voice.* Cambridge, Mass.: Harvard University Press.

Hanmer, J. (1981). Sex predetermination, artificial insemination, and the maintenance of male-dominated culture. In H. Roberts (Ed.), *Women, health and reproduction.* London: Routledge and Kegan Paul.

Haraway, D. (1985). Science, technology, and socialist feminism in the 1980s. *Socialist Review,* 80, 65–107.

Harris, H. (1974). *Prenatal diagnosis and selective abortion.* Cambridge, Mass.: Harvard University Press.

Henshaw, S., & Martire, G. (1982). Abortion and the public opinion polls. *Family Planning Perspectives,* 14, 53–62.

Hilton, B., et al. (1973). *Ethical issues in human genetics.* New York: Plenum.

Hook, E. B. (1973). Behavior implications of the human XXY genotype. *Science,* 179, 139–49.

Hook, E. B. (1981). Rates of chromosome abnormalities at different maternal ages. *Obstetrics and Gynecology,* 58, 282–85.

Hook, E. B., Cross, P. K., & Schreinemachers, D. M. (1983). Chromosomal abnormality rates at amniocentesis and in live-born infants. *Journal of the American Medical Association,* 249 (April 15): 2034–38.

Hsu, L. (1982). *Keeping genetic service accessible.* Report from a conference on the continuing role of the prenatal diagnosis laboratory of New York City, June.

Joans, B. (1980). *Dilemmas and decisions of prenatal diagnosis.* Symposium at the New York City Technical College, April.

Lipkin, M., and Rowley, P. (Eds.). (1974). *Genetic responsibility.* New York: Plenum.

Marion, J. P., et al. (1980). Acceptance of amniocentesis by low-income patients in an urban hospital. *American Journal of Obstetrics and Gynecology,* 138, 11–15.

Oakley, A. (1979). A case of maternity: Paradigms of women as maternity cases. *Signs,* 4, 607–31.

Oakley, A. (1980). *Becoming a mother.* New York: Schocken.

Oakley, A. (1981). *Woman confined: Sociology of childbirth.* New York: Schocken.

Petchesky, R. (1984). *Abortion and women's choice.* New York: Longman.

Powledge, T., and Fletcher, J. (1979). Guidelines for the ethical, social and legal issues in prenatal diagnosis. *New England Journal of Medicine,* 300, 168–72.

Prenatal Diagnosis Laboratory of New York City. (n.d.). Counseling protocols, charts, and tables.

Pueschel, S. (1978). *Down syndrome: Growing and learning.* Kansas City: Sheed Andrews and McMeel.

Rapp, R. (1984). Amniocentesis: The ethics of choice. *Ms. Magazine,* April, 97–100.

Rothman, B. K. (1982). *In labor: Women and power in the birthplace.* New York: Norton. (Reprinted as *Giving birth: Alternatives in childbirth.* New York: Penguin, 1985).

Rothman, B. K. (1986). *The tentative pregnancy.* New York: Viking/Penguin.

Sadovnik, A. D., & Baird, P. (1981). A cost-benefit analysis of prenatal detection of Down syndrome and neural tube defects in older mothers. *American Journal of Medical Genetics,* 10, 367.

Shaw, N. S. (1974). *Forced labor: Maternity care in the United States.* New York: Pergamon.

Snow, L. F., Johnson, S. M., and Mayhew, H. (1978). The behavioral implications of some old wives' tales. *Obstetrics and Gynecology,* 51(6), 727–32.

Sokal, D. C., et al. (1980). Prenatal chromosome analysis, racial and geographic variation for older women. *Journal of the American Medical Association,* 244, 1355–547.

Thompson, S. (1983). Felicita Garcia: I just came out pregnant! In A. Snitow, C. Stansell, & S. Thompson (Eds.), *The powers desire*. New York: Monthly Review Press.

Wertz, D., and Wertz, R. C. (1977). *Lying in: A history of childbirth in America*. New York: Free Press.

MARGARET HONEY

13 The Maternal Voice in the Technological Universe

When I think about the world of technology, I think about a world that is rigidly gendered—that is, a world that is the exclusive province of men and is governed by a form of logic that is abstract, calculable, and depersonalized. To my way of thinking, the technological universe is characterized by a type of rationality that in certain schools of thought is known as instrumental, in which the means are divorced from the ends or the ends from the means and there is a preoccupation with issues of domination and control. These are the negative images I have. I also have images that might be characterized as envious and somewhat desirous—in this respect, the technological universe is powerful, tough-minded, and strong. People who have entered this universe have the goods; that is, they have something I don't have, but I want. As a result, they are decidedly different from me—they have succeeded in gaining access to a world that remains attractively Other.

There are other domains that are similar to the world of technology—sports, including games like football and basketball, the military, the world of high finance, and so on. I tend to

This chapter reflects the work and thinking of a number of my colleagues; thus, I use the plural *we* in representing the ideas and thoughts that evolved in collaboration with them. I would like to thank Katie McMillan for her work on the transcripts, her contributions to the development of the interpretive frameworks elaborated here, and her careful reading and rereading of the manuscript. Cornelia Brunner's, Jan Hawkins's, Peggy Clement's, and Babette Moeller's ideas had a major impact on the content and shape of the chapter. And our weekly discussions around the women and technology project at the Center for Children and Technology served as an important developmental space in which a number of ideas contained here emerged.

think of such worlds as phallic universes—this is my shorthand and it means something specific. They are worlds that systematically exclude the maternal, they are indifferent to personal needs, and they banish values such as nurturance and care to the privatized domestic world of the home. The phallic universe is characterized by a slippery amalgam of means and ends: Winning is everything and yet when victory is not realized the means are quickly accorded their own triumphant status. And yet, because these phallic universes also signify power, potency, and prestige, they are in this respect a source of envy.

Historical approaches to the study of women's involvement with technology have focused on the ways in which women have been at the mercy of technology rather than being empowered users or creators of technology, or contributors toward technological change (McGaw, 1982; Wright, 1987). During the 1970s and 1980s, however, women entered the skilled end of the computer industry in increasing numbers. As of 1990 they held 32.4 percent of the systems analysts jobs and 41.1 percent of the jobs in operations and systems; they made up 35.7 percent of our nation's mathematical and computer scientists (Frankel, 1990). Despite these inroads, computer science continues to be a professional arena that is perceived and experienced as hostile to women (Pearl et al., 1990).

For the past several years a group of us at Bank Street's Center for Children and Technology has been doing research on adult technology experts.[1] Our inquiry was designed to counter traditional deficit model studies, which claim that women are excluded from technological professions and thus have limited knowledge about technology as a whole. We were interested in the women who had gained access to and achieved a certain level of professional stature within technological worlds. In particular, we wanted to investigate their interpretive and meaning-making processes—what significance did they attribute to their work and what did they find compelling about it?

We began this research with certain theoretical suppositions about the nature of technological objects. Technological objects are symbolic and as such they are overdetermined. The task of decoding the symbolic nature of technologies is a hermeneutic endeavor that involves an intellectual process of deciphering and uncovering hidden or latent meanings (Ricoeur, 1970). The computer serves as an interesting case in point. Like all symbolic objects, computers have meanings attached to them that are both manifest and latent, and perhaps more than any other object on the contemporary horizon computers have been used to both illustrate and embody different aspects of human potential and human imagination. Computer scientists working in the area of artificial intelligence attempt to breathe life into technology by endowing machines with aspects of

1. This research was originally funded by the Spencer Foundation (Women and Technology: A New Basis for Understanding). Jan Hawkins was the principal investigator; Cornelia Brunner, Peggy Clements, Margaret Honey, and Babette Moeller were the project staff.

human intelligence, the prototypic example of this being the intelligent chess-playing computer.[2]

In his research on "The Army and the Microworld," Paul Edwards (1990) makes the point that "computer work—programming, computer engineering, systems analysis—is more than a job. It is a major cultural practice, a large-scale social form that has created and reinforced modes of thinking, systems of interaction, and ideologies of social control" (p. 102). As part of a larger cultural discourse, the computer and, increasingly, information technologies in general, embody a kind of hyperrationality that is privileged in our culture as a whole. The work of the computer scientists takes place within a rule-bound, logical universe that is freed from the constraints and messiness of day-to-day life. The culture of computer science is thought of as rigorous, intellectually demanding, and requiring "hard" knowledge to both participate and succeed in. As Sherry Turkle and Seymour Papert (1990) note, "both popular and technical culture have constructed computation as the ultimate embodiment of the abstract and the formal." And indeed, the rationalist tradition within which the work of the computer scientist is embedded has long been associated with maleness and masculinity—with a kind of hard mastery that is opposed to the softer, more interpersonally oriented world of women (Cohn, 1987; Edwards, 1990; Keller, 1985; Turkle, 1984, 1988, 1990). In this sense, then, the computer is the ultimate technological object, and it embodies in exaggerated fashion those aspects of technology that are most phallic in nature.

In her research on programming styles, Sherry Turkle has written extensively about the ways in which the dominant computer culture—the world of culturally produced meanings—supports and legitimates a certain way of appropriating technology, which she characterizes as "hard mastery." As Turkle (1984) describes it, "hard mastery is the imposition of will over the machine through the implementation of a plan. A program is the instrument of premeditated control" (p. 104). For the hard master, there is a perfect fit between the cultural promise of technology and its personal realization, and it is this fit that allows for the articulation of personal desires that are more often than not divided along gender lines. Soft mastery, on the other hand, is more like the give-and-take of conversation; rather than imposing ideas on the machine, ideas emerge and evolve through the process of interaction. As a cultural practice, however, this kind of conversation with technology is not privileged. As Turkle's work documents, when women attempt to appropriate technology they more often than not find themselves in situations of conflict—hence, the woman who assumes that if she does something wrong with her computer it will explode in her face.

In a different but related domain, Carol Cohn (1987), a feminist scholar and peace activist, writes about the discursive culture of defense intellectuals, those individuals who articulate the theory that informs and legitimates America's

---

2. For an excellent discussion of the history of artificial intelligence see Turkle (1984, pp. 239–47).

nuclear arms policies. Cohn was one of a group of college teachers who attended a summer workshop on nuclear weapons, nuclear strategic doctrine, and arms control. Her involvement led her to undertake an analysis of the language of this culture, a language she calls technostrategic. Cohn not only documents the obvious and expected aspects of this culture, such as the use of phallic and gender-laden imagery (long discussions took place on the relative value of different "penetration aids" or how to "get more bang for your buck"), but also analyzes the more subtle role that the language of strategic defense analysts plays in masking the *reality* of nuclear death and devastation. As Cohn writes:

> In the ever-friendly world of nuclear weaponry, enemies "exchange" warheads; one missile "takes out" another; weapons "marry up"; "coupling" is sometimes used to refer to the wiring between mechanisms of warning and response, or to the psycho-political links between strategic (intercontinental) and theater (European-based) weapons. The patterns in which a MIRVed missile's nuclear warheads land is known as a "footprint." These nuclear explosives are not dropped; a "bus" "delivers" them. (1987, p. 698)

Cohn's point is that this kind of talk serves to domesticate and tame the forces of nuclear destruction. The metaphors that these men use to characterize their work minimize the horrific deadly nature of the weapons they describe—"they are a way to make phenomena that are beyond what the mind can encompass smaller and safer, and thus they are a way of gaining mastery over the unmasterable" (p. 698). Cohn describes her experience, as she became more enmeshed in the language of the defense community, of losing sight of the reality that she had originally come to study. It was no longer possible for her to hold onto the images of devastation and destruction that most of us associate with nuclear war.

Cohn's research is a poignant example of the ways in which gender, language, and technology can combine to shape and inform the cultural practices of a community. Her work illustrates, in turn, the ways in which cultural practices allow certain patterns of meaning to flourish while excluding or banishing others. In our own research on gender and technology, we were interested in investigating how the technological cultures within which women worked would impact on the ways in which they would appropriate and make meaning out of different areas of technological expertise. As Teresa de Lauretis (1986) has stated, "the relation of experience to discourse is what is at issue in the definition of feminism" (p. 5).

What is at stake in this inquiry is the larger issue of women's desire. We are all well aware of Freud's famous query: what does woman want? Indeed, the very fact that Freud posed such a question has been the villain in much feminist debate. Rather than trying to address a question that was born of a one-sided orientation to the problem of desire itself, psychoanalytically oriented feminists have begun to shift our focus away from the object of desire (the father or phallus) to the subject of desire (Benjamin, 1986, 1988; Chodorow, 1978; Gilligan, 1982, 1986; Gilligan & Stern, 1986). The question then changes: it is not *what*—in what object do we locate our desire—but rather *how*—how do we as women articulate our needs and wants? But as I said earlier, the discursive practices that constitute the technological universe complicate the ways in which meanings and expressions can arise. The question of women's desire, then, becomes especially problematic when we attempt to articulate it in relation to a universe that is so clearly phallic in nature. Thus, in our own research, we were curious about how these technological experts would navigate such slippery terrain—how would they make meaning and derive pleasure out of a phallic universe?

In part, we were suspicious. These were women who had gained access to a technological domain and entered a universe that required hard-core knowledge. Although we were not altogether sure what these women would sound like, we were fairly certain they would not sound like women. We thought we would hear them engage in a kind of hyperlogical talk; we imagined they would stride efficiently through our interviews in a clean and concise manner. We were thus surprised when we began to hear echoes of a different kind of discourse, one that was distinctly maternal in tone.[3]

The Research

We conducted twenty-eight in-depth interviews with seventeen women and eleven men who were deeply engaged in computer-related activities as programmers, computer engineers, computer scientists, and aerospace engineers. They worked in industry and in private and public research and development centers, as well as for hardware manufacturers and software development houses. The women ranged in age from twenty-one to forty-four, and the men from twenty-seven to thirty-nine.

One of the questions that we explored in depth with our interviewees was what they found exciting or compelling about their work. Both the women and the men talked about deriving pleasure from the processes that their work involves. They described their enjoyment in the routines, the problem solving, and the detail work that computer programming often entails. When the women spoke about being compelled by the process of the work, however, they also spoke about getting pleasure out of problems or processes that circled around someone else's enjoyment and involvement. Their orientation was distinctly interpersonal—the pleasure they found in their work came from embedding technology in the larger context of human relationships and interactions. The men, in contrast, were much more likely to talk about the immense enjoyment

3. I see the term *maternal voice* as a component of what Sara Ruddick (1989) has identified as *maternal thinking*—the kind of reflective thought that develops around the demands of motherhood for preservation, growth, and social acceptability. I also see the term *maternal voice* as bearing a direct relation to the ideas that Gilligan (1986) developed in *In a Different Voice,* and to the Women's Ways of Knowing Collective (Belenky et al., 1986).

they derived from the technology itself. They described the pleasure they got out of working on particularly complex technical problems—problems that moved them further away from the user toward the technology itself.

My colleague Jan Hawkins (1990, 1991) first called attention to these different perspectives in terms of what she called the *aesthetics* of understanding. Drawing on the work of aesthetic philosophers, she has characterized the difference between men's and women's orientations as *opaque* and *transparent,* respectively. In her interpretation, the men tend to get *arrested by the technological devices* themselves, whereas the women tend to *see through the objects* to the larger context of human interactions.

In this chapter I shall explore this issue from another perspective—one that is grounded simultaneously in an analysis of the discourse of technological culture and the work of psychoanalytically oriented feminist theory. In particular, I shall examine the distinctive features of the interpretive frameworks that women and men use to characterize the pleasure they get out of their work with computer technology, paying close attention to their language and metaphors.

The Women

Of the seventeen women we interviewed, thirteen of them expressed an orientation toward their work that contained elements of a maternal voice that has as its focus the needs and experiences of others. Their orientation can be further characterized by four interpretive frameworks: (1) pleasure in technology's communicative potential; (2) pleasure in making technology more accessible; (3) pleasure in the collaborative nature of technological work; and (4) pleasure in the personal accomplishments that can result from computer-based work.

Pleasure in Technology's Communicative Potential

I'm excited about the potential that it opens up for people. Having the video connection between our two sites was really exciting to me—it was incredibly thrilling. I thought that the way that it allowed people to be brought together who wouldn't have been otherwise was fantastic. And I still feel that way about it a lot. So I'm certainly excited about what it can offer and intrigued by the fact that often it offers you something that you didn't anticipate. (Computer scientist, corporate research and development center, age forty-two)

One of the things I really liked doing, and that's probably why I transferred actually, was the space stuff—working on building networks that would interface people. I worked on one project for the space station people, to manage all their information. And that was really exciting, because we were designing a new network, we were going across the country, we were hooking all the networks together. I think the wide-area networks and interaction with other people always were exciting to me.

(Systems engineer, government research and development center, age twenty-seven)

The communications stuff I do: the fact that I can be talking with people around the world easily, and the sort of chance interactions I have with people are quite exciting. (Computer scientist, software company, age forty)

The three women who speak here cite the *potential* of the technology, and they locate this potential in what it can *open up* for people. What is compelling about the computer-based technologies with which they work are the possibilities for communication and exchange between people that they facilitate. Words like *exciting, thrilling,* and *fantastic* are used to describe the technologies' capacity to bring people together. Metaphors that have to do with creating and fostering connections are also used: *building, interfacing,* and *hooking* are the capacities of the technology they talk about. Encountering the unexpected is also a source of pleasure, particularly when it leads to an unanticipated exchange between individuals.

The portrait that these women paint is expansive in tone, and we are left with an image of *technology as possibility,* as something that can expand and enhance the range of communicative activities among people. There is a surprising absence of "tech talk." There is no mention of *file transfer protocols, satellite hook-ups, internet access, TCP/IP connections,* or any number of terms that often roll off people's tongues when they are talking about telecommunications technologies.[4] Rather than calling attention to their knowledge of sophisticated technical undertakings, these women choose to emphasize the communicative and relational capacity of the technology.

Pleasure in Making Technology More Accessible

The whole concept of expert systems and artificial intelligence hits me wrong for a couple of reasons. First, I think it's really scary that we're attempting to replace human expertise with machines. I can't see how you could ever get the knowledge that is in people's heads or the knowledge in a discipline into a group of discrete facts in a computer system. I don't see how that would be possible to do objectively. My whole goal in doing this business and in getting into technical writing is ultimately to make technology more accessible to people. And I think that what we're always trying to do in this work is to make people understand complicated sys-

---

4. *File transfer protocols* allow you to send and receive information over telecommunications networks; *satellite hook-ups* is generic terminology used to describe a range of different systems that allow for the transfer of video images; the *internet* is an electronic mail system connecting governmental institutions, military branches, educational institutions, and commercial companies throughout the world; *TCP/IP connections* stand for Transmission Control Protocol/Internet Protocol.

tems and show them that things really aren't all that complicated and people can understand them. And so having the opportunity to design the user interface for a system was a golden opportunity. (Computer scientist, technical consulting company, age twenty-eight)

My day-to-day activity is focused on how we get the technology into our place. And that is not as driven with the technology being an exciting part. It's the capability that it brings to you; getting the new machine in is very exciting, because it has additional capability. It's not because it has some kind of special components. My excitement comes because if my organization and I can do those things well, then the users have better tools, and with the users having better tools, they can accomplish their research projects. My focus is always on the user, the researcher, the people who have the needs. (Chief of computer systems, government research and development center, age thirty-five)

My interest in user interfaces comes from two areas. One reason I took psych courses (I majored in psychology) is I find people interesting, and there are people who are afraid of computers. Computers are wonderful toys, all right. To a large extent that's how I feel about them. They can do amazing things, and they can free you up to do really good fun stuff. But a piece of software is only as usable as the interface on it. If I can help somebody, if I can put together something that takes the mundane drudgery out for somebody, then I've really done something to help them. I've helped them be more creative and relieved them of a tedious task. You know, computers are good for tedious tasks; they don't care. But people get bored—it's not fun. (Computer scientist, corporate research and development center, age thirty-seven)

I think what I like best is when you look at some of the prototypes and show them to other people, they get really excited. It isn't like it's something hard—it doesn't look hard to them; it looks like something very easy and usable and valuable. That's the biggest satisfaction. There are two aspects: There's a lot of satisfaction in doing it and then seeing how other people respond to it. (Multimedia developer, software and hardware manufacturer, age forty-four)

The women in this group locate the value in their work in making technology more transparent and accessible for others. They derive genuine pleasure from taking into account the user's point of view, demystifying the technology so that productive engagement is possible. In general, these women see technology as a facilitator and enhancer of human potential rather than as a more efficient substitute for human capabilities. Indeed, attempts to use the computer to replace human thought and action are seen as frightening.

Computers can bring *relief* from *tedious* tasks. They can be used to *free people up* and help people become more *creative*. The interpretive emphasis is on the technology's expansive and liberating potential; helping others to make use of this potential is a source of satisfaction. These women talk about making technology less *hard*. Their goal is to make technological objects friendlier and more conversant with people's needs. And they derive genuine pleasure from witnessing other people's satisfaction in their work. The impression one gets is that these women want to turn technological objects into companionable partners—helpmates that will improve the quality of human life.

Pleasure in the Collaborative Nature of Technological Work

I think for me the most exciting projects are ones where you are building up something that's new, where you're building up a new capability, or you're participating with a group of people to put something together—anything that would involve that sort of thing. Right now we're getting into space station work, and for me that's really exciting. (Computer scientist, government research and development center, age thirty-three)

In terms of the things that are most satisfying about my job, they're probably more people things than technology things. I really enjoyed running the conference I ran this week. I like being the person who sees what things fit together and which groups of people should talk to each other. I like having a sense of what the technology's good for, but in fact I don't get tremendously turned on by making that be real myself. (Computer scientist, software company, age forty)

One thing I enjoy doing—something that I've been doing today—is at the initial conception of an idea, trying to find the different people I need to talk to and gather the information necessary. I enjoy that. I also enjoy, once there is a problem, sitting down and actually stepping it out—how logically does this problem get solved—not as much the big picture at that stage, but the specifics of sitting down and saying, "Okay, I need to read from a file. How do I do that?" I like the broad picture when it's with people and I like the very specific picture when it's with the computer. (Knowledge engineer, industry, age twenty-six)

I think of what I enjoy in two categories. One is things that I physically do myself at the computer. For example, I like debugging software. If a programmer says, "Okay, here's a new version, try it out," and I have a data set that I've been working with and I try it out and something works a little strangely, part of me says, "Oh, my God, we've got another bug in the software!" But part of me regards it as a fun problem to work on. The other thing that's been interesting to me lately, since I've moved beyond the actual programming, is thinking about the design of software, and having ideas that can then be worked out in more detail with other people. I think that's a more collaborative process. (Computer scientist, corporate research and development center, age thirty-eight)

The four women who fall into this group talk about *collaborative* processes and *building up* knowledge in conjunction with others. It is the generative process of working with and gaining information from others that they find satisfying. Creating a *new capability,* bringing to life something that hasn't existed before, is exciting, and the fact that this happens in collaboration with others is valued.

It is the *people aspects* of their work that are satisfying. Bringing out other's capabilities, gathering information from others, and communicating with and learning from other people are all seen as pleasurable parts of the design process. The locus of satisfaction is found not in the technological objects themselves but in the kinds of discursive communities that form around technological projects and in problem solving that involves talking with and learning from others. Once again, the metaphors are generative and connective—*building, creating, collaborating* are the descriptors that these women use.

Pleasure in Knowledge

What intrigues me the most is when you've got something that works and you fix it to make it better, and then suddenly it doesn't work anymore. You have to go back and trace over it, and figure out where you went wrong, and correct it from there—the fact that you have to sit there and work at it until it works, and there's really no one you can ask, and you have to figure it out yourself. Because if you bring something you've written to somebody, they'll look at it, and it's very difficult for someone to understand someone else's code. And so it's yours, and you have to figure it out. (Computer engineer, industry, age twenty-one)

I like being handed a program that doesn't fit, say, into the space available, and I have to look through it and rewrite it to try to make it fit smaller—which reminds me of journalism. That's a task that I find pleasing. I like the general feeling of being faced with a problem that hasn't been figured out, where there's a lot of specs written that have technical information but no one's ever actually done this task. I go into it knowing it's possible, and then spend enough time with the information until it sinks in—what is needed to get it done and then have it done. I like to feel the difference between when I thought I would never figure this out and then when I have. I think that's why at some point along the line I succeeded and understood that if I spent long enough figuring it out, I would get it. (Programmer, software company, age forty-three)

Any time my program doesn't work, it's a problem I enjoy solving. And I get particular satisfaction when I've worked really hard on a problem and gotten discouraged, and wanted to get help, and I didn't get help, and I ended up solving it myself. That's very satisfying to me. It isn't so much any particular kind of problem, because all the problems I work on seem to be similar. (Programmer, software company, age thirty-six)

The flow physics is what I get into. What I've been working on is vertical take off aircraft, the harriers that take off straight up. There's a specific part, the lift jets, that I've been looking at. Instead of putting in a whole aircraft, you put in just the lift jet and a flat surface that resembles this plane, and look at the physics that makes these things work. Nobody really understands all the small-scale features of this flow; experimentally we don't have things that can measure it in detail. And yet I'm getting some of these details. That kind of thing really excites me. Anything I can do to dig into that kind of thing is my favorite problem to work on. (Aerospace engineer, government research and development center, age twenty-seven)

The women in this group derive pleasure from the feeling of self-reliance they experience while problem solving. They talk about the importance of *figuring things out themselves,* of getting some of the details—a process that results in ownership of knowledge, which is satisfying. In particular, challenging their own capabilities, proving to themselves that indeed they can do it, is gratifying. To feel the difference between when they think they can never figure something out and when they do is especially rewarding to them. And for at least one of these women, there is also pleasure in the competitive advantage that knowledge buys: "I'm getting some of these details," she says.

The metaphors they use describe a process that is a mixture of patience and perseverance. They talk about sitting and working at something until it works, and spending time with the information until it sinks in. One is left with the impression that their relation to technology is largely contemplative in nature. Like an accomplished teacher who assesses each student according to his or her individual needs, they spend time with their computer programs tracing over, figuring out, and correcting.

The Men

When asked to describe the aspects of their work that they found exciting or compelling, the eleven men we interviewed all described processes that in one way or another moved them closer toward the technology. As a group they can be characterized by three types of interpretive frameworks: (1) pleasure in the process of abstraction; (2) pleasure in deciphering the mysteries of technology; and (3) pleasure in the process of design.

Pleasure in the Process of Abstraction

Every once in a while, I come on a problem that really excites me and gets me running. I sort of eat, drink, and sleep it for a period of time. I can give you an example of one that obsessed me for a while and that I certainly enjoyed. Five years ago, we needed to go into large-scale software production, and we needed to have software tools with which to do that. I was the guy charged with coming up with the software tools, either finding them on the market or creating them. I had been able to find these things called assemblers on the market, and we even ordered a quarter-million-dollar machine that would be able to run some assemblers. But I wasn't very happy with the performance of any of these assemblers. They all seemed to run too slow, and they would inhibit the creative process. So one night I was thinking, well, couldn't I make it faster? And I reduced the problem to a matter of what I call symbol look-up. Symbol look-up's got to be the critical thing. How fast can I do symbol look-up on our little home computers, on our IBM PC's? So I worked on that problem for a little while, kicking it around in my head, and got it down to about an eight-instruction loop. Eight little instructions, and from those, I immediately extrapolated and figured out that I could make an assembler that ran closer to a hundred times faster than anything else existing. (Programmer, software company, age thirty-two)

We had a situation at the beginning of last year, where we had to think about how to represent the types of interactions people do on a computer, and hired some people to work at a plan I had for representing videotext interactions, or computer interactions. And we built this whole system—it was really quite elegant. It caused us to have to abstract a lot of the types of things you do on computer, the types of interactions and types of responses, and what you do with that information. It was very good work; it was the type of work I like to do, trying to abstract and represent it, knowledge representation. That's something I really like—to draw the design phase, to solve the design problems. (Programmer, software company, age twenty-eight)

We've always had the attitude that if it could be done on computer, we could do it. There came a time when I was doing the main editor core, which the other parts of the editor use to edit text and put up different windows and things like that. It came to a point where we wanted to allow as much functionality as possible. It was very slow, unacceptably slow. And I remember thinking "we're really in a jam now. It does a lot, but we're working on a machine that runs very slowly. What can we do?" We put our minds together and came up with a way of speeding it up. Then I came up with some hardware scrolling and some other things that together sped up the program to the desired speed. To me that was problem solving in its simplest form. We saw a problem that we had no idea how to solve, and just by thinking about it, we were able to come up with some great ideas. It was very encouraging (Programmer, software company, age twenty-seven)

The software we did was pretty technically complicated compared to most kids' software—that is, the underlying models were complicated. I don't know whether it shows up on the screen, but there was a lot of math and problem solving in the programming that I liked and that was pretty difficult for me. But it was the kind of stuff I thought I should be able to do, because I couldn't see anything that I obviously didn't know how to do. I enjoy that kind of well-defined, highly specified problem, which was very obvious if you got it right and very obvious when you got it wrong. Computers are marvelous things to let you go all night at them, so I spent a lot of enjoyable time just locked in to problems. Solving some of the programming problems was the most enjoyable part for me. (Programmer, educational development group, age thirty-nine)

The pleasure these four men derive from their work comes from a kind of mental wrestling they engage in with the ideas and procedures they generate in relation to the technology. They delight in mental effort, in kicking ideas around in abstraction and extrapolation. There is a sense that these men see themselves as taking risks, that they alone are challenging themselves, and that the projects they work on involve a great deal of technical sophistication. The enterprises these men work on are large and their missions difficult; they carry the burden for success and failure, and they deeply enjoy the challenges involved. There is also an obsessive quality to what they do: They eat, drink, and sleep their problems. There is talk about being *locked in,* and one gets a sense as well that they even derive erotic pleasure from these obsessive and engaging tasks— "computers are marvelous things to let you go all night at them."

Their descriptions are laden with technical terminology—there is talk of target machines, symbol look-ups, and instruction loops. Technology is the topic of conversation; there are no human reference points. The universe that gives them satisfaction is an exclusively technical one.

Pleasure in Deciphering the Mysteries of Technology

The real problems that excite me are on all sorts of levels. Any computer is a system, and within this system there's a lot of other little things. The real hard problems are interactions where the cause of the problem is not where the problem shows itself. There's this trail that comes round and shows you you don't understand the system. So it takes a rethinking about the problem and what causes it, the chain of events that leads to the problem. The longer the chain, the more interesting it is. (Software engineer, software company, age thirty-two)

There's an area where something that I didn't consider is causing problems down the road, and I'd like to get an answer to it. In my business I get problems from testing, from quality assurance on the product, and they can be very complicated scenarios that cause really disastrous things to happen. To track something like that down is satisfying. One approach that we often take is a sort of binary search method. You get a report from a tester that has, say, twenty steps in the sequence of events that finally leads to the problem. To actually fix the thing, it could be any one of the twenty steps that are causing the problem to occur. (Software engineer, software company, age twenty-nine)

What I've always found curious about computers is that you can use them to program, but you can also spend time to find out more about the computer and how it operates—and so you discover things. You're discovering something that someone made, as opposed to science, where you're discovering something that has occurred naturally. When a computer system is designed, the designer is not fully aware of all the ways that it can be used and all the little things that'll happen, all the little idiosyncrasies. That's kind of fun in itself. But the most fun, what got me into it, was being able to set up a series of steps to solve a problem. You had full control, and that machine would follow your orders exactly. It was a really nice tool, and it was a nice kind of environment to work in. (Programmer, software company, thirty-three)

I like designing the structure of the system. You take a problem, and you try to solve the problem based on the structure that the problem seems to have. It's looking at the situation and trying to eliminate the irrelevant aspects of it or the parts that at the first level of development may not be relevant. It's trying to get to the core of the problem. (Computer scientist, university research and development center, age thirty)

The men who fall into this category derive pleasure from extracting the secrets that the computer harbors. Despite the fact that technological objects are manmade, they are accorded a mysterious—as yet undiscovered—elusive character that is reminiscent of the scientist's relationship to the natural world (Keller, 1985). Indeed, one of the men articulates this: "When a computer system is designed, the designer is not fully aware of all the ways that it can be used and all the little things that'll happen, all the little idiosyncrasies." Hence, for the programmer, the computer is a puzzle that must be solved.

Not surprisingly, then, the problems that are most exciting for these men are the ones that are not obvious. Like a detective, one engages in the task of tracking down the root of the trouble, ferreting it out by stepping through a chain of events. And the longer the chain, the more interesting the problem. Trying to get to the core of the problem—a process that takes you further and further into the interstices of the technological environment—is most compelling. Missions that entail tracking things down are especially satisfying. The appeal lies in making the invisible visible; and the computer is an especially satisfying environment to do this in because logic and order can be used to unearth the mystery. Programming allows you full control, and the fact that the computer follows your orders exactly is a source of pleasure because of the certainty that systematic activity will reveal the machine's idiosyncrasies.

Pleasures in the Process of Design

Making things understandable is something that gets me excited. When I'm building a system, I think a lot about how people are going to use it, and try to develop it in a way that people will relate to and that will be meaningful to them. I try to think of what the right metaphors are to make it work. For example, one project we're working on is programmable bricks. One way to use them is to link them to a computer and send a program down into the brick and then disconnect it, and then the program's in the brick. But it might be nice not to have the computer at all, but to have a bunch of buttons on the brick, and by pushing these buttons you can write a program. So maybe this brick with a computer inside has a two-line display, and maybe it has twenty buttons. So it's relatively small. Maybe it's the size of a deck of cards or the size of a calculator. (Programmer and designer, university research and development center, age thirty-two)

One interesting thing is the way the tool actually gets used. For example, I talked to somebody who told me that the way this thing is supposed to work is you have these data streams, which run in columns. One of them might be verbal transcript, which would be text, and each of these is chronologically ordered. Another column might not have text at all, but graphics, little lines, and whatever notation system you might have, representing whatever you're interested in, like when somebody's gaze changes. One interesting thing that could happen is, say, if we were talking at the same time and we had a little overlap in the conversation on the order of three or four words that we said at the same time: If you looked at the two columns, you'd see a line that had your words and mine lined up together. But within that, we don't know how they actually line up, right? I don't know which words were on top of which other words. You might want it to flip from being vertical to being horizontal. So those three or four words that you say and the three or four words that I'd say would then line up like this, and we could actually align much more finely, if you will. And I thought that was a cute idea. (Computer scientist, corporate research and development center, age thirty-five)

The notion of how someone navigates the space of possibilities in any given computer program is something you have to ask every time, and it's always a fascinating question requiring different answers. You want to give somebody some functionality, and you want to figure out how to give them as much functionality as possible, but hand it to them in such a way that it's something that they can get control over very easily. That's the high level and most interesting problem. (Computer scientist, software and hardware manufacturer, thirty-one)

At first glance, the men who fall into this category appear to be focused on the user in a way that seems similar to the women who take pleasure in making technology more accessible. But though these men articulate interest in creating technological environments that meet the needs of users, as their descriptions of what they find compelling progress the user tends to disappear from view. What they appear to be genuinely interested in are the design issues involved in creating computer-based environments.

Their focus is on the surface structure of the technology—how many buttons a programmable object should have, how many lines of display should appear, how big the object should be, how words that denote different conversational structures might line up, and so on. What is intriguing for these men is figuring out the details of the object, thinking through the ways in which its various devices will function. Although they talk of wanting to find out how someone navigates the space of possibilities and voice a desire to create as much functionality as possible, it is as though they cannot resist the allure of the technological objects themselves. They are unable to keep their gaze centered on the user, and their focus shifts to the objects they are designing. Even when they talk about user-oriented design issues, their talk is abstract, and unlike the women it is not about demystifying the technological universe. Rather, the sense one gets is that they are interested in controlling and containing the object for the naive user.

Conclusion

In a related study (Honey, 1988), I investigated the ways in which adolescent boys and girls appropriated and made meaning out of a computerized fantasy role-playing game modeled on Dungeons and Dragons. The fantasy scenarios that boys constructed as they interacted with this simulated world elaborated and expanded upon the symbolic content of the game. Indeed, the boys were able to use the game environment as a source of narcissistic satisfaction and confirmation. The girls, in contrast, constructed multiple interpretations of the game, some of which resisted the fantasy content or refused it altogether.

The metaphors that such games embody—metaphors of conquest, domination, and control—allow young boys to slide effortlessly into the universe of play, so that the process of developing expertise and triumphing over the game world is a much more seamless experience for them than it is for girls. Video games are both simulated worlds that hold out to the player the possibility of ultimate control through the elimination of ambiguity, and fantasy spaces in which dramas unfold, often leading the player on a heroic quest of one sort or another. The appeal of video games resides in their unique blending of these two dimensions of experience.[5]

For the men in our study, computers embody both of these elements. They are unpredictable, mysterious, and deeply puzzling, and yet they are environments in which control can be achieved through systematic analysis and problem solving. It is the blending of these two processes—mystery and mastery—that makes computers particularly alluring objects for the men. Like the boys playing video games, the men are comfortable with the discourse that surrounds the technological universe; they appropriate its procedures and practices and make use of its terminology. They locate the source of their satisfaction and

---

5. I owe this insight to Sherry Turkle, who first articulated it in her book *The Second Self* (1984).

pleasure in the instruments with which they work, and for the majority of them the quest that is most satisfying is one that takes them deeper and deeper into the soul of the machine.

What, then, might we make of the other voice we hear, the voice that is distinctly maternal in tone? It is not an expression of innate femininity, an indication that by virtue of our sex we are more nurturing and peace loving. As Sara Ruddick (1989) points out, this kind of "rhetoric and the theory run up against two facts: men are not so warlike and women are certainly not peaceful" (p. 151). Rather, the fact that we hear these maternal voices suggests both a way in which we locate ourselves in our work as women and a means whereby we domesticate or "make safe" technologies that are otherwise experienced as threatening. The former is expressive, the latter defensive—and these postures are taken up simultaneously; one does not exist without the other.

In her work on the question of women's desire, Jessica Benjamin (1986) suggests that what is needed is not an alternative symbol in which to locate the expression of desire but an alternative way of thinking about how the psyche is structured. She proposes a nonphallic mode of psychic organization that takes account of the development of self in relation to others. If we realign the discursive boundaries of psychoanalytic theory, it becomes possible to rethink the articulation of women's desire in terms of an intersubjective space. What we as women want, then, is no longer merely a matter of a symbolic dance around the quest to either *have* or *be* the phallus. Desire can be articulated in relation to an intersubjective reality in which the self's creative processes are linked to and shared with the experiences of others. Benjamin is clear, however, that this understanding of psychic development is only one piece of the developmental puzzle; the intersubjective mode both complements and contradicts the more phallically structured intrapsychic mode. As she states:

> The self that develops and accumulates through such experiences of rec-ognition is a different modality that sometimes works with, but some-times is at cross-purposes to, the symbolized ego of phallic structuring. It is essential to retain this sense of the complementary, as well as the contrasting, relationship of these modes. Otherwise, one falls into the trap of choosing between them, grasping one side of a contradiction that must remain suspended to be clarifying. (1986, p. 94)

Retaining a sense of the complementarity as well as the contradiction that exists between the intrapsychic and intersubjective modes of experience allows us to avoid the pitfall of labeling women's desire as exclusively maternal. Indeed, it helps us see the paradox that is inherent in giving voice to our desire within a phallic universe, for it is impossible to know the truth of desire given the patriarchal nature of the social world in which we live. The paradox, then, is that women's desire is always both expressive and defensive.

As Sherry Turkle and Seymour Papert (1990) have found, "Women are too often faced with the not necessarily conscious choice of putting themselves at odds with the cultural associations of the technology or with the cultural constructions of being a woman" (p. 151). The maternal voice is born of this conflict. While allowing us to position ourselves as women in relation to technology, the maternal voice also serves to domesticate and tame the cultural discourse of technology. Thus, the presence of this voice suggests both possibilities and limitations.

The tendency demonstrated by the women in our study to locate the value of their work in making technology more transparent and accessible to others is a humanizing influence on a domain that is often experienced as inhospitable to the needs and concerns of nontechnical users. The other side, however, is that this kind of maternal talk also functions like a safety valve, ensuring a well-trodden path out of a domain that frequently puts us in conflict. As result, we tend to resist deep engagement with technology, a phenomenon that Sherry Turkle (1988) has termed *computational reticence*. Thus, the degree to which we can imagine creative and far-reaching uses to which technology can be put is limited.

In a related piece of research (Brunner et al., 1990), we asked this same group of technological experts to write a reply to the following scenario: *If you were writing a science fiction story in which the perfect instrument (a future version of your own) is described, what would it be like?* The results of this research complemented the interpretive frameworks that emerged in our interviews. In their fantasy scenarios the women tended to see technological instruments as people connectors or communication and collaboration devices. The men, in contrast, tended to envision technology as extensions of their power over the physical universe. Their fantasies were about absolute control, tremendous speed, and unlimited knowledge. Here are two scenarios that illustrate these different orientations; the first was written by a woman and the second by a man:

> The "keyboard" would be the size of a medallion, formed into a beautiful piece of platinum sculptured jewelry, worn around one's neck. The medallion could be purchased in many shapes and sizes. The keyed input would operate all day-to-day necessities to communicate and transport people (including replacements for today's automobile). The fiber optic network that linked operations would have no dangerous side effect or by-product that harmed people or the environment. (Computer engineer)

> A direct brain-to-machine link. Plug it into the socket in the back of your head and you can begin communications with it. All information from other users is available and all of the history of mankind is also available. By selecting any time period the computer can impress directly on the user's brain images and background information for that time. In essence a time-machine. The user would not be able to discern the difference between dreams and reality and information placed there by the machine. (Perhaps this is all a nightmare.) (Computer programmer)

The kinds of devices that the women dreamed up were friendly and inviting. They tended to be small, robust, companionable objects that fit fluidly into the daily context of women's lives. The men's fantasies, on the other hand, were grandiose. They imagined devices that had both tremendous power and tremendous speed, devices that resulted in instantaneous, brain-zapping gratification. Indeed, the men's fantasies often contained dangerous and militaristic images that we associate with the deadly potential of technology.

As my colleague Cornelia Brunner (1991, 1992) has noted, both voices are necessary components of what might be thought of as a technological worldview. By itself, the masculine voice leads to technological advance, which, however, can be enormously destructive and deadly in its potential. And the maternal voice has a downside as well; it "does not seem, on the surface, to promise the kinds of breath-taking (in the positive as well as negative sense) advances in technology we have witnessed" (Brunner, 1992, p. 10).

As we have noted, however, the discursive reality that constitutes the technological universe leaves little room for the presence, let alone the realization, of the maternal voice. Indeed, many of the women we interviewed spoke about feeling marginalized and isolated within their professional communities. Our goal in carrying out this research was to identify the pathways and points of view that characterize women's entry into and relationship with technological work, so that we might articulate a different framework for thinking about issues of gender and technology. What we have discovered is that it is essential to hold in sight both the complementary and the contradictory aspects of these gender-laden perspectives on technology. It thus becomes possible to imagine the ways in which the maternal voice might serve to humble and humanize the grandiose (and frequently destructive) nature of technological discourse, and the ways in which this grandiosity might, in turn, be used to stretch the imaginative potential of the maternal voice.

References

Belenky, M. F.; Clinchy, B. M.; Goldberger, N. R.; & Tarule, J. M. (1986). *Women's ways of knowing: The development of self, voice, and mind*. New York: Basic Books.

Benjamin, J. (1986). A desire of one's own: Psychoanalytic feminism and intersubjective space. In T. de Lauretis (Ed.), *Feminist studies/critical studies*. Bloomington: University of Indiana Press.

Benjamin, J. (1988). *The bonds of love: Psychoanalysis, feminism, and the problem of domination*. New York: Pantheon.

Brunner, C. (1991). Gender and distance learning. *Annals of the American Academy*, 514.

Brunner, C. (1992). *Gender and technological desire*. Paper presented at the annual meeting of the American Educational Research Association, San Francisco.

Brunner, C.; Bennet, D.; Clements, M.; Hawkins, J.; Honey, M.; & Moeller, B. (1990). *Gender and technological imagination*. Paper presented at the annual meeting of the American Educational Research Association, Boston.

Chodorow, N. (1978). *The reproduction of mothering*. Berkeley: University of California Press.

Cohn, C. (1987). Sex and death in the rational world of defense intellectuals. *Signs,* 12(4), 687–718.

de Lauretis, T. (1986). Feminist studies/critical studies: Issues, terms, and contexts. In T. de Lauretis (Ed.), *Feminist studies/critical studies.* Bloomington: University of Indiana Press.

Edwards, P. (1990). The army and the microworld: Computers and the politics of gender identity. *Signs,* 16(1), 102–27.

Frankel, K. (1990). Women and computing. *Communications of the ACM,* 33(11), 34–46.

Gilligan, C. (1982). *In a different voice.* Cambridge, Mass.: Harvard University Press.

Gilligan, C. (1986). Remapping the moral domain: New images of self in relationship. In T. Heller, M. Sosna, and D. Wllbery (Eds.), *Reconstructing individualism: Autonomy, individuality, and the self in Western thought.* Stanford: Stanford University Press.

Gilligan, C., and Stern, E. (1986). *The riddle of femininity and the psychology of love.* Paper presented at a seminar on the psychology of love, Douglass College.

Hawkins, J. (1991). *The aesthetics of understanding.* Paper presented at a conference on women, work and computerization, Helsinki, Finland.

Hawkins, J.; Brunner, C.; Clements, P.; Honey, M.; & Moeller, B. (1990). *Women and technology: A new basis for understanding—Final report to the Spencer Foundation.* New York: Center for Children and Technology, Bank Street College of Education.

Honey, M. (1988). Play in the phallic universe: An analysis of adolescents' involvement with a fantasy role-playing computer game. Ph.D. diss., Columbia University.

Keller, E. (1985). *Reflections on gender and science.* New Haven: Yale University Press.

McGaw, J. A. (1982). Women and the history of American technology. *Signs,* 7(4), 798–828.

Pearl, A.; Pollack, M.; Riskin, E.; Thomas, B.; Wolf, E.; & Wu, A. (1990). Becoming a computer scientist. *Communications of the ACM,* 33(11), 37–57.

Ricoeur, P. (1970). *Freud and philosophy: An essay on interpretation.* New Haven: Yale University Press.

Ruddick, S. (1989). *Maternal Thinking.* Boston: Beacon Press.

Turkle, S. (1984). *The second self: Computers and the human spirit.* New York: Simon and Schuster.

Turkle, S. (1988). Computational reticence: Why women fear the intimate machine. In C. Kramarae (Ed.), *Technology and women's voices.* New York: Routledge and Kegan Paul.

Turkle, S., & Papert, S. (1990). Epistemological pluralism: Styles and voices within the computer culture. *Signs,* 16(1), 128–57.

Wright, B. (1987). *Women, work, and technology.* Ann Arbor: University of Michigan Press.

ADRIA SCHWARTZ

14 Taking the Nature Out of Mother

On August 14, 1990, Anna Johnson, a twenty-nine-year-old pregnant surrogate mother, filed suit in a California state court for
custody of the child she was carrying, a genetic offspring of Mark
and Crispina Calvert. The Calverts had donated sperm and ova to
create an embryo, which was then transferred from a petri dish
in the laboratory to the womb of Ms. Johnson, a single parent of a
three-year-old. She was to turn the baby over to the Calverts for
ten thousand dollars. At the time of the filing, the baby was due
in two months. She, like Elizabeth Kane, the first known woman
to sign a legal contract for surrogacy, and Marybeth Whitehead-
Gould, genetic and gestational mother of Baby M, attempted to
renege and claim her parental rights. In the case of Anna Johnson, the court denied that right, ruling that the child she was
carrying had "no biological relation to her" (based on her lack of
genetic connection) and therefore that she must be looked upon
as a "foster parent" providing a temporary home via her womb.
They denied her claims to motherhood by devaluing her gestational relation to the child and likening her uterus to a temporary fetal shelter.[1]

In that same month another article appeared in the *New York
Times* hailing recent advances in bioengineering that would
open the doors of motherhood to postmenopausal women
through in vitro fertilization with donated ova. In that case, it
seems, the medical profession assumes that, contrary to the
ruling in the surrogacy case, the gestational mother is to be the
real mother, and the genetically connected mother who was
legitimized by the court in the Johnson case is to be reduced to
the status of "anonymous donor."

The culture's commitment to and investment in reproductive
technology in the past thirty years has shaken the very founda-

1. Quoted in the *New York Times,* August 13, 1990.

tion of our notions of motherhood and seems to have taken the nature out of Mother Nature. The development and use of fertilization aids, ovulatory tracking with its concomitant opportunity for gender selection, alternative insemination, in vitro fertilization, and surrogacy have cast a long shadow over the "naturalness" of the reproductive process. Mother Nature can no longer be counted on as the arbiter of fertility, the provider of care. Neither nature nor mothers can be assumed to be what they were, and what they are forms the province of substantial debate.

The argument as to essentialist versus social constructionist views of gender (masculinity and femininity and their various attributes within ideology and culture) and sexual difference has constituted much of the discourse within feminist theory. It has been the subtext in much of the psychological writing about women and men as well. Essentialism, here, can be said to refer most generally to those theories of sexual difference that are primarily biologically determined, and so look to discover, define, and describe innate elements of the masculine and the feminine. Social constructionists look to culture and the language and ideology embedded therein as the historically determined creators of gender and gender role. Although women's mothering and their reproductive capacities are often used as ammunition in the arsenals of the opposing camps, the subject of mothers and motherhood rarely stands as the object of analysis in and of itself.

As reproductive technology developed and entered the mass culture, our theoretical inadequacies became glaringly obvious. We struggle to understand the changes in the very foundations of our thinking about mothers, mothering, and motherhood. Through a discussion of some of the problematics raised by issues of surrogacy as illustrative of the technologizing of reproduction, and through a brief look at Margaret Atwood's *The Handmaid's Tale* as feminist parable, I hope to highlight the inadequacy of the essentialist–social constructionist polarity as a vehicle of analysis.

Will the Real Mother Please Stand Up?

The question of the relation of kinship to motherhood is not new. For thousands of years, cultures have had adoptions whereby the "biological" or "natural" mother has given up her offspring to be reared by an "adoptive" mother. Here, "natural" or "real" is equated with "biological." But with advances in biotechnology we have increased the possibilities: the genetic mother (donor of the ova), the gestational or birth mother, the adoptive or social mother. Even surrogacy is distinguished by whether it is traditional or not. In traditional surrogacy, a male donates sperm for alternative insemination to a surrogate who is the genetic mother of the ensuing offspring. In gestational surrogacy, the surrogate is not genetically related to the offspring, but has become pregnant through in vitro fertilization.

According to recent estimates there have been four thousand births via traditional surrogacy since its inception in the 1970s, and eighty births through gestational surrogacy from 1987 to 1990. The total cost of gestational surrogacy is approximately forty thousand dollars as opposed to ten thousand dollars for traditional surrogacy.[2]

The year 1978 marked the first birth of a child (Louise Brown) through in vitro fertilization. Since that time, and despite the fact that 90 percent of in vitro fertilizations fail (Rothman, 1989a), according to a 1990 report in the *Fertility and Sterility Journal* as many as ten thousand embryos are frozen by women each year for future use.

What does this all mean?

Women are increasingly rejecting the constraints placed upon them by biology. The associative link between women, fertility, and motherhood is being eroded, if not broken, in the laboratory. The traditional shame of barrenness, the inevitable sterility of menopause, the onerous ticking of the biological clock, the very legitimation of womanhood by reproductive function, are all called into question by alternative modes of reproduction.

Women also are rejecting heterosexuality as the necessarily exclusive pathway to motherhood. Lesbian couples co-mother children either adopted or born of alternative insemination from known or unknown donors. When couples co-parent there are often two mothers, either of which may or may not be genetically related to the child.

Doesn't it mean, then, that our increased knowledge of reproductive functioning and the technology that has been created out of that knowledge liberate women from their bodies, their history of objectification and exclusive identification with motherhood and nurturance? Alternative paths to motherhood *seem* to offer previously disfranchised groups new options while allowing women even greater control over their bodies and how they are to be used.

On the Cusp of the Gender Divide

Let us look for a moment at the now famous case of Baby M, a trial that captured the nation's attention and split the feminist community asunder as the phenomenon of paid surrogacy dramatized the way in which technology could call motherhood into question.

The case of Baby M was and continues to be the focus of furious debate because it raises fundamental questions about the meaning of motherhood within the culture. Is motherhood a right of ownership, and if so, upon what is that based? Is it a relationship of caring or caretaking? Is it an instinct or a mandate? Is motherhood a construction of femininity or constitutive of womanhood?

In 1986, Marybeth Whitehead, wife of a sanitation worker and mother of two, agreed to be artificially inseminated by William Stern, to bear the child thus

2. These statistics are provided by the Center for Surrogate Parenting in Beverly Hills, California.

conceived, and to deliver that child to William and Elizabeth Stern for the contractually agreed-upon sum of ten thousand dollars. Elizabeth Stern, a pediatrician, had self-diagnosed multiple sclerosis and thus felt a pregnancy would be life endangering. Marybeth Whitehead was to act as Elizabeth's surrogate in the creation of the Stern family.

Toward the end of her pregnancy, Marybeth Whitehead became convinced that she could not give up *her* baby. She had made a grave mistake and vowed to keep the child. The Sterns, as well as a great proportion of the American population, were outraged that Marybeth felt she could so blatantly ignore or violate the terms of a legal contract. She was legally bound. The fact that she promised to return all monies received and forfeit those promised made no difference. The fact that it is elementary in contract law that performance may not be enforced, but merely affects the damages collected, made no difference. By threatening to keep her child, Marybeth proved herself to be outside the moral pale first by offering to sell her child and then by changing her mind and trying to keep it. Clearly she was unstable and unfit to be a mother.

We seemed to be back in King Solomon's court when Marybeth kidnapped her baby and kept her hidden from the Sterns, and then the Sterns, in conjunction with the authorities, stole the baby back and returned it to the jurisdiction of the court, which in turn delivered the baby back to them.

At the initial trial, where the Sterns sought to terminate all parental rights to the surrogate, one of their expert witnesses, psychologist Lee Salk, informed the court:

> I don't see that there were any "parental rights" that existed in the first place. As I see it . . . Mr. Stern and Mrs. Whitehead entered into an agreement that was clearly understood by both. The agreement involved the provision of ovum by Mrs. Whitehead for artificial insemination in exchange for ten thousand dollars . . . and so my feeling is that in both structural and functional terms, Mr. and Mrs. Stern's role as parents was achieved by *a surrogate uterus and not a surrogate mother.* (Chessler, 1989, p. 231; emphasis added)[3]

In this surrogacy arrangement, Elizabeth Stern was able to transcend her biological limitations (the multiple sclerosis, which was said to be health endangering in case of pregnancy) and achieve motherhood. She would become a mother by virtue of her relation to Baby M's genetic father and, presumably, by her caring for and mothering the child. But for Marybeth, the situation was quite different. Far from being liberated from her body, in the state's eye, Marybeth Whitehead became her body or rather a disembodied part-object, an instrumental construct to fulfill the needs of a man who wishes a genetic offspring. If she was only her body or, rather, a body part, then she could not be a mother.

In the preliminary surrogacy agreement signed by both, William Stern is

---

3. For Marybeth Whitehead Gould's own story, see Whitehead with Schwartz-Nobel (1989).

referred to as the "natural father" or "natural and biological father," and Marybeth Whitehead is referred to exclusively as "surrogate" (Chessler, 1989, pp. 167–173). Here, it seems, only the male is held to be privy to nature, the woman having sold her claim for ten thousand dollars. Clearly, in this case, the womb is no longer considered essential to the biological process of reproduction. It is merely a temporary shelter that may even soon be replicated or subsumed by reproductive technological advance.

Who is the real mother of Baby M? Marybeth Whitehead, of whose flesh she is, who conceived and carried her, who offered to sell her for a goodly sum of money? Elizabeth Stern, mostly silent throughout the prolonged media circus that accompanied the trials, who did not wish to bear the risks of childbirth but who claimed to want and love Baby M? The trial evoked tremendous passion on both sides with essentialists championing women's biological rights to motherhood and social constructionists rejoicing at their liberation from the primitive bonds of women's reproductive capacities.

Not surprisingly the state limited the discourse. There was no discussion about the possibility of Baby M having two mothers in legal parity, two mothers who are equally valued, without one being more real, more primary, than the other. Legally today this is not an option—the court recognizes only one legal father and one legal mother. There is an unspoken moral purview. A child is to be conceived from a monogamous heterosexual union and the value of that union is to be indemnified by the court.

Should it have been possible for both Elizabeth Stern and Marybeth Whitehead to be Baby M's mother(s)? Might not they be awarded equal access to and time with Baby M, and share equally in all decisions concerning her upbringing, as in traditional joint custody divorce cases?

But what of the psychological ramifications? Can a child have two mothers, two primary objects of internalization and identification? Psychoanalysis has been struggling over the past ten years in its shift from a one-person (intrapsychically focused) to a two-person theory (relational theory with its interpersonal, intersubjective, and object relations components) of development resulting in an increased emphasis on the mother-infant dyad as the cradle of selfhood. How might relational theory accommodate the basic triad of one infant–two mothers that could have occurred had the court awarded joint custody to Elizabeth Stern and Marybeth Whitehead-Gould?

Neither classical Freudian-based theory nor relational theory has addressed itself to alternative families where there can be no automatic presumption as to who is or what it means to be the mother. There are families where there are two mothers, neither of them biologically connected to the offspring. In lesbian families, for instance, one parent might legally adopt a newborn (as only one woman can) while the other shares equally in primary caretaking responsibilities. Who is the mother then?

Our legal system, embedded in a "naturally" heterosexual matrix, maintains that there can be only one mother. There is no legal recognition of the co-parent as mother for fiscal, medical, or other guardianship purposes. Nor is there continued legal recognition of the birth mother (who is most often in these families the genetic and gestational mother) in the adoptee's life. The state prefers to eradicate the birth mother. After an adoption becomes legal, the newborn infant's birth certificate will list the adoptive parent as mother while the birth mother's name is sealed in the court's records and lost to the child, possibly forever. Although this procedure was supposedly instituted in order to protect the birth mother and ensure the integrity of the adoptive family, it also serves as a reaffirmation of sexual conservancy. Babies are not born outside of marriage; mothers do not give up their babies.

To return to Baby M. Ultimately, the New Jersey Supreme Court restored the parental rights to Marybeth Whitehead-Gould that were terminated in a lower court, but allowed the Sterns to keep custody in "the best interests of the child."

This case was one of the most journalistically popular in the years of 1987 and 1988. Not only did it raise fundamental issues about the culture's changing attitudes toward mothers, mothering, and motherhood, but, as Harold Cassidy, Marybeth's lawyer, pointed out, the case raised the subterranean issues of class and caste, so rarely addressed in popular American discourse. "What we are witnessing, and what we can predict will happen, is that one class of Americans will exploit another class. And it will always be the wife of the sanitation worker who must bear the children for the pediatrician" (Chessler, 1989, p. 160).

Barbara Katz Rothman has written extensively about what she terms the commodification of motherhood. According to Rothman, we have become victims of an ideology that treats people as objects, commodities for sale, and the fetus as a product subject to quality control. Women (and men) are treated as producers without emotional ties to their products. Women sell their ova and rent their wombs. She suggests that surrogate mothers who are content with their role "have accepted the alienation of the worker from the product of her labor; the baby like any other commodity does not belong to the producer but to the purchaser" (Rothman, 1988, pp. 95–100). In this analysis, surrogates who recant ultimately could not accept this commodification of their motherhood.

Rothman decries an ideology in which the relation of a mother to her own body is no longer esteemed and suggests that the valuation of genetics over the gestational relation operates primarily as a boon to the baby brokers. Rothman demands that the gestational relation be elevated to primacy, which is surely intended to undo women's growing alienation from her body and its further commodification and objectification. In her more recent writing Rothman states clearly that she rejects traditional kinship ties with their claims to ownership. She rejects surrogacy, because in her analysis it negates interpersonal relationship in the service of mercantilism.[4]

While Rothman decries the evil of reproductive technology as an alienating representative of our commodity culture, Bassin (1989) argues that reproduc-

4. See Rothman (1988), p. 99. For the fullest account of her thinking, see Rothman (1989b).

tive technology may be situationally traumatic without necessarily being symbolic or carry a negative psychological impact to the integrity of the self. Citing clinical material, Bassin suggests that reproductive technology may be experienced as alienating or not, depending on one's subjectivity.

Could it be that reproductive technology might alienate women from feelings of authenticity and the integrity of their bodies *or* provide an opportunity to free themselves from the restraints of the body and transcend the biological differences between the sexes? Another way of approaching that question might be to ask, is it possible for science and technology to stand outside the berth of ideology, or is one's comfort with the constraints of ideology dependent on psychic structure?

The Handmaid's Tale

Margaret Atwood's novel *The Handmaid's Tale* (1986) appears to embody a strange admixture of Rothman's concern for women's increasing alienation from her body and the exploitation of her reproductive capacities, coupled with a nightmarish vision of an essentialist feminism gone awry. In some ways a classic feminist dystopia, *The Handmaid's Tale* tells of a time when a return to militaristic protestant fundamentalism born of an environmental apocalypse has created a society in which reproduction is considered the sole province and responsibility of women. Toxic contamination has rendered most women (and men) infertile, although men, in keeping with the idealization of their powers and the concomitant splitting of sexuality and reproduction, were never presumed to be so. The handmaids act as surrogates, a class of women whose sole function is to provide offspring for infertile couples. Elizabeth Kane's personal story echoes Atwood's vision, when she declares, "We have become a society that demands instant gratification, and now we are demanding instant babies by expecting healthy women to become our breeding stock. The fact that our society has accepted using breeders to create children for wealthy people frightens me."[5]

The novel takes place in the Republic of Gilead, a small section of what might be New England, given the reference to the Salem witch trials; but as Aunt Lydia (the prototype for the co-opted woman who embraces her oppressor and willingly passes on that oppression in the name of love) so wisely repeats to her young charges, "The Republic of Gilead knows no bounds. Gilead is within you." As the Handmaid tells us, in Gilead women are valued and assigned caste solely for their reproductive capacities. Fertility determines one's usefulness to a society that discards or exiles lower-class women—unwomen, who have been unwilling or unable to bear fruit for the ruling elite, commanders and their wives. The women have generic names only. They are their function. The Marthas

5. Elizabeth Kane (a pseudonym) has published a book about her experience entitled *Birth Mother: America's First Legal Surrogate Mother, Her Change of Heart.*

serve. They are domestic servants who are too old to reproduce or who, in one case, had a tubal ligation before it had become illegal.

The handmaids, the lucky fertile ones, are called Ofglen, Ofwarren. They have no identity other than that of reproductive appendixes to the men they are temporarily servicing. Dressed in red (a reference to Hawthorne's *Scarlet Letter*), they are spoken of as vessels. In a wonderful touch in the book, it is noted that the wives have forbidden the use of face cream or lotion for the handmaids. They are considered vanities. "We are containers, it's only the insides of our bodies that are important. The outside can become hard and wrinkled, for all they care, like the shell of a nut. . . . they don't want us to look attractive" (Atwood, 1986, p. 124). The aunts, the women who imprison, train, and condition other women, tell them they are a national resource. And there is envy and false competition among them for parturition. But mostly there is shame and despair and, for those who can remember other times, a longing for personhood and a self that existed independently of the uterus they have become.

Within the feminist discourse, essentialist Jane Alpert argues strongly for the mother right, for women being defined and empowered by their unique biology.

> Feminists have asserted that the essential difference between women and men does not lie in biology but rather in roles that patriarchal societies (men) have required each sex to play. . . . However, a flaw in this feminist argument has persisted: it contradicts our felt experience of the biological difference between the sexes as one of immense significance. . . . The unique consciousness or sensibility, the particular attributes that set feminist art apart, and a compelling line of research now being pursued by feminist anthropologists all point to the idea that female biology is *the basis of women's powers.* Biology is hence the source and not the enemy of feminist revolution. (Snitow, 1989, p. 77)

What is so interesting about Margaret Atwood's treatment of the problematic of the relationship of women to their reproductive capacities is that she demonstrates in a most harrowing fashion the ways in which we can pervert a position through its radical extension. Overvaluation of the biological potential of women to bear young and finding that reproductive potential to be constitutive of womanhood lead ultimately to the objectification of woman as body/nature and to the obliteration of her subjectivity. Alternatively, as women seek to transcend the constraints of a biologically determined existence, we risk the disembodied commodification and exploitation of our bodily selves.

Ultimately, Atwood finds the condition of patriarchy preemptive of even the formulation of that contradiction. There is only one woman who retains her name throughout the narrative: Moira. Moira is a resister from the outset. She attempts many escapes from the Red Center (training ground for the Handmaids), is captured, beaten, and finally remanded to work at Jezebel's, a brothel servicing the ruling class of men. Is the irony here that Moira is a lesbian and therefore a long-standing resister, as Adrienne Rich might say, to our culture's compulsory heterosexuality (Rich, 1980)? Or, that given the choice of how to service men in our patriarchy, sexually or through reproduction, she chooses her sexuality as a more secure means of retaining some measure of autonomy, integrity, and wholeness? In either case, Atwood seems to say that it is the historical condition of patriarchy that defines what a women or a mother is, and there can be no truly feminist conception until that condition is removed.

Similarly, feminist theorist Ann Snitow asks, "To what extent is motherhood a powerful identity? . . . To what extent is it a patriarchal construction that inevitably places mothers outside the realm of social, the changing, the active?" (Snitow, 1989, p. 49). In Atwood's novel, female existence is defined and circumscribed by one's relation to motherhood. Some wives are biological and functional mothers. Others simulate intercourse, right beside their Handmaids, in bizarre conceptual rituals, and likewise simulate childbirth backed by a chorus of laboring Handmaids. These wives then become instant mothers as they grab the newborn infant from its now anonymous birthgiver, as a prize product to be shown to the attendant wives of society. No matter how it is to be accomplished, one either is a mother or is servicing a mother-to-be. For a woman, there is no other role, no other option.

Is it possible, Snitow asks, for biological difference to wither away as a basis for social organization, or are the sexes endurably different biologically, and therefore psychically, requiring different cultural organization?

Psychoanalysis and Motherhood

For Freud and his disciples within classical psychoanalysis, the psychology of motherhood rested on a foundation of anatomy and desire. Freud proclaims a fundamental though not totally inflexible biological determinism in psychosexual development and describes what he assumes to be the likely progression of the young girl toward femininity/heterosexuality and the wish to have a baby, based largely on the child's perception of the obvious and universal superiority of the penis. Thus, the realization and acknowledgment of the anatomical differences between the sexes propels the preoedipal girl to abandon her mother as a primary love object, renounce her active/clitoral "masculine" sexuality and embrace her passive/vaginal "feminine" sexuality, which can produce a baby as its consolation prize.[6]

Subsequent psychoanalysts have pointed out that Freud had mistaken the concrete anatomic penis for a culturally privileged phallus, that girls seem to

6. In "Some Psychical Consequences of the Anatomical Distinctions between the Sexes" Freud discusses the little girl's discovery of the penis and her immediate envy of what she considers to be a superior organ. Freud's clearest statement as to how the girl's alleged penis envy is translated into a wish for a baby from her father can be found in his essay on "Femininity" in *New Introductory Lectures on Psychoanalysis*.

have an early awareness and positive valuation of their own genitals that is not reactive to a phallic stance, and that he was wrong about the importance of the so-called oedipal stage in the development of female gender role identity (Fliegel, 1973, 1982; Grossman & Stewart, 1976; Kleeman, 1976; Schwartz, 1984). But these claims for a girl's primary femininity still retain an essentialist bias that will again lead us to a conclusion that women are mothers because they are anatomically female. That is, their mothering will ultimately be equated with their reproductive capacities.

Nancy Chodorow, in an attempt at a feminist revision of Freud's original formulation, utilizes an object relations structure to ask why women mother (Chodorow, 1978). What psychological operations occur to ensure the reproduction of mothering by females in our culture? She deals with processes of identification and internalization, but her frame of reference is a traditionally mimetic gender/sexed model of heterosexuality comprised of two-parent nuclear families where traditionally feminine mothers give birth to and care for the young who are sired by traditionally nonnurturant masculine fathers. Although she speaks of identification and internalization, Chodorow largely ignores the unconscious communications that occur between women and their daughters and sons about their feelings about their womanhood and their role as nurturer, which, especially in traditional households, are rarely unconflicted.

How is it that some men assume the role of primary caretakers and nurturers? Clinical experience tells us that in many families it may be the man who is felt to be the real nurturer even though he does not take on the usual domestic responsibilities. Who is the mother there? How might Chodorow's model apply in gay male families where both men take equal parenting responsibilities, or where roles are divided along more traditional expressive and instrumental parameters? Would the male children in such families become the nurturers and females the repressed nonrelational ones, in reaction to their positional identifications as "not-like" their primary caretaker?

As compared to Freud and the ensuing arena of classical psychoanalysis, the object relations school of psychoanalytic thinking does contain the roots of a more flexible, less essentialist understanding of development, based as it is on the strength and influence of early caretaking dyads that need not be gender-specific or gender-continuous. It is within these early caretaking dyads that internalizations evolve that are historical, idiosyncratic, and dependent on the confluence of mothering styles and the congenital-temporal needs of the infant.

If one looks to Winnicott as the object relations theorist who dealt most specifically with mothering, we find him speaking in actuality of early "mothering work," where mother is the provider of the facilitating environment, a good-enough mother who is able to hold the infant (protect from physiological insult, take account of the infant's various tactile and kinesthetic sensitivities, and accommodate the infant's rhythms) and mirror appropriately to provide the ground for ego relatedness and a sense of going-on-being.

In his essay on the parent-infant relationship, Winnicott (1960) divides the functions of the parents along traditionally gendered lines in keeping with the socioeconomic custom of his milieu. Mother cared for the infant while father cared for the mother by protecting her environment. There is, however, no sustained discussion of "fathering work" as it relates specifically to development, nor any reason to suppose that men are any less able to provide a facilitating environment than women. Unlike Chodorow, who tells us specifically that our patterns of asymmetrical parenting reproduce women who mother and men who do not because the men have repressed the relational-nurturant aspects of themselves that are female-identified, Winnicott tends not to deal with issues of gender or sexual difference (Chodorow, 1978). With Winnicott, as with other British object relations theorists, as well as with Kohut and fellow American self psychologists, we are left with theories describing internalized object relations and the development of the self that are essentially genderless, not by intent, but by omission.

The Postmodern Critique

The postmodern critique of feminist theory questions the very primacy of sexual difference as a field of inquiry. Focusing on male-female differences obscures other issues, such as power relations, and assumes that unitary categories of male/female are valid ones. Snitow speaks of the "divide" that keeps forming in feminist thought between the need to build an identity of women and the need to dismantle the category entirely. The same can be said of motherhood where women, it seems, have always resisted being confined and defined by cultural representations of motherhood, and yet are loathe to give up their mother right.

In *Gender Trouble* (1990), Judith Butler offers a provocative critique of the genealogy of gender categories in an attempt to subvert what she perceives to be the oppression of gender hierarchy and compulsory heterosexuality on our thinking. Most of what Butler questions about the category of women within feminist theory—that is, the very construction of a unitary and presumedly universal category—applies to mothers and motherhood as well.

As Butler attempts a deconstruction of the category of women, we might ask in a similar vein, does the term *mother* denote a common identity, a stable signifier that commands the assent of those it purports to describe and represent? Or is the construction of the category "mother," like that of "women," an unwitting regulation and reification of gender relations that furthermore attains stability and coherence only in the context of a traditional heterosexual matrix? Butler's critique would suggest that the category of mother *is* a constructed subject based on a questionable category of gender.

Butler argues that there is no necessity for gender to retain a mimetic relationship to sex, given that the former is presumed to be culturally constructed and the latter biological. Thus, man and masculine might just as easily signify a female body as a male one; and woman and feminine might just as easily signify a male body as a female one. Culture has always recognized this in fact, and we have always had our "masculine women" and "feminine men" with differing roles and differing levels of approbation or proscription depending on the culture.

Butler extends her analysis even further, however, and calls into question the very distinction between a supposedly biologically given sex and a culturally constructed gender.

> Can we refer to a "given" sex or a "given" gender without first inquiring into how sex and/or gender is given, through what means? And what is "sex" anyway? Is it natural, anatomical, chromosomal, or hormonal? . . . Does sex have a history? Does each sex have a different history, or histories? Is there a history of how the duality of sex was established, a genealogy that might expose the binary options as a variable construction? Are the ostensibly natural facts of sex discursively produced by the various scientific discourses in the service of other political and social interests? If the immutable character of sex is contested, perhaps this construct called "sex" is as culturally constructed as gender; indeed, perhaps it was already gender, with the consequence that the distinction between sex and gender turns out to be no distinction at all. (Butler, 1990, pp. 6–7)

Through Butler's voice, one could envisage a new parenting subject that would be less unitary and more conditional, free of constrictions of gender altogether.

Is Motherhood a Gendered Relation?

Is motherhood a gendered relation? Our brief look at the problematic raised by the advent of reproduction technology and its representation in culture suggests that motherhood is a matter of relation. But just what that relation is, and who will define and legitimize it, remains unclear. Butler's analysis further complicates the issues, as the very identification of motherhood with women becomes eroded, if not entirely erased. The term *mother* might signify a feminine male body or a masculine one just as it might signify a feminine female body or a masculine female body. How then might one identify a mother or mothering?

In a somewhat different vein, Sara Ruddick introduces a concept of mothering as work that transcends gender. She distinguishes between birthing labor, which only women do, and mothering work. Birthing labor remains the special province of women (thus far) and women might choose to celebrate this, just as in a particular situation, genetic parents might choose to be recognized in a specific fashion. But for Ruddick, mothers and mothering work need not be gendered. A mother is

> a person who takes on responsibility for children's lives and for whom providing child care is a significant part of her or his working life. I *mean*

"her or his." Although most mothers have been and are women, mothering is potentially work for men and women. This is not to deny . . . that there may be biologically based differences in styles of mothering. . . . I am suggesting that whatever difference might exist between female and male mothers, there is no reason to believe that one sex rather than the other is more capable of doing maternal work. (Ruddick, 1989, pp. 40–41)

Ruddick suggests that the push toward ever increasing sophistication of reproductive technology stems from *envy* of female reproduction capacities and the wish to strip that capacity from the exclusive province of women. This notion stands, in a way, as the inverse complement of Freud's, whereby a woman's urge to procreate stems ultimately from her penis envy in that often maligned unconscious equation of penis = baby.

Concluding Thoughts

In our culture, mothers/mothering no longer universally signifies a woman's essential biological relation to her child. By examining the impact of reproductive technology and its cultural reflections, and through the prism of postmodern critique, we have deconstructed the category "mother" as a "natural," biologically rooted gendered relation to genetic offspring. What are the consequences of that deconstruction for theories of psychological development?

There are clearly consequences for our notions of femininity and womanhood as they interface with our assumptions about motherhood. By taking the nature out of mother, we rend a tectonic shift in our parallel assumptions about the universal meaning of menarche, menopause, and fertility within women's lives, and concomitantly, of the importance of traditional marriages and heterosexual intercourse for achieving reproductive goals.

Psychoanalytic theorists have been interested in the internalization of early maternal experience as the wellspring for the emergence of self and self-in-relation, with the implicit understanding that that experience is grounded in a traditional triangular heterosexual matrix. Its focus has been largely on the development of the child (Winnicott's essay on "Primary Maternal Preoccupation" [1956, pp. 300–305] notwithstanding), with little emphasis on maternal subjectivity.

Recent developments in intersubjective theory involving patterns of attunement and the evolution of mutual recognition between the infant and mother also assume that the all-important infant–mother-caretaker dyad occurs within the context of a fairly traditional heterosexual triangular matrix (Benjamin, 1988; Stern, 1985). Although Benjamin recognizes in a footnote that a large proportion of children in our culture do not grow up with a "mommy and daddy in stereotypical families with a conventional sexual division of labor," she maintains that psychic structure must be understood within a context of the "dominant culture and its gender structure" (1988, p. 105). So although she acknowledges that the figures of mothers and fathers are "cultural ideals" that "need not be played by 'biological' mothers and fathers, or even by women and men," she reproduces those cultural ideals as she generates new theory and imbues the maternal with an almost predetermined lack of subjectivity.

If we could transcend our tremendous resistance to altering the traditional representations of motherhood based on our collective anger, envy, idealization, and objectification of our female mothers, then we might begin to ask some historically germane and potentially more interesting questions about being and experiencing motherhood.

Can a father be a mother? What might distinguish mothering and fathering work, and are those differences necessarily gender-related? What happens in the growing number of single-parent families that exist today? A single parent of either sex retains the more familiar role of negotiating in the public arena, traditionally the father's role, while a large proportion of the daily intimate care is often provided by a substitute caretaker, usually a female. Is the single-parent mother really the father then? What is the experience of a single-parent father who is responsible for the nurturance and daily care of his child or children? Does that father experience himself as "the mother" or "the father"? Obviously each family constellation is different depending on the nature and quality of the child care, the age and developmental stage of the child, and most important, the *subjective experience* of the parenting one.

What is being suggested here is that males and females might have different mothering styles and those differences might supersede or converge with individual differences, but that being a mother is a subjective experience rather than an objective category of definition.

Psychoanalysis as a developmental model has been interested in parenting primarily from the vantage point of the infant. We might ask, then, how does the infant internalize the earliest dyad, where the mothering one is male? Is there a difference, or is maternal function, generically assumed to be female, actually without need of gender (Moss, 1989)?

Is there a difference in maternal subjectivity between a "biological mother" (including both gestational and genetically related mothers) and a mother who is not genetically related to her offspring? Is that difference internalized by the child, and if so, what form does it take? Our only current point of reference is the literature of adoption studies, and these tend to focus on the adjustment of adoptees and occasionally on that of the surrendering birth mother (Brodzinsky & Schecter, 1990). The distinction of different maternal objects, based on the internalization of differing modes of maternal subjectivity, speaks to a level of experience and sophistication not yet reported in the psychoanalytic consulting room.

These and other questions suggest a radical shift from the notion of mother and motherhood to notions about mothering. The shift reflects an active identity that exists within a temporal frame that transcends gender. It is a relational entity and one whose subjectivity is implicit. For women, it is the nature of their relation to their biology rather than the biological nature of their relation to motherhood that should concern us. Freed of the bonds of discrete gender/sex roles, we can begin to think of mothering in a far more complex and textured fashion, occurring as it does in a continuum of multiple subjectivities and relations. It is the task of an enhanced psychoanalytic inquiry to discover how these relations are internally represented.

References

Atwood, M. (1986). *The handmaid's tale.* New York: Houghton Mifflin. (Working text, New York: Ballantine Books, 1987.)

Bassin, D. (1989). Woman's shifting sense of self: The impact of reproductive technology. In J. Offerman-Zuckerberg (Ed.), *Gender in transition: A new frontier.* New York: Plenum.

Benjamin, J. (1988). *The bonds of love: Psychoanalysis, feminism and the problem of domination.* New York: Pantheon.

Brodzinsky, D. M., & Schecter, M. D. (Eds.). (1990). *The psychology of adoption.* New York: Oxford University Press.

Butler, J. (1990). *Gender trouble: Feminism and the subversion of identity.* New York: Routledge.

Chessler, P. (1989). *The sacred bond: Legacy of Baby M.* New York: Random House.

Chodorow, N. (1978). *The reproduction of mothering: Psychoanalysis and the sociology of gender.* Berkeley: University of California Press.

Fliegel, Z. (1973). Feminine psychosexual development in Freudian theory. *Psychoanalytic Quarterly, 42,* 385–409.

Fliegel, Z. (1982). Current status of Freud's controversial views on women. *Psychoanalytic Review, 69,* 7–28.

Freud, S. (1925). Some psychical consequences of the anatomical distinctions between the sexes. In *Standard Edition.* Vol. 19, 243–58. London: Hogarth Press.

Freud, S. (1933). Femininity. In *Standard Edition.* Vol. 22, 112–35. London: Hogarth Press.

Grossman, W., & Stewart, W. (1976). Penis envy: From childhood wish to developmental metaphor. *Journal of the American Psychoanalytic Association, 24*(5), 193–212.

Kane, E. (pseud.) (1988). *Birth mother: America's first legal surrogate mother, her change of heart.* New York: Harcourt Brace.

Kleeman, J. (1976). Freud's views on early female sexuality in light of direct childhood observations. *Journal of the American Psychoanalytic Association, 24*(5), 3–28.

Moss, D. (1989). On situating the object: Thoughts on the maternal function, modernism and post-modernism. *American Imago, 46*(4), 350–69.

Rich, A. (1980). Compulsive heterosexuality and lesbian existence. In C. Stimpson & E. Person (Eds.), *Women, sex and sexuality.* Chicago: University of Chicago Press.

Rothman, B. K. (1988). Reproductive technology and the commodification of life. In D. H. Baruch, A. D'Adamo, Jr., & J. Seager (Eds.), *Embryos, ethics and women's rights.* New York: Harrington Park Press.

Rothman, B. K. (1989a). On surrogacy: Constructing social policy. In J. Offerman-Zuckerberg (Ed.), *Gender in transition: A new frontier.* New York: Plenum.

Rothman, B. K. (1989b). *Recreating motherhood: Ideology and technology in a patriarchal society.* New York: Norton.

Ruddick, S. (1989). *Maternal thinking.* Boston: Beacon Press.

Schwartz, A. (1984). Psychoanalysis and women: A rapprochement. *Women & Therapy,* 3(1), 3–12.

Snitow, A. (1989). A gender diary. In A. Harris & Y. King (Eds.), *Rocking the ship of state: Feminist peace politics.* Denver: Westview.

Stern, D. N. (1985). *The interpersonal world of the infant.* New York: Basic Books.

Whitehead, M., with Schwartz-Nobel, L. (1989). *A mother's story.* New York: St. Martin's.

Winnicott, D. W. (1956). Primary maternal preoccupation. In D. W. Winnicott, *Collected Papers: Through Paediatrics to Psychoanalysis.* New York: Basic Books, 1958.

Winnicott, D. W. (1960). The theory of the parent-infant relationship. In D. W. Winnicott, *The Maturational Processes and the Facilitating Environment.* New York: International Universities Press, 1965.

E. ANN KAPLAN

15 Sex, Work, and Motherhood: Maternal Subjectivity in Recent Visual Culture

In this chapter I shall trace a movement that has taken place in films during the past fifteen years—from a renewed focus on the mother-as-subject to a remarginalization of the mother-subject in favor of the fetus/baby as the *real* subject. In addition, I shall note and account for the paucity of films addressing the difficulties facing white women as they attempt to combine sex, work, and motherhood.[1]

Representations of the mother-as-subject have become far more common in films because of the various women's movements and their impact on a largely white middle-class audience of women.[2] Stated briefly, women have been working personally, politically, and academically on themselves and on issues pertaining to women generally, and, as a result, female subjectivity has changed. Some films portray a new mother-subject, since there is an audience for her. Others focus on mothers and daughters, who have been encouraged by the women's movements to take satisfaction and joy in one another (see films like *Terms of Endearment,* 1988; *Postcards from the Edge,* 1991; and *Stella Dallas,* 1990). *Shoot the Moon* (1986) set the trend for images of the divorced mother with children and was followed by

1. This chapter focuses on the white maternal subject that is so much the preoccupation of recent Hollywood films. I am fully aware of the interdependency of black and white maternal constructs, however, and shall point out some of the basic contrasts between black and white mothers that arise automatically as one focuses on white motherhood. My future research will seek to explain differences between black and white maternal figures.

2. Men stand in a different relation to the impacts of the women's movements and therefore to both conscious and unconscious change.

films like *The Good Mother* (1988), which exemplify the new interest in images of women seeking to combine satisfaction in motherhood with sex outside marriage.

The absence in recent films of either angelic, self-sacrificing mothers or evil/whore ones—the binary mother figures that have haunted film history from its beginnings—has been significantly positive. Some evil mothers appeared in the early eighties (for example, *Frances, Mommie Dearest*), and one recent angelic mother emerged in the 1990 version of *Stella Dallas*. But more typical of the nineties is a spoof on the whole family melodrama genre, *Throw Momma from the Train* (1988).

The negative classical paradigms are not being represented as often in surface narratives of angel/whore white mothers. This does *not* mean, however, that the unconscious processes that produced these images are no longer operating. An incredible split exists between what has happened to women's *conscious* processes regarding mothering and daughtering as a result of the various women's movements and what *unconscious* desires still remain in American culture generally. Much of this unconscious unease regarding the mother has been displaced into the horror film (Creed, 1986, 1992); but the displacement is also obvious in the fetal interpellation which, borrowing neo-Marxist Louis Althusser's (1971) concept, I will explore later in this chapter.[3] To counter sentimentalized images of the mother safely located in her nuclear family, images of the father displacing the mother, images of the fetus/baby displacing the mother, and finally, images of the mother as monstrous and displaced into horror genres, feminists now face the challenge of producing images of a radically transformed maternal subject.

Part of the unconscious difficulty that still haunts the American imagination in relation to women is evident in the paucity of films dealing with motherhood and work. Films that address women's struggles to combine sex, work, and motherhood are even more absent. By the mid-1980s, statistics about the increasing number of working mothers had proliferated in newspapers and magazines. Growing attention was paid to single-parent families. In 1987, 5.6 million single American women were said to be working while rearing children, while only 900,000 single men were doing the same. The figures cited in the later 1980s and early 1990s showed 24 percent of American children living with one parent, with the number expected to rise to 50 percent by the time those children have reached adulthood (*New York Times,* May 9, 1987; June 16, 1988; *Newsweek,* June 4, 1990). Although the writers expressed the most concern about the *single* working mother, they also worried over the impact of professional working mothers on their children, even when there were two parents in

3. By *interpellation*, Althusser (1971) meant the process through which a subject is "called" or "hailed" into being via dominant ideology. Dominant institutions demand certain kinds of subjects at specific historical moments, and these institutions produce discourses that in turn produce the needed kinds of subject. An example is the recent "hailing" of the fetus as subject because it satisfies certain cultural needs.

the home. Typically, the statistics cited as cause for concern, originating what I will call the "concern discourse," did not distinguish mothers according to class and race. This is equally true of the most recent figures cited: 75 percent of women with school-aged children are in the work force and, in the course of the 1990s, 60 percent of children in the United States are predicted to spend some part of their childhood in a single-parent family (Silverstein, 1991; Weitzman, 1985).

It must be emphasized that although minority women have long been single working mothers, no concern discourse emerged in relation to them.[4] Thus the recent concern discourse must arise because more and more *white* women are raising children alone. The majority of *professional* mothers who are married are assumed to be privileged white women. The concern discourses for the white maternal subject, whether single mother or career woman, are constituted so as to marginalize the black/minority maternal subject.[5]

In this chapter, I shall consider the plethora of films dealing with white mothers and babies as their subjects in the eighties and early nineties. Although there is no monolithic discourse about sex, work, and white motherhood in this period, the number of films about motherhood do have to be accounted for, as do the ideological investments their narratives reveal. *Genre* should also be addressed, as it plays an important role in governing the shape that a narrative will take and constraining what is ideologically included or excluded within a particular film.

Underlying all these films about white mothers and children is anxiety in relation to white women and the cultural changes in sex, family, and work spheres that are emerging in tandem with changes in the technological, economic, and industrial spheres. This anxiety partly has to do with the fact that childbirth and child care are no longer an automatic, "natural" part of the white woman's life cycle. This centrally affects women's sex and work lives; they not only may be sexual before marriage but need not have children at all. Meanwhile, they can compete with men in the work sphere.

4. I speculate that the few images of minority mothers as subjects of a dominant narrative until recently resulted from white culture's ensuring, through its economic arrangements, that black women occupied the maternal (domestic) space—the space of caring for white children as well as their own, of cleaning white women's houses as well as their own, and of nurturing society's needy as nurses, teachers, and social workers. That is, while the white mother has traditionally occupied the place of the Kristevan "abject" (Kaplan, 1993; Kristeva, 1982), the black woman was positioned as *object*. See the discussion (below) on *Imitation of life*.

5. I do not have the space here to make a comparison of black and white maternal subjects in contemporary film, a topic that merits full attention. My new research, influenced by Hazel Carby's volume *Reconstructing Womanhood*, will, however, explore ways in which white maternal figures are closely intertwined with black maternal constructs. Both figures evolved out of the "slaves" and "mistresses" constructs and interrelationships in the antebellum South.

In this situation, the American cultural imagination produces new images of women fulfilling themselves through bearing children and living in a traditional nuclear family. Movies have always represented women as mothers, but images of motherhood have often been peripheral to the main narrative. In earlier decades there was little focus on self-fulfillment for women in childbearing and rearing. On the contrary, feminist scholars researching women's own records (letters, diaries, fiction) have found that the main nineteenth-century mother-hood discourse concerned suffering and self-sacrifice in the service of a *duty* to mother that goes unquestioned.

A brief discussion of Fanny Hurst's 1934 novel *Imitation of Life* and its subsequent film versions will illuminate how remarkable that narrative was in raising some of the conflicts between sex and motherhood for the white mother, as well as the impossibility of the black woman escaping construction in white discourse as the maternal *and nothing else*—as maternality personified. Bea Pullman, a white widowed working mother and heroine of the 1934 narrative, offers an unusual Hollywood image as she struggles at the start of the film to ready herself for her low-paying job and her daughter, Jessie, for day care. A black mother's opportune knock at the door, keeping her own little girl out of sight, solves Bea's dilemma in trying to combine motherhood and work. Sex, as usual, is not yet an issue. The black mother, Delilah, and her daughter move in with Bea and Jessie, and in this way the traditional nuclear family division of labor is reconstituted. The white woman's work life is made possible through the black woman's *unpaid* domestic labor (Bea does not yet have enough money to pay Delilah). But even this story assumes that it is the white woman's "duty" to mother and, if she is "good," to sacrifice her desires for her child. Also, the film is not satisfied with Delilah's uncomplaining acceptance of her relegation to the maternal personified: it insists that her mulatta daughter rescind the desire to pass for white and accept her black maternal status.

In this 1930s narrative, motherhood is not conceived as a willing choice in the face of alternatives, as it is in our period. Sirk's 1959 film version of *Imitation of Life* is somewhat different. In the period just prior to the feminist eruptions of the late sixties, Lana Turner's desire to subordinate mothering to her career is severely critiqued (Kaplan, 1992). Significantly, such desires are again critiqued in 1991 in *Postcards from the Edge* (discussed below). The late-twentieth-century reification of mothering not as a duty (women no longer *have* to mother) but as fulfilling in and of itself is something new.

In addition, the plethora of films about motherhood has been fueled by a new market that film producers have located—namely, baby-boomers in their mid-thirties, many of whom have recently decided to start families. The baby-boom numbers are sufficient to warrant refining old melodrama formulas into new mothering and parenting films. Market reasons may also be behind the paucity of images of black maternal figures. The black youth audience is currently being addressed in a spate of youth films, but it is not clear that Hollywood has accepted that there is an audience for images of black mothers equivalent to the audience that exists for images of white mothers.[6]

Although this question lies beyond my focus here, let me briefly allude to John Berry's 1974 film *Claudine,* which is unusual because it presents a narrative focused on a black maternal figure. The image of Claudine, a single working mother, is allowed agency within the social and economic constraints of her class. As the heroine, her conflicts between sex and motherhood drive the narrative. But two questions immediately arise: why is it that conflicts between motherhood and sex, so late in being addressed in relation to white women, were vividly presented in a film about a black maternal subject as early as 1974? And second, why was this film such a sleeper and apparently is still not available on video? The answer to the first question would entail exploration of the constitution not only of black maternity but of black sexuality in white culture. Possibly, the black mother can be openly (and realistically) sexual in this film because American culture is not invested in her Symbolic Virginal Mother status. The answer to the second question would entail a detailed analysis of the film's exhibition history. I suspect part of the problem of the film for current audiences is not its domestic content but its reliance on black stereotypes and its complicity with expectations that blacks will be represented only in those roles that white society desires for them. By 1974, blacks could be "subjects" and not "objects" if they were good, hardworking subjects. The black mother's conflicts among sex, work, and motherhood were not threatening because black women still have few real *alternatives* in society. In this situation, the boundaries of the maternal do not have to be policed. But I shall leave these complex questions for future research.

It was in connection with the white baby-boomer group that films in the mid-eighties began to present satisfaction in mothering and the choice of mothering over career (see *The Good Mother* and *Baby Boom* discussed below). *Heartburn* (1986) also depicted pleasure in mothering and the choice of children over an

6. See Jacqueline Bobo "'The Subject Is Money': Reconsidering the Black Film Audience as a Theoretical Paradigm," *Black Literature Forum* (Summer 1991): 421–32; and Bobo's "The Construction of Black Sexuality: Towards Normalizing the Black Cinematic Experience," a paper read at the MLA meeting in New York, December 1992. The desire for images of African-American families, including a diversity of female and maternal images, is evident in the extraordinary interest in Julie Dash's film *Daughters of the Dust* (1992), at least on the East Coast. Bobo discusses the relatively small investment Hollywood made in *The Color Purple* (1986) because of uncertainty about the potential audience for the film. In fact, the film was an overwhelming success, despite (or because of) the controversy it sparked among both black and white viewers. But the *construction* persists that black audiences are not interested in domestic melodramas. This must be linked to negative stereotypes about the African-American family—to notion that it has been "destroyed" or that there are no middle-class African-American families! Such constructions on the part of Hollywood—still a while male patriarchal institution—require fuller treatment than I can give here. See my forthcoming book on *Race, Psychoanalysis, and Cinema.*

unsatisfactory marriage. A comedy like *Raising Arizona* (1988) showed the extreme lengths (in this case, kidnapping) that parents will go to in order to have a baby. On television, meanwhile, there were sentimental images in *Thirtysomething, Baby Boom* (started after the film's success), and *Almost Grown* of "yuppies" who are satisfied in rearing children.

As is clear from this brief list, films have not responded to the statistics concerning work and motherhood, nor have they dealt seriously with role conflicts and practical issues that arise when mothers, especially single ones, work. It is difficult to find Hollywood films that address the fact that many mothers, especially single ones, simply have to work in order to support themselves and their children. It is also difficult to find films that focus on the fact that many mothers *want* to work, for a whole series of reasons, including wanting a degree of independence within a marriage, needing fulfillment through work, and needing the social adult community one can find in a workplace. Rare films by socially conscious directors coming out of the sixties, like Martin Ritt (*Norma Rae*, 1979), have dealt with strong working-class heroines and, to a degree, with tensions among sex, work, and motherhood. The few recent and popular Hollywood films that take the working woman as subject, such as Mike Nichols's *Working Girl* (1988), do not portray the central characters as mothers. Indeed, this particular film absolutely excludes any reference to motherhood or children, as these roles might interact with or make problematic female needs for satisfaction in work. Hollywood has been ready to broach the tensions between sex and motherhood, perhaps because sex always sells, no matter what the context. But the Hollywood mother pays a price for breaking the code between "mother" and "sex," much as Bea Pullman did in the 1934 version of *Imitation of Life*.

To further explore these issues, I shall focus on six recent representative films about mothers, including two melodramas, *The Good Mother* (1988) and *Fatal Attraction* (1989); three comedies, *Baby Boom* (1988), *Three Men and a Baby* (1988), and *Look Who's Talking* (1990–91); and *Postcards from the Edge* (1991), a film that falls in between melodrama and comedy. I shall use these films to demonstrate varied kinds of motherhood discourses, along with the contradictory ideological positions they portray, and shall speculate on why these discourses arise now. I shall show how they emerge from a concern discourse that, in turn, arises from anxiety about who will care for the children (and for men, too?), given women's newly won choices.

The following two films are chosen to contrast a "high modernist" approach to issues regarding mothering with a "postmodern" one.

The Good Mother (1988), a melodrama, addresses important contemporary issues having to do with divorce, child custody, and female sexuality within a high modernist frame. Made from Sue Miller's 1981 novel of the same name, the film critically exposes the degree to which traditional mother images and myths remain deeply embedded within the laws and legal institutions of the United States. How these codes constrain what the heroine, Anna, is able to become— how they force her into traditional maternal positions that she has in some ways moved beyond—is exposed. In this film, Anna's sexuality is highlighted in a way that within the traditional family it need not be. Certainly, within the legal nuclear family, sexuality is considered a private matter. But the novel shows that this is not the case with the single mother. Her right to be fully sexual comes under criticism from the state, an issue that is introduced by her former husband during the custody battle.

Liberatory discourses about single motherhood, female sexuality, child custody, and the state are evident. But they exist in complex relation to what I am here calling a renewed sentimentalizing of motherhood discourse. Even in the novel, mothering is presented as a woman's only satisfying activity. Anna is destroyed when she loses primary custody of her child, Molly. She leaves her lover, Leo (who has stayed by her through the excruciating court case), and she does not take up any professional interests.

The film exacerbates the subdued tendencies in the novel, placing even more emphasis on the idyllic mother-child relationship. The visual representation of the New England grandparents' home (not unlike that in *Baby Boom*) is almost embarrassingly nostalgic and stereotypical, as are the grandparents themselves. Despite being an archaic representation, this premodern, Thoreauvian world still haunts the American imagination.

In its construction of the ambivalent image of the lover and his relationship with the child, the film slants things in favor of the husband. It supplies a scene, not in the novel, in which Anna flares up at Leo when he complains that her life is too narrowly focused on the little girl. Anna, interestingly, points out that men previously wanted and got a homebody; now they want a woman with broader interests. She demands to know why nurturing is not enough; what is wrong with this focus? The scene prepares for the ending of the film, when Anna, having lost primary custody of the child, acts almost as if the girl had died. Her life is now seen to be empty and pointless; she is left to yearn for the child.

Nevertheless, the film is progressive in letting us see how legal institutions construct mothers according to old patriarchal codes—codes that the film itself has partly surpassed. Anna's lawyer suggests that the only hope of victory is to blame Leo. When Anna argues for telling the truth, she is persuaded that the jury is not yet ready for a truth that involves openness about sexuality, particularly outside of marriage. The film explores situations—such as losing a custody case—that women in the seventies experienced, and thus usefully exposes remaining double standards.

But film is not life. The politics of representation has taught us that images are always arbitrary and selective; many alternative images are possible, whereas in life women often do not have choices. Choosing to represent the heroine's overreaction to the outcome of the case as her passive renunciation of her life to the loss of custody does not provide a helpful model. There is insufficient analysis in the film of the dominant ideologies that govern institutions like the law courts. It would have been interesting to have a heroine who was a fully fledged career woman, who cared about her work as well as about her role as mother. We have yet to see Hollywood address the conflict between work and parenting from the mother's point of view as was done for fathers in *Kramer versus Kramer* (1981).

This film, then, betrays contradictory discourses. It is progressive and unusual in showing Anna as a mother enjoying impassioned, extramarital female sexuality, but ultimately falls into a sentimental discourse in which the heroine finds self-fulfillment in mothering alone. The maternal sacrifice paradigm may be glimpsed returning here. Anna has, like the heroines in *Imitation of Life*, sacrificed herself for the sake of her child. The underlying definition of woman as nothing-but-mother slyly returns. In a contradictory manner, the film supports both this and the discourse of liberated female desire in a high modernist manner, critiquing the old-fashioned nuclear family and the legal institutions still embedded in it. It is a modernist film because it assumes that Anna's "truth" is achievable, if only legal institutions were rational.

Fatal Attraction (1989) is perhaps the clearest example of a new ideological construction of the family in opposition to the "liberated" career woman. It is postmodernist, for it looks back nostalgically at a public fantasy rather than exploring institutional relations in the manner of *The Good Mother*. It is also postmodern in its deliberate mixing of the woman's film with the horror genre (Jameson, 1981, 1985, 1991; Kaplan, 1988, 1992).

"Liberation" in most Hollywood films still means "sexual promiscuity." Glenn Close is shown at the start of the film as an independent career woman who objects to being made a sex object, but who also has an intense sexual drive. The female spectator is invited to identify with the figure at the start of the film, only to have this identification sickeningly wrenched away as the viewer watches Glenn Close turn into a monster of horror film proportions. Viewers are forced to identify with both the besieged husband and the abused wife and, finally, with the wretchedly tortured child. Glenn Close, the repressed underside of the nuclear family, becomes intolerable. Like the ghastly mutations of science fiction and horror genres, she must be eliminated as the representative of everything that threatens the biological nuclear family. Like those mutations, she keeps returning in ever more vile forms, with ever more monstrous purposes, until, finally, husband and wife manage to eradicate her together. The sanctity of the nuclear family returns, albeit badly scarred (the wife, contaminated by Glenn Close, has had to resort to undesirable violence; the child is damaged). Nevertheless, the trio reconstitute their little community once evil (the liberated woman) is exorcised.

Fatal Attraction combines melodrama with the horror film—the genre into which the most extreme anxieties about mothering have often been displaced—and it develops its position through producing intense emotion in the spectator. Strategies of identification, suspense, and fear are effectively utilized. In contrast, a second set of films—*Baby Boom, Three Men and a Baby,* and *Look Who's Talking* are comedies and situate the spectator quite differently vis-à-vis the image. These films diffuse anxiety about mothering through comic devices. Nevertheless, comedies develop ideological positions as much as melodramas do. A brief comparison of *Three Men and a Baby* (1988) and *Baby Boom* (1988) is instructive in this regard, illustrating the different ways in which contemporary culture *thinks* about fathering versus mothering.

Both *Baby Boom* and *Three Men* begin with a comic satire on New York yuppie life. *Baby Boom* satirizes the new "working girl," in showing Diane Keaton as a hustling, nervous, high-powered executive woman. She lives in a smart, well-equipped apartment, where she eats take-out food. Her lawyer boyfriend is equally wired and pressured and has equally little time for relaxation. Keaton and he take their work to bed with them and *time* their sexual intercourse to seconds. Nothing could be further from family life and domestic concerns. By some fluke, Keaton inherits a baby, who is brought to her and then left with her. She tries unsuccessfully to get rid of the baby, but in the meantime grows increasingly fond of it. The baby has awakened, it seems, Keaton's assumed-to-be-dormant maternal self. Before we know it, she has quit her high-powered job and bought a rambling old house in the country.

Three Men sets up a similar situation. The men are roommates and have hectic, active lives; only in this film the focus is more on their promiscuity and their libidinal pleasures than on their work drives. The comparison of these films suggests that the new woman is overinvested in her work. Keaton is serious and devoted, whereas the three men delight in bodily pleasures; they are playful, carefree, and sensual. Here, too, a baby arrives unannounced on their doorstep, and they have to deal with it. But since men are not supposed to know about babies or to have parental yearnings, there is far more comedy around dealing with the baby's eating, defecating, and cleaning than in *Baby Boom*. In fact, taking care of the baby becomes the film's main content, although there is a significant side-step into the detective genre through a subplot about smuggled drugs, as if to allude to the more serious matters that normally involve men. A certain sexualizing of the baby reflects a distaste for "mature womanhood" (Modleski, 1988, p. 71) and also the need to keep the aging men in the romantic mode. Unconscious anxiety about men in the domestic setting may be glimpsed here—an anxiety that has to do with women's new demands that men share child care. The anxiety is diffused, however, through the comedy and through making sure that nothing is actually at stake for these men in relation to the baby. Fathering is not seen as part of any identity they *need* to assume. The film shows how understandable it is that the men would want to rid themselves of the baby, but also understandable that some attachment to the baby might develop. In this film, fatherhood is shared and chosen, not demanded.

The case is very different for Diane Keaton. Since women are still *assumed* to be innately linked to childbearing and rearing, the film shows Keaton quickly altering her personality and life-style. Indeed, the focus of her life changes completely; she becomes so absorbed in the baby that she neglects her work and is eventually fired. The film underscores expectations of women in contrast to those of men.

The second part of the film does offer a critique of single motherhood. Keaton's idea of an idyllic country retreat turns into a nightmare when she and the baby are marooned in a ramshackle house in a severe northeastern winter.

She is soon climbing the walls with loneliness and boredom. This does not last long, however. The depressed mother needs only sex and romance to bring her back to life. Keaton finds this in the figure of the local veterinarian called in, for want of someone better, to treat her depression. Through his love, Keaton is reenergized and the American pastoral fantasy begins again.

Keaton hits upon the idea of producing healthy homemade baby applesauce and soon has a highly successful business. So much so, that her old corporation pleads for her to come back and bring them her business. Here the film engages in a comic critique of the corporation in favor of small entrepreneurship. Keaton, looking svelte and efficient, refuses to return. Again, in tune with the American nostalgia for small enterprise (a fantasy that here conveniently fits in with the desire for heterosexual coupling), Keaton chooses her country life, motherhood, and her horse doctor over hectic city life. Of course, her city entrepreneurial skills come in handy—she has found a job that she can conveniently combine with mothering—but the family is idyllically reconstituted at the film's end.

The contrast with *Three Men* is dramatic. It is not that the men do not grow fond of the baby (they do), or that they are not sorry to see it leave (they rush to the airport to try to prevent the girlfriend from taking the baby away). It is the film's cavalier, comic, distanced treatment of these emotions that makes the difference. Men cannot be truly invested in a baby, and their yuppie city jobs are never in jeopardy. This would deny their masculinity and their virility (hence the anxiety beneath the comedy). Indeed, it is the *woman's* maternal investment— she finds that she cannot leave the baby—that threatens to disrupt the three men's life with baby. In the end, this film allows everyone's fantasy to come true. The woman returns, and they all decide to set up a sort of communal family around the baby.

American culture seems ready, as is evident in *Baby Boom*, to cast a critical eye on its drive for more money, more markets, and the aggressive pursuit of careers.[7] But it seems unable to find a way in which to do this without returning (especially in *Baby Boom*) to earlier American myths about nature as better than the city and the family as better than the single life. These films play out unconscious fantasies of abandonment (the bad mothers in these films drop off their babies), of unrestrained libidinal desire (parenting is a responsibility for another, and is good for you), and end conventionally, reinserting the mother into the narrative, even if we are left with a slightly unconventional "family."

These eighties images are contradictory. They validate the domestic sphere for women who have been successful in careers while also promoting the woman who finds fulfillment only in mothering. No longer is combining career and motherhood thought to be desirable; nor is choosing career over mothering seen positively. Indeed, this possibility has rarely been shown, nor have there ever been regular images of the mother-woman's satisfaction in work or her needs for self-fulfillment through work. It is clear that in the late eighties

7. See, e.g., a film like *Wall Street* for a full development of this theme.

choosing the child over career (as happens in *Baby Boom*) or going to college or taking up some kind of business only after the daughter is grown (the situation of most mothers in the 1989 and 1990 "Mother-Daughter Pageant") represents the new ideal. As in the fifties, the domestic is idealized after a period in which women entered the work force in large numbers. The difference now is that the *single* working woman still has a hold on the social imagination, as is evident from the success of Mike Nichols's *Working Girl.*

The end of the eighties seems to have marked a return to rigid polarization of sex, work, and motherhood in the movies. But there are important variations in the films' images from those in earlier ones. Single women are now more often represented in high-level career positions, although they are usually depicted as masculinized or unpleasant (such as in Nichols's *Working Girl*). Mothers are represented as sexual, but not career women, or as career women and not sexual. It appears that there is only one universal way in which to mother and that motherhood is still too deep and problematic a topic to be given complex treatment.

One film that begins to explore mother-daughter relations in some of their lived complexity is Mike Nichols's *Postcards from the Edge* (1990). The film functions on a psychological level; intense jealousies and rivalries flourish between Meryl Streep and her mother, played by Shirley MacLaine. The film begins to disrupt the old evil witch–mother paradigm by examining the positions of both mother and daughter in their jealousies, narcissism, and competition.

Postcards from the Edge, made from Carrie Fisher's successful novel, was widely believed to refer to Fisher's own experiences with her star-mother, Debbie Reynolds. It is perhaps because this story emerges in the context of contemporary psychological sophistication about family relationships—or at least in the context of a certain vocabulary about them—that the film is able to delve more deeply than earlier ones into complex mother-daughter ties. But the film nevertheless remains within some of the conventions of the *Imitation of Life* paradigm, especially in regard to the constraints placed on mothers. The relationship between Shirley MacLaine (mother) and Meryl Streep (daughter) has clear overtones of the Lana Turner (mother) and Jessie (daughter) relationship in Sirk's 1959 film. As in Sirk's film, the mother is an ambitious film and vaudeville star who is proud of having made it and who, like most stars, is highly narcissistic. The biggest change, however, is in the daughter. Indeed, the Meryl Streep character has more in common with Sarah Jane, the mulatta daughter in Sirk's film, than with the meek and mild Jessie, who adheres to dominant values and provides part of the critique of the Lana Turner figure. Like Sarah Jane in Sirk's 1959 film, Streep is in revolt against her mother, although for very different reasons.

Whereas Sarah Jane revolts against the powerlessness of being black—against relegation to a submissive maternity like her mother's—Streep feels completely overshadowed by her mother. *Postcards* broaches a little-attended-to series of issues about mother-daughter rivalry and jealousies. Streep feels unloved and neglected, as well as overshadowed and controlled. Her way of dealing with this is to follow in her mother's footsteps—she is a film star—but to short-circuit any hopes of really making it through self-destructive drinking and drug-taking.

Significantly, this film does not complicate the mother-daughter relationship through husbands or ongoing love affairs, as did *Imitation,* although it does insert father and lover figures in order to preclude a world in which women can take care of themselves. Nevertheless, the film leaves the mother-daughter relationship and the working through of conflicted emotions at the center of the narrative. *Postcards* is partly about the difficulty of aging for the narcissistic but, significantly, not evil mother. In the course of the film the mother struggles with aging and losing her beauty and comes to recognize that it is time to cede center-stage to her daughter. The film is about the daughter's learning to empathize with her mother's difficulties with aging and her need to be the center of attention. A scene in a hospital after the mother is in an accident captures the daughter's growing ability to help her mother through this stage of life. The daughter finds her mother looking weary and plain without her wig and makeup. She pulls out her cosmetics and gradually constructs the mother's image for her so that she can go out and face reporters.

As noted, the film does insist on father and lover figures to help Streep along. Gene Hackman plays a stern but ultimately well-meaning film director who gives Streep just the right kind of peptalks at just the right moments; Dennis Quaid is an attractive but unreliable boyfriend; and Richard Dreyfuss, the doctor who first pumps Streep's stomach when she overdoses at the start of the film, remains in the wings ready to provide her with the needed heterosexual coupling at the film's end. But Streep is also allowed, finally, to be a successful film star, while her mother looks on now with generative pleasure rather than competitive jealousy.

Postcards manages to deal with a new level of mother-daughter emotional intensity and addresses struggles around combining motherhood and career as they are worked through by an adult. The quality of the mother-daughter relationship echoes that already noted in Sirk's 1959 film, although the contexts for the two sets of relationships are constituted very differently: The first involves black women, the second, privileged white women. Sarah Jane, the mulatta daughter in *Imitation of Life,* has no opportunity to work things through with her aging, weary, deeply saddened mother. Rather, her abrupt departure and severing of the relationship with her mother brings about her mother's premature death. Sarah Jane is forced to shoulder her guilt and return to the place her mother occupied, the submissive black maternal position.

As this summary shows, *Imitation of Life* was ahead of itself, a fact that makes clear that many of the images that seem "new" are not, except in their overall emphasis regarding woman's deliberate self-fulfillment in mothering. What really is new in our own period is, first, the role that fathers are made to play in child rearing and, second, the focus on the fetus and baby. Fathers are beginning to steal the show in regard to parenting: That they are the new heroes in this role is fascinating just because the narratives of so many traditional maternal melodramas precisely show mothers and daughters *alone,* and the fathers dead, unknown, or absent. I have elsewhere argued that the mother is overinstalled in the Symbolic because she never can satisfy in lived experience (Kaplan, 1992). Does the new insistence on *fathers* as parents reflect a new despair about the mother's ability to satisfy? The need to situate Fathers in the Symbolic to safeguard the child from the neglectful Mother?

However that may be, the fetus/baby has recently begun to steal the show from both mothers and fathers. The fetus has entered into film, where it threatens to displace the mother as subject. Amy Heckerling's 1990 comedy, *Look Who's Talking,* shows us the actual moment of conception. Spectators view the inside of what we later realize is the heroine's body. An egg matures and drops into the fallopian tube (these images accompany the film titles). The camera then pans right to focus on a male hand feeling the heroine's leg. The adulterous couple are at work, but are about to have sex. At this point, the camera pans left again, now showing sperm racing through the fallopian tubes. The sperm are given male voices, which sound like men chasing and competing for women in a dance hall. The "winner" is seen diving into the egg, while tones of satisfaction fill the sound track.

The camera continues to take us, periodically, into the heroine's womb, where the *male* fetus talks to us about what it feels like in there. The world outside the body returns as the heroine struggles with her baby's father over whether or not to marry. Things the heroine does are registered by the fetus in the womb. At one point, the thirsty fetus suggests "we get some orange juice down here"; a moment later, the heroine is seen finishing a gallon of juice.

The birth is presented from the fetus's perspective, and, after birth, the baby continues to talk to the viewer, as if a fully cognizant being from the start. He has opinions about the heroine's boyfriends, and he helps her choose the right one. While this makes for good comedy, the underlying significance of displacing the mother-as-subject and of assigning to fetus and baby thoughts and perceptions of adulthood should not be taken lightly. Indeed, the choice of a boy baby sets up an automatic oedipal rivalry between the baby and the heroine's boyfriends and means that once again, woman/mother is an object of exchange between, if not "men," then "males." In the end, the baby and lover become the *real* couple until the heroine gives in and agrees to marry the lover who is now bonded to the baby. The mother's authority and centrality are at stake, again, in such images.

Look Who's Talking, Too appeared in 1990. The success of the first film, as with *Three Men and A Baby,* spurred Hollywood to make a follow-up movie. This time, the fetus is female, but as before, it fills the screen and is given cute features and Roseanne Arnold's deep voice; it is made a full subject, with thoughts and language, long before birth. After the birth, both the baby and her brother are given perceptions, thoughts, and language, and the voices of adults. The film's world is seen from their points of view. Although theoretically this film could be seen to convey a certain empowerment of children, the way in which the scenes are done is closer to exploitation. The film does not represent young children's inner worlds, but only adult play with adult concepts of children's lives. As with the first film, *Look Who's Talking, Too* reinforces the nineties fashion of decentering adults and making children the heroes. Particularly troubling is the representation of the fetus as *person,* and the disjunction between the image of the womb and that of the mother's body.

Accounting for such fantasies of the fetus as person is too complex an issue to treat fully here. As I have argued elsewhere, the new fetal images have been in part produced through the abortion debates and images like those in the pernicious *A Silent Scream,* as well as through the relatively innocent photography of Lennart Nilsson (see Ginsburg, 1990; Petchesky, 1986; Squier, 1991; Kaplan, 1993). But we may well ask if this form of fetal interpellation, in the Althusserian sense mentioned earlier, fulfills human beings' need for a hero. Is the fetus the new savior of humanity, delivering us from all the messes we have made? Is the focus on the fetus part of man's dream to make the perfect being? Is the focus on the fetus the latest form of the age-long male utopian urge to control reproduction, to control the body, perhaps to the extent of eliminating it altogether?

Focus on the fetus may indeed indicate a renewed desire to write the mother out of the story and serves to marginalize and negate her subjectivity (Kaplan, 1993). This new discourse appears to contradict a nostalgic return to a sentimentalized mother-child relationship, but in fact colludes neatly with it. Instead of an intense mother-child relationship being idealized, we have obsession with conception and gestation, with fetal life within the mother. But the discourses are linked insofar as they both indicate a return to an obsession with the biological child.

The differences between these discourses are also important. The sentimental-mother discourse portrays a mother who is absorbed in nurturing. However oppressively (*The Good Mother*), it situates the mother as a subject recognizing the pleasure that can be gained from nurturing. In contrast, the reproductive-mother discourse marginalizes the mother in favor of the fetus and redefines *subjectivity,* raising anew issues about what constitutes subjectivity in the first place.

Fetal interpellation manifests a new form of the old desire to absent (or deny) the mother. The fetus is represented as an entity in its own right, unattached to the mother, or at least rendering her irrelevant to what is going on in the womb. Primal male fears of woman's ability to reproduce are partially responsible for producing the mother images I have discussed here.

All of the discourses mentioned above collude in privileging the biological nuclear family. North American culture feels threatened by the legacies of the women's, gay, and other liberation movements of the sixties. As a result, it counters with images of couples happily united around the biological baby. Images of a radically transformed family are needed to help move us toward new institutional forms for the postmodern era—forms that would finally accept, and make possible, white women combining sex, work, and motherhood. The struggles facing women of color must also be addressed and analyzed in relation to an oppressive politics of representation that I have been able to allude to only briefly here. Comparison and contrast between the politics of representing white and black mothers is urgent research that I am currently pursuing. Such research is already revealing the complex interdependency of white and black maternal constructs: The pernicious power hierarchy that privileges white over black maternal figures is clear, but research also reveals how white patriarchy controls both sets of figures. But that is a future story.[8]

References

Althusser, L. (1971). Ideology and ideological state apparatuses. In *Lenin and philosophy and other essays*. (Trans. B. Brewster). New York and London: Monthly Review Press.

Creed, B. (1986). Horror and the monstrous-feminine: An imaginary abjection. *Screen,* 27(1), 44–71.

Creed, B. (1991). Monstrous women. Ph.D. diss., La Trobe University, Bundora, Australia. Forthcoming from Routledge.

Flitterman-Lewis, S. (1988). Imitation of life: The black woman's double determination as troubling other. *Literature and Psychology,* 34(4), 44–57.

Ginsburg, F. (1989). *Contested lives: The abortion debate in an American community.* Berkeley: University of California Press.

Jameson, F. (1981). *The political unconscious: Narrative as a socially symbolic act.* Ithaca, N.Y.: Cornell University Press.

Jameson, F. (1985). Postmodernism, or the cultural logic of late capitalism. *New Left Review,* 146, 53–92.

Jameson, F. (1991). Nostalgia for the present. In *Postmodernism, or the logic of late capitalism.* Durham, N.C.: Duke University Press.

Kaplan, E. A. (1987). Motherhood and representation: From post–World War II Freudian figurations to postmodernism. *Minnesota Review,* N.S. 29, 88–102.

Kaplan, E. A. (1988). *Postmodernism and its discontents: Theories and practices.* London: Verso.

Kaplan, E. A. (1992). *Motherhood and representation: The mother in popular culture and melodrama.* London and New York: Routledge.

Kaplan, E. A. (1993). Look who's talking, indeed!: The meaning of fetal images in recent USA visual culture. In L. Forcey & E. Glenn (Eds.), *Contested terrains: Social constructions of mothering.* London and New York: Routledge.

Kristeva, J. (1982). *Powers of horror: An essay on abjection.* (Trans. L. S. Roudiez). New York: Columbia University Press.

Modleski, T. (1988). Three men and Baby M. *Camera Obscura,* 17, 71.

Petchesky, R. (1987). Fetal images: The power of visual culture in the politics of reproduction. *Feminist Studies,* 13(2), 263–92.

Silverstein, L. B. (1991). Transforming the debate about child care and maternal employment. *American Psychologist,* 46(10), 1025–32.

8. Since writing this essay, I have started research on the new project, which addresses omission of African-American maternality. See my essay on "Mothering in the Movies Revisited: Race, Psychoanalysis, and Cinema" (forthcoming).

Squier, S. (1991). Fetal voices: Speaking for the margins within. *Tulsa Studies,* 10(1), 17–30.

Squier, S. (Forthcoming). *Babies and bottles.* New Brunswick, N.J.: Rutgers University Press.

Taylor, J. (1989). The public fetus and the family car: From abortion politics to a Volvo advertisement. *Public Culture,* 4(2), 67–80.

Weitzman, L. (1985). *The divorce revolution: The unexpected social and economic consequences for women and children in America.* New York: Free Press.

SUSAN RUBIN SULEIMAN

16 Playing and Motherhood; or, How to Get the Most Out of the Avant-Garde

A mother who stays in her place is the Law.
  Philippe Sollers (1982)
Now, I-woman will blow up the Law.
  Hélène Cixous (1981)

Julia Kristeva (1974) has argued that the male avant-garde writer (in her model, the avant-garde writer is always male) uses his mother, and even appropriates her place, in his "battle against the Name-of-the-Father."[1] This appropriation, which may be called perverse, leads, Kristeva argues, to a revulsion from genitality and a putting into question of "family structures and the rules of filiation," but it does not imply that the son/subject gives up his "phallic position" (p. 471). In fact, sadism and aggression against the mother's body accompany the son's appropriation of it. Kristeva concludes that the son's "implacable war against an absolutely present father" signals a historical crisis of identity for the phallic subject (p. 472)—which may be another way of saying that the son's battle against the father is rendered ambiguous by their mutual fascination with the phallus.

Kristeva's densely argued prose should not blind us to the continuing relevance of the question it raises: What is the rela-

1. Unless otherwise indicated, all translations from the French are my own. This chapter is a drastically shortened version of chapter 7 of my book *Subversive Intent: Gender, Politics, and the Avant-Garde* (Cambridge, Mass.: Harvard University Press, 1990). It has been revised especially for this volume.

tion between innovative, rule-breaking artistic practices associated with "the avant-garde" and changes in psychic and social configurations that we associate with modernity, or even with the "crisis of modernity" heralded by such thinkers as Freud, Marx, Nietzsche, Einstein? In this chapter, I shall present an argument about one aspect of that relationship, focusing on the figure of the mother. In brief, my argument is that playful inventions of avant-garde writing, starting with surrealism and continuing to present work, can provide an impetus, perhaps even a metaphor or model, for reimagining the mother in her social and child-rearing role. This reimagining takes the form of a displacement, from what I call the patriarchal mother to the playful mother. Just what is at stake in that displacement is a question I shall save for the end.

The Patriarchal Mother

Among the so-called historical avant-gardes, surrealism stands out by its combination of political truculence, directed largely against what the surrealists saw as the bankrupt culture of bourgeois Europe—a culture that had culminated in the carnage of World War I—and aesthetic playfulness, emphasizing verbal and visual punning, parody, and collage, often scatological or otherwise "scandalous" in nature. Family, church, and state were the institutions the surrealists most gleefully and persistently attacked: Buñuel and Dalí's famous (for some, still notorious) 1930 film *L'Age d'or* offers a good example, in both substance and manner, of the surrealist critique of that sacrosanct trinity. Composed of wildly discontinuous fragments that nonetheless tell a story, the film celebrates "mad love" between a man and a woman, hindered by bourgeois conventions, government interference, and Catholic inhibitions.

The impetus of surrealist activity, whether in the domain of writing, film, or painting and photography, was avowedly antipatriarchal. Like Marx and Engels before them, the surrealists saw the patriarchal family as an institution closely linked to the capitalist economy and state; but paradoxically, this family was often embodied in their works not (or not only) by the figure of the stern father but by that of the petty, repressive mother. Throughout its life as an organized movement, the surrealist group published a great many collective declarations, political and polemical. It was a way of asserting surrealism's role as an avant-garde movement with a social as well as an aesthetic program. One of the most vitriolic documents, signed by every major male surrealist (thirty-two signatures in all, an unusually large number), was an eight-page diatribe against Mrs. Charlie Chaplin, who in 1927 sued her husband for divorce and a large financial settlement (she was the mother of his two children).

Entitled "Hands Off Love!" the declaration was an impassioned defense of poetry and free love, embodied in the person of Charlie Chaplin, and an attack on the petit bourgeois mentality of "those bitches who become, in every country, the good mothers, good sisters, good wives, those plagues, those parasites of every sentiment and every love," represented by Chaplin's wife (Nadeau, 1964, p.

256).[2] Narrow-minded, money-grubbing, moralizing, deriving her raison d'être solely from the "manufacture of brats," Mrs. Chaplin as painted in this surrealist portrait is the very embodiment of what I am calling the patriarchal mother—a figure not bound by time or place, for one also finds her (for example) in the fiction of William Burroughs. Robin Lydenberg (1987) has written, apropos of Burroughs, that "it is the figure of the mother who arouses his most vitriolic resentment," because he "perceives that the mother, as defined by conventional notions of sexual difference and family structure, is a necessary instrument in a larger system of patriarchal power which seeks to dominate the individual from his earliest moment of life" (p. 168).

Although surrealism in its heyday (roughly, 1924–1935) was virtually all male, imbued with deeply—even if unconsciously—misogynistic attitudes toward women, the movement eventually became quite open to women artists. This did not, however, change the surrealists' view of the family or of mothers. Whitney Chadwick (1985) has noted that very few women surrealist artists became mothers and that most had quite negative feelings about motherhood. This attitude can be seen as part of their revolt against the conventional female roles prescribed by their largely middle-class backgrounds, at a time when a woman who wished to pursue a full-time career, not to mention an artistic career, outside the bounds of wifehood and motherhood was still considered a dangerous anomaly. In addition, the male surrealists' image of woman as erotic partner (in *l'amour fou,* "mad love") or as free spirit (in *la femme enfant,* the "child-woman") also militated against surrealist women's self-image as mothers.

In surrealist writing by women, mothers are generally either absent or negative figures. Leonora Carrington (whose two sons were born in the late 1940s, after she had left the movement) may be the only surrealist woman writer who has represented a mother (albeit a rather untypical one) as a heroine, not only positive but self-consciously playful, in her novel *The Hearing Trumpet* (1976). In her stories of the 1930s, however, Carrington's portrayal of the mother, insofar as she is portrayed at all, fits the usual patriarchal stereotype. Nelly Kaplan, my other favorite surrealist woman writer (of the postwar generation), has written extremely funny parodies of sacred texts, including the Gospels (for example, "Aimez-vous les uns sur les autres," a rewriting of Christ's betrayal by Judas as a story of homosexual jealousy, in *Le Réservoir des sens*). But Kaplan writes exclusively as a daughter, and indeed the father's daughter; her attitude toward mothers, as well as toward motherhood, is unambiguously negative. This is particularly apparent in her comic erotic novel (published under the pen name Belen), *Mémoires d'une liseuse de draps,* whose heroine's exploits include the discovery and marketing of a carnivorous plant that eats fetuses—a real service to pregnant women, the heroine claims.

One might conclude from all this that contemporary feminist avant-garde practices—those that define a certain "feminist postmodernism"—have little to

2. "Hands Off Love!" was first published in *La Révolution surrealiste,* no. 9–10 (1927). It is reprinted in its entirety in Nadeau (1964, pp. 252–60).

gain from being associated with surrealism, whose dominant views were, and remained even after women entered the movement, chiefly male. Gayatri Spivak (1981) has argued that contemporary feminist works derive all of their power from "their substantive revision of, rather than their apparent formal allegiance to, the European avant-garde" (p. 167). That may be true in some cases; but in others, one finds both a formal allegiance, as in the explosive use of humor or parody, and a substantive agreement, as in attacks on family, church, and state or in negative views of the mother, who is once again imagined only as a patriarchal mother.

Take the young British novelist Jeanette Winterson, for instance. Born in 1959, Winterson has no historic ties to the surrealists. Yet her first two published novels—*Oranges Are Not the Only Fruit* and *Boating for Beginners,* both appearing in 1985—display the explosive humor of much surrealist narrative; and her portrayal of the heroine's mother in *Oranges Are Not the Only Fruit* is negative for the same substantive reason as theirs: the mother is perceived as the narrow-minded defender of the law (in this case, the law of heterosexuality), even when the male figures around her have given up on that policing role.

A scene toward the beginning of the novel thematizes, in a wonderfully comic way, the antipatriarchal impetus of feminist-postmodern parody. Significantly, the scene occurs in a chapter entitled "Genesis" (all of the novel's chapters bear titles corresponding to books of the Old Testament) and involves a little girl's playing with a sacred text. The female first-person narrator recounts this incident, which occurred when she was seven years old. Brought up by her strictly evangelical adoptive mother, the little girl spends a lot of time in church. One day, a visiting pastor, eager to make a point about the ubiquity of evil, points to our innocent heroine and intones: "This little lily could herself be a house of demons." As it happens, the heroine will grow up to be a "house of demons" (in her mother's and the pastor's eyes) by becoming a lesbian. In the meantime, her unorthodox penchants reveal themselves in play:

> I felt a bit awkward . . . so I went into the Sunday School Room. There was some Fuzzy Felt to make Bible scenes with, and I was just beginning to enjoy a rewrite of Daniel in the lions' den when Pastor Finch appeared. I put my hands into my pockets and looked at the lino.
>
> "Little girl," he began, then he caught sight of the Fuzzy Felt. "What's that?"
>
> "Daniel," I answered.
>
> "But that's not right," he said, aghast. "Don't you know that Daniel escaped? In your picture the lions are swallowing him."
>
> "I'm sorry," I replied, putting on my best, blessed face. "I wanted to do Jonah and the whale, but they don't do whales in Fuzzy Felt. I'm pretending those lions are whales."
>
> "You said it was Daniel," He was suspicious. "I got mixed up."
>
> He smiled. "Let's put it right, shall we?" And he carefully rearranged the lions in one corner, and Daniel in the other. (1985, p. 13)

The pastor is outraged, then mollified; the little girl, wily—a contrast to the open defiance of graffiti-drawing boys. The overall effect is humorous, at the pastor's expense; in the end, the little girl leaves him playing out his own biblical fantasies in Fuzzy Felt.

As the novel progresses, more and more old stories enter its texture: other Old Testament stories, fairy tales, Perceval's quest for the Holy Grail. Their presence, increasingly unmotivated in realist terms, fragments the text and gives it something like the heterogeneity of collage or the hybrid or carnival. The narrator's humor, however, gives way to anger and eventually to a kind of despair—as if the parodic lightness of the beginning could not be sustained after she becomes an outcast from home and church, both of them her mother's house.

And her mother? Repressive and fanatical, she looms large; as a fictional creation, she is a triumph for the novelist. As a character within the fiction, however, she is more disastrously hampering to her daughter than any male (the male characters all appear weak or ridiculous). Although I am simplifying somewhat for the sake of the argument, I think it is not a misreading to say that the mother is represented here as being wholly on the side of patriarchy, indeed as the most vigorous defender of patriarchal values. Surrounded and sustained by women friends and totally dominating her husband, the mother is nevertheless in thrall to male authority figures: God and his earthly representatives, a few fundamentalist pastors. Fortunately for her, these authorities are quite distant, allowing her to wield considerable local power even while disclaiming it.

Winterson's novel allows us to see with particular clarity why the figure of the mother has fared so badly in the work of some radical artists, whether male or female. To the extent that she is perceived as a defender and an instrument of patriarchy, the mother takes on all of the father's negative attributes even while lacking his power; as such, she is the perfect target for both the son's and daughter's anger. Furthermore, in the absence of a strong father, the mother functions as a repressive authority, thus doubly betraying her daughter—and at the same time fulfilling Philippe Sollers's (1982) epigrammatic formula: "A mother who stays in her place is the Law" (p. 12).

A similar dictum underlies the sharp distinction between Amazons and mothers in Monique Wittig and Sande Zeig's mock "history of the world," *Brouillon pour un dictionnaire des amantes* (translated as *A Lovers' Dictionary*, 1976). The sedentary heterosexual mothers function as upholders of the father's law and are therefore inimical to the roaming Amazons. A slightly revised version of the separation between lesbian daughter/warrior and heterosexual mother occurs in *Virgile non* (1985), Wittig's rewriting of Dante's *Inferno*. Like her great male predecessor's comedy, Wittig's is not funny, but by turns sarcastic, angry, lyrical, vituperative, sorrowful. The damned souls that Wittig's poet-protagonist (who bears the author's name) sees during her journey—all of them women, most of them willing victims of the patriarchal system—elicit her pity or her scorn, and none more so than the creatures "permanently accompanied by one or several annexes." To Wittig's continual surprise, the women actually love these millstones around their necks. "Will we ever be able to rid them of their damned annexes?" she asks Manastabal, her guide who is "not Virgil." Manastabal replies that she and Wittig are "not in hell to blame the damned souls but to show them the way out, if necessary" (p. 51). In this work, mothers have become the alienated victims of patriarchy rather than its self-righteous accomplices. Not much progress, from the Amazon's point of view. And nothing to laugh about.

Nancy K. Miller (1988a), in her study of a certain tradition of fiction by French women writers (which she calls a "feminist literature of dissent"), remarks that in the typical feminist plot the heroine not only refuses to marry but also refuses to become a mother. "Is this bypassing of maternity the ultimate effect of the indictment of patriarchy?" Miller asks rhetorically (p. 10). Judging by the figure of the patriarchal mother, it would indeed seem to be the case that a woman cannot be a mother and outside the father's law at the same time: whether as alienated victim or as self-righteous accomplice, the mother appears necessarily on the side of patriarchy. As such, she is a figure of both derision and hatred for the avant-garde.

Reimagining the Mother

It was partly in reaction to this view—which sees all mothers as patriarchal—that theorists like Hélène Cixous and Luce Irigaray began, in the mid-1970s, to elaborate the "maternal metaphor" for innovative women's writing and women's cultural politics. Cixous's (1981) simultaneous affirmation, in her famous manifesto "The Laugh of the Medusa," that "a woman is never far from 'mother'" (p. 251) (*"La femme n'est jamais loin de la 'mère'"*) and that "Now, I-woman am going to blow up the Law" (p. 257) (*"Maintenant, je-femme vais faire sauter la Loi"*) seems directed specifically against the notion that the mother is always patriarchal. In Cixous's text, it is the mother who, newly defined ("I mean outside her role functions: the 'mother' as nonname and as source of goods," p. 251), allows the woman to oppose both the Name-of-the-Father and the father's parsimonious economy.

In the above quotation, the mother is essentially a metaphor ("outside her role functions"), but elsewhere in the manifesto motherhood is treated more concretely. A woman who wants a child should not be afraid of falling into the patriarchal trap, "engendering all at once child—mother—father—family. No; it's up to you to break the old circuits" (p. 261). Cixous thus suggests, in a significant reversal of the avant-garde (and sometimes avant-garde feminist) stereotype, that a woman can be politically radical, artistically innovative, and yet a mother.

Domna Stanton (1986), who has submitted the maternal metaphor to a thoroughgoing critique, admits that it served in its time as an "enabling mythology." I would say that (among other things) it enabled a number of French women writers to imagine a feminist avant-garde practice that would retain the historical avant-gardes' subversive/parodic energy, but would revise and critique their negative attitude toward women—an attitude that, as Cixous and others rightly understood, had its source in and was exemplified by their repudiation of the mother.

It is just such a critical revision that is effected by Cixous's (1981) famous evocation of the Medusa:

> Too bad for them if they fall apart upon discovering that women aren't men, or that the mother doesn't have one. But isn't this fear convenient for them? Wouldn't the worst be, isn't the worst, in truth, that women aren't castrated, that they have only to stop listening to the Sirens (for the Sirens were men) for history to change its meaning? You only have to look at the Medusa straight on to see her. And she's not deadly. She's beautiful and she's laughing. (p. 255)

The punch line is in the last sentence—and I do mean "punch line," because its effect is similar to the aggressive and scandalous effect of surrealist parody. The difference is substantive rather than formal: Cixous's figure of the beautiful and laughing Medusa, a reversal of the traditional hideous image, is formally equivalent to any number of surrealist reversals—whether positive or negative, like Max Ernst's punitive Virgin in *The Blessed Virgin Chastising the Infant Jesus* (1926), or negative to positive, like Lucifer in Louis Aragon's 1924 preface to his earlier work, *Le Libertinage*. It is the meaning of the "reversed" Medusa, as determined by the context of the paragraph and by that of the essay as a whole, that is different.

Within the paragraph, the Medusa figure alludes both to the Greek myth and to Freud's reading of it. According to the myth, as retold by Ovid (1955), the Gorgon Medusa was once beautiful, "the hope of many an envious suitor," until one day Neptune raped her in Minerva's temple, whereupon the goddess, "punishing the outrage as it deserved," turned Medusa into a monster (an early form of blaming the victim). Ovid also tells us that after the hero Perseus severed the Gorgon's head, "from that mother's bleeding / Were born the swift-winged Pegasus and his brother" (p. 106). The Gorgon's head became a powerful weapon, turning all those (men) who looked at it to stone. In Cixous's revision, Medusa is restored to her beautiful state before the rape, and her head invites looking at (by men and women: "*Il suffit qu'on la regarde,*" *on* being an impersonal pronoun).

Freud, as is well known, read the decapitated Medusa's head as a symbol of the mother's (and by extension, women's) castrated genitals seen from the "terrorized" point of view of the male spectator. Cixous's revision of this reading consists in imagining a female spectator who finds the very notion of women's castration laughable, and who, looking at her body through her own eyes rather than the man's, finds all of it beautiful. (Does the equation of the Sirens with men suggest that once women stop listening to them they will become Odysseuses—explorers and heroes?) Cixous's Medusa, in short, figures the woman who laughs at being taken for the Medusa, that "symbol of horror."

Enlarged to the context of the essay as a whole, the laughing Medusa becomes a powerful trope for women's autonomous subjectivity and for the necessary irreverence of women's writing—and rewriting.

But if the maternal metaphor (and recall that in the Greek myth Medusa actually became a mother, giving birth to Pegasus) was empowering to many French women writers of the 1970s, opening up to them possibilities for verbal invention and free play, little of the writing thus produced was playful in the ordinary sense of lighthearted or just plain funny. Annie Leclerc (1974), Chantal Chawaf (1979), and Julia Kristeva (1977), who all at some point wrote about motherhood and maternal love not (or not only) as a metaphor but as an actual experience, opted for the expansive lyric mode when writing as mothers. Although lyric can be full of invention, it does not offer much possibility for humor or parody.

The lyric genre is also, of course, in contrast to the epic—that is, to narrative. Cixous's fictions immediately following "The Laugh of the Medusa" exploited the maternal as a metaphor for the mutually nurturing relations between women and as a metaphor for Cixous's own writing (the author giving birth to her texts). These works delight in verbal invention, including puns and other "play of signifiers"; they are intertextual, reworking Greek myths—*Illa* and *Promethea* (Cixous, 1980, 1983)—or texts by contemporary writers—*Vivre l'orange* (Cixous, 1979). But their overall effect is effusively lyrical, or else essayistic, rather than narrative; and although they may at times provoke laughter, they are not comic works.

Am I being obtuse, desiring that women's play be humorous and narrative, as well as inventive—and especially humorous about, and in the voice of, the mother? Erma Bombeck's self-deprecating humor is not what I have in mind; it is not a matter of mothers grinning and bearing the age-old travails of motherhood. I have in mind, rather, something closer to Freud's notion that humor is both pleasure producing and rebellious. In his short 1927 essay "Humor" (which immediately follows the essay on fetishism in the *Standard Edition*), Freud emphasizes the liberating function of humor and contrasts it to mere jokes, humor possessing, according to him, "grandeur" and "dignity," whereas jokes (which, as he analyzes them in *Jokes and Their Relation to the Unconscious* [1905], are always at someone else's expense) do not. Even more interestingly in the present context, Freud suggests that the origin of humor is in the superego, not in the unconscious as is the case with jokes. Given that in Freud's system the superego usually has a repressive rather than a rebellious or liberating function, I find this ascription of the origin of humor to the "parental agency" extremely suggestive. And it becomes even more so if the parental agency is identified as the mother, not the father.

I have in mind, finally, a desire for laughter coupled with a desire for story. (Metaphors are fine, but stories spun out are better—does this thought mark me as "postmodern" or merely as having lived too long in the country of Hollywood?) Not the same old story, to be sure, or if the same old story, then rewritten, rewritten. But something that takes place in time, no matter how unlinear; that tells about events occurring in a world with characters (and "characters"), no matter how preposterous (the more preposterous, the better). In short, something that moves and changes, yet continues too.

Had I the space here, I would offer a full-fledged reading of Carrington's *The Hearing Trumpet,* an outrageously inventive and comically carnivalesque novel that occupies a significant historical place between surrealism and feminist postmodernism, and that, uniquely to my mind, associates the subversive laughter of carnival with the figure—perhaps even more important, with the narrative voice—of the mother. If I am right in thinking that the emblematic subject of male avant-garde practice (both in the historical avant-gardes and later) is a transgressive son who may, in Roland Barthes's famous words, "play with the body of his mother" but who never imagines, let alone gives voice to, his mother playing, then the "character" of a transgressive, laughing mother in the work of an innovative woman writer will appear new indeed. More than new, it may be revolutionary.

The Mother Playing

But why, other than for aesthetic reasons, should we care about this? Why are the stakes as regards the image—or, if you will, the enabling myth—of the laughing mother political (in the broadest sense) as well as aesthetic?

Playing, as Freud (1905, 1927) and Winnicott (1971) among others have shown us, is the activity through which the human subject most freely and inventively constitutes herself or himself. To play is to affirm an "I," an autonomous subjectivity that exercises control over a world of possibilities; at the same time, and contrarily, it is in playing that the I can experience itself in its most fluid and boundaryless state. Barthes (1975) speaks of being "liberated from the binary prison, putting oneself in a state of infinite expansion" (p. 137). Winnicott (1971) calls the play experience "one of a non-purposive state, as one might say a sort of ticking over of the unintegrated personality" (p. 55)—and adds a few pages later that "it is only here, in this unintegrated state of the personality, that that which we describe as creative can appear" (p. 64).

To imagine the mother playing is to recognize her most fully as a creative subject—autonomous and free, yet (or for that reason?) able to take the risk of "infinite expansion" that goes with creativity. Some feminist critics have expressed worry over the idea of the female subject, mother or not, playing with the boundaries of the self, given the difficulties women in our culture have in attaining a sense of selfhood to begin with. Nancy Miller (1988b), who has forcefully argued this view, has remarked about the signature, "Only those who have it can play with not having it" (p. 75); and as she points out, women's signatures, even for those who "have" them, are still undervalued. Naomi Schor (1987) has argued in a similar vein that feminists should not abandon the notion of feminine specificity in favor of "the carnival of plural sexualities" (p. 109).

Although I share Miller's and Schor's desire to hold on to a notion of female selfhood, it still seems important to me to admit the possibility of playing with the boundaries of the self, especially if Winnicott is right in seeing such play as a necessary part of artistic creativity. I believe that women—women artists in particular—must be strong enough to allow themselves this kind of play; one way to achieve such strength is for girls to imagine (or see) their mothers playing. Jessica Benjamin (1988) has argued that if the mother were really recognized in our culture as an independent subject, with desires of her own, that would revolutionize not only the psychoanalytic paradigms of "normal" child development (which have always been based on the child's need to be recognized by the mother, not on the idea of mutual recognition) but the actual lives of children in this culture as they develop into adults. Could it be that it would change the way we in the West think about the constitution of human subjectivity?

That may be too big a claim, or at least one that would have to be argued more fully than I am doing here. In fact, I will be content with a more modest vision: of boys (later to be men) who actually enjoy seeing their mother move instead of sitting motionless, "a peaceful center" (Barthes, 1978) around which the child weaves his play; and of girls (later to be women) who learn that they don't have to grow up to be motionless mothers.

To imagine the mother laughing as she plays brings a touch of lightness to what otherwise could appear as too pious a dream. (There is nothing so self-defeating or so grim as the idea of required or regimented play.) And it may allow us to envision a new mode of play that is lighter—though no less inventive and free—than the sadistic, narcissistic, angst-ridden games of transgressive children.

Patricia Yaeger (1988) quotes Herbert Marcuse paraphrasing Friedrich Schlegel: "man is free when the 'reality loses its seriousness' and when its necessity 'becomes light'" (p. 228). As Yaeger points out, this is not a recipe for learning to live with the way things are, but rather one possible recipe for wanting to change them.

References

Barthes, R. (1975). *Roland Barthes par lui-même*. Paris: Editions du Seuil.

Barthes, R. (1975). *Leçon*. Paris: Editions du Seuil.

Benjamin, J. (1988). *The bonds of love: Psychoanalysis, feminism, and the problem of domination*. New York: Pantheon.

Carrington, L. (1976). *The hearing trumpet*. San Francisco: City Lights.

Chadwick, W. (1985). *Women artists and the surrealist movement*. London: Thames and Hudson.

Chawaf, C. (1979). *Maternité*. Paris: Stock.

Cixous, H. (1979). *Vivre l'orange*. Paris: Editions des Femmes.

Cixous, H. (1980). *Illa*. Paris: Editions des Femmes.

Cixous, H. (1981). The laugh of the Medusa. (Trans. K. Cohen & P. Cohen). In E. Marks & I. de Courtivron (Eds.), *New French feminisms*. New York: Schocken.

Cixous, H. (1983). *Li livre de Promethea.* Paris: Gallimard.

Freud, S. (1905). Jokes and their relation to the unconscious. In *Standard Edition.* Vol. 8. London: Hogarth Press.

Freud, S. (1922). Medusa's head. In *Sexuality and the psychology of love.* New York: Collier Books, 1963.

Freud, S. (1927). Humor. In *Standard Edition.* Vol. 21. London: Hogarth Press.

Kristeva, J. (1974). *La Révolution du langage poetique.* Paris: Editions du Seuil.

Kristeva, J. (1977). Héréthique de l'amour. *Tel Ouel,* 74.

Leclerc, A. (1974). *Parole de femme.* Paris: Livre de Poche.

Lydenberg, R. (1987). *Word cultures: Radical theory and practice in William Burroughs' fiction.* Urbana: University of Illinois Press.

Miller, N. K. (1988a). *Subject to change: Reading feminist writing.* New York: Columbia University Press.

Miller, N. K. (1988b). The text's heroine. In N. K. Miller, *Subject to change: Reading feminist writing.* New York: Columbia University Press.

Nadeau, M. (1964). *Histoire du surréalisme.* Paris: Editions du Seuil.

Ovid (1955). *Metamorphoses.* (Trans. R. Humphries.). Bloomington: Indiana University Press.

Schor, N. (1987). Dreaming dissymmetry. In A. Jardine & P. Smith (Eds.), *Men in feminism.* New York: Methuen.

Sollers, P. (1982). L'Assomption. *Tel Ouel,* 91.

Spivak, G. S. (1981). French feminism in an international frame. *Yale French Studies,* 62, 154–184.

Stanton, D. (1986). Difference on trial: A critique of the maternal metaphor in Cixous, Irigaray, and Kristeva. In N. K. Miller (Ed.), *The poetics of gender.* New York: Columbia University Press.

Suleiman, S. (1990). *Subversive intent: Gender, politics, and the avant-garde.* Cambridge, Mass.: Harvard University Press.

Winnicott, D. W. (1971). *Playing and reality.* New York: Basic Books.

Winterson, J. (1985). *Oranges are not the only fruit.* New York: Atlantic Monthly Press.

Wittig, M. (1985). *Virgile non.* Paris: Editions de Minuit.

Yaeger, P. (1988). *Honey-mad women: Emancipatory strategies in women's writing.* New York: Columbia University Press.

Contributors

Donna Bassin is a clinical psychologist and psychoanalyst in private practice. Her writings, which have appeared in psychoanalytic journals and books, center around the contribution of feminism to psychoanalytic theory and practice. She is an associate member of the Institute for Psychoanalytic Training and Research and a member of the International Psychoanalytic Association.

Jessica Benjamin is a practicing psychoanalyst and a fellow of the Institute for the Humanities at New York University. She is the author of *The Bonds of Love: Psychoanalysis, Feminism and the Problem of Domination.* Her articles have been published in feminist and psychoanalytic journals and are widely anthologized.

Janine Chasseguet-Smirgel is a training analyst with the Paris Psychoanalytic Society and an honorary member of the Philadelphia Psychoanalytic Association. She holds a diploma in political science. She is also a psychologist and docteur des lettres des sciences humaines at the Sorbonne.

Patricia Hill Collins is associate professor of African-American studies and sociology at the University of Cincinnati. Her book *Black Feminist Thought* received the C. Wright Mills Award in 1991 as the best new publication in social problems research.

Jean Bethke Elshtain is the centennial professor of political science and professor of philosophy at Vanderbilt University. Her books include *Public Man, Private Woman: Women in Social and Political Thought; Mediations on Modern Political Thought; Women and War;* and *Power Trips and Other Journeys.*

Elsa First is associate clinical professor of psychology at New York University's postdoctoral program in psychoanalysis and psychotherapy and a psychoanalyst in private practice. She received her training in child psychoanalysis at the Anna Freud Centre of the Hampstead Clinic in London.

Myra Goldberg teaches fiction writing at Sarah Lawrence College. Her stories have appeared in *Ploughshares, Transatlantic Review, Feminist Studies,* and other periodicals in America and abroad. *Whistling,* a collection of her stories, was recently published.

Marianne Hirsch is professor of French and comparative literature and a member of the Women's Studies Program at Dartmouth College. She is the author of *The Mother/Daughter Plot: Narrative, Psychoanalysis, Feminism* and co-editor of *The Voyage In: Fictions of Female Development* and *Conflicts in Feminism.*

Margaret Honey is associate director of the Center for Children and Technology, a research and development group based in New York City. She is a developmental psychologist and has spent the past ten years researching issues of gender, culture, and technology.

E. Ann Kaplan is professor of English and comparative studies at SUNY, Stony Brook, and director of the Humanities Institute there. She has written and lectured internationally on women in film, postmodernism, psychoanalysis, feminist theory, music television, and cultural studies. Her many books include *Women in Film: Both Sides of the Camera; Rocking around the Clock: Music Television, Postmodernism and Consumer Culture; Psychoanalysis and Cinema;* and *Motherhood and Representation: The Mother in Popular Culture and Melodrama.*

Meryle Mahrer Kaplan is the founding coordinator of the Women's Center at William Paterson College. She is a developmental psychologist and author of *Mothers' Images of Motherhood.* She has worked as a consultant to businesses throughout the United States.

Barbara Kruger is a contemporary artist and activist whose work combines images and text. Her work has been widely exhibited in the United States and in Europe. She writes and lectures about the impact of media on popular culture. She is currently represented by the Mary Boone Gallery in New York City.

Jane Lazarre's books include *The Mother Knot, The Powers of Charlotte,* and *Worlds beyond My Control.* She is the director of the writing program at the Eugene Lang College of the New School for Social Research, where she teaches writing and literature.

Therese Lichtenstein is visiting assistant professor of art and art history at Rice University. She has done research on the Nazi photographer Hans Bellmer.

Rayna Rapp is professor of anthropology at the New School for Social Research and an editor of *Feminist Studies.* She has been active in the reproductive rights movement and the development of women's studies for over twenty years.

Sara Ruddick teaches feminist studies and philosophy at the New School for Social Research. She is the author of *Maternal Thinking: Toward a Politics of Peace.*

Adria Schwartz is a psychoanalyst in private practice. She is on the faculties of the Mount Sinai Medial Center, the Institute for Contemporary Psychotherapy, the Psychoanalytic Psychotherapy Study Center, and the Institute for Expressive Analysis. She is the author of numerous articles on issues of psychoanalysis and gender. Her most recent work focuses on the internalization of maternal representations.

Susan Rubin Suleiman is professor of Romance and comparative literatures at Harvard University. Her books include *Authoritarian Fictions: The Ideological Novel as a Literary Genre; Subversive Intent: Gender Politics and the Avant-Garde;* and the edited volume *The Female Body in Western Culture.*

Index